College
Reading and
Study Skills

College Reading and Study Skills

Second Edition

Kathleen T. McWhorter

Niagara County Community College

Little, Brown and Company

Boston   Toronto

Library of Congress Cataloging in Publication Data

McWhorter, Kathleen T.
　　College reading and study skills.

　　　Bibliography: p.
　　　Includes index.
　　　1. Reading (Higher education)　　2. Study, Method of.
　　3. Note-taking.　　4. Examinations — Study guides.
　　I. Title.
　　LB2395.M435　　1983　　　　　428.4′07′11　　　82-22853
　　ISBN 0-316-56405-2

Library of Congress Catalog Card No. 82-22853

ISBN 0-316-56405-2

9　8　7　6　5　4　3　2　1

SEM

Published simultaneously in Canada by Little, Brown & Company (Canada) Limited

Printed in the United States of America

ACKNOWLEDGMENTS

　The author wishes to thank the following authors and publishers for permission to reprint their material throughout the text.
　George Abell, *Exploration of the Universe,* 2nd ed. Copyright © 1964, 1969 by Holt, Rinehart and Winston, Inc. Reprinted by permission of Holt, Rinehart and Winston, CBS Educational and Professional Publishing.
　Advertising Age, advertising tables on pages 342, 349, and 353. Reprinted with permission from the February 1978, September 1978, January 1981, February 1981, and March 1981 issues of *Advertising Age.* Copyright © 1978, 1981 by Crain Communications, Inc.
　American Airlines ad reprinted by permission of American Airlines.
　Andrew Althouse, Carl Turnquist, and Alfred Bracciano, *Modern Refrigeration and Air Conditioning.* Copyright © 1975 by Goodheart-Wilcox Company, Inc. Reprinted by permission.
　"Army Husband," in TIME, 16 April, 1979. Copyright © 1979 Time Inc. All rights reserved. Reprinted by permission from TIME.
　Robert Arnold et al., *Introduction to Data Processing.* Copyright © 1966 by John Wiley & Sons, Inc. Reprinted by permission of John Wiley & Sons, Inc.
　Sissela Bok, "To Lie or Not to Lie — The Doctor's Dilemma." Copyright © 1978 by The New York Times Company. Reprinted by permission.

　Richard H. Buskirk, *Principles of Marketing,* 3rd ed. Copyright © 1961, 1966, 1970 by Holt, Rinehart and Winston, Inc. Reprinted by permission of Holt, Rinehart and Winston, CBS Educational and Professional Publishing.
　Mary Calderone, "It's Really the Men Who Need Liberating," Guest Editorial, LIFE 69 (4 September 1970). Copyright © 1970 by Life (Time, Inc.). Reprinted by permission.
　John F. Cuber, *Sociology: A Synopsis of Principles,* 6th ed. Copyright © 1968 by Appleton-Century-Crofts. Reprinted by permission.
　Gordon B. Davis, *An Introduction to Electronic Computers.* Copyright © 1965 by McGraw-Hill Book Company. Reprinted by permission.
　Andreas Feininger, *The Complete Photographer.* Copyright © 1968, 1975 by Prentice-Hall, Inc., Englewood Cliffs, New Jersey 07632. Reprinted by permission.
　Ford Escort ad reprinted by permission of Ford Division, Ford Motor Company.
　James Geiwitz, *Looking at Ourselves: An Introduction to Psychology.* Copyright © 1976 by Little, Brown and Company (Inc.). Reprinted by permission.
　"A Good Word for Bad Words," in TIME, 14 December, 1981. Copyright © 1981 Time Inc. All rights reserved. Reprinted by permission from TIME.

For Thomas and Brette

Preface

Beginning college students require a foundation in reading and study skills that will enable them to handle college level work. *College Reading and Study Skills* presents the basic techniques for reading comprehension and efficiency, study, notetaking, written assignments and research papers, and taking exams. The reading and study skills I have chosen to present are those most vital to the student's success in college. Each unit teaches skills that are immediately usable — all have clear and direct application to the student's course work.

More than fourteen years of teaching reading and study courses in both two-year and four-year colleges have demonstrated to me the need for a text that covers *both* reading and study skills and provides for *both* instruction and application. This text was written to meet those needs.

Reading and study skills are inseparable. A student must develop in both areas in order to successfully handle college work. With this goal in mind, I have tried to provide complete coverage of both skills throughout the text, and to show their relationship and interdependency. In doing so, my emphasis has been on direct instruction. My central aim is to teach reading and study through a "how to" approach.

The units are interchangeable, enabling the instructor to adapt the material to a variety of instructional sequences. Part One provides an organizational framework for approaching the college experience, including such topics as organizing activities, managing time, learning about the campus, and developing effective learning techniques. Parts Two and Three focus on good reading habits and comprehension and help students apply these comprehension skills to sample textbook passages. Part Four teaches study skills — how to use textbook organization and how to underline and mark the textbook — and reading-study systems. Part Five helps students improve their ability to perform in the classroom by describing how to take notes in lectures, how to prepare for and take exams, how to participate in class discussions, and how to prepare written class assignments and research papers. Because vocabulary development is critical for improved reading and mastery of course content, Part Six focuses on improving vocabulary. The final section, Part Seven, discusses techniques for reading efficiency, the physical process of reading, and skimming and scanning.

A worktext format was chosen to provide ample instruction as well as practice. Explanation of each new technique is followed by exercises that illustrate the use of that technique and allow the student to test its effectiveness. With this method, students are given the opportunity first to understand the ideas and then to try out each new skill. Each chapter first presents and explains a technique and then helps the student learn it by giving practice exercises. The most commonly used type of exercise quotes excerpts from a wide range of college texts, providing realistic examples of college textbook reading. A second type of exercise uses a unique feature of this book — the sample textbook chapter, included in the appendix. Portions of the sample chapter are used throughout the book so that the student can practice skills with actual textbook material. A last type of exercise requires the student to apply each skill in his or her own course work.

Several features make this book well suited to the needs of beginning college students. First, the sample textbook chapter, described above, provides a link, or intermediate step, between in-chapter practice and independent application of new techniques. Second, comprehensive chapters on principles of learning and concentration are included in Parts One and Two. This coverage is essential: Students frequently complain that they cannot remember what they read, a problem that is often at the root of reading/study difficulties. Also, the principles of learning and remembering effectively provide a rationale for many of the reading and study techniques presented. Third, the level of writing and of practice exercises has been carefully controlled, and the sample textbook chapter was selected for its nontechnical content and general interest.

An Answer Key is included to make the text adaptable to self-instruction and to provide immediate feedback for students as they work through the practice exercises. An Instructor's Manual gives the instructor a detailed description of the text and specific suggestions for classroom use.

The second edition of this text includes changes and additions that allow the instructor to address more effectively the learning-study needs of college students. Recognizing that writing is an essential classroom performance skill as well as a vital mode of learning and expression, I have included a chapter on preparing written assignments and research papers. The chapter on concentration and recall has been revised, expanded, and divided into two chapters. A new sample textbook chapter has been chosen to be more widely representative of freshmen level college texts. The sentence comprehension chapter includes new material on modifiers and sentence patterns. Chapter 6 now focuses on reading efficiency techniques and has been broadened to include a discussion of attitudinal factors. Skimming exercises have been added as well as additional exercises requiring students to apply skills to their own text and course materials.

I wish to thank my colleagues for their many useful suggestions on the development and revision of this book. My typist, Joyce Pawelczyk, has consistently provided excellent professional manuscript services, as well as demonstrated patience, interest, and support in the revision of this text. My editor, Molly Faulkner, and my production editor, Kathryn Daniel, deserve special thanks for their encouragement, valuable comments, organization, and attention to the many complexities of producing this text.

K.T.M.

Contents

Contents

**College
Reading and
Study Skills**

Part One
Succeeding in College

Many students find their first few weeks in college a confusing and frustrating period. Even excellent students who achieved high grades in high school discover that college is a difficult and challenging experience.

Getting started in college may be difficult for you because it is a completely new situation. The physical surroundings are new and it is easy to feel lost. Many times, too, you don't have many friends with whom to share experiences and ask questions. Also, college classes are conducted differently from high school classes. Your professors may not act like high school teachers, and they seem to expect different things from you. Finally you find that you have not only a lot more work and responsibility, but also a lot more freedom. You find that the amount of reading, writing, and studying required is much greater than you expected, and you realize you have a lot of choices and decisions to make. You choose your own courses, your own time schedule, and even whether or not to attend class.

The purpose of Part One of the text is to give you some tips on how to minimize the frustration and confusion that most students experience as they begin college. This part includes specific suggestions which will help you start your courses in an effective and organized way.

Each chapter discusses a particular aspect of getting started in college. Chapter 1 offers many specific suggestions on what to do before classes begin, during the first week of classes, and throughout the semester. Chapter 2 addresses the problem of how to learn your way around the campus by showing you how to find information, how to become familiar with policies and procedures that affect you, how to get help with problems, and how to take advantage of services available on campus. Chapter 3 is concerned with time efficiency and is designed to help you handle the extra demands of the heavy work load required in most of your courses. Chapter 4 identifies the ability to learn as the key to academic success, describes how learning occurs, and presents the basic principles of learning. This chapter explains how these principles are behind many of the techniques presented throughout this text.

1. How to Succeed

Use this chapter to:

1. *Get organized before classes begin.*

2. *Make the best use of the first week of the semester.*

3. *Find out what to do throughout the semester to insure your success.*

This chapter is intended to provide you with some tips about succeeding in college. The chapter lets you find out these things the easy way — by reading about them. Most college students, unfortunately, have learned them the hard way — by making mistakes and paying for them with extra work or considerable inconvenience and disorganization.

BEFORE CLASSES BEGIN

There are several things that need to be done before classes actually begin. Usually, these can be taken care of the week before the opening of school.

1. Obtain your schedule of classes if it is available. If you don't know where to get your schedule, call the college's main switchboard and ask. This will save you time the first morning, for you will know ahead of time where and when your first class begins.
2. If you have a part-time job, get your hours rearranged ahead of time. Your employer needs some notice to change the schedule, and you want to be free the week classes begin. Changing your work schedule a week in advance gives you some lead time in case your employer takes longer than you thought in rescheduling you. If things go as planned, you'll have some time to get used to your new schedule before classes begin.
3. Unless you live on campus, arrange for transportation to and from campus. If you'll be involved in a car pool, organize it now. If you do not, you may be sitting at home some morning when you have a class, or you may end up wasting valuable time the first week, frantically trying to get a ride. Check the bus schedules, even if you don't plan to take the bus regularly, for an alternative means of transportation. If you have your own car, get it in good working order. You wouldn't want to miss several days during the semester dealing with car repair.
4. Get your finances in order. During the first week of classes you will

need money to pay your tuition (if not required in advance) and to purchase textbooks. Make arrangements to have adequate cash available before classes begin. You can find out how much tuition you owe by calling the Bursar's Office or the Business Office. As for textbooks, estimate that you will need at least one text for each course and that the average cost per text will be from $16 to $20.

5. Visit the campus and learn your way around. This will make your first day much less hectic and will enable you to get to classes on time. Once you have your schedule of classes, take the time to locate each of your classrooms. Also, find the snack bar, the bookstore, and the student center.

6. Get your living arrangements settled (unless it was not necessary to relocate to attend college). If you are moving into an apartment or dormitory, move in as early as possible. Try to be completely settled before classes start. You will be very busy once they begin!

7. Get a copy of the college catalog. The college catalog is the student's contract with the college. It tells you exactly what you are entitled to for the tuition you pay. It also contains the "rules of the game" — curriculum requirements, procedures to follow, graduation requirements, financial aid information, and the academic calendar (including holidays, deadlines, and dates). Course descriptions are usually included in the catalog too. They can help you select courses you're interested in taking and help you get an idea of what required courses are about.

8. If the college offers any orientation activities, such as campus tours, a get-acquainted-with-the-college workshop, or a back to school social event, try to attend. The activity will give you a chance to meet faculty and students and pick up a great deal of useful information about the college.

THE FIRST WEEK

Attend the First Class

Attending the first class of a course is crucial to surviving in that course. Attend it at all cost, even if you are late because you could not locate the room. Many students think that nothing is taught the first day. They may be correct in that the instructor does not present his or her first lecture, but they fail to realize that something much more important occurs. It is during the first meeting that the instructor introduces the course, discusses the organization of the course, and explains course requirements (tests, exams, papers).

Get to Know Someone in Each Class

During the first week, try to get to know someone in each of your classes. You will find it helpful to have someone to talk to, and you will feel you are part of the class. In case you miss a class, you will have someone from whom you can get the assignment and borrow notes. Also, this person may be able to explain ideas or assignments that are unclear or you may be able to study with him or her.

Purchase Your Textbooks

As soon as possible after the instructor assigns the text, go to the bookstore and purchase it. Do this even if you do not have an assignment to complete right away. The reason for doing this is that some bookstores run out of texts — more students may have signed up for the course than was anticipated, the texts may not have arrived, or another instructor's students may have purchased books that were intended for your class. In any case, it is usually worth your waiting in line at the bookstore to avoid the risk of having to wait five to six weeks for your textbook to be reordered.

Get Materials for Each Course Organized

You should have a notebook for each class — either spiral bound or loose leaf. You will use it to take lecture notes and to record outlines or summary-study sheets you might prepare from the text or lecture. Be sure to keep the instructor's course outline, or syllabus, as well as the course assignment and/or requirement sheets in a place where you can readily refer to them. The syllabus is particularly useful because it specifies course objectives and it provides an overall picture of the course. Also, date and organize day-to-day class handouts; these are important when studying and reviewing for an exam. Be sure to organize and date all of your class homework assignments and to keep returned quizzes, exams, and written assignments. Specific use of all of these materials will be discussed in Part Five, Chapter 17, "Studying for and Taking Exams."

Organize an Assignment Notebook or Pocket Calendar

College instructors frequently give long-term assignments and announce dates for papers, assignments, and exams much in advance. They frequently do not feel it is their responsibility to remind students as the dates approach. Consequently, you will need to develop some system for keeping track of what assignments need to be done and when each is due.

Many students keep small notebooks in which they record all their assignments as they are given. If you keep one, you can see at a glance when particular assignments are due and what tests and quizzes are coming up. Crossing assignments off as they are completed will give you a sense of accomplishment and help you feel you are getting things done. Other students use a pocket calendar and record due dates in the appropriate date blocks. Most useful are the monthly calendars which display a full month on one page. These allow you to see upcoming due dates easily without flipping pages. Both assignment notebooks and pocket calendars will eliminate the problem many students experience — realizing, at the last moment, that an assignment is due and then frantically trying to meet the deadline.

Using either your assignment notebook or pocket calendar, write out, at the beginning of each week, a "Must-Do List." Include in this list, in priority order, all the things you need to accomplish during that week.

THROUGHOUT THE SEMESTER

Get to Know Your Advisor

Most colleges assign each student an advisor to help the student plan his or her academic program. Your advisor can help you with more than just selecting courses and being certain you meet curriculum requirements for graduation. She or he can tell you whom to see to solve a particular problem, give you advice on how to handle certain courses, and provide a perspective on jobs within his or her field or refer you to someone who has more information. Many advisors consider it the student's responsibility to read the college catalog. So, before you make an appointment with your advisor, be sure that you have read the college catalog and are familiar with the information it contains.

Attend Classes Regularly

Instructors vary in their attendance policy. Some require regular attendance and frequently penalize students who exceed a specified number of absences. Others do not have a specific limit on absences and leave it to the students' own discretion to attend class. You should not assume that regular attendance is not important just because an instructor does not require attendance. Classes provide new information, interpretation, and discussion of information presented in the text, as well as vital synthesis, review, and repetition necessary for learning. Studies have indicated that successful students attend class regularly, while unsuccessful students do not.

Get to Know Your Instructors

If you become seriously ill or know you will be absent due to a family emergency, notify your instructor and give a general reason — not all the details of your situation. It is important for you and your instructor to get to know each other. You will find that your instructors are better able to help you if they know something about your background, your career goals, or your special difficulties with the course. You can get to know your instructor by stopping to ask a question after class or by talking with him or her during office hours.

Use the Instructors' Office Hours

Usually, each college instructor posts a list of several hours per week during which he or she will be available in his or her office to meet individually with students. It is usually not necessary to make an appointment to see an instructor during these times, but if you feel uncomfortable just walking in, you might mention to the instructor after class that you'd like to talk with him or her during office hours.

You can talk with the instructor during office hours about anything related to the course — how you are doing, trouble you are having with the course, difficulty you are having with a particular assignment — or to get further information or explanation about a certain topic.

Make Good Impressions

Based on how you act and react (how much you participate in class, how alert and interested you seem, how serious you are about learning), your instructors will form lasting impressions of you. They are naturally more willing to help a serious, conscientious student than one who seems not to care about learning. Serious students, too, frequently are given the higher of two grades if their semester test average is exactly between two grades — a high C or low B, for example.

Keep Up with Daily Assignments

Because many instructors do not check or require you to complete assignments as they are given, it is very easy to let things go and, as a result, have work accumulate as the semester progresses. As you will see in Chapter 4, "Becoming a Successful Learner: Principles of Learning," you learn and retain more information if you spread out your study time than if you try to do everything all at once at the end of the semester. There is a danger, too, in allowing work to pile up as the semester goes on; you may get so far behind that you'll become discouraged and will not want to or be able to spend the time required to catch up. Many students drop or withdraw from a course for this exact reason. One excellent way to be sure you will keep up with your courses is to follow a study-time schedule. Developing this schedule is discussed in the next chapter of this part of the text.

EXERCISE 1

Directions: *Read each of these situations. Then determine what caused the problem and place a check mark beside the best possible solution.*

1. Sally has been working hard in a required math course but has been confused all semester. She now realizes that the course is too advanced for her. What is the first thing she should do?
   - ____ a. just stop attending class
   - ____ b. see her advisor
   - ____ c. talk with her instructor
   - ____ d. hire a tutor
2. During the first week of classes, Tim realizes that he has signed up for too many courses and decides he should drop his chemistry class. Tim wants to know if he is eligible for a tuition refund. How should he find out?
   - ____ a. ask his instructor
   - ____ b. ask his faculty advisor
   - ____ c. check the college catalog
   - ____ d. ask a friend
3. Because of an error in his class schedule, Sam missed the first class meeting of his criminal justice course. What should he do?
   - ____ a. try to find someone who did attend and ask what was covered
   - ____ b. just hope that he did not miss too much
   - ____ c. explain to the instructor why he was absent and ask for copies of any handouts

4. Suppose that you are confused about what is expected of you for a term paper assignment given by your botany instructor. You decide to talk to your instructor but discover that you have other classes scheduled during each of his office hours. What should you do?

    —— a. skip one class and try to see your instructor
    —— b. forget about seeing your instructor
    —— c. ask your instructor for help after class
    —— d. see if you can make an appointment with your instructor at a time when you are both free

5. Suppose you are taking a chemistry course in which a weekly lab is required. You find that lab involves set-up instructions, experimental procedures, guidelines for evaluating your results, and a lab report. Your instructor usually discusses these topics during class sessions. What would be the best way to organize handouts, procedure sheets, and lab information and materials?

    —— a. keep these things together with everything else from the course
    —— b. keep them together only until the lab is held; then discard them
    —— c. create a separate section of your chemistry notebook for lab materials
    —— d. keep the information folded in the back of your textbook so that it is readily available

SUMMARY

The chapter presented numerous practical suggestions for achieving success in college. Before classes begin, it is important to arrange all the details related to attending college. These details include arranging work schedules, transportation, living arrangements, and finances. Before classes begin is also a good time to visit the campus, learn your way around, and become familiar with your schedule of classes.

The first week of classes can be used in getting organized for the remainder of the semester. It is a time for purchasing texts and organizing materials for each course. The first week is also the appropriate time to learn about each course you are taking, to understand the course requirements, and to get to know your instructors.

2. Learning Your Way Around

Use this chapter to:

1. *Learn your way around campus.*

2. *Become aware of all the services the college offers to help you.*

There is substantial evidence that students who are active and involved with the college scene around them are more likely to be successful than those who participate only by attending class and returning home. In order to get involved, however, you have to learn your way around. It is important to become familiar with the various offices, services, and student activities on campus. It is equally important to be fully familiar with the rules and policies that may affect you. Take the following quiz. It will give you an idea of how aware you are of what's going on around you.

DO YOU REALLY KNOW YOUR WAY AROUND?

1. What is the last day that you can withdraw from a course this semester?

    _____

    Do you have to pay for the course anyway?

    _____

2. Where would you go if there were a mistake on your tuition bill?

    _____

3. Where would you go first if you wanted to change from one curriculum to another?

    _____

4. Does the college allow you to take courses on a Pass/Fail or Satisfactory/Unsatisfactory basis instead of receiving a letter grade?

    _____

If so, what is the limit on the number of these courses you can take?

_____

5. What is meant by *grade point average* or *quality point average* and how do you figure it out?

_____

_____

6. How would you request a transcript to be sent to an employer?

_____

7. To whom should you talk if you think you received the wrong grade in a course?

_____

8. If you were in a car accident and know you'll be out of school for three weeks, whom should you notify?

_____

9. Is the library open on Saturday and/or Sunday afternoon?

_____

10. In the event that you or a friend became suddenly ill while on campus, where would you go for help?

_____

11. Does the college sponsor

a tennis team? _____

a women's tennis team?_____

a backgammon club?_____

If not, what activities does it sponsor?

_____

_____

How did you score? If there were two or more questions that you could not answer, you need to sharpen your awareness. Try some of the suggestions in the rest of this chapter to improve your knowledge of the college of which you are a part.

GENERAL SUGGESTIONS FOR LEARNING YOUR WAY AROUND

The expression *learning your way around* means several things. First, it means learning the location of various buildings, offices, and classrooms on campus. Second, and more important, it means knowing where to go for things you need, what policies affect you, whom to talk to, and how and where to get information you need. It also means being aware of what is going on around you — things such as new courses being offered, a new sports team forming, a freshman class picnic on a Saturday afternoon, visiting lecturers on campus, and the schedule for free movies.

Learning Where Things Are

Here are some ideas for learning the physical location of places:

1. If you are on the campus of a large college or university, you will need some type of campus map. Check to see if one is included in the college catalog. If not, ask for one at the visitor's information center or the reception area in any of the office buildings.
2. Once you find a particular room or office, jot down the building and room number.
3. During your first week, spend a lot of time walking around, looking, and asking questions.
4. If you have difficulty finding a certain room, ask anyone you see. (This is a good way to meet people too.)

Learning About College Activities

The college provides several sources of general information for all students. These are described under the next four headings.

The College Catalog: The college catalog contains the official information about the college that students need. It contains the rules and policies students are expected to know as well as course and curriculum information.

The Student Newspaper: Most colleges subsidize, or financially support, a student newspaper published at least weekly during the academic semester. In addition to feature articles about issues and events on campus, you will find notices of upcoming activities sponsored by various student groups, announcements about changes in college policies, and information concerning changes in academic policies. The student paper is usually free. Pick up a copy each time it is issued and look through it.

Brochures and Pamphlets: Pick up and read all brochures and pamphlets that you see. They provide a quick way of learning about some of the new and unusual groups or events on campus. Some offices which offer services to students — such as the Counseling Center, financial aid offices, and learning labs — prepare and distribute brochures as a means of advertising or making students aware of their services.

Bulletin Boards: On bulletin boards near or outside various department offices, you will find several types of important information. Last-minute information such as room changes and class cancellations may be posted. Departmental information such as faculty office hours, course changes, and student-advisor assignment lists may also be posted.

HOW TO GET INFORMATION AND HELP YOU NEED

A large portion of every college's budget goes toward providing a variety of support services for students and for the staff and offices needed for these services.

Learning About College Services

Under the headings below, some of the most common student-service offices are named along with a brief description of what they offer. Try to locate each of these offices on your campus, and become familiar with the specific services offered by each. You might, as you locate each office, pick up any available brochures which describe the services offered and the hours the office is open.

The Counseling Center: This office offers help to students with personal problems and to students having trouble deciding what they want to do, what career they should choose, or in which curriculum they should enroll. While most of the counselors will not make decisions about particular problems, students find that counselors often know the right questions to ask to help them think through the problems.

The Financial Aid Offices: Because obtaining tuition assistance awards, loans, and scholarships is sometimes quite complicated, most colleges have a special office whose primary function is to help students receive all possible financial assistance. Smaller colleges sometimes designate one staff member in the Counseling Center to help with financial aid. In any case, find out who is responsible for financial aid at your college and visit that person's office. Don't be one of the many students who finds out too late, after the deadline for application, that he or she was eligible for some type of aid.

The Library: Most students think of the library only as a place where books are stored, but a library also offers many valuable services. The library may loan records and/or films; it often houses coin-operated photocopying machines; it may provide listening rooms, typing rooms, and study rooms. Some libraries offer an interlibrary loan system whereby they can borrow books from other libraries for your use.

The people who work in a library are perhaps more important than any particular thing which is kept there. While you may think of librarians as people who check out and shelve books, you will find that college librarians are valuable to talk to. They frequently have college degrees in two or more subject areas as well as in library science. They can help you locate information, suggest a focus and direction for approaching a topic, and help you organize your research. Even though librarians always look busy, do not hesitate to ask them questions. There is always at least one librarian, usually located in the reference area, whose primary responsibility is to assist students.

Visit the library, look around, and be ready to use it effectively when you get your first class assignment this semester.

The Placement Office: Although you are not looking for a full-time job right now, it is wise to learn what services the Placement Office offers. (At small colleges this office may be part of the Counseling Center.) Placement Offices maintain a listing of current full- and part-time job openings. Some Placement Offices also, upon request, establish a placement file containing a student's background information, transcripts, and references. While at the college a student can use this service to collect and organize job-related information. Later, when applying for a job, a student can request that his or her file be sent to potential employers.

The Student Health Office: Most colleges have some type of health clinic or office to help students who become ill or injured while on campus. Find out what particular services your clinic offers. Does it dispense medicines? Make referrals to area physicians? Offer free tests?

The Reading-Learning Lab: Most colleges now have a center which offers students help with reading-learning-studying for their college courses. While the services offered by learning labs vary greatly from college to college, check to see if the lab at your college offers tutorial services, self-instructional learning modules, or minicourses at any time during the semester. Some labs offer brushup courses in skills like spelling, punctuation, and usage; basic math computation (percentages, fractions, and so forth), and term paper writing. Check to see if your college's lab offers anything that could help you to become a more successful student.

The Student Center: This building or area houses many of the social and recreational services available to students. Snack bars, theaters, game rooms, lounges, and offices for student groups are often located there. The Student Center is a good place to meet people and to find out what is happening on campus.

College Administrative Offices

Many offices on campus are primarily concerned with operating the college. While these administrative offices do not offer services to students, they keep records and make policies which directly affect you. These offices may have different names at various colleges. Here are a few you should become familiar with:

The Registrar's (Student Records) Office: This office keeps records on courses you take as well as grades you receive and mails your grades to you at the end of each semester. These records keep track of when you graduate and what degree you receive.

The Bursar's (Student Accounts) Office: All financial records are kept by this office. The people who work there send tuition bills and collect tuition payments.

Department Offices: Each separate discipline or subject area usually has a department office which is located near the offices of the faculty members who are in that department. The department secretary works there, and the department chairman's office is usually in the same location.

The Student Affairs Office: The Student Affairs (or Student Activities) Office plans and organizes all student extracurricular activities. This office can give you information on various athletic, social, and religious functions that are held on campus.

EXERCISE 1

Directions: *If you have learned your way around your campus, you should be able to answer the following questions:*

1. Beyond loaning books, what services does your library offer? List as many other library services as you were able to discover.

   _____

   _____

2. During what hours is the library open?

   _____

3. What office on your campus handles financial aid to students?

   _____

4. Does your college have a placement office?

   _____

5. Where is the Student Health Office located?

   _____

6. How often is the student newspaper published?

   _____

7. Where is the Counseling Center located? What services does it offer?

   _____

8. Where is the Registrar's Office located?

   _____

9. Did you find in the college catalog a listing of course descriptions offered by each subject area department?

_____

10. Does the college offer any brushup courses in skills such as spelling, punctuation, or basic math computation?

_____

11. Does your department office have a bulletin board or other ways to communicate information to its students?

_____

SUMMARY

In order to benefit most from your experience in college, it is important to be aware of all the services the college offers and the activities it sponsors. This chapter first presented specific suggestions for learning the physical location of places on campus. Next, the chapter discussed how to become familiar with activities the college sponsors and the services it offers. Finally, the chapter addressed a problem most students face — how and where to get information. The chapter listed various offices on campus and described the kinds of information and services they provide.

3. Organizing Your Time

Use this chapter to:

1. *Analyze how you currently use your time.*

2. *Find out how much time is needed for reading and study.*

3. *Learn to use your reading and study time more effectively.*

An essential factor in getting organized and succeeding in college is being able to use your time effectively. For most college students (for most adults too), finding enough time to do everything they *should* do and everything they *want* to do is nearly impossible. Most people continually face a series of conflicts over use of their time and are forced to make numerous decisions about what to do at specific times. Examples of such time conflicts include:

Watching the late movie
vs.
getting a good night's sleep

Taking your car to the garage for inspection
vs.
attending a local football game

Taking your sister shopping
vs.
keeping your dental appointment

Some time conflicts involve choosing between equally pleasant and enjoyable alternatives. Most likely, you would enjoy deciding whether to go bowling or to see a film on a particular evening. Other conflicts and the choices you make are determined by particular circumstances and needs. If you have the flu, for instance, you may have to decide to skip classes so you can see your doctor.

Still other day-to-day decisions, however, can be frustrating and take up valuable time as you weigh the alternatives. Probably the most frustrating are "want to" versus "should" decisions. These decisions become necessary when you want to take part in an enjoyable activity that is taking place at the same time you should be doing something else. College students have varied interests, social commitments, and family responsibilities. These interests frequently conflict with completing assignments, writing papers, studying for exams, or other things that should be done. Here are some examples of this type of conflict:

Want to	*Should*
Go out with friends	Finish reading textbook chapter
Have coffee in snack bar	Do library assignment
Go bowling	Study for psychology test

Not only is it difficult and time-consuming to face these choices, it is also easy to give in to an immediate "want to" and leave a "should" until later. Unfortunately, this only creates further problems. Not only is work still left to be completed, but the student ends up feeling guilty about the choice and doesn't fully enjoy the activity chosen.

ANALYZING YOUR TIME

There is a way to eliminate this constant struggle between what you would like to do and what needs to be done. The answer is to plan your time in advance — to develop a schedule or routine which allows time for both leisure activities and college course work. In such a schedule, you can set up a time to study for an exam in psychology, a time for library research, and a time for reading biology assignments. Following a schedule like this eliminates hard-to-make choices and ensures that you'll get everything done.

In order to develop an effective time schedule, it is first necessary to determine how much time you have available and then decide how you use it. Many students say they don't achieve high grades in their courses because they don't have enough time to study. Others have part- or full-time jobs, social interests, and family commitments, and they claim that these things take up all their time.

To begin developing a schedule, make some rough estimates. First, quickly estimate how many hours per week you have available for reading and studying, and write the number of hours on the blank below.

Estimated study hours available per week: _____ hours

Next, estimate the number of reading-study hours you need per week. For each course that you are taking, estimate how many hours per week you would need to spend, outside of class time, in order to get the grade you want to earn. Be honest; indicate what grade you really want to work for. When estimating time, take into consideration how much time you need to study, how many assignments there are, how fast you normally read, and how difficult the subject is for you. Write the grade and time estimates on the chart in Figure 3-1. When you are finished, add up the hours and fill in the total.

Name of course	Desired grade	Hours per week needed

Total hours _____

FIGURE 3-1

Now, let's see how realistic and practical your estimates were. Were you correct about how much reading-study time you have available each week? Do you have enough reading-study hours available each week to earn the grades you indicated on the chart? To find out, analyze your actual time commitments. Fill in Figure 3-2, estimating the time you need for each activity. Remember to indicate how much time each actually takes. Do not indicate an hour for lunch if you usually take only ten or fifteen minutes for a quick sandwich. When you have completed the chart, total the hours per week to discover your actual weekly time commitment.

	Hours per day	Hours per week
Sleep	_____	_____
Breakfast	_____	_____
Lunch	_____	_____
Dinner	_____	_____
Part- or full-time job	_____	_____
Time spent in classes	_____	_____
Transportation time	_____	_____
Personal care (dressing, shaving, etc.)	_____	_____
Household/family responsibilities (cooking dinner, driving mother to work, etc.)	_____	_____

Total committed time per week _____

FIGURE 3-2

Now that you have totaled your committed time per week, it is easy to see how much time you have left to divide between reading-study for your courses and leisure activities. There is a total of 168 hours in each week. Just copy your total committed time from Figure 3-2 and complete the subtraction:

168   hours in one week

– _____   total committed time

_____   hours available

Are you surprised to see how many hours per week you have left? Write this number of hours on the second and fourth blanks below. How does this total number of available reading-study hours compare with your earlier estimates? Look back to page 17 to see how many hours you estimated you have available for reading-study, and write the hours on the first blank. Look back to Figure 3-1 and see how many hours you estimated you needed to earn a particular grade in each course, and write the hours on the third blank. Now, answer this question: Do you have enough time available for reading and study to achieve the grades you want?

Estimated study hours available	_____ hours
Actual study hours available	_____ hours
Estimated hours needed for grades	_____ hours
Actual study hours available	_____ hours

If your answer to the question was no, one of two things is probably true. Either you were unrealistic in your estimate of committed time, or you really are committed to such a point that it is unrealistic to take as many courses as you are taking and aim toward the grades you indicated. There are several alternatives to consider if your time is overcommitted. Can any activity be dropped or done in less time? Can you reduce the number of hours you work, or can another family member split some time-consuming responsibilities with you? If you are unable to reduce your committed time, you should consider taking fewer college courses or adjusting your expected grades to more achievable levels.

If your answer to the question was yes, you are ready to begin to develop a schedule that will help you use your available time most effectively. You are probably concerned at this point, however, that the above time analysis did not take into account social and leisure activities. That omission was deliberate up to this point.

While leisure time is essential to everyone's well-being, it should not take precedence over college course work. Most students who develop and follow a time schedule for accomplishing their course work are able to devote reasonable amounts of time to leisure and social activities.

BUILDING YOUR TIME SCHEDULE

A study-time schedule is a weekly plan of when and what you will study. It identifies specific times for studying particular subjects as well as times for writing papers, conducting library research, and completing homework assignments for each course.

The major purpose in developing a study-time schedule is to allow you to decide in advance how you will divide your available time between study and leisure activities. A schedule will eliminate the need to make frustrating last-minute choices between "should" and "want to" activities.

The sample study-time schedule in Figure 3-3 was developed by a freshman student. Read it through carefully.

Your Own Schedule

Now that you have seen a sample schedule, you can begin to build your own schedule. Fill in the blank schedule, Figure 3-4, following steps 1–5.

1. Write "class" in all the time blocks that you spend attending classes and labs.
2. If you have a part-time job, write "work" in the appropriate time blocks.
3. Write "trans." in those portions of the time blocks in which you travel to and from campus and to and from work.
4. Block off with an *X* realistic amounts of time for breakfast, lunch, and dinner.
5. Also block off and write *F-H* in blocks of time committed to inflexible family/household responsibilities.

The empty time blocks are those available for study and for leisure activities. Look through the following hints before you attempt to decide what subject you will study at what time.

1. Study difficult subjects first. It is tempting to get easy things and short little assignments out of the way first, but do not give in to this approach. When you start studying, your mind is fresh and alert and you are at your peak of concentration. This is the time you are best equipped to handle difficult subjects. Thinking through complicated problems or studying complex ideas requires all the brain power you have, and you have most at the beginning of a study session.
2. Leave the routine and more mechanical tasks for last. Activities like recopying papers or alphabetizing a bibliography for a research paper do not require a high degree of concentration and can be left until you are tired.
3. Schedule study for a particular course close to the time when you attend class; that is, plan to study the evening before the class meets or at a time after the class meeting. If a class meets on Tuesday morning, plan to study Monday evening, or Tuesday afternoon or evening. By placing study time and class time close together, you are making it easier to relate class lectures and discussions to what you are reading and studying.

4. Build into your schedule a short break before you begin studying each new subject. Your mind needs time to refocus — to switch from one set of facts, problems, and issues to another.

5. Short breaks should also be included when you are working on just one assignment, but for a long period of time. A ten-minute break after 50–60 minutes of study is reasonable.

6. When reading or studying a particular subject, try to schedule two or three short, separate blocks of time for that course rather than one long, continuous block. As will be explained in the next chapter, on principles of learning, you are able to learn more by spacing or spreading out your study time than you are by completing it in one sitting.

7. Schedule study sessions at times when you know you are usually alert and feel like studying. Do not schedule a study time early on Saturday morning if you are a person who does not really wake up until noon, and try not to schedule study time late in the evening if you are usually tired by that time.

8. Plan to study at times when the physical surroundings are conducive to study. If the dinner hour is a rushed and confusing time in your household, don't attempt to study then if there are alternative times available.

9. Do not wait for the mood to strike or until you feel like studying.

Using the suggestions above, plan a tentative study-time schedule for the week and fill in the empty time blocks on the schedule in Figure 3-4. First, identify only the times when it would be best to study. Then decide what subjects you will study during these times and in what order you will study them. You will need to refer to Figure 3-1 to check the total number of hours per week that each course requires. Try to be as specific as possible in identifying what is to be done at particular times. If you know, for example, that there is a weekly homework assignment in math due each Wednesday, reserve a specific block of time for completing that assignment.

Now that you have identified study times, the remaining time can be scheduled for leisure and social activities. Analyze this remaining time to determine how it can best be used. What things do you enjoy most? What things do you do just because you have nothing else to do? Plan specific times for activities that are most important to you.

USING YOUR TIME SCHEDULE

Using your schedule will be a challenge because it will mean saying no in a number of different situations. When friends call or stop by and ask you to join them at a time when you planned to study, you will have to refuse, but you could let them know when you will be free and offer to join them then. When a friend or family member asks you to do a favor — like driving him or her somewhere — you will have to refuse, but you can suggest some alternative times when you will be free. You will find that your friends and family will accept your restraints and may even respect you for being conscientious. Don't you respect someone who gets a lot done and is successful in whatever he or she attempts?

Try out the schedule that you have built for one week. Be realistic and make adjustments where they are obviously needed. Mark these

	Monday	Tuesday	Wednesday	Thursday	Friday
8:00	✕	✕	✕	✕	✕
9:00	←——— TRANSPORTATION TIME ———→				
	History class	Psychology class	History class	Psychology class	History class
10:00	review History notes; read assignment	study	review History notes; read assignment	TRANSPORTATION	review History notes
11:00	Math class	Psychology	Math class	study Psychology	Math class
12:00	LUNCH	LUNCH	English Composition	LUNCH	English Composition
1:00	Math homework	review lab procedures	class.	Math homework	class
2:00			LUNCH		LUNCH
	Chemistry class		Chemistry class	read Chemistry	Chemistry class.
3:00	TRANSPORTATION	Chemistry Lab.	TRANSPORTATION		TRANSPORTATION
4:00					
5:00					
	DINNER	TRANSPORTATION	DINNER	DINNER	DINNER
6:00		DINNER			
	WORK	Write lab	WORK		WORK
7:00		report; start reading new Chemistry chapter; type		read English assignment	
8:00		English Composition		revise returned Composition	
9:00					
10:00					
11:00					

FIGURE 3-3

	Saturday	Sunday
8:00		
9:00		
10:00	type Chemistry Lab report	revise English paper
11:00	(other typing)	review history assignment
12:00		
1:00	draft English paper	
2:00	read Psychology chapter	Math homework
3:00		read and study Chemistry
4:00	review Psychology notes	
5:00		
6:00		
7:00		plan next week's study
8:00		
9:00		
10:00		
11:00		

	Monday	Tuesday	Wednesday	Thursday	Friday
8:00					
9:00					
10:00					
11:00					
12:00					
1:00					
2:00					
3:00					
4:00					
5:00					
6:00					
7:00					
8:00					
9:00					
10:00					
11:00					

FIGURE 3-4

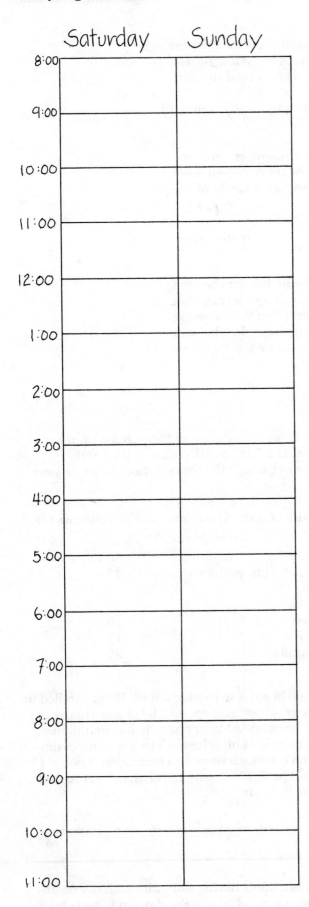

	Saturday	Sunday
8:00		
9:00		
10:00		
11:00		
12:00		
1:00		
2:00		
3:00		
4:00		
5:00		
6:00		
7:00		
8:00		
9:00		
10:00		
11:00		

changes on the schedule itself. Do not stop to decide if you should follow or change each block on the schedule. Doing so forces you back into the "want to" versus "should" conflict the schedule was designed to eliminate.

After using the schedule for one week, evaluate it by asking yourself the following questions:

1. Did you overestimate or underestimate the amount of time you needed for each course? (The time will vary, of course, from week to week, so be sure to allow enough for those heavy times of the semester — midterm and final exam weeks.)
2. Did you find some conflicts? Can they be resolved?
3. Did you find some scheduled study-times particularly inconvenient? Can they be rearranged?

Revise your schedule and then try the revised schedule for the next week. Within a week or two you will have worked out a schedule that will carry you through the remainder of the semester. You will be using your time effectively and getting the grades that you have decided you want. Best of all, day-to-day frustrating conflicts over time will be eliminated.

EXERCISE 1

Directions: *Read each situation described, and then decide what could be done to solve the problem. Discuss your decisions with another student and place a check mark beside the best solution, or write your answer on the line below.*

1. In analyzing his amount of committed time, George Andrews filled in a chart as follows:

Sleep	56
Breakfast, lunch, dinner (total)	14
Part-time job	35
Time in classes	23
Transportation	10
Personal care	15
Household/family	20
Total	173

George has to have a job in order to pay for school. He is enrolled in Science Lab Technology, so he must spend a lot of class hours in lab. He estimates that he needs 30 hours per week to maintain a high B average this semester. If he schedules this amount of time, he will have virtually no time for leisure and recreation. Look at his chart again. What could he do? What are his choices? Try to find as many alternatives as you can.

_____

_____

2. Susan is a serious student but is having difficulty with her botany course. She has decided to spend all day Sunday studying botany.

She plans to lock herself in her room and not come out until she has reviewed four chapters. What is wrong with her approach? What study plan would be more effective?

_____

_____

3. Mark realizes that he has three assignments that have to be completed in one evening. The assignments are to revise an English composition, to read and underline ten pages in the anatomy and physiology text, and to recopy a homework assignment for sociology. He decides to get the sociology assignment out of the way first, then do the English composition (because English is one of his favorite subjects), and to read the anatomy and physiology text last. Evaluate Mark's plan of study.

_____

_____

4. You are taking a course in music appreciation, and your instructor often asks you to listen to a certain part of a concert on FM radio or to watch a particular program on TV. Since you cannot predict when these assignments will be given or at what time you need to complete them, what could you do to include these assignments in your weekly study schedule?

_____

_____

5. Suppose that, just as you are beginning your math homework, your younger sister asks you to drive her to a nearby shopping mall. You explain to her that you must complete your assignment, but she suggests that you bring it along and finish it while she shops. Evaluate each of the following alternatives:
   ____ a. follow her suggestion — take the work with you
   ____ b. simply refuse
   ____ c. go to the mall — plan on doing the assignment when you get back
   ____ d. refuse, but suggest another time when you are free to take her

6. Consider your plans for this evening. List as many "want to" activities as you can with their corresponding "should" activities.

_____

_____

7. John used the study schedule shown in Figure 3-5 for one week but found that he wasn't getting as much accomplished as he should and had difficulty studying when he was supposed to. Why

	Monday	Tuesday	Wednesday	Thursday	Friday
8:00					
9:00	Business Organization + Management class		Business Organization + management class		Business Organization + Management class
10:00		Business Math class	do Data Processing Lab work	Business Math	do Data Processing Lab work
11:00	English Composition class		English Composition class		English Composition class
12:00					
1:00	Data Processing class	Psychology class	Data Processing class	Psychology class	Data Processing class
2:00					
3:00			SWIM TEAM PRACTICE		
4:00					
5:00					
6:00			do Math	type English Composition	
7:00	read Psychology assignments		homework	read Data Processing chapter	
8:00			draft English composition		
9:00					
10:00					
11:00					

FIGURE 3-5

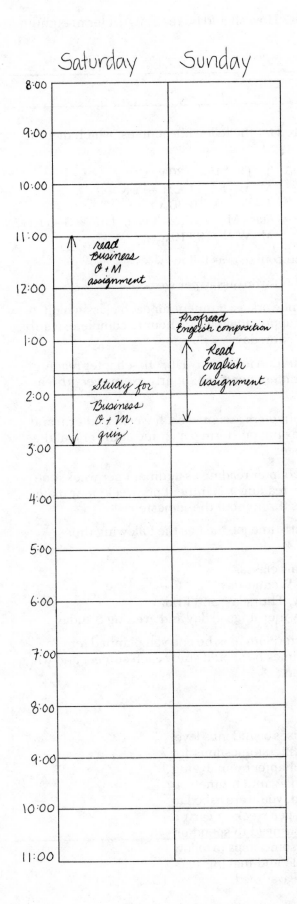

is he having problems? How should he rearrange it for maximum efficiency?

_____

_____

8. Sam Smith is registered for the following courses, which meet at the times indicated:

Bus. Management 905   T–Th   12–1:30 P.M.
English 101   M–W–F   11 A.M.–12 NOON
Math 201   T–Th   9–10:30 A.M.
Biology 601   class M–W–F, 2–3 P.M.; lab W, 3–5 P.M.
Psychology 502   M–W–F   9–10 A.M.

The work load for each course is as follows:

English	One 250-word essay per week
Math	A homework assignment for each class which takes approximately one hour to complete; a quiz each Thursday
Biology	Preparation for weekly lab; one-chapter reading assignment per week; hourly exam every three weeks
Business Management	Two chapters assigned each week; midterm and final exam; one term paper due at the end of the semester
Psychology	One-chapter reading assignment per week; one library reading assignment per week; four major exams throughout the semester

Because Sam has a part-time job, he has the following times available for study:

the times between his classes
evenings: Tuesday, Wednesday
afternoons: Monday, Thursday, and Friday
weekends: Saturday morning, all day and evening Sunday

Plan a study schedule for Sam like the one you planned for yourself. Include the times he should study each subject and what tasks he should work on.

SUMMARY

The ability to use time effectively greatly increases a student's level of success in college. This chapter presented specific suggestions for analyzing and organizing your time. You began the chapter by analyzing your current time commitments and determining how much time you have available to meet college course demands. Next, you were asked to estimate the amount of time each course requires per week to earn a certain grade and to determine the total amount you need to spend on course work each week. Finally, the chapter offered some steps to follow in planning and using a weekly study-time schedule and making necessary adjustments to meet the course load you have assumed.

4. Becoming a More Successful Learner: Principles of Learning and Memory

Use this chapter to:

1. *Find out how forgetting, learning, and memory work.*

2. *Learn principles that will help you learn.*

Now that you are involved with your courses and have become familiar with your campus, it is time to consider how to be successful in your courses.

Think of the courses you are taking this semester and why you are taking them. Most likely, some are required courses, and others you have elected on the basis of interest, convenience, advice, or need. Now, think of what you want from each course. Of course, at the very minimum, you want to pass each course. To do so, you must *learn* enough to complete assignments, to pass exams, and to write acceptable papers. You are probably taking certain courses to *learn* a skill, such as math, writing, accounting, or data processing. In others you are *learning* a new academic discipline, such as anthropology, psychology, ecology, or sociology. Regardless of the type of course you are taking, you have one overall goal — to learn.

Since learning is at the core of success, the first step is to learn how to learn. The main purpose of this chapter is to suggest practical ways you can learn and remember more efficiently.

FORGETTING

Have you ever wondered why you cannot remember what you have just read? Have you noticed students in your classes who seem to remember everything? Do you wonder why you can't? The answer is *not* that these other students are brighter than you are or that they have studied twice as long as you have. Instead, these students have learned how to learn and to remember; they have developed techniques for effective learning.

Forgetting, defined as the loss of information stored in memory, is a normal, everyday occurrence. It occurs because other information interferes with or prevents you from recalling the desired information. Psychologists have extensively studied the rate at which forgetting occurs. According to Geiwitz in his text entitled *Psychology: Looking at Ourselves*, forgetting, for most people, occurs very rapidly immediately after learning and then levels off over time. To demonstrate to you just how fast forgetting normally occurs and how much information is lost, Figure 4-1 has been included. It is called the retention curve, and it shows how much you are able to remember over time.

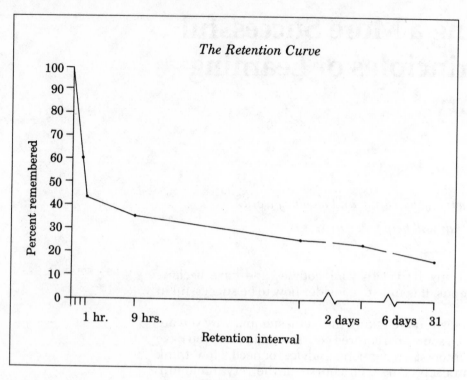

FIGURE 4-1

This retention curve has serious implications for you as a learner. Basically, the curve suggests that unless you are one of the lucky few who remember almost everything they hear or read, you will forget a large portion of the information you learn unless you do something to prevent it. For instance, the graph shows that your recall of information learned drops to below 50 percent within an hour and to about 30 percent within two days.

Fortunately, there are specific techniques to prevent or slow down forgetting. These specific techniques are what the remainder of this book is all about. Throughout the book you will learn techniques to enable you to identify what to learn (pick out what is important) and to learn it in the most effective way. Each technique is intended to help you remember more and to slow down your rate of forgetting. For instance, in Chapter 15 you will learn how taking notes during class lectures can help you learn and remember what the lecture is about. In Chapter 13 you will learn a system for reading to learn and remember more.

However, before learning these specific techniques it is useful to understand a little about the learning and memory process and why forgetting occurs. Once you know how learning occurs, you will be able to see why and how the various techniques suggested throughout the book are effective. Each reading and study technique presented is based on the learning and memory process and is designed to help you learn in the most efficient way.

EXERCISE 1

Directions: *Apply the information you have learned about the rate of forgetting to each of the following reading-study situations. Refer to the retention curve (Figure 4-1).*

1. How much information from a textbook chapter can you expect to recall two days after you read it?

   _____

2. How much information presented in a lecture last week can you expect to remember this week if you do not take any notes on the lecture?

   _____

3. What do you think your level of recall would be if you took notes on a particular lecture but did not review your notes for two weeks?

   _____

4. Why would it be necessary to take notes on a film shown in class if you have to write a reaction paper on it that evening?

   _____

HOW PEOPLE LEARN AND REMEMBER

There are several steps or stages involved in the learning-memory process. First, information enters the brain from a variety of sources. In reading-study situations, information is entered primarily through reading and listening. Second, the information is either discarded or remembered momentarily. The momentary or brief memory is called *short-term memory*. Next, information in your short-term memory is either discarded and forgotten, or it is transferred into your permanent memory. This permanent memory is called *long-term memory*. Anything you want to remember for more than a few seconds must be stored in your long-term memory. To place information in your long-term memory it must be *learned*. Finally, not all information which you learn and have stored in your long-term memory stays there in a form that can be easily recalled. Some information is forgotten or lost; other information can be brought back or retrieved.

How Short-Term Memory Works

Your immediate, or short-term, memory is very limited and cannot be relied upon for any type of permanent learning. It is limited in both the length of time that it can hold information and in its capacity (the amount of information it can hold at one time). Items or facts stay in your short-term memory only about 15 seconds. Then they are either lost or they must be transferred to long-term memory, through a learning process.

The nature of short-term memory can provide an explanation for many puzzling day-to-day situations. Have you looked up a phone number and then walked to the next room to dial the number only to find that you could not remember it? You probably forgot the number because more than fifteen seconds elapsed and your short-term memory discarded the information. Or, when you are looking up a person's phone number, you look directly at the address as well as the number. Why don't you remember the address? You were not looking specifically for the address, so it was discarded instead of being stored in your short-term memory.

Short-term memory also plays an important role in reading-study situations. Short-term memory can explain why you cannot remember facts and details in a chapter you have just finished reading. It also explains why you cannot remember the content of a lecture given last week. As you are reading, then, you must make direct efforts to identify information that is worth remembering and transfer it to your long-term memory. Information you do not identify as important will drop out of your short-term memory and never reach your long-term memory.

Learning: The Transfer from Short-Term to Long-Term Memory

Learning, or the process by which you are able to remember information, involves the transfer of information from short- to long-term memory. In fact, how completely and how thoroughly you learn a piece of information, in part, determines how well and how long you will be able to remember it.

Psychologists often refer to this transfer of information from short- to long-term memory as *rehearsal*. The term "rehearsal" will become more meaningful if you think of a choir rehearsing a song or a group of actors rehearsing for a play. Members of the choir learn the songs by practicing them. Actors also learn their parts through practice and repetition. At first they work on scenes and acts; eventually they perform the entire show in dress rehearsal. Rehearsal, then, involves some type of *repetition* of information in order to learn and remember it. In learning information from your textbook or class lecture notes, this repetition might be accomplished by saying the information aloud or silently, by writing the information, or by reading a summary of the information.

Effective learning, however, involves much more than the dull repetition of information. Information can be organized or structured to make it easier to remember. Also, new information can be connected or related to learned information that already is stored in your long-term memory. For example, after looking up a phone number, if you want to remember it while you are walking to the phone, you might repeat it over and over, or you might note that there is a pattern to it, such as 877-8777. Also, you might recognize that, except for the last digit, it is the same as your sister's phone number. Each of these suggested techniques — repetition, organization, and connection to previously learned information — is a form of learning, or rehearsal.

In general, you might think of learning as a process of storing information so that you can retrieve it, or pull it out of your long-term memory, easily and quickly.

As you work through the various chapters in the text, you will see that rehearsal is the underlying principle on which many of the study techniques presented later in this book are based. In Chapter 14, for example, a technique for underlining and marking textbooks is presented. This technique requires that you identify and underline important ideas and facts and that you make marginal notes about paragraph or passage content. The technique of underlining is, however, actually a form of rehearsal. By selecting information to be underlined, you are repeating the information and sorting the important from the unimportant. By making marginal notes, you may be classifying, organizing, labeling, or summarizing information; all of these techniques are part of rehearsal.

As you take classroom lecture notes (discussed in Chapter 15), rehearsal is taking place. In order to know what to write down as you listen, you are sorting the important ideas from the details and examples. Then, as you write the notes, you are repeating the information. Unless you copied down every word of the lecturer, you were also rearranging, paraphrasing (putting into your own words), and interpreting the information given in the lecture.

Long-Term Memory

Your long-term memory contains hundreds of thousands of facts, details, impressions, and experiences that you have accumulated throughout your life. Exactly how this memory works is still being debated by learning psychologists. Some researchers think memory is a chemical process and is related to the production in the body of a chemical called RNA. Others think memory has to do with the body's neurological structure (electrical connections and movements within neurons). Despite the uncertainty as to how long-term memory works, there are definite factors that affect how well and how long we can remember things.

Whether you will be able to remember something is determined partly by how thoroughly and completely you learned it. Of course, if you never made any attempt to learn a piece of information, it is unlikely that you will remember it. For example, you have probably forgotten whether it was raining last June 25th or whether you went to the store on May 25th of last year.

Similarly, if you made no special effort to learn a textbook's content as you read it, you cannot expect to be able to remember it. You can only expect to remember something if you take special steps to store the information in your long-term memory. If, however, you study and attempt to remember a body of information and still cannot remember it, it is likely that you have not learned the material thoroughly or completely. Let's consider an example from everyday life. Suppose you have a job as a file clerk in a business office and your responsibility is to store and locate when needed all correspondence, bills, and purchase orders. If you didn't file at all and just let the material pile up on your desk, soon you would not be able to find anything. Or if you filed the material incompletely by piling it into one of five file cabinet drawers, you still would not be able to locate material rapidly and easily. However, if you did your job completely and thoroughly, filing everything in the appropriate cabinet, drawer, and file folder, you would be able to retrieve any information at a moment's notice. You can probably see how this situation parallels learning. Learning is, in a sense, a type of filing in which you store (or file) information in your memory. The more thoroughly and accurately the information is filed, the more easily you will be able to remember it. Applied to reading-study situations, this factor strongly suggests the need for reviewing and checking your learning to be certain it is thorough and complete. Throughout the text you will find numerous techniques that have a built-in check or test-yourself factor.

A second factor that controls how well you will be able to learn something is called *interference*. This can mean that you forget something you have learned because something new interferes with it. Suppose you have one friend named Bill Atkins, and you never have trouble remembering his name. Then you make another friend whose name is Bill Atkinson, and now you often mistakenly call your older friend Atkinson. The second person's name interfered with your recall of the first, even though it was, at one time, thoroughly and completely learned. Similar interference can occur between various subject areas or between similar content in one subject area. It is easy, for instance, to confuse "endomorph" and "ectomorph" — terms that refer to basic body types — when studying human physiology, because the terms look alike.

Interference can also refer to a situation in which it is difficult to learn something new because something you already know gets in the way. For instance, you may have trouble, after moving, remembering a new phone number, especially if it is similar to your old one. In learning a second foreign language, you may have difficulty learning the French word for "sister" if you already know the Spanish word.

PRINCIPLES OF LEARNING

Now that you know how the learning-memory process works, it is appropriate to consider ways in which you can learn most effectively. This section presents a summary of the most useful principles of learning. Each has specific applications for learning material contained in college texts or presented in class lectures.

Principle 1: Intent to Remember

What were you wearing seventeen months ago at this time? What did you eat for lunch on March 18, 1982? Why can't you answer these questions? The answer, of course, is simple: because you did not store the information. At the time you saw no need to remember what you were wearing or eating. One of the most obvious principles related to memory is that you remember only what you intend to remember — that which you identify as worth remembering.

To further illustrate this principle, draw the face side of a one dollar bill in the space provided below before you read any farther.

Now, did you include each of the following: the face of George Washington, the seal of the Department of the Treasury, the Federal Reserve Bank seal, the signature of the Treasurer of the United States, the signature of the Secretary of the Treasury, the words *Federal Reserve Note*, serial numbers, the series date, the words *UNITED STATES OF AMERICA*, and so on? Did you put all of these things in the right places? Most likely you were not able to reproduce a dollar bill accurately, and just think of how often you have looked at one. You did not remember the details on the bill because, whenever you looked at one, you had no *intention* of remembering it.

Application: Intent to remember has direct applications to both textbook reading and lecture notetaking. As you read or listen, you should select what you intend to remember by sorting out the important ideas from those that are relatively unimportant.

This principle also provides the basis for the techniques of pre-reading and establishing a purpose (presented in Chapters 7 and 8). You will learn that prereading is a method of getting an overview, or advance picture, of what is important and worth remembering in a textbook chapter before reading it completely. Prereading really tells you, in advance of a complete reading, what material you should intend to remember. Suppose you discover through prereading a chapter in an astronomy text that the chapter discusses the location, physical properties, and appearance of eight planets. Then you can establish an intent to remember. As you read, you will plan on identifying and remembering the name, location, properties, and appearance of each planet. The technique of establishing a purpose involves forming questions to guide your reading. It requires that, for each dark print (or boldface) heading within a textbook chapter, you form a question. And then, as you read, you try to find the answer to the question. The answer to your question is what you intend to remember.

Principle 2: Meaningfulness

Material that is meaningful, or makes sense, is easier to learn and remember than meaningless information. It would be easier to learn a list of meaningful words than a list of nonsense words. Try the following experiment to test the accuracy of the last sentence.

EXPERIMENT

Directions:
1. Read through list 1 on page 38, spending a maximum of 15 seconds.
2. Now, cover list 1 with your hand or a piece of scrap paper, and write down in the space provided as many items as you can remember.
3. Follow steps 1 and 2 for each of the other three lists.
4. Check to see how many items you had correct on each of the four lists.

List 1	List 2	List 3	List 4
KQZ	BLT	WIN	WAS
NLR	TWA	SIT	THE
XOJ	SOS	LIE	CAR
BTK	CBS	SAW	RUN
YSW	NFL	NOT	OFF

List 1	List 2	List 3	List 4
_____	_____	_____	_____
_____	_____	_____	_____
_____	_____	_____	_____
_____	_____	_____	_____
_____	_____	_____	_____

Did you recall more items on list 2 than on list 1? Why? Did you remember more items on list 4 than on list 3? As you must now realize, after list 1, each list became more meaningful than the one before it. The lists progressed from nonsense syllables (1) to meaningful letter groupings (2) to words (3) and, finally, to words that, when strung together, produced meaning (4). This simple experiment demonstrates that you are able to remember information that is meaningful more easily than information that has no meaning.

Let's look at some other examples of the principle of meaningful learning. Consider phone numbers. Some are easy to remember; others are not. Would it be easy to remember the phone number of your local takeout pizza shop if the phone number were 825-3699? Probably not. Would it be easier to remember if you realized that the digits in the phone number correspond to letters on the phone dial that spell *takeout*? Yes. The word *takeout* has a particular meaning to you because you are using the phone number to order a takeout item.

Application: The principle of meaningful learning is critical in all textbook reading situations. It affirms the necessity of understanding (comprehending) what you read. If you do not understand a concept or idea, it is not meaningful, and you will not be able to remember it. As you read, to be sure that you are comprehending, try to explain what you have read in your own words. If you cannot, you probably have not understood the material.

Several of the reading-study techniques presented in this text are, in part, based on the principle of meaningfulness. The technique of prereading, in which you become acquainted with the overall organization and content of a selection before you begin to read it, makes the reading process more meaningful. Establishing a purpose also makes reading more meaningful: you are reading to find specific information. The techniques of underlining and marking textbooks and taking lecture notes also give further meaning and organization to the materials to be studied.

Now suppose that, while learning vocabulary for an astronomy course, you discover you have to learn the terms for the lower, middle, and upper layers of the atmosphere. The terms are *troposphere, mesosphere,* and *exosphere*. One way to learn these words would be to memorize each word and its corresponding meaning. A better way would be to recognize that the root *sphere* in each refers to a three-dimensional object — in this case, the earth. The prefix, or beginning part of each word, in some way describes the atmosphere in relation to the earth. *Tropo-* means "change," and it is in this lower layer of the earth's atmosphere that the temperature changes with increasing altitude. The prefix *meso-* means "center or middle," so *mesosphere* is the center layer of the atmosphere. The prefix *exo-* means "outside or external," so it is the exosphere which is the uppermost or outer layer of the atmosphere. It is by learning the meanings of the root *sphere* and the prefixes as well as connecting them with specific meanings in astronomy that the terms become more meaningful and are easier to remember.

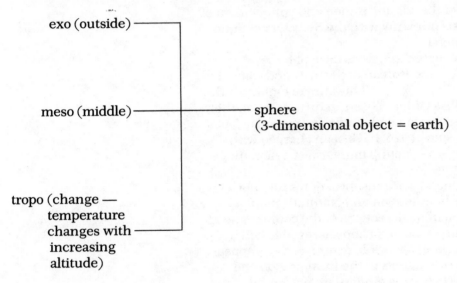

Principle 3: Categorization and Labeling

Categorization is the restructuring, or reorganizing, of information into meaningful groups for easier recall. Suppose you had to remember to buy the following items at the supermarket and couldn't write them down: apples, milk, toothpaste, eggs, pepperoni, shampoo, celery, deodorant, salami, cheese, pork chops, and onions. What could you do to make recall of the items easier? One thing you could do is classify the items by organizing them in the categories shown in these headings:

Toiletries	*Dairy*	*Meat*	*Fruits/ Vegetables*
toothpaste	milk	pepperoni	apples
deodorant	cheese	salami	onions
shampoo	eggs	pork chops	celery

By classifying the items in these categories, you are, first of all, making the information meaningful — it is organized according to aisles or departments within the store. Second, you have placed a label on each group of items. The labels "Toiletries," "Dairy," and so forth can serve as "memory tags" that will help you to remember to buy the items you classified under each category. Using memory tags may be compared to knowing which cupboard door to open in your kitchen when you are looking for something. If you know which cupboard door to open, locating a can of soup is relatively easy. But if you do not know where the canned items are stored, locating the soup could be difficult. In trying to remember your list of supermarket shopping items, if you can remember the category "Dairy," recalling the particular items you want to buy becomes a simpler task.

Application: Try to categorize information as you read it — either in your mind or on paper. In the following passage, you could classify the information into the two categories indicated by the headings in the diagram below.

> Responsibility for the administration and enforcement of immigration laws rests primarily with the Secretary of State and the Attorney General.
>
> The Secretary of State discharges most of his responsibilities through the Bureau of Security and Consular Affairs authorized by the 1952 act. This bureau embraces the Passport Office and Visa Office. These, in turn, carry on their work with the aid of American diplomatic and consular officers abroad, who, since 1924, have been charged with primary responsibility for selecting immigrants before they embark.
>
> The Attorney General performs most of his functions in this field through the Immigration and Naturalization Service, which has a staff in all sections of the country and at important ports of entry. A board of appeals, established by the Attorney General and responsible to him, reviews appeals from orders and actions of agents of the Immigration and Naturalization Service. Hearing officers are not bound, however, to observe the standards of fairness prescribed by the Administrative Procedures Act.
>
> —Ferguson and McHenry, *The American System of Government,* p. 213.

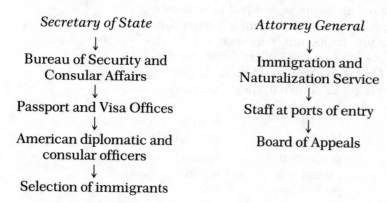

Secretary of State	*Attorney General*
↓	↓
Bureau of Security and Consular Affairs	Immigration and Naturalization Service
↓	↓
Passport and Visa Offices	Staff at ports of entry
↓	↓
American diplomatic and consular officers	Board of Appeals
↓	
Selection of immigrants	

Several reading-study techniques suggested in this book employ the principle of categorization. As you take lecture notes (Chapter 15), for example, you are arranging, classifying, and categorizing information. As you use the recall clue system for studying those lecture notes, you continue applying the principle of labeling and grouping — categorizing information. As you underline and mark a textbook (Chapter 14), you are performing a similar task.

Principle 4: Association

New information is easier to learn and remember if you can connect it with previously learned or familiar information. For instance, it is easy to remember your new license plate number if it is 1776 US. You can associate, or connect, the new license plate with an already well-learned date and event, in this case the date the United States became independent. Or you can remember and recognize the shape of Italy on a map if you associate it with a boot.

In an American history course, it would be easier to understand and recall various battles in the Civil War if you had visited the cities in which they occurred and could form associations between the details of the battles and specific geographic points that you recall from your visits.

Application: As you read, always try to make connections between the new material and what you already know. You will see that the recall clue system for studying your notes (Chapter 15) relies heavily upon the principle of association. As you read each recall clue you wrote in the margins of your notes, you attempt to relate, or associate, the clue with the corresponding facts in the notes.

Principle 5: Spaced Study

The length of time and spacing between reading-study lessons directly affects how much you learn. Generally, it is more effective to space or spread out study sessions rather than to study in one or two large blocks of time. In fact, research has shown that when periods of study were divided into units separated by breaks, the total time necessary to memorize information was significantly reduced.

Spaced learning and study has several advantages. First, it is likely that by spacing out your study you are reducing the possibility of becoming fatigued — both physically and mentally. Second, there is some evidence that, even when you stop studying and take a break, a certain amount of rehearsal continues to take place.

Finally, dividing your study time into small blocks is psychologically rewarding. When you finish a block, you will feel as if you are making progress and accomplishing something.

Application: The most direct application of this principle occurs as you organize daily and weekly study schedules, as discussed in Chapters 3 and 5. In addition, the use of the study card system described in Chapter 17 will also help you apply this learning principle to your work.

Principle 6: Mnemonic Devices

Mnemonics are memory tricks, or aids, that you can devise to help you remember information. Mnemonics includes such things as rhymes, anagrams, words, nonsense words, sentences, or mental pictures that aid in the recall of facts. Do you remember this rhyme: "Thirty days hath September, / April, June, and November. / All the rest have thirty-one / except February, alone, / which has twenty-eight days clear / and twenty-nine in each leap year"? The rhyme is an example of a mnemonic device. It is a quick and easy way of remembering the number of days in each month of the year. You may have learned to recall the colors in the spectrum by remembering the name *Roy G. Biv;* each letter in this name stands for one of the colors which make up the spectrum: *R*ed, *O*range, *Y*ellow, *G*reen, *B*lue, *I*ndigo, *V*iolet.

The Chicago Police Department once developed an anagram to help officers remember what steps to follow when called to the scene of a crime. The officers' responsibility is to make a *preliminary* investigation by following the procedure below. Notice the word that is spelled by the first letters of the steps in the procedure.

P — Proceed to the scene.
R — Render assistance to the injured.
E — Effect the arrest of the perpetrator.
L — Locate and identify witnesses.
I — Interview complainant and witnesses.
M — Maintain the scene and protect evidence.
I — Interrogate suspects.
N — Note all conditions, events, and remarks.
A — Arrange for collection of evidence.
R — Report the incident fully and accurately.
Y — Yield responsibility to detectives.
      —Wilson and McLaren, *Police Administration,* p. 353

Application: Mnemonic devices are useful when trying to learn information that has no inherent organization of its own. You will find the principle useful in reviewing tests and lecture notes as you prepare for exams.

EXERCISE 2

Directions: *In answering the following questions about practical situations, think of or write answers that are most consistent with what you have learned about the memory process.*

1. If you are taking an introductory course in criminal justice and you have to learn the different types of jurisdiction that apply in various court cases, how could you learn them effectively? The types of jurisdiction are limited or special, general, appellate, concurrent, and exclusive. How could you remember them easily?

    _____

2. Suppose you had to remember to bring all of the following items the next time you attended a workshop on automobile maintenance: tire gauge, car repair manual, grease remover,

jumper cables, car service record, flashlight, course textbook, wrench, soap, notebook, hand towel, screwdriver, paper towels. How could you remember all the items easily?

_____

3. If you had to review a twenty-page chapter in your physics textbook, how should you schedule your study? Underline the appropriate answer.
    a. Review ten pages, take a break, then review another ten pages.
    b. Review the entire twenty pages at one sitting.
    c. Take a break after every five pages, do some math problems, then return to studying physics.

4. If you were taking a course in nursing care for infants and children, and you had to remember the following nutritional requirements for newborn babies, what memory technique would you use?

    calories   minerals
    protein   iron
    fat   fluoride
    carbohydrates   vitamins
    fluid

_____

_____

SUMMARY

This chapter presents an overview of learning and memory processes and offers practical ways to learn more efficiently. Forgetting occurs very rapidly unless specific steps are taken to retain the information.

To prevent forgetting, it is necessary to understand how your learning and memory work. The chapter summarizes the stages in both short-term and long-term memory. As you encounter information, it is either stored in short-term memory or discarded and forgotten. Then, you must either transfer information into the more permanent long-term memory or allow it to be forgotten. Transferring facts from short- to long-term memory involves a process called rehearsal. A number of principles of learning influence how well information is stored in long-term memory. These include the intent to remember, how meaningful the information is, how well organized and categorized the information is at the time of storage, how the information is associated with previous knowledge, the scheduling of learning sessions, and the use of mnemonic devices to aid learning.

Part Two
Techniques for
Effective Reading

Most college students have a basic competency in reading. They have acquired a core vocabulary and have developed an understanding of language structure which allows basic understanding (comprehension) of units of written expression. Yet many students frequently complain that they have difficulty getting through the required reading in a course, that they cannot keep their mind on what they read, or that they cannot remember what they have read.

This seeming contradiction can be explained by the fact that most students have not developed (or have not been taught) necessary reading and study techniques that can influence and greatly alter the ability effectively to read and retain textbook material. In addition, many students have developed reading habits which actually interfere with efficient reading. The primary purpose of this part of the book is to discuss reading habits and strategies that can enhance a student's ability to concentrate and to read and learn more effectively.

Chapter 5 presents techniques for improving your level of concentration by eliminating distractions and focusing your attention on the task at hand. Chapter 6 discusses physical habits and mental attitudes that contribute to reading efficiency. Chapter 7 presents the technique of prereading, which provides a means of becoming familiar with the content and organization of a chapter before beginning to read it. Chapter 8 offers an easy method for keeping your mind focused on what you are reading and increasing the amount of information you can recall — establishing a purpose for reading. The chapter describes how the reader can use this procedure to determine what he or she intends to learn from reading material before beginning to read.

5. Improving Your Ability to Concentrate

Use this chapter to:

1. *Learn how to exclude distractions.*

2. *Develop skill in focusing your attention.*

Concentration is the ability to keep your mind on what you're doing. In the framework of a college course, concentration refers to the ability to keep your mind on what you are reading and studying; it can also mean keeping your mind tuned into a lecture, class discussion, or on a written assignment or research paper.

Developing your power of concentration is a first step to becoming a more efficient, careful reader. Unless you are able to keep your mind on what you are reading, you will not be able to understand or remember the material. Lack of concentration, then, is often a major reason why some students experience difficulty understanding or remembering what they read.

The ability to concentrate involves two major skills or abilities — exclusion and focusing. *Exclusion* is the ability to exclude, or keep out, distractions and interruptions that take your mind off your reading or studying. *Focusing* is the skill of directing your attention to the material you are studying. If you can master some techniques in using each of these skills, you will notice a change in your level of concentration.

EXCLUDING DISTRACTIONS

It will be impossible to eliminate all the sources of distraction and interruption; but if you can control several of the factors which interfere with concentration, you will improve your ability to concentrate. Several effective ways to control, if not eliminate, distractions are discussed in this section.

Choose a Place with Minimum Distraction

The place or physical location you choose for reading and study determines, in part, the number of distractions or interruptions you will have. If you try to read or study in a place where there is a lot of activity (doors slamming, people talking, a radio playing, machines running, and so forth), you will probably find that your mind wanders. Even though you may not really want to listen to a nearby conversation, you cannot help but overhear certain parts. And you cannot help but think and react to what you hear.

Choose a place where there is a minimum of distraction. If your home or dorm is too busy and noisy, study in a quiet place on campus. Try various student lounge areas, or check out study areas in the library. Empty classrooms are also good possibilities.

Read in the Same Place

Try to read and study in the same place rather than wherever it seems convenient at the time. There is a psychological advantage to working in the same place regularly. As with many other activities, you build a mental association, or connection, between an activity and the place where it occurs. If you sit down at a table set for dinner, for example, you expect to eat dinner. If you always sit in the same comfortable chair to watch TV, eventually you expect to relax and watch TV every time you sit in that chair. This same psychological expectation applies to reading and studying. If you become accustomed to working at a particular desk, you build up an association between the place — your desk — and the activity — reading and studying. Eventually, when you sit down at the desk, you expect to read or study. Your expectation makes tasks at hand much easier; you do not have to convince yourself to work. Instead, you are almost automatically ready to read or study when you sit down at the desk.

In choosing a regular place to read, be sure you do not select a place which you already associate with a different activity. Don't try to read in your TV chair or stretched out across your bed; you already have built associations with your chair and bed as places to relax or sleep.

Read at Peak Periods of Attention

The time of day or night when you read or study also influences how easy or difficult it is to shut out distractions. Most people have a time limit for how long they can keep their minds on one thing. This is called *attention span*. Attention span changes from subject to subject, from book to book, from lecturer to lecturer, and from one time of day to another. People experience peaks and valleys in attention span at different times of the day. Some people are very alert in the early morning; others find they are most alert at midday or in the early evening. To make concentration easier, try to read and study during the peaks of your attention span. Choose the times of day when you are most alert and when it is easiest to keep your mind on what you are doing. Avoid working at times when you know you will be easily distracted. If you are not aware of your own peaks of attention, do a quick analysis of your effectiveness. Over a period of several days, keep track of when you read and studied and how much you accomplished each time. Then look for a pattern.

Control the Noise Level

Some students find it difficult to concentrate in a completely quiet room. Others need some background noise in order to concentrate. Most students find some middle ground, or compromise, between total silence and a loud, noisy background. Research suggests that the volume of background music which interferes with concentration varies with individuals. A noise level which is distracting to one student may not disturb another.

The best way to find out how much background noise you can take is to try out different levels and see which seems best suited for you. Try studying in complete silence; then try soft music; then try other types of music. Keep trying different noise situations until you have found that which is least distracting. Then, deliberately choose a place with the appropriate noise level, or adjust the level to suit you.

Pay Attention to Your Physical State

How you feel physically greatly influences how well you can concentrate. If you are tired or sleepy, concentration will be difficult. If you are hungry, you will find that your thoughts drift toward what you'll have to eat when you're finished. If you feel sluggish, inactive, and in need of exercise, concentration will also be difficult. Try to schedule reading or studying at times when your physical needs are not likely to interfere. Also, if, while reading, you find that you are hungry, tired, or sluggish, stop and try to correct the problem. Take a break, have a snack, or get up and walk around. However, if you are physically or mentally exhausted, it is usually best to stop and find a better time to complete the assignment.

Have Necessary Materials Available

When you sit down to read or study, be sure that all the materials you need are readily available. This might include a dictionary, pen, pencils, paper, a calculator, index cards, calendar, clock, and so on. Surrounding yourself with these materials will also help to create a psychological readiness for reading or studying. Further, if you have to get up to locate any of these items, you are breaking your concentration and taking the chance of being distracted from the task at hand.

EXERCISE 1

Directions: *Decide what might be wrong with each of the following study situations. Write your answer in the space provided.*

1. You are studying while stretched out on your bed.

   _____

2. You begin studying immediately after you get home from a vigorous basketball team practice.

   _____

3. You start studying just before you get ready to go out to a party that you have been eagerly looking forward to attending.

   _____

4. You are studying while playing a record album that you just purchased.

_____

5. You are studying in an easy chair in front of the television.

_____

6. You are studying on campus in the snack bar or cafeteria at noon, between your eleven o'clock and one o'clock classes.

_____

7. You are studying at a table next to the circulation (check out) desk at the library.

_____

8. You decide to study at your friend's house while you are waiting for her to get ready to go shopping.

_____

EXERCISE 2

Directions: _As you read an assignment this evening, be alert for distractions. Each time you lose your concentration, try to identify the cause. List below the items that distracted you and, if possible, a way to eliminate the distraction._

1. _____

2. _____

3. _____

4. _____

FOCUSING YOUR ATTENTION

Focusing your attention on what you are reading or studying is another skill which can be learned and used to improve your concentration. There are a number of tricks and techniques you can use to direct your attention to what you are reading or studying. As you apply these techniques, you will find that your mind wanders less often, and that you are able to complete reading and study assignments more efficiently.

Give Yourself a Goal

Psychologically, reaching or achieving a goal is a positive, rewarding experience. It makes you feel good and proves that you are accomplishing something. Use this psychological principle to help you focus on what you are reading or studying. For each reading assignment you have to do, give yourself a goal to work toward. Instead of just sitting down and beginning, first figure out how much you can accomplish in a specific amount of time. Set a time limit and work toward meeting it. Working under time pressure will help you focus your mind on what you are doing because you will be aware that distractions and day-dreaming will cost you time and delay you in meeting the time limit you set as a goal. Also, when you meet your goal, you will feel positive and know that you have accomplished something worthwhile.

Choose Goals That Are Easy to Accomplish

As you set a goal — what you will try to accomplish within a given time frame — be sure to choose relatively small amounts of material which can be read or studied in correspondingly short amounts of time. When you finish, take a short break. Then set another time goal for the next unit of material. Setting several limited goals and reaching them is more rewarding than accomplishing one overall, more ambitious goal, and certainly more rewarding than not reaching your goal at all. Janice set the following goals for herself for one evening of study:

Read Business Management
p. 101-122   1½ hrs.

Do Math Problems
p. 161-162
#1-5   40 mins.

Read Short Story for English   1 hr.

It is possible to establish long-range as well as evening-by-evening goals. George, for example, set up the following study goals for the week.

WEEKLY READING/STUDY GOALS

Data Processing	Review Chapters 2+3 Edit and review 3 sets of class notes
English	Type paper due Wed. Do draft of ideas for next paper.
Ecology	Prepare for Lab on friday. Read and understand Chapter 6. Review Chapter 5.
Anthropology	Start research for 1st project. Review for quiz #1 on friday
Speech Comm.	Do draft of ideas for Speech #2 Submit reaction paper to film shown on Tues.

Notice that George made his weekly goals more specific and detailed and that he set time goals, day by day, for completing each assignment. Then he divided the long-range goals into more specific daily/nightly study goals.

DAILY READING/STUDY GOALS

Mon.	Read Data Processing Chap. 2	1 hr.
	Edit Monday's class notes (D.P.)	10 mins.
	Draft ideas for Speech reaction paper	½ hr.
	Read Economics Chap. 6	1½ hr.
Tues.	Type English composition	½ hr.
	Proofread composition	15 mins.
	Review Chaps. 2·3 Anthropology for quiz	1 hr.
Wed.	Read Data Processing Chap. 3	1½ hr.
	Edit Wed. class notes in D.P.	10 mins.
Thurs.	Draft ideas - English composition	½ hr.
	Read Lab manual p. 152-160 and list procedures	45 min.
	Review Chapters 4·5 for Anthropology quiz.	1 hr.
Fri.	Edit Fri's class D.P. notes	10 min.
Sat.	Review Economics Chap. 5	½ hr.
	Write and revise reaction paper for speech.	1½ hr.
Sun.	Go to library · start Anthropology research.	2 hrs.

EXERCISE 3

Directions: *Review your class assignments, reading assignments, quizzes, and papers, including exams, for the next week of classes. Write a set of weekly reading/study goals that list what you hope to accomplish for each of your courses.*

EXERCISE 4

Directions: *Using the weekly reading/study goals you prepared for Exercise 3, develop a set of daily reading/study goals that specify when you will complete each assignment and how much time you expect to spend on each.*

Reward Yourself

Setting and meeting goals within a time limit is one type of reward which can help you focus your attention. Other types of rewards can be used to help you keep your mind on what you are doing: daily activities which you enjoy — such as watching TV, eating, making phone calls — can be used as rewards if you arrange them to follow periods of reading and studying. You might, for example, plan to call a friend after you finish working on your math problems. In this situation, calling a friend becomes a reward for finishing your math assignment. Or, if you plan to rewrite your English composition before watching a favorite TV program, the TV program becomes a reward for finishing your revision of the written assignment.

Get Interested in the Subject

Interest is a major factor in keeping your attention focused on the subject you are studying. Hardly anyone has difficulty concentrating on a magazine article that is highly interesting or keeping his or her mind on a film or TV show he or she wants to see. It is when the subject matter is not extremely interesting that the problem of daydreaming occurs. While you cannot change a dull subject to make it interesting, there are a few things you can do to create or develop your interest in the subject. Try the following suggestions:

1. Read critically. As you read, look for ideas that you can question or disagree with. Look for points of view, opinions, statements which are not supported.
2. Try to predict or anticipate the author's thought. See if you can predict what the author is leading up to or what point he or she will make next.
3. Try to connect, or see the relationship between, new material and information you already have learned. Does the new material expand, alter, or contradict ideas you had before?

Combine Physical and Mental Activities

Physical activities — such as writing and underlining — when combined with the mental activities of reading, reviewing, and memorizing, will help you focus your attention. Many of the reading and study techniques which will be suggested in this text include some type of physical action to be used in conjunction with reading or studying. Techniques for marking and underlining textbooks, writing notes in the margin, and studying for exams all include both writing and reading. By underlining important ideas or taking notes on important things you read, you are forcing yourself to keep your mind active and involved. As you read, you have to react to or evaluate each idea and decide whether it is important enough to underline or write down. To test the value of writing as you learn, try the following:

EXPERIMENT

Directions: *Below are listed two sets of words which you will try to memorize. Follow each of the three steps right after you read it. Do* not *read through all the steps before beginning.*

1. Read the words in set A once. Then reread them. Without looking, write down as many of the words as you can remember on a separate piece of paper.
2. Read the words in set B once. Then copy the words on a piece of paper. Without looking at the words or your copy of them, write down as many words as you can remember.
3. Check to see how many words you had correct on each list.

Set A				Set B		
MOM	COP	MOP		CAT	TAR	PAT
FAT	TAP	ARE		SAM	DAD	HOP
RAM	FAR	LAP		MAT	CAR	HAS
	RAM				RAT	

Most likely, you were able to remember more words in set B. Although you spent approximately the same amount of time learning the words in sets A and B, writing the words in B improved your ability to remember. This experiment demonstrates the value of combining the physical activity of writing with the mental processes of reading and remembering.

Vary Your Activities

Ability to focus on a particular subject will improve if you try not to force your concentration on only one type of activity for a long period of time. You might plan your study schedule so that you read sociology for a while, then work on math problems, and finally switch to writing an English paper. This plan would be much more effective than all reading activities — reading sociology, then reading chemistry, then reading an essay for English. As you vary the type and nature of your study activities, you are using different mental processes and different skills. The change from one skill or mental process to another will be refreshing and make concentration easier.

Keep a Distractions List

As you are reading or studying, often you will think of something you should remember to do. If, for example, you are trying to remember a dental appointment you've scheduled for the next afternoon, you will find that a reminder occasionally flashes through your mind. Actually, this flash is a good way to remember something. It is only a problem when it interferes with your concentration. To overcome these mental reminders flashing through your mind as you study, keep a distractions list. Have a separate sheet of paper nearby as you read or study. Each time that one of these mental reminders occurs, jot it down. You will find that by writing it down on paper, you will temporarily eliminate it from your memory. Use the same paper to record other ideas and problems that distract you. A distractions list might look like this:

dentist - Tues. 2 p.m.
call Sam
buy birthday presents
return library books

Use the Tally System to Build Your Attention Span

As mentioned earlier, your attention span is the length of time you can keep your mind focused on a particular subject without any interference or distraction. An easy way to increase your attention span is to monitor, or keep track of, how many times you are distracted during a specified period of time (half an hour). Make a tally, or count, of distractions. Each time you think about something other than what you are studying, make a mark on the paper. Total up your marks at the end of the specified time. Check yourself again, and try to reduce the number of distractions by ten percent. Do not keep this tally every time you read or study anything, or you will rely on the technique to force your concentration. Instead, use it once every few days until you have sufficiently increased your concentration.

EXERCISE 5

Directions: *Over the next week, try to build your attention span using the tally system suggested above. Record the results below.*

	Reading/Study Assignment	Time Period	Number of Distractions
1.	_____	_____	_____
2.	_____	_____	_____
3.	_____	_____	_____
4.	_____	_____	_____

SUMMARY

Improving concentration involves two major skills or abilities — excluding distractions and focusing your attention. There are a number of ways to eliminate distractions. These include choosing a place with minimum distraction, reading in the same place, choosing an appropriate noise level, and paying attention to your physical state. To help you focus your attention, or concentrate, on the subject at hand, a variety of techniques are presented. Setting a goal and rewarding yourself when you achieve it is often an effective way of forcing yourself to keep your mind on your work. Getting yourself interested in the subject also aids in concentration. If you vary the subjects you study as well as the skills and abilities (both physical and mental) you use in studying, your mind will wander less. By keeping a distractions list on which you jot down appointments and other things you need to remember, you will keep them from interfering with your concentration. Concentration can also be improved by a concerted effort to build your attention span — the length of time you are able to focus on your subject without distraction.

6. Effective Reading Habits

Use this chapter to:

1. *Learn how to control the physical aspects of reading.*

2. *Learn how to develop a positive approach to reading.*

Reading is both a physical and a mental process. The movement of your eyes across a line of print is a physical activity. Understanding and getting meaning out of what your eyes see is a mental activity. Basically, your eyes pick up visual images and transmit them to your brain. Then your brain sorts and connects these impressions and attaches meaning to them, using its store of knowledge and experience.

Over the years you have developed a set of reading habits, both physical and mental. You read in a particular way, handle problems that arise as you read in a particular way, and approach the process of reading in a particular way. Some of these habits have served you well in the past but are no longer useful and may be preventing you from becoming an effective reader. Other habits are inefficient and if changed, can enable you to read faster and with higher comprehension. Still other habits are effective and require no change. The purpose of this chapter is to emphasize habits that are effective and positive, to help you overcome habits that are holding you back and to help you change or modify those that are inefficient.

DEVELOPING PHYSICAL READING HABITS

Since reading begins with the physical process of recognizing words on a printed page, it is important that this physical part of reading occur efficiently and in a manner that will enable you to understand what you read easily and rapidly. In fact, poor physical habits are a primary reason why some students read slowly and understand little of what they read. Lacking good physical habits, these students find reading to be a difficult task for which they have developed a strong dislike. Several suggestions for developing effective physical reading habits are offered in the following sections.

Use Effective Eye Movement Patterns

As will be discussed in greater detail in Part Seven ("Reading Efficiency Techniques"), the eyes move and stop, move and stop, as they go from left to right across the line. When the eyes stop, or fixate, they see a part of a word, a word, or perhaps a group of words. Then the eyes move farther to the right and stop again.

Sometimes, however, the eyes move backward instead of going on to the next word. They move backward, or regress, to a word already read, either in the same line or in a previous line. This kind of backward movement is called a *regression*. While an occasional regression is necessary, some readers make two or three regressions per line. Such regressions cause a reader to see a sentence in scrambled order and may prevent the reader from understanding the sentence meaning. Regression is best overcome by forcing your eyes to move forward across the line. Do not regress unless there is a phrase or sentence that you do not understand. Remember that the idea expressed in a sentence is not complete until the sentence is finished. If in midsentence you feel insecure and think you do not understand the meaning, you are probably right. You will not get the full meaning until you have finished the sentence. Force yourself to read the whole sentence before going back. If you are confused after finishing the sentence, then reread it.

Use an Appropriate Angle of Vision

Many students feel physically tired after reading for an extended period of time. Although partially caused by the high level of concentration, fatigue may also result from reading with an inappropriate angle of vision. Most students read with the book lying flat on a desk or table. Although this may seem comfortable for a while, it eventually contributes to eye strain due to the angle of vision created. Ideally, there should be a 90-degree angle formed by your line of vision and the surface of the printed page. When the book is lying flat and you are sitting upright, the angle is less than 90 degrees. When the angle is less than 90 degrees, reflection, glare, and distortion of print produce eye strain. To avoid eye strain, try to hold your book in your hands, tilted slightly to produce a comfortable angle of vision.

Avoid Conflicting Physical Activities

You probably are aware that certain physical activities interfere with one another, especially if they are patterned or rhythmical. Try patting your head while rubbing your stomach. Each activity is easy when done separately, but when done together, they become confusing.

A similar interference may occur with reading when it's done in conjunction with other physical activities. Activities such as gum chewing or tapping the foot to music tend to create a rhythm which can interfere with the rhythm of your eyes moving across a line. Even listening to someone type in the background can be distracting. If you chew gum while you read, you may find yourself reading at the same pace you chew, or you may chew at the same rate you read.

Take a moment to be sure that your own actions or things around you are not interfering with your reading. If you find some of your actions or certain background noise distracting, stop the actions or change the time and/or place of your study.

Avoid Roadblocks to Reading Efficiency

There is a group of poor reading habits that are carry-overs from when you first learned to read. These are (1) moving your head as you read, (2) moving your lips as you read, and (3) using your finger or other object to keep your place on the line. Each of these habits can slow you down and can contribute to poor comprehension.

Moving your head: When children learn to read, they have difficulty moving only their eyes straight across a line of print. Due to this lack of eye control, many children move their entire head from left to right as they proceed across the line. While this habit may be necessary for children, it is not necessary for adults with adequate visual control. However, some adults have never eliminated the habit. Moving the head rather than just the eyes prevents adult readers from reading at even a normal reading rate and also creates strain and muscular fatigue. Ask someone to check to see if you move your head while reading; this person should check when you are not consciously thinking about this problem.

If you have this habit, it is probably a very old one that will take serious effort to overcome. One of the easiest ways to break it is to sit with your elbow up on your desk with your hand cupping your chin. If you start to move your head, you will feel your hand and forearm move, and this will remind you to try to stop.

Moving your lips: Lip movement while reading silently is also a carry-over from beginning reading experiences. When you were first learning to read, did you read orally (out loud) or silently? Most students are taught to read orally first, partly so that the teacher can know if the children are identifying words correctly. Later on, in second or third grade, the teacher tells students to read silently. At this stage, while making the change over from mostly oral to mostly silent reading, many children move their lips. Eventually, when the change-over is completed, lip movement should be eliminated. For some students, however, this habit hangs on. For an adult, lip movement results in an extremely slow silent reading rate. The average adult rate of speech (pronouncing words out loud) is 125 words per minute, while the average adult rate for silent reading is 250–300 words per minute. You can see that moving your lips can really slow your silent reading down — by as much as half. However, there is one situation in which lip movement may be appropriate. When you are reading something that is extremely difficult or complicated, you may find that moving your lips or even whispering aloud as you read helps you to understand the material.

Young children are sometimes broken of the habit of lip movement by having them hold a pencil horizontally between their lips as they read. When their lips move, the pencil wiggles or drops. Since this technique is not exactly appropriate for adults, you may wish to try a more sophisticated version. Sit in a position so that part of your hand or your fingers touch your lips. If you move your lips while reading, you will feel the movement on your hand or fingers.

Keeping your place on the line: Another bad habit left over from childhood reading is keeping your place on a line of print by moving your finger or a pen, pencil, or index card across the line as you read. Children are sometimes allowed to do this because they lack the eye control to keep their eyes from jumping from line to line or to move their eyes straight across one line smoothly. For adults, however, this habit results in a very slow word-by-word reading.

The solution to this one is simple — tightly grasp the book with both hands. This will prevent you from following across the line with your finger or another object. Be careful you don't cheat and slide your thumb down the margin as a guide to where you are on the page. If you have tried unsuccessfully to control this habit, an eye exam is advisable. Inability to keep one's place on the line is one symptom of a need for corrective lenses.

EXERCISE 1

Directions: *Now that you are aware of the physical habits that are important to effective reading, evaluate your own reading habits. Use the following checklist to indicate whether each item applies to you often, sometimes, or never.*

Habit	Often	Sometimes	Never
Regression	☐	☐	☐
Poor angle of vision	☐	☐	☐
Conflicting physical activities	☐	☐	☐
Head movement	☐	☐	☐
Lip movement	☐	☐	☐
Losing place on line	☐	☐	☐

DEVELOPING A POSITIVE APPROACH TO READING

Throughout this unit and the next several, you will learn specific techniques for understanding and remembering what you read. However, unless you approach the task of reading with a positive and realistic frame of mind, reading will always seem difficult and time consuming. Several suggestions for approaching reading that will help you become a more effective reader are discussed below.

Recognize that Reading Takes Time

Although you may never have thought of it as such, reading is one of the fastest means of acquiring facts and ideas. In an hour of reading often you can cover much more information than in an hour of listening, or in an hour spent viewing a filmstrip, videotape, or movie. Even though reading is one of the most efficient ways to acquire information, it still does require a time commitment. To read most effectively you must be willing to spend time. You should be prepared to spend time rereading difficult or complicated material, cross-checking ideas, or asking a friend or your instructor to clarify what you do not understand. It is also necessary to take time out from reading to study maps, graphs, charts, and pictures as well as to jot down important ideas, figure out unknown words and consider answers to questions the author may pose.

The amount of time that reading requires depends on two factors: your purpose for reading and the difficulty of the material. Reading a book for general information may take you less time than reading to recall details. Reading a paperback for pleasure may take less time than reading a textbook chapter on which you must pass an exam. Also, you may be able to read a newspaper article of 2000 words in less time than it takes you to read the same number of words in a chemistry text. Generally speaking, a newspaper article is written at an easier level and discusses less complicated ideas than does a chemistry text.

Thinking of Reading as Communication

A writer writes to express an idea to his reader, while a reader reads to understand the idea expressed by the writer. Through the medium of print, a writer and a reader are able to communicate or share a message. As a reader, it is your responsibility to try to understand the message thoroughly and accurately.

One true test of whether you have understood what you read is to summarize or restate the ideas using your own words. If you have understood an idea, you should be able to explain it without using the author's wording. In cases when you cannot restate an idea, you can be fairly certain that you have not fully mastered the concept or that the meaning of a particular term is blocking your comprehension.

As a check, then, that you are really understanding what you are reading, stop occasionally and mentally review or summarize what you have just read. Be sure that your restatement is specific. It is not sufficient to say, for example, that you have just read a paragraph about newspaper advertising when, in fact, the paragraph explained the three audiences to which newspaper ads appeal.

Look for the Person Behind the Print

As you read textbooks and other course material, it is easy to think of a printed page as cold and impersonal. Of course, everything in print was written by someone, and it often helps to try to "see" the person behind the print. The author has attitudes, opinions, biases, as well as particular ways of expressing ideas. You should be aware of a writer's slant on a particular subject. As you begin reading the work of a particular author, too, take some time and effort to adjust to his or her style. Once you are familiar with the author as a person and with his or her particular writing style, you will find the material somewhat easier to read. In textbooks, an easy way to become familiar with the author is to read the preface. Here the author explains a little about the book and why it was written.

Consider Reading as Thinking

To get the most out of what you read, it is useful to consider reading as a thinking process. Reading is much more than routinely moving your eyes across lines of print and understanding the meaning of each word and sentence. In a sense it is a two-step communication process in which you first understand the author's message and then react to, evaluate, and apply that message. Once you understand the author's meaning, you must think about it, relate the ideas to your background knowledge and experience, and use the information you have acquired.

To develop the habit of thinking about what you are reading, start by asking questions as you read. Ask yourself such questions as these: How does this information fit in with what I already know? How or when can I use this information? Is the information consistent with other sources I have read?

Treat Reading as the First Step in Learning

The first step in learning is to identify the information to be learned. In most college courses, reading is the primary means of finding out what information is important to learn. You are expected to read textbooks, supplementary readings, handouts, and exams. Your success in a course largely depends on your ability to read course material accurately and thoroughly. Only when you have read the material are you ready to study, review, and organize the information for later recall.

SUMMARY

Each person has his or her own particular set of reading habits. Some habits may prevent one from becoming an effective reader; others may be inefficient. New habits can produce faster and more efficient reading. Physical habits are important to effective reading and include using effective eye movement patterns, using an appropriate angle of vision, avoiding conflicting physical activities, and avoiding roadblocks to reading efficiency. In addition to physical habits, the reader's frame of mind also determines his or her effectiveness. It is important to recognize that reading takes time, that reading is communication, that reading is thinking, that written material is personal and individualized, and that reading is the first step in learning.

7. Prereading

Use this chapter to:

1. *Learn a way to get interested in what you are reading and to remember more.*

2. *Find out how to become familiar with what you are going to read before you begin.*

Do you check for traffic before crossing a street? Do you check the depth of a pool before diving in? What do you do to an article or chapter before you read it, before you "jump in"? In this section you will become acquainted with the technique of prereading — a useful way of checking any written material before you read it. Just as most people check traffic before crossing a street or water depth before diving, efficient readers check printed materials before reading to become generally familiar with the overall content and organization.

HOW TO PREREAD

Your overall purposes in prereading are to identify the most important ideas in the material and to note their organization. You look only at specific parts and skip over the rest. The portions to look at in prereading a textbook chapter are listed below. Later, you will learn how to adapt this procedure to other types of material.

Read the Title and Subtitle

The title provides the overall topic of the article or chapter; the subtitle suggests the specific focus, aspect, or approach toward the overall topic.

Read the Introduction or the First Paragraph

The introduction, or first paragraph if there is no introduction, serves as a lead-in to the chapter. It gives you an idea of where the material is starting and where it is heading.

Read Each Boldface (Dark Print) Heading

The headings function as labels or topic statements for what is contained in the sections that follow them. In other words, a heading announces the major topic of each section.

Read the First Sentence Under Each Heading

The first sentence frequently tells you what the passage is about or states the central thought. You should be aware, however, that in some types of material or in certain styles of writing the first sentence does not function as a central thought. Instead, the opening sentence may function as a transition or lead-in statement, or may be written to catch your interest. If the first sentence seems unimportant, read the last sentence; often this sentence states or restates the central thought.

Note Any Typographical Aids

Italics are used to emphasize important terminology and definitions by using slanted (italic) type to distinguish them from the rest of the passage. Graphs, charts, pictures, and tables are other means of emphasis and are usually meant to point out what is important in the chapter. Be sure to read the captions for pictures and the legends on graphs, charts, or tables. Notice any material that is numbered 1, 2, 3, lettered a, b, c, or presented in list form.

Read the Last Paragraph or Summary

The summary or last paragraph gives a condensed view of the chapter and helps you identify the key ideas. Often the summary outlines the key points in the chapter.

Read Quickly Any End-of-Article or End-of-Chapter Material

This might include references, study questions, vocabulary lists, or biographical information about the author. These materials will be useful later as you read and study the article or chapter, and it is important, as part of prereading, to note if such materials are included. If there are study questions, it is useful to read them through quickly since they will indicate what is important in the chapter. If a vocabulary list is included, rapidly skim through it to identify terms which you will need to learn as you read.

DEMONSTRATION OF PREREADING

The following textbook chapter excerpt has been included to demonstrate to you what it is like to preread. This chapter excerpt is taken from an introductory text, *Marketing,* by Frederick Russ and Charles Kirkpatrick (Boston: Little, Brown, and Co., 1982). Features of this text are referred to frequently; the complete chapter is included in the Appendix (page 335). To illustrate how prereading is done, these pages have been specially marked. Everything that you should look at or read has been shaded. Preread this excerpt now, reading only the shaded portions of each page.

Table 19-4   The United States' largest advertising agencies

U.S. income rank	Agency	U.S. gross income, 1980	U.S. billing, 1980	Total U.S. employees, 1980
1	Young & Rubicam	$200.0	$1,333.7	3,804
2	J. Walter Thompson Co.	137.8	918.9	2,474
3	Ogilvy & Mather	125.5	837.1	2,160
4	Foote, Cone & Belding	109.1	749.3	2,330
5	Leo Burnett Co.	108.2	734.6	1,481
6	Ted Bates & Co.	108.0	720.3	1,884
7	BBDO International	105.8	806.4	2,049
8	Doyle Dane Bernbach	98.1	671.0	1,800
9	Grey Advertising	78.7	524.9	1,522
10	Benton & Bowles	$ 73.8	$ 492.0	1,447

NOTE: Billings and gross income are in millions; these figures do not include foreign billings.

SOURCE: *Advertising Age,* March 18, 1981, p. 8.

The Creative Side of Advertising

When advertising people refer to the "creative" side of advertising, they mean the activities involved in the actual preparation of advertisements: deciding how to appeal to the buyer, what specific headlines and illustrations to use, and what written copy will accomplish best the objectives. Seemingly small differences in an advertisement can have a dramatic impact on its effectiveness. As just one example, it has been shown that some ads are 150 percent more effective when placed on the back page of a newspaper than when placed on an inside page. Thus, choosing these elements and determining how they should be pulled together is a critical marketing activity.

The most important ingredient in an ad is the promise it makes. Why? Because the buyer responds favorably or not to what the advertiser claims its product or service will deliver. Remember, buyers do not buy products or services as such; instead, they exchange their money for what a product or service will do to or for them, for satisfaction of some sort. If consumers want a kitchen cleanser that will be gentle to their hands, that is what the product should offer and what the ad should promise.

Visualization and Layout

Once an ad's objective has been determined and its promise selected, the actual building of the ad can start. This calls for visualization and layout. Determining what elements or units an ad shall contain is called visualization. The common elements are headline, subheads, illustrations, and copy. Laying out the ad is a matter of position and relationships. Visualization decides *what* the ad will

Advertising / 433

65

contain, layout decides *where* each of those elements will be placed. Should a retailer's name be at the top of a newspaper ad but a manufacturer's name at the bottom of a magazine ad? If several illustrations are to be included, where should each be placed? Well laid-out ads are sound and simple; their attractiveness invites reading. The expert selection and placement of illustrations can increase advertising effectiveness and the response the advertiser wants.

Copy

The most important element in an ad's copy message, the promise, is often expressed in the headline. The major jobs of headlines are to make contact with and attract the attention of the seller's prospects — also a responsibility of the ad's illustration — and to induce prospects to read the ad.

Most strong headlines have either news content or buyer-benefit — self-interest — content "The K Cars are here," for example, a newsy headline from Chrysler, or "A better mileage rating than Audi 5000 for $1,699 less!" for the Pontiac Bonneville, stressing benefit to the buyer. Many headlines are a question — "What's Continental Telephone doing way out here?" — or a command: "Let Kelly work for you." Headlines may try to help prospects identify themselves as prospects by including such words as "motorists," or "students." Other words believed to be powerful in headlines include "free," "how to," "you," and "which."

Body copy is much like a salesperson's presentation in that it should expand on and explain the promise on which the ad is built. It should be built on a strong, persuasive sales idea. Product facts, product satisfaction, and product price are main ingredients. Body copy must be clear and believable, sincere yet interesting.

Ads should try to "close" just as salespeople do, and an ad's close is second only to its headline in importance. The close should urge some sort of immediate favorable action: "Fill out the coupon and mail it today"; "Visit your nearest dealer and ask for a demonstration"; or simply, "Try it, you'll be glad you did." Words such as "go," "try," and "ask" are often found in closes. The advertiser's name and address or the brand name are often prominent in closes.

Illustrations

Illustrations — drawings, photos, or cartoons — share with headlines the assignment of attracting the attention of prospects. They can tell a story, make a point quickly and clearly, or prove a claim; "before-and-after" photographs are an example. Art directors are always debating illustration strategies. Should the ad contain a single, dominant illustration or several small illustrations? When should the product be shown, and when should some feature or part of the product be shown? Should people be included, perhaps using the product? Proven answers are rare for these questions; as in so much of advertising, experience is often the best guide.

434 / Chapter 19

Now that you have seen what it is like to preread, you are ready to test out the technique and observe its benefits. Turn to the sample textbook chapter, "Advertising," in the Appendix. You have already preread two pages. Preread the entire chapter. You should not spend more than five minutes. When you finish, answer each question in the following Exercise.

EXERCISE 1

Directions: *Answer each of the following questions after you have preread the sample textbook chapter, "Advertising," in the Appendix. Mark T after statements that are true and F after those that are false. Do not look back in the chapter to locate the answers. When you finish, check your answers in the Answer Key and write your score in the space indicated.*

1. Each advertisement has a specific objective. _____
2. One important concept discussed in the chapter is the various media that advertisers use. _____
3. The most important element of an advertisement is stated in the last line. _____
4. The primary purpose of illustrations (photos, drawings) is to attract the attention of the reader. _____
5. The chapter discusses the function of advertising agencies and the services they provide. _____
6. The chapter does not discuss the cost and budgeting of advertising. _____
7. The creative side of advertising is concerned with designing the layout, copy, and illustrations. _____
8. The article discusses government regulation of advertising. _____
9. All ads make a promise to the buyer. _____
10. The ultimate goal of advertising is to increase profits. _____

Score (number right): _____

Look back at your score on the quiz in Exercise 1. Most likely you got at least half of the questions right, perhaps more. This quiz was a test of the main ideas that were presented in the chapter. You can see, then, that prereading does familiarize you with the chapter and enables you to identify and remember many of the main ideas it contains. Actually, each part of the chapter that you read while prereading provided you with specific information about the organization and content of the chapter. The following exercise emphasizes how each step in the prereading process provides you with useful information about the material to be read.

EXERCISE 2

Directions: *Listed on page 68 are various parts of an actual textbook chapter or article to which you would refer in prereading. Read the parts; then answer the question which follows.*

1. *Sample text*

Title:	*Introductory Psychology*
Subtitle:	*Selected Case Studies and Readings*
Question:	What further information does the subtitle provide about the text content? About its organization?

_____

_____

2. *Sample article*

Title:	"Psychologists Have Proof of ESP"
Source:	*Today's Women* magazine
Question:	Answer with yes or no. Would you expect this article to

    a. be technical?
    b. be highly factual with careful references?
    c. contain accounts of individuals with ESP?
    d. contain opinions?
    e. contain references for further study?

3. *Sample text*

Section heading:	Culture and Technology
Consecutive headings:	Historical Roots and Trends Recent Technological Changes Predicted Long-Range Effects
Question:	What clues do you have about how the author arranged ideas or about the organization of this section of the text?

_____

_____

4. *Sample text*

Title:	*Business Management*
Subtitle:	*An Organizational Perspective*
Copyright:	1951
Question:	What does this information tell you about the usefulness and limitations of the material contained in this text?

_____

5. *Sample text*

Title:	*Introduction to Psychology*
Chapter title:	"Human Learning, Remembering, and Forgetting"
Chapter introduction:	This chapter stresses learning that is characteristically human — especially the learning of verbal and symbolic materials.

Such learning is particularly important to you, the student: you have learned such material throughout all your school days, and you will continue to for the rest of your academic and professional careers. Although verbal learning is our main concern here, something is said also about the learning of manual skills — driving a car, using a typewriter, repairing radios, and so on. In this chapter, too, we consider the problem of forgetting — the problem raised in the quotation from William James. Finally, we discuss techniques of study and programmed learning, applying some of the principles derived from laboratory experiments to the problems of studying that the student faces, and providing some hints to the skill of successful studying. (Morgan, p. 115)

Question: Based upon the information presented in the chapter introduction, what can you tell about the content and organization of the chapter?

_____

_____

_____

6. *Sample text*

Title: *Introduction to Psychology*

Chapter title: "Principles of Learning"

Chapter summary: We have emphasized three different processes by which changes in behavior may come about. These three processes are classical conditioning, instrumental learning, and perceptual learning. Avoidance learning is not listed here because it seems to be dependent upon classical and instrumental conditioning. Rather than attempt to bring all learning under one process, as was done in the heyday of learning theory, we have emphasized that learning occurs by different processes. Much of the knowledge about these processes has come from studies with lower animals. The exact results cannot be applied to human beings; rather, the processes uncovered by animal research can be applied to human learning. We have attempted to show when, and in what areas, classical conditioning, instrumental learning, and perceptual learning are important in human life. (Morgan, p. 112)

Question: Based on the information included in this chapter summary, what are the major points you would expect to be covered in the chapter?

_____

_____

_____

7. *Sample text*

Title: *Our Changing Economy*

Subtitle: *An Introduction to Economics*

Chapter title: "Why Are There Economic Systems?"

Graphic aids: The chapter includes the following graphic aids:
  a. a graph showing the relationship between production of various types of goods and price
  b. a "Beetle Bailey" cartoon that illustrates that choice is associated with cost
  c. a picture of various objects that have been used as money in various cultures throughout the world

Question: What clues do the graph, cartoon, and picture give you about the chapter content?

_____

_____

8. *Sample text*

Title: *The World Today*

Subtitle: *Its Patterns and Cultures*

Chapter title: "The Orient"

Section headings: This chapter is divided into four major sections. The section titles are as follows:
  a. The Heritage of the Past in the Orient
  b. How the Millions of the Orient Make a Living
  c. New Directions for India, Pakistan, and Southeast Asia
  d. Red China, Democracy, and the Uncommitted Orient

Question: By noting the section titles within this chapter, what do you expect about the organization and content of the chapter?

_____

_____

HOW TO PREREAD ARTICLES AND CHAPTERS WITHOUT HEADINGS

Earlier in this chapter you learned that when prereading you should read boldface (dark print) headings. However, much material is written without these convenient labels of section content. In articles and chapters without headings, prereading does become somewhat more time-consuming because you must read the first sentence of each paragraph. As you will see later in the text, by reading the first sentence of each paragraph, you are often reading the main idea of each paragraph. Articles or chapters without headings may still have introductory and concluding portions, graphic material, and questions at the end. You can also get ideas from the organization of the material. Is it a list of ideas on the topic? Is it a series of events? If you can see this, you will know what to expect in the rest of the article or chapter.

PREREADING SPECIFIC TYPES OF MATERIAL

Textbooks

Whenever you purchase a new textbook, it is useful to preread it before you begin to read specific assignments. If you are familiar with the overall organization, purpose, and content of the text, you will find that the individual chapters make more sense. You might think of individual chapters of a text as the pieces of a picture puzzle. When the pieces of the puzzle are put together, you can see the function of each piece, but each piece by itself has little meaning. Similarly, textbook chapters become more meaningful when seen as a functioning part of the entire text.

To preread a text, check the following:

1. The title and subtitle.
2. The author(s). In many cases, the name will be unfamiliar. But, as you acquire knowledge in new fields of study, you will begin to recognize names of authorities.
3. The publication or copyright date. It is always useful to be aware of how up to date the text is. Especially in rapidly developing fields, a chapter written several years ago may be seriously outdated.
4. The table of contents. The table of contents provides a brief outline of the entire text. It lists all the major topics covered in the text and indicates how the text is organized.
5. The preface or "Note to Students" at the beginning of the text. This introductory portion of the text often contains important information about the text's organization and use.
6. Learning aids. Numerous learning aids are included within or at the end of each chapter and at the end of the text. Chapter 12, "Textbook Aids to Learning," discusses these aids in detail.

Textbook Chapters

The technique of prereading is highly effective when used in reading textbook chapters. When approaching a lengthy textbook chapter, first preread it entirely, noting only major groups of ideas. Then, divide the chapter up into smaller segments or sections and preread, then read, each section.

Articles and Selections

When prereading magazine articles, reading selections, or excerpts included within a book, in addition to the items listed earlier under the section "How to Preread," be sure to pay particular attention to:

1. The title. It often suggests the topic and author's focus, although sometimes it is intended to catch your interest.
2. The author. Check to see who wrote the material. If you are able to recognize the author's name, then you can form a set of expectations about the content of the article.
3. The source. When prereading material reprinted from another source, use the footnote or acknowledgment at the beginning or end to determine where the material was originally published. How much you accept of what is said depends on the type of publication the article appeared in. For example, you would expect an article on aggression published in the *Journal of Psychology* to be more research oriented than an article on the same topic published in a weekly news magazine.

Research and Reference Material

When you are collecting information for a class assignment or research paper, prereading is a valuable technique to use to identify sources that contain the information you need. When you have identified a book that appears to contain information on the topic you are researching, take a few moments to preread before checking it out of the library or using valuable time reading it unnecessarily. By prereading you may find that the source does not contain information you need, that it is too general or too detailed for your purpose, or that it only contains information you already have collected from another source.

To preread reference material, first check the index and table of contents. Then, if your topic is listed, quickly preread the appropriate sections or chapters to determine if they contain information that suits your purpose.

Newspapers

Information in newspaper articles is structured differently from most other types of writing. In contrast to most material in which the first few sentences are introductory, the opening sentences in news stories frequently carry the *most* important information. As the article progresses, the facts presented become more and more detailed, and you find more background information. To preread a news article, then, read the headline, the first few lines, and section headings; then glance through the rest of the article, picking up such details as names, dates, and places.

LIMITATIONS OF PREREADING

Prereading is used best with expository, factual material which is fairly well organized. Knowing this, you can see that prereading is not a good strategy to use when reading such materials as novels, poems, narrative articles, essays, or short stories. However, you will find it fairly easy to adapt the prereading technique to various types of writing you read.

DOES PREREADING WORK?

Research studies suggest that prereading does increase comprehension and improve recall. Several studies have been conducted which show that prereading is a useful technique for reading textbook chapters. In a study done by McClusky,* college students were divided into two groups: one group was taught how to use headings and summaries for prereading; the other group received no instruction. Both groups were given a selection to read and comprehension questions to answer. Results of the study indicated that the group which used headings and summaries read 24 percent faster and just as accurately as the students who did not preread.

WHAT DOES PREREADING ACCOMPLISH?

First, prereading helps you get interested in and involved with what you will read. Through prereading, you become familiar with the material or gain advance information about it. You become acquainted with the general subject of the material, you discover who wrote it, and you learn when and where it was published. You also become aware of the main subtopics and how they are organized. Because you know what to expect, then, reading the material completely will be easier.

Second, prereading provides you with a mental outline of the material you are going to read. As you read the headings of a chapter, you are actually forming a mental outline of the chapter. You begin to anticipate the sequence of ideas; you see the relationships of topics to one another; you recognize what approach and direction the author has taken in writing about his or her subject. With this outline in mind, the actual reading is a much simpler task: reading the chapter becomes a matter of filling in the parts of the outline with the proper details.

Third, prereading is useful because it enables you to apply several principles of learning. Through prereading you identify what is important, thus establishing an intent to remember. Prereading also facilitates meaningfulness by allowing you to become familiar with the basic content and organization of the material. Because prereading also provides an additional repetition of the major points, it functions as a type of rehearsal that enhances recall.

* H. Y. McClusky, "An Experiment on the Influence of Preliminary Skimming on Reading," *Journal of Educational Psychology,* 25 (1934): 521–529.

EXERCISE 3

Directions: *Select a chapter from one of your own textbooks. To be practical, select a chapter which will be assigned to be read in the near future. After prereading it, answer the following questions.*

1. What is the major topic of the chapter?

_____

2. How does the author subdivide or break down this topic?

_____

3. What approach does the author take toward the subject? (Does he or she cite research, give examples, describe problems, list causes?)

_____

4. Can you construct a very general mental outline of the chapter?

_____

SUMMARY

Prereading is a technique which allows the reader to become familiar with the material to be read before beginning to read it completely. The technique involves checking specific parts of an article or textbook chapter which provide the reader with a mental outline of the content of the material. Prereading makes the actual reading of the material easier and helps the reader to understand and remember what he or she reads. In prereading, the reader should note such items as the following: title and subtitle; the author and source; publication or copyright date; introduction or first paragraph; each boldface (dark print) heading and the first sentence under it; typographical aids (italics, maps, pictures, charts, graphs); summary or last paragraph; and end-of-chapter or end-of-article materials.

8. Establishing a Purpose for Reading

Use this chapter to:

1. *Help you concentrate on what you are reading.*

2. *Learn how to ask questions before you read.*

Did you ever read a complete page or more and then not remember a thing you read? Do you wander aimlessly through paragraph after paragraph, section after section, unable to remember key ideas you have just read, even when you are really trying to concentrate? If these problems sound familiar, you are probably reading without a specific purpose in mind. That is, you are not looking for anything particular as you are reading. Perhaps the single most important thing to do to ensure understanding and recall of what you read is to establish a purpose — to decide what information you are looking for — for everything you read, and then read to find it.

By now, you are probably beginning to see the relationship of prereading — discussed in the last chapter — to establishing a purpose for reading. Prereading helps you find the topics that are included in an article or chapter; it tells you what you should be looking for. Then it is only a small, but deliberate and active, step to establishing a purpose: asking a specific question which you will try to answer as you read.

HOW TO ESTABLISH A PURPOSE

For written material with boldface headings, the simplest way to establish a purpose for reading is to change each heading into a question which you will try to answer as you read — for a section with the heading "Limitations of Hypnotism," you could ask the question: What are the limitations of hypnotism? Then, as you read that section, you would actively search for the limitations. In the following section, you might ask the question: How are crimes classified? Then you would read to find out the different ways crimes can be classified.

CLASSIFICATION OF CRIMES

On the basis of the seriousness of the offense, crimes may be divided into two general classes, felonies and misdemeanors. The term *business crimes* is applied to crimes committed in the course of business operations. Usually such crimes are committed with the intent of acquiring money or property unlawfully. Business crimes may be either felonies or misdemeanors, depending upon the seriousness of the offense.

Felonies

Felonies are criminal offenses of a serious nature, generally punishable by death or imprisonment in a penitentiary. Crimes classified as felonies are usually committed with wrongful intent. Murder, robbery, and forgery are common felonies.

Misdemeanors

Misdemeanors are criminal offenses of a less serious nature which are punishable by a fine or by imprisonment in a county jail or workhouse. Crimes classified as misdemeanors are sometimes committed without wrongful intent. Among the most common misdemeanors are violations of traffic rules, drunkenness, and disorderly conduct.

—Goodman, *Today's Business Law*, p. 36

As you read the section, you would find out that there are two major types of crimes — felonies and misdemeanors.

As they develop their questions, some students jot down their questions in the margins of their texts, next to the appropriate heading. Writing the questions is a good way to get yourself into the habit of establishing purposes. Many students also find them useful later for study and review.

Who, What, When, Where, Why, How

Questions that begin with Who, What, When, Where, Why, and How are especially helpful as purpose questions. Who, When, and Where questions are perhaps the least useful of this type. They are frequently *closed questions*. They often can be answered through superficial reading and may lead to simple factual or one-word answers. What, Why, and How questions might be more useful questions. They are frequently *open questions*. They require detailed answers that demand more thought, and, as a result, they force you to read in more depth in order to come up with acceptable answers.

A section entitled "The Fall of the Roman Empire" could be turned into a closed question like: When did the Roman Empire fall? This question could give you a goal or purpose for reading the section. As you can see, an acceptable answer for this question could be merely a date. Closed questions like this one probably would not do a good job guiding you through or testing your understanding of most college textbook chapters. On the other hand, open questions (such as: How did the Roman Empire fall? What brought about the fall of the Roman Empire? or Why did the Roman Empire fall?) would require more detailed answers that might include a number of important events or a series of causes or reasons. If you go into the reading of each chapter section with open questions like these in mind, you will be on the lookout for and will identify the most important information in the chapter.

Below are a few headings from one chapter of a text and possible purpose questions to form:

Text: CHILD PSYCHOLOGY
Chapter: "Language Learning and Development in Children"

Heading	*Questions*
Development of Use of Words	How do children use words? How does this ability develop?
Construction of Sentences	How do children form sentences?
Memory and Sentence Formation	What does memory have to do with sentence formation?
Types of Sentence Structures	What are the types of sentence structures children use?

When it is not possible to form open questions using *What, Why,* and *How,* try to keep your purpose questions as open as possible. Purpose questions that can be answered with a simple yes or no, a single name, date, or place, or only a few words will rarely provide you with the guidance that leads to full understanding.

EXERCISE 1

Directions: *Assume that each of the following is a boldface heading within a textbook chapter and that related textual material follows. In the space provided, write a purpose question that could be formed. Compare your questions with those listed in the Answer Key.*

Boldface heading	Question
1. Types of Logic	_____ _____
2. Characteristics of Test Anxiety	_____ _____
3. Nondirective Therapy	_____ _____
4. Physical Changes in Adolescence	_____ _____
5. Sociological Factors Related to Delinquency	_____ _____
6. Adolescent Need for Dependence	_____ _____

7. Influence of "Experts" on Child
   Rearing Practices

   _____

   _____

8. Language and Memory

   _____

   _____

9. Inheritance of Physical
   Characteristics

   _____

   _____

10. Language of Disadvantaged
    Children

   _____

   _____

WRITTEN MATERIALS WITHOUT HEADINGS

In articles and chapters without headings, the title should provide a general overall purpose, and the first sentence of each paragraph can be used to form a question about each paragraph. In the following paragraph, the first sentence would be turned into a question which would guide your reading by telling you what to look for as you read.

Despite its recent increase in popularity, hypnotism does have serious limitations which restrict its widespread use. First of all, not all people are susceptible to hypnotism. Second, a person who does not cooperate with the hypnotist often will not fall into the hypnotic trance. Finally, there are limits to the commands a subject will obey when hypnotized. In many cases, subjects will not do anything which violates their moral code.

From the first sentence you could form the question: What are the limitations of hypnotism? Then, in reading the remainder of the paragraph, you would find three limitations: (1) some people cannot be hypnotized, (2) the subject must cooperate or hypnosis does not occur, (3) subjects will not follow commands to do what they believe is wrong.

EXERCISE 2

Directions: *Assume that each of the sentences below is the first sentence of a paragraph within an article which does not have boldface headings. Beside each sentence, write a purpose question which you would attempt to answer as you read. Compare your responses with those given in the Answer Key.*

First sentence   *Question*

1. Historically, there have been
   three major branches of
   philosophical analysis.

   _____

   _____

2. Scientists who are studying the earthquakes attribute their cause to intense pressures and stresses which build up inside the earth.

_____

_____

3. Information which is processed by the human senses is either physical or chemical in nature.

_____

_____

4. Democracy has not been fully realized in the United States for a number of reasons.[1]

_____

_____

5. Astronomers have learned most of what we know about the stars and the galaxies by analyzing light and how it behaves.[2]

_____

_____

6. The different types of drill presses for performing drilling and allied operations vary in design and specific function.

_____

_____

7. In refrigeration work, the physics of latent heat is especially important.[3]

_____

_____

8. All societies have rules or norms specifying appropriate and inappropriate behavior, and individuals are rewarded or punished as they conform to or deviate from the rules.[4]

_____

_____

9. The electrical terminals which carry the circuit through the dome must be electrically insulated from the dome or housing.[5]

_____

_____

10. Although most studies of work groups concentrate on "problem" behavior, such as turnover, absenteeism, morale, and low productivity, they offer insights into the basic processes underlying behavior in organizations.[6]

_____

_____

DOES ESTABLISHING A PURPOSE WORK?

A number of research studies have been conducted to test whether establishing purposes or forming questions based on the text improves understanding and recall of the information contained in the text. These studies confirm the effectiveness of purpose-setting and indicate that students who read with a purpose have a higher percentage of recall of factual information than students who read without specific purposes.

For example, in one experiment conducted by Frase and Schwartz,* sixty-four college students were divided into two groups. Both groups were given a passage to read and study. One group (Group A) was directed to construct and write out questions based on the text; the other group (Group B) was simply directed to study the material. The results were as follows:

Group	Percentage of recall
Group A	72
Group B	53

The results show that the group that established a purpose for reading by forming questions recalled 19 percent more than the group that read without establishing a purpose.

WHY ESTABLISHING A PURPOSE WORKS

There are several reasons why establishing a purpose is an effective technique.

1. It focuses your attention on what is important, on what you are supposed to read and remember. Let's consider an example from everyday experience which, in some ways, parallels the process of reading. Suppose an instructor asks you to take a walk around the building and when you return, asks you how many office doors were open. Although you could probably guess, you would not be able to provide the specific answer. Suppose, on the other hand, the instructor had asked you to take a walk around the building and, as you walked, to count the number of open office doors. Upon your return, you could easily provide the specific answer. The two situations described differ in the purpose given. When you didn't know what to look for, you didn't find anything specific. When you knew what to look for, it was easy to supply the answer. The same is true when reading a paragraph. If you wander aimlessly through a paragraph, you probably will not remember much about it. If you read with a specific purpose question in mind, if you know what you are looking for, finding and remembering the answer will be simple.

2. Setting a purpose is effective, too, because it forces you to become active — to sort out, process, and evaluate what you read to determine if it answers your purpose question. This processing helps you concentrate and keeps your mind on what you're reading.

3. Unless you have a purpose, it is very easy to slip into the habit of reading without thinking, more or less mechanically recognizing words and ideas. Poor readers frequently recognize an idea but do not respond or react to it; they do not process it. This lack of response may be the prime cause of poor recall.

* L. T. Frase and B. J. Schwartz, "Effect of Question Production and Answering on Prose Recall," *Journal of Educational Psychology*, 67 (1975): 628–635.

EXERCISE 3

Directions: *Turn to the sample textbook chapter included in the Appendix of this text (page 335). For each heading on each of the first six pages, form a question that would be useful in giving you a purpose for reading. List the questions you formed in the space provided below. Then read the sample chapter and answer your questions in the space provided.*

	Questions	Answers
1.	_____	_____
2.	_____	_____
3.	_____	_____
4.	_____	_____
5.	_____	_____

EXERCISE 4

Directions: *Choose a three-to-four-page selection from one of your textbooks. Select pages that you already have been assigned or that you anticipate you will be asked to read. For each heading, form a question that would help you establish a purpose for reading. List the questions you constructed in the space provided. Then read the selection and answer the questions you wrote.*

	Questions	Answers
1.	_____	_____
2.	_____	_____
3.	_____	_____
4.	_____	_____
5.	_____	_____

SUMMARY

Establishing a purpose for reading is a reading habit which significantly affects how well you read, how easily you can concentrate, and how much you can remember. The chapter emphasized that, before beginning to read, you should have in mind specific information that you will be looking for as you read. You may form particular questions to which you expect to find specific answers.

In a textbook chapter, establishing a purpose for reading is relatively simple. Most texts contain boldface headings which can be easily converted into questions. For texts and other types of reading materials which do not have headings, the first sentence of each paragraph can be used to form a purpose question.

Research studies cited in the chapter suggest that having a purpose for reading improves your ability to retain and recall information you read. The chapter ended with some ideas about why and how setting a purpose for reading is an effective technique.

Part Three
Comprehension Skills

Can you remember how you were taught to read? Do you remember going to a reading class or having reading groups in elementary school? Can you remember using readers (series of books with stories) and then answering questions on what you read? Did you use workbooks with drills and exercises that taught you about vowel sounds and syllables? You probably can remember some or all of these things because reading was a regular part of each day's instruction in elementary school.

Now, do you remember going to a reading class in junior or senior high school? Probably not. Most secondary schools throughout the country do not offer reading classes as a regular part of each year's curriculum. In effect, then, reading instruction stopped for you at the end of grade six. This general practice of discontinuing reading instruction at the end of elementary school has serious implications and has directly affected how well you can read now, as you enter college.

When you finished sixth grade, you probably were reading at least at sixth-grade level. You achieved this level through the direct instruction and practice you received in grades one through six. Then, after you entered seventh grade, reading was no longer taught. Instead, it was left up to you to raise your reading skills to the seventh-grade level by the end of seventh grade, to the eighth-grade level by the end of eighth grade, and so forth. The assumption that you could improve your reading skills on your own continued throughout the remainder of your secondary education.

What occurs as a result of this lack of direct instruction is that some students are able to increase their own reading ability while others are not. Most students are able to make some improvement; that is, not many students still read at a sixth-grade level when in the twelfth grade. But, on the other hand, a large percentage of students do not read at a twelfth-grade level at the end of twelfth grade. While estimates and reports which indicate how many students do not read at grade level vary, some statistics show that as many as 30 to 40 percent of a high school graduating class do not read as well as they should. Further, it has been estimated that as many as 60 percent of the freshmen entering New York State's community colleges do not read at a college level.

The purpose of Part Three is to help make up, or compensate, for the lack of reading instruction over the past six years. This part of your text will present some of the most important higher-level reading skills that should have been taught to all students as they began to read more complex and difficult assigned material. The chapters are primarily concerned with how to read better and how to remember more most efficiently. Chapters 9, 10, and 11 will focus on common units of meaning — the sentence, the paragraph, and the passage. Techniques for accurate and effective comprehension of each of these units are presented.

9. Understanding Sentences

Use this chapter to:

1. *Learn how to grasp quickly the meaning of a sentence.*

2. *Learn how to use punctuation as an aid to comprehension.*

Along with words and phrases, sentences are basic units of meaning to consider when improving reading rate and comprehension. Clear and accurate understanding of sentences is essential to all other comprehension skills and to the effective reading and study of textbook chapters.

A sentence is commonly defined as a group of words that express a complete thought or idea. A sentence must be about one thing — the *subject* — and some action that happens in relation to the subject — the *verb*. In some situations the verb, instead of expressing action, links or connects two parts of the sentence. Together, the subject and verb form the *core parts* of the sentence and carry its essential meaning. However, sentences can contain many other parts, and they can vary widely in pattern and complexity. To read a sentence effectively, it is necessary to develop the ability to recognize the structure of a sentence as well as to identify the core parts which convey the essential meaning of the sentence.

RECOGNIZING COMPLETE SENTENCES

Even before beginning to develop skill in recognizing core parts of a sentence, it is important for a reader to understand the difference between complete and incomplete thoughts. A complete thought is one that supplies enough information to give you the full meaning being expressed by the writer. Incomplete thoughts give you only partial information. After reading an incomplete thought, you are left with a question about (1) what happened or (2) to whom or what something happened. The following examples show the difference between groups of words which are complete sentences and those which are not complete sentences because they do not fully express the writers' meanings.

> *Example 1A:* Slipped off the side of the road into the ditch during a winter storm.

In this sentence, you know what happened (something or someone slipped into the ditch), but you do not know what or who slipped. You do not know whether it was a truck, bus, car, or careless driver that went into the ditch.

Example 1B: The tractor-trailer slipped off the side of the road into the ditch during a winter storm.

Sentence 1B is complete. Now you know that the something which slipped off the road and went into the ditch was a tractor-trailer.

Example 2A: This chapter, an excellent summary of the current economic problems in Russia.

In this sentence, there is a subject, "chapter," and some information is given about the subject — "an excellent summary of current economic problems in Russia." The sentence is not complete because there is no action; nothing is happening in relation to the chapter. You do not know what is being said about the chapter — whether it is boring, or whether it is difficult to read.

Example 2B: This chapter, an excellent summary of the current economic problems in Russia, presents some very useful graphs.

Example 2B is a complete sentence because you now know what the chapter does — it presents useful graphs.

You can see that unless a group of words contains a subject and a verb, it does not express a complete thought.

EXERCISE 1

Directions: *Read each of the following groups of words. Mark an S in the blank if the words form a sentence. Mark an N if they do not form a sentence.*

_____ 1. Twenty years ago this month, the President's Council of Economic Advisors reopened for business under a new management after nearly a year in limbo.[1]

_____ 2. A second feature of the pre-operational stage of child growth and development.

_____ 3. Becoming less dependent on sensory-motor responses and more capable of processing language.

_____ 4. One can exert a relatively small force through a large distance and lift a heavy weight through a relatively short distance.[2]

_____ 5. The energy that is used in business and industry in the form of electricity.

_____ 6. Added to the problem of racial unrest caused by court-ordered busing.

_____ 7. In the military-like atmosphere created in many public schools by so many rules and regulations, students easily become bored.[3]

_____ 8. Islands and peninsulas that are inhabited by fewer than one hundred people.

_____ 9. Just as water pressure is caused by the weight of water, atmospheric pressure is caused by the weight of air.[4]

_____ 10. Recitation is both the most neglected aspect of study and the single most important aspect of study.[5]

IDENTIFYING CORE PARTS

As you can see from the above examples and exercise, the two core parts of the sentence — the subject and the verb, or the subject and the action — must be present for a group of words to convey a complete thought. For a group of words to be considered as a sentence in written English, three conditions must be met. The group of words must (1) contain a subject, (2) contain a verb, and (3) express a complete thought. To read and understand a sentence, you should be able to quickly identify these core parts. In short, simple sentences, the core parts are easy to identify. Often simple sentences have only the core parts and a few additional descriptive words or phrases. Read this sentence: The battleship sank. The sentence consists only of the core parts: the subject — battleship — and the verb or action — sank. Now read this sentence: After the battle, the ship sank. The core parts are still easy to identify — ship and sank. However, in addition to conveying the basic message that the ship sank, the sentence contains one additional piece of information — *when* it sank.

In each of the following examples, the core parts are underlined. Read through the sentences, using the following steps. First, read only the underlined words and notice how these give you the basic meaning of each sentence. Then read each sentence through completely. This time, notice what additional information you receive.

Examples:
1. The children lined up according to height.
2. The books fell off the desk.
3. Psychological principles can be applied by everyone.[6]
4. The average American consumes six gallons of beer each year.
5. After her own illness, the physician was more sympathetic to her patients' concerns and fears.

As you read the above examples, you probably noticed the words and phrases that were not core parts of the sentences and contained additional information that in some way described or further explained the chief thought in the sentences. In sentence 5, for example, the important thought is that the physician was sympathetic. The other parts of the sentence tell *when* she was more sympathetic (after her own illness), suggest *why* she was more sympathetic (due to her experience with illness), and tells *to whom* she was more sympathetic (to her own patients).

In longer, more complicated sentences, the verb has an object or thing it refers to which further completes the meaning of the sentence. For example, read this sentence: The thief stole my car. The subject is thief and the action is stole; however, what the thief stole is also important — my car. In reading core parts, then, it is useful to include the complete predicate rather than just the verb itself.

Sentence Modifiers

Once you have identified the core parts of a sentence, the next step is to determine how the meaning of those core parts is changed or modified by the remainder of the sentence. These remaining parts, called *modifiers,* provide you with further information about one of the core parts. Notice how each of the underlined modifiers expands, alters, or limits the meaning of the following sentences.

> After showing the film, the instructor gave a quiz.
> —The modifier tells *when* the quiz was given.

> Dr. Ling, my philosophy instructor, assigns one chapter per week.
> —The modifier indicates who Dr. Ling is.

> Everyone except engineering majors is required to take a philosophy course.
> —The modifier limits by giving an exception.

Multiple Core Parts

Some sentences may have more than one subject and/or more than one verb. Read this sentence: The bookstore and library were closed. There are two subjects — *bookstore* and *library*. Next, consider the following sentence: The professor gave an assignment and canceled class. The instructor performed two actions — *gave* and *canceled*. Here are a few more examples of sentences that contain multiple core parts.

1. Diet and exercise both contribute to weight loss.
2. Quick weight loss schemes deceive consumers and discourage them from trying legitimate plans.
3. Local businesses and private citizens organized the scholarship fund and solicited donations throughout the community.

You should have noticed that sentence 1 contains two subjects, sentence 2 has two predicates, and sentence 3 contains both two subjects and two predicates.

To read a sentence accurately, you must notice and understand the relationship between the modifiers and the core parts. In some cases modifiers provide relatively unimportant additional information to which you should pay little attention. At other times, modifiers qualify, limit, or restrict the meaning of the core parts and significantly alter their meaning, as in the following sentence:

> Those Congressmen hoping for a pay increase voted against the budget cut.

Here the underlined portion is essential; you would not fully understand the sentence unless you knew that not all Congressmen, but only those hoping for a pay increase, voted against the cut.

EXERCISE 2

Directions: *Read each of the following sentences and underline the core parts, the subject and verb (including the object).*

1. My sister took her car to the garage for repairs.
2. The library was closed for the entire week due to a flu epidemic.

3. The textbook contains exercises intended to increase reading speed.
4. Divorce is now more common than in the past because our norms, or behavioral guidelines, concerning divorce are changing.[7]
5. An external force is required to change the momentum of a body.[8]
6. The relationship between buoyancy and displaced liquid was first discovered by the ancient Greek philosopher Archimedes.[9]
7. Safe streets, good schools, clean food are political decisions influenced by who participates in them, who is prevented from participating, and who chooses not to participate.[10]
8. When two elements react with each other, a chemical reaction occurs, and a compound is formed.[11]
9. With the new abortion laws, women of all ages, married or unmarried, with and without previous children, request therapeutic abortions.[12]
10. In looking at the writing of the Constitution, we saw how the colonists drew from the tradition of English political thought, the models of colonial government, and experience with the Articles of Confederation in shaping the Constitution.[13]

RECOGNIZING RELATIONSHIPS AMONG IDEAS

Many sentences that you read in textbooks and reference material express more than one idea. Often, a writer combines closely related ideas into one sentence to make the connection between them clearer and easier to understand. For instance, in the following example notice that the longer, combined sentence provides more information than do the two shorter ones.

1. Sam wanted to see a movie.
2. Sam stayed home and studied.

Combined sentence:
Although Sam wanted to see a movie, he stayed home and studied.

The combined sentence shows that the two actions are alternatives and occur within the same time frame.

There are two basic sentence patterns commonly used to combine ideas. It is useful to be familiar with each type because they provide the reader with very useful clues about the relationship and relative importance of the ideas.

Sentences That Combine Ideas

When two or more equally important ideas are very closely related, a writer may combine them into a single sentence. This is done for three reasons: (1) to emphasize their relationship, (2) to indicate their equal importance, and/or (3) to make the material more concise and easier to read. In the following example notice how two related ideas are combined.

1. Marlene was in obvious danger.
2. Joe quickly pulled Marlene from the street.

Combined sentence:
> Marlene was in obvious danger, and Joe quickly pulled
> her from the street.

In this case the combined sentence establishes that the two equally important events are parts of a single incident.

As you read sentences of this type, be sure to locate two sets of core parts. If you do not read carefully or if you are reading too fast, you might miss the second idea. Often you can recognize a sentence that combines two or more ideas by its structure and punctuation. Although a later section of this chapter discusses punctuation in more detail, basically, equal ideas are combined by using either a semicolon or a comma along with one of the following words: *and, but, or, either-or, neither-nor.* Here are a few examples:

1. The students wanted the instructor to cancel the class, <u>but</u> the instructor decided to reschedule it.
2. The union members wanted to strike<u>;</u> the company did nothing to discourage them.
3. Some students decided to take the final exam<u>, and</u> others chose to rely on their semester average.

Sentences That Relate Ideas

Often a writer expands a sentence by adding related, but less important, ideas to the base sentence. While these less important ideas have their own core parts, they depend on the base sentence to complete their meaning. For example, in the following sentence you do not fully understand the meaning of the underlined portion until you read the entire sentence.

> <u>Because Diane forgot to make a payment,</u> she had to pay a late charge on her loan.

In this sentence, the more important idea is that Diane had to pay a late charge. The reason for the late charge is presented as background information that amplifies and further explains the basic message.

As you read sentences of this type, be sure to notice the relationship between the two ideas. The idea of lesser importance may describe or explain a condition, cause, reason, purpose, time, or place. Here are a few additional examples of sentences that relate ideas. In each the base sentence is underlined and the function of the less important idea is indicated in parentheses above it.

(description)
1. <u>My grandfather,</u> who is eighty years old, <u>collects stamps.</u>

(time)
2. <u>American foreign policy changed</u> when we entered the Vietnam War.

(condition)
3. Unless my class is dismissed early, <u>I'll be late for my dental appointment.</u>

(reason)
4. Since I failed my last history exam, <u>I decided to drop the course.</u>

EXERCISE 3

Directions: *Read each of the following sentences and decide whether the sentence combines two equally important ideas or whether it expresses a relationship between two ideas, one of which depends on the other. Mark C in the space to the right if the sentence combines two or more ideas. Mark R if it relates two unequal ideas, and underline the more important, base idea.*

1. The personnel office eagerly accepted my application for a job, and I expect to receive an offer next week. _____

2. Since it is difficult to stop smoking, the individual who wants to quit may find group therapy effective. _____

3. Birth control is interference with the natural rhythms of reproduction; some individuals object to it on this basis. _____

4. Computers have become part of our daily lives, but their role in today's college classrooms has not yet been fully explored. _____

5. Marriage consists of shared experiences and ambitions, and both are influenced by the values of each partner. _____

6. As far as we can tell from available evidence, humankind has been on this earth for several million years.[14] _____

7. Because sugar is Cuba's main export, the Cuban economy depends upon the worldwide demand for and price of sugar. _____

8. The personnel manager who accepted my application is well known for interviewing all likely candidates. _____

9. Even though a feather and a brick will fall equally fast in a vacuum, they fall quite differently in the presence of air. _____

10. The anthropological linguist is concerned primarily with languages that have no written form, although languages are not ignored by any means.[15] _____

EXERCISE 4

Directions: *Choose a page from one of your textbooks. Read each sentence and underline any or all sentences that combine two or more ideas. Place brackets [ ] around all sentences that relate two or more ideas.*

IDENTIFYING CORE PARTS IN COMPLICATED SENTENCES

Identifying core parts as you read becomes more difficult as sentences become longer and more complicated and as additional information is added.

Complete sentence — simple:
Burger World plans to start work on a new restaurant.

Complete sentence — complicated:
Burger World, which operates some 2000 fast food restaurants, plans to start work this spring, or at the latest by early summer, on a new self-service restaurant in Rochester, New York, which is designed to test many new ideas in energy saving and customer convenience.

The above examples show how a lot of additional information can be added to a simple sentence. Reread the example of a complicated complete sentence, noticing how much extra information has been added to the simple sentence. If each fact added to the simple sentence had to be written as a separate sentence, how many additional sentences would be necessary? Let's find out:

Core:
Burger World plans to start work on a new restaurant.

1. The new restaurant will be self-service.
2. Burger World operates 2000 fast food restaurants.
3. Burger World plans to start work this spring.
4. If Burger World does not start work in the spring, it will start in early summer.
5. The new restaurant will be located in Rochester, New York.
6. The new restaurant is designed to test many ideas in energy saving and customer convenience.

Now you can see why sentences are written in complex ways. By writing a long, complicated sentence, the author eliminates the need to write many short, simple sentences; the information is expressed in a shorter, more compact way, and repetition is difficult. You must sort out each important thought in these long and complicated sentences.

EXERCISE 5

Directions: *First, identify the core parts of each complicated sentence below and write them in the space provided. Then, write as many new sentences as you can using the remaining information in the sentence.*

1. Besides teaching the rules of behavior that are acceptable in our society, the family supplies children with the affection and love they need to feel that they are complete and happy persons.[16]

   Core parts: _____

New sentences:

a. _____

b. _____

c. _____

d. _____

e. _____

2.   Segregation occurs within the school as well, because students are usually assigned to different tracks, or programs, according to ability and achievement.[17]

Core parts: _____

New sentences:

a. _____

b. _____

c. _____

d. _____

e. _____

3.   The Gulf Stream, the warm waters of the northward-flowing ocean current, has influenced much of the life of the Gulf and Atlantic shores as far north as Newfoundland.

Core parts: _____

New sentences:

a. _____

b. _____

c. _____

d. _____

e. _____

4.   As the Gulf Stream passes between Cuba and Florida on its way back to the Atlantic, the stream is of immense size — its width nearly a hundred miles, its depth a mile, and its volume equal to several hundred Mississippi Rivers.[18]

Core parts: _____

New sentences:

a. _____

b. _____

c. _____

d. _____

e. _____

5. Although the relationship between pressure and weather is not so simple as some barometers imply (high pressure equals fine weather, low pressure means rain, in between means variable), nevertheless, the rising and falling of the barometer is an expression of atmospheric processes which determine future weather.[19]

Core parts: _____

New sentences:

a. _____

b. _____

c. _____

d. _____

e. _____

EXERCISE 6

Directions: *Turn to the sample textbook chapter included in the Appendix of this text. Beginning with the section headed "Media Strategy," read each sentence and underline the core parts of each. Continue reading and underlining until you finish the page.*

EXERCISE 7

Directions: *Select one page from a chapter in a textbook you are currently reading. After you have read each sentence, underline its core parts.*

EXERCISE 8

Directions: *Select several pages from one of your more difficult textbooks. Quickly look through these pages and locate ten long or complicated sentences. Then, underline the core parts in each sentence.*

PUNCTUATION: AN AID TO SENTENCE COMPREHENSION

Most readers tend to be unaware of the purpose of punctuation as they read. They do not realize that punctuation is an important aid to understanding sentences. Punctuation can be a guide, or marker, for the location of sentence core parts. It may also separate the core parts of the sentence from other words and phrases in the sentence.

To demonstrate the importance of punctuation, try reading the following material, from which all punctuation has been deleted.

> The major challenge facing newborn children is to come to know the world in which they live this assignment may not seem difficult to us after all the world is so familiar that we take for granted its many facts and aspects we know there are objects of various types rocks trees and animals books records and films women men and children we expect these to behave in customary ways a rock falls to the ground when dropped a tree changes in form over the years men and women often marry and procreate above all we believe that objects are permanent they will continue to exist in some form even if hidden from us for a considerable time

Now, read the same material with punctuation restored and notice the difference.

> The major challenge facing newborn children is to come to know the world in which they live. This assignment may not seem difficult to us; after all, the world is so familiar that we take for granted its many facts and aspects. We know there are objects of various types: rocks, trees, and animals; books, records, and films; women, men, and children. We expect these to behave in customary ways: a rock falls to the ground when dropped; a tree changes in form over the years; men and women often marry and procreate. Above all, we believe that objects are permanent: they will continue to exist in some form, even if hidden from us for a considerable time.[20]
> –Gardner, *Developmental Psychology*, p. 57

As you can see from reading these two versions of the same paragraph, punctuation makes a real difference and helps you read in several ways. First, it marks the end of sentences and separates them from one another. Second, it separates the various parts of a sentence. Finally, punctuation tells you specific things about the arrangement and relative importance of the various parts of a sentence. Punctuation marks can, for example, separate the core parts from the remainder of the sentence. The relationship of the core parts to the remainder of the sentence may also be suggested by various types of punctuation. Each of these uses of punctuation will be discussed under the headings that follow. The uses of specific punctuation marks will be described. You will see that each type of punctuation mark has specific uses within a sentence and that each provides you with certain clues about the meaning of the sentence.

The Comma

The comma has a number of different uses, but in each case it separates some type of information from other parts of the sentence. The different uses of the comma are explained below.

The Introductory Use: The comma can be used to separate introductory, beginning, or opening parts of a sentence from the main part of the sentence. Sentences often begin with some type of introductory phrase that connects what will be said in one sentence with what has already been said in a previous sentence, that provides some background information, that sets the scene or time frame, or that offers some qualifying information or considerations. Introductory phrases, such as *as you know, upon careful consideration, after it rained,* all serve to introduce or lead into the main idea presented in the core parts of the sentence. The following examples show how commas can be used to separate introductory phrases from the main sentence.

Example: To my surprise, most people attending the party were over thirty years old.

In this sentence, the important idea is that most people at the party were over thirty. The introductory phrase adds additional qualifying information about the writer's reaction to the main idea.

Example: At the age of thirteen, he began to give piano concerts.

In this example, information regarding the time frame is added to the sentence through the introductory phrase. Notice, again, that the phrase is separated from the main part of the sentence by a comma.

The Parenthetical Use: The comma can be used to separate additional information from the main part of the sentence. Writers occasionally interrupt the core sentence to add some extra (parenthetical) information which is important but not crucial to the sentence meaning. They use a comma before and after this parenthetical information. To you as a reader, this use of a comma should help you tell important from less important information and should aid you in identifying the sentence's core parts.

Each of the sentences in the examples below illustrates the use of the comma to separate extra (parenthetical) information from the main part of the sentence. As you work through each example, first read the entire sentence. Then reread all parts of the sentence except the parenthetical phrase which has been underlined. You will notice that even when the parenthetical phrase is left out, the sentence is complete and conveys meaning.

Examples:
1. My sister, Jane Samuels, plans to run for mayor of Philadelphia.
2. Dolphins, as a matter of fact, are very friendly creatures which frequently come to the rescue of people.
3. Drugs and alcohol, experts warn, are an unsafe and dangerous combination.

The Serial Use: Whenever several items are presented in a list, or series, in a sentence, they are separated by commas. Many different types of items may be given in a series. Single words, such as nouns or adjectives, as well as clauses and phrases, are all separated by commas when they are part of a list. In all cases, the items in a series are equal and consistent in how they are connected or related to the core parts of a sentence. As you are reading, if you notice many items separated by commas, you might expect that they are a series of related facts or ideas. You should also realize that, because they are separated from the core parts of the sentence, they can help you in locating the core parts.

Read each of the following sentences, which are examples of the serial use of the comma. Notice how the underlined items in the series have a parallel or equal relationship to one another and to the core parts of each sentence. Each item in the list is of the same class or category.

Examples:

1. After I saw the film, I was <u>bored,</u> <u>tired,</u> and <u>angry.</u>
2. Each state retained its "<u>sovereignty,</u> <u>freedom,</u> and <u>independence.</u>"[21]
3. Social adjustment refers to <u>the ability of the individual to maintain himself independently,</u> <u>to be gainfully employed,</u> and <u>to conform to social standards set by the community.</u>[22]

Related Ideas: The comma can be used to join two closely related, and complete, ideas within a single sentence. When used in this way, the comma must be used with a conjunction, or connecting word. Some of the most commonly used conjunctions are *and, or, nor, but,* and *for.* This use of the comma tells you that there are actually two complete but related ideas within a sentence. This use of the comma also indicates that there are two sets of core parts within the sentence.

Read the examples below. Notice how the first sentence in each example can be divided into two separate, complete sentences.

Examples:

1. We walked two miles into the woods, but we did not see a single wild animal.

or

We walked two miles into the woods. We did not see a single wild animal.

2. Divorce is increasing in popularity and acceptance, but many negative feelings about it continue.

or

Divorce is increasing in popularity and acceptance. Many negative feelings about it continue.

EXERCISE 9

Directions: *In each sentence that follows, cross out the part or parts of the sentence that you can identify as of lesser importance in the sentence based on the use and placement of commas.*

1. In the nineteenth century, industrialization made its impact on society for better or worse.[23]

2. That is, no member of the Congress could serve more than three years in any six.[24]
3. If we put together everything we have discussed about the incidence and distribution of mental retardation, we can draw some tentative conclusions.[25]
4. All societies are held together by a system of *norms*, which are defined as rules of acceptable behavior that are upheld by tradition and custom, as well as by law.[26]
5. Man has been labeled a political animal, a tool-using animal, a social animal, a speaking animal, and a creature that is aware of itself.[27]
6. How is it, then, that we perceive depth, the third dimension?[28]
7. Perhaps even more important, when humans think, they know they are thinking.[29]
8. Language can be recorded, either on paper or in the folktales that survive by constant retelling, and can thus provide a bond with the past.[30]
9. Graphite, on the other hand, is made of a lot of carbon layers stacked one on top of the other, like sheets of paper.[31]
10. When a gas is cooled, it condenses (changes to a liquid) at its condensation point, which is the same temperature as the boiling point.[32]

The Semicolon

The primary use of the semicolon is to separate two very closely related ideas which have been combined into a single sentence. Sentences 1 and 2 in the examples below can be combined using a semicolon to form sentence 3.

Examples:

1. They bought the house at a very low price.
2. The former owner had to sell immediately and move to another city.
3. They bought the house at a very low price; the former owner had to sell immediately and move to another city.

You may notice that this use of the semicolon is similar to the use of the comma to separate complete and related ideas in one sentence. Both are used to separate closely related ideas within a sentence. One main difference is that a conjunction, such as *and* or *but,* must be used along with the comma, but the semicolon can be used alone — without a conjunction.

When you are reading a sentence which contains a semicolon, be alert for two separate ideas and two sets of core parts. When a semicolon is used, you know that the two ideas have equal weight or importance. Each of the following sentences contains two related ideas separated by a semicolon. The core parts of each sentence are underlined.

Examples:

1. The fishermen caught fifteen trout; they cooked them over an open fire.
2. The job had to be finished on time; we found we had underestimated the amount of work involved.

3. All <u>objects</u> <u>radiate</u> or <u>absorb</u> some form of
    electromagnetic radiation; the <u>kind</u> and <u>amount</u> <u>depend</u>
    on their temperature and physical state.[33]

Occasionally, a semicolon is used to separate sentence parts which,
if divided by commas, would be confusing or difficult to read. To illustrate this use of the semicolon, the sentence below has been written in
two versions.

Versions:

1. Speakers at the conference included Dr. Frank, a
    biologist, Dr. Flock, a philosopher, and Professor Smich,
    a geneticist.
2. Speakers at the conference included Dr. Frank, a
    biologist; Dr. Flock, a philosopher; and Professor Smich,
    a geneticist.

As you read the first version of the sentence, you are not sure whether
the speakers include Dr. Frank and a biologist or whether it was Dr.
Frank who was being described as a biologist. The use of the semicolon
in the second version makes it clear that it is Dr. Frank who is the
biologist.

The Colon

The colon is most often used to introduce a list, statement, or quotation. The colon tells you, the reader, that some type of additional information which further explains the main idea of a sentence is to follow.
The colon also serves as a marker indicating that the sentence's core
parts precede the colon.

Examples:

1. Books that I have enjoyed recently include the following:
    Pride and Prejudice, Sons and Lovers, and *Bleak House.*
    (In this sentence, the colon introduces a list of book
    titles.)
2. The causes of the war can be divided into three
    categories: social, economic, and political. (Here, the
    colon indicates that a list of categories will follow.)
3. Finally, Chomsky described two levels of language: one
    underlying or deep structure involved with meaning,
    and a surface level produced and heard in ordinary
    conversation.[34] (The colon in this example signals that
    an explanation of the two levels of language is to follow.)

The Dash

The dash is most commonly used in a sentence to separate unessen-
tial or parenthetical elements from the core sentence, when using a
comma would be confusing. This usage also assists the reader in separating core parts from supporting information.

Example: At least three sports — basketball, football,
and tennis — are continually gaining television fans.

EXERCISE 10

Directions: *For each of the sentences listed below, use punctuation as an aid in locating the sentence's core parts. Draw a line through all elements within the sentence which, according to punctuation used, can be identified as nonessential to the sentence's main meaning.*

1. Steel, for instance, is mostly iron, with various other metals added, such as chromium, nickel, vanadium, manganese, molybdenum, or zirconium, depending on what the steel is to be used for.[35]

2. Among the physical traits that, added together, separate humans from all other animals, there are three of overwhelming significance: a skeleton built for walking upright; eyes capable of sharp, three-dimensional vision in color; and hands that provide both a powerful grip and nimble manipulations.[36]

3. Unfortunately, though, for all the biomedical advances, the cause of mental retardation in most cases cannot be established.[37]

4. For a hundred years, changes in the environment, wrought by humans burning fossil fuels, clearing large forests, and cultivating and excavating the land, have tremendously accelerated.[38]

5. A common theme in many social process theories is that like any other kind of social behavior, criminal behavior is learned; accordingly, they place much emphasis on the manner in which learning takes place and on the factors thought to affect the content of learning.[39]

EXERCISE 11

Directions: *Using punctuation as a guide, underline the core part(s) in each sentence.*

1. The periodic table is the backbone of chemistry, and we'll be using it again and again throughout this book.[40]

2. Your brain sits at the top of your spinal cord, in your head, protected by a thick layer of bone called the skull; most of your brain lies higher than your nostrils.[41]

3. Throughout history, man has been puzzled and exasperated by the strange duality of his nature — half animal, half angel — and much religious and philosophic teaching has been an attempt to understand and integrate these two sides of human nature.[42]

4. Atomic physicists, for example, have determined that certain radioactive elements discharge at a constant rate and, in the process, turn into certain other materials.[43]

5. Poverty and mild retardation go hand in hand, yet the vast majority of individuals from poverty neighborhoods are not mentally retarded.[44]

SUMMARY

The sentence, one of the basic units of meaning, is defined as a group of words that expresses a complete thought or idea. In order to be complete, a sentence must contain sufficient information so the reader is not left to question what happened or to whom or to what something happened.

All complete sentences must have two essential components; these are called core parts. First, a sentence must have a subject; it must be about a person, thing, or idea. Second, a sentence must express some type of action; something must happen to or be done by the subject. To understand a sentence, the reader must be able to recognize these core parts. Many sentences combine two or more sets of core parts for the purpose of showing relationships between them. In long, complicated sentences, identifying the core parts is more difficult because it is necessary to separate the core parts from other words, phrases, and clauses which provide additional information about the core parts.

Punctuation is an aid to the reader in comprehending sentence meaning and identifying the core parts of the sentence. Each type of punctuation mark gives the reader specific information about the relative importance of ideas and the location of core parts within the sentence:

Comma: The comma separates additional, less important, information from the main part of the sentence.

Semicolon: The semicolon separates two complete and very closely related ideas which have been combined into a single sentence. The semicolon indicates the presence of at least two sets of core parts within the sentence.

Colon: The colon usually indicates that a list, statement, or quotation is to follow.

Dash: The dash separates additional or nonessential elements of the sentence from the core parts of the sentence in instances in which a comma would be confusing.

10. Understanding Paragraphs

Use this chapter to:

1. Find out what to look for as you read a paragraph.
2. Increase your recall of paragraph content.

The *paragraph* can be defined as a group of related sentences about a single topic. Just as sentences have specific components — core parts — paragraphs also contain particular elements that are necessary for complete meaning to be conveyed.

THREE ESSENTIAL ELEMENTS OF A PARAGRAPH

Topic: the one thing the paragraph is about. The topic is the unifying factor, and every sentence and idea contained in the paragraph relates to the topic.

Main idea: what the author wants to communicate about the topic. The main idea is the central or most important thought in the paragraph. Every other sentence and idea in the paragraph is related to the main idea. The sentence that expresses this idea is called the *topic sentence.*

Details: the proof, support, explanation, reasons, or examples that explain the paragraph's main idea.

Each of the following examples contains a group of sentences, but only *one* is a paragraph. Only that one has the three essential elements. Identify the paragraph.

Examples:
   Cats frequently become aggressive when provoked. Some plants require more light than others due to coloration of their foliage. Some buildings, due to poor construction, waste a tremendous amount of energy.

   Some plants require more light than others due to coloration of their foliage. Some plants will live a long time without watering. Plants are being used as decorator items in stores and office buildings.

   Some plants require more light than others due to coloration of their foliage. Plants with shades of white, yellow, or pink in their leaves need more light than plants with

102

completely green foliage. For example, a Swedish ivy plant
with completely green leaves requires less light per day than
a variegated Swedish ivy that contains shades of white,
yellow, and green in its leaves.

In the first example, the group of sentences were unrelated; each sentence was about a different thing, and there was no connection among them.

In the second example, each sentence was about plants — the common topic; however, the sentences together did not prove, explain, or support any particular idea about plants.

In the third example, each sentence was about plants, and all sentences were about one main idea — that some plants need more light than others due to colors in their leaves.

Thus, the third example is a paragraph; it has a topic — plants; a main idea — that plants require varying degrees of light due to coloration; and supporting details — the example of the Swedish ivy. The first sentence functions as a topic sentence.

In order to understand a paragraph, a reader must be able to identify the topic, main idea, and details easily. In the following paragraph, each of these parts is identified:

Topic sentence {
As societies become industrialized, the distribution of workers among various economic activities tends to change in a predictable way. In the early stages, the population is engaged in agriculture and the collection of raw materials for food and shelter. But as technology develops, agricultural workers are drawn into manufacturing and construction.

Topic: distribution of workers

Details

HOW TO IDENTIFY THE TOPIC OF A PARAGRAPH

The topic of a paragraph is the subject of the whole paragraph. It is the one thing that the whole paragraph is about. Usually, the topic of a paragraph can be expressed in two or three words.

To find the topic of a paragraph, ask yourself this question: What is the one thing the author is discussing throughout the paragraph?

Example:
In recent years, the importance of vending machines has rapidly increased. Actually, vending is little more than an extension of the self-service trend except that added locational flexibility is realized. The vending industry has now developed a machine that can read and handle bills; therefore, it is only a matter of time before goods with larger unit value will be sold in vending machines.
–Buskirk, *Principles of Marketing*, p. 124

In the example, the author is discussing one topic — vending machines — throughout the paragraph. Notice how many times the word *vending* is repeated in the paragraph. Frequently, the repeated use of a word can serve as a clue to the topic of a paragraph.

EXERCISE 1

Directions: *Read each of the following paragraphs and then underline the topic of the paragraph.*

1. Family relations are characterized by identification, which is a process of experiencing the actions of another person as if one had performed them himself. Some identification is a part of any group membership, but it is especially important to the primary group. The pride which a family member feels because of the accomplishments of any other member is an important source of solidarity in the family relationship. On the other hand, identification is also a source of disharmony, since it leads the individual to feel the same discomfort when another member of the family commits a social error or violates a social norm that he would if he had committed it himself, except that he may perceive its inappropriateness even more clearly.
   —Broom and Selznick, *Sociology*, p. 376

   a. pride
   b. identification in family relations
   c. family relations
   d. social norms

2. Morbidity refers to the occurrence of disease, and the morbidity rate is usually expressed as the incidence of a disease per 100,000 of population. The gathering and interpretation of medical statistics is an exceedingly complex operation. For example, changing classifications of diseases impose difficulties in the interpretation of morbidity rates over a period of time, and diseases that are socially stigmatized are often not correctly reported. The lists of disease are being reviewed and revised constantly, and the continuing National Health Survey has greatly improved morbidity records in the United States.
   —Broom and Selznick, *Sociology*, p. 331

   a. classification of disease
   b. population statistics
   c. National Health Survey
   d. morbidity rates

3. Whenever a test of water is involved, its condition is expressed in pH. This factor indicates the activity of the hydrogen ion whenever there is moisture present. The term *pH* followed by a number is used to indicate whether water tends to be acidic or alkaline. Distilled water at 77°F. (25°C.), neither acidic nor alkaline, has a pH of 7. It is said to be neutral. Numbers above 7 and up to 14 express increasing alkalinity. Numbers decreasing from 7 (6 to 0) indicate increasing acidity.
   —Althouse et al., *Modern Refrigeration and Air Conditioning*, p. 876

   a. pH factor
   b. acidity in water
   c. alkalinity in water
   d. distilled water

4. Heat is the safest and most usual agent for sterilization in hospitals. Methods of applying heat for sterilization are exposure to steam under pressure (autoclave), dry heat, boiling, and occasional flaming. In using heat, consideration is given to the nature of the materials to be sterilized, to the time of exposure to the heat, and, with the autoclave, to pressure. Most pathogenic microorganisms can be killed by a temperature above 140°F. (60°C.), but mature spores may survive many hours of boiling temperature. All living organisms can be killed by exposure to moist heat at a temperature of 250°F. (121°C.) for fifteen minutes. Disinfection with heat at home may be accomplished by using the oven, by boiling, by using a pressure cooker, and, for small materials, by ironing with a hot iron or flaming with a match.
   —McClain and Gragg, *Scientific Principles of Nursing,* p. 108

   a. steam sterilization
   b. sterilization by heat
   c. sterilization methods in hospitals
   d. pathogenic microorganisms

5. New species of plants are being discovered every year. It is estimated that the yearly average for the higher groups of plants alone is approximately 4700 proposed new species. It is obviously necessary, from a practical as well as from a scientific standpoint, that attention be given to the naming and proper classification of the vast assemblage of plants, both native and cultivated. The scientists who do these things are systematic botanists or taxonomists. Most certainly it is essential for those working the various fields of plant science — whether they are agriculturists, florists, foresters, physiologists, or morphologists — to know which plants they are dealing with; they must know their proper scientific names and their relationships.
   —Robbins et al., *Botany,* p. 7

   a. the role of taxonomists
   b. new plant species
   c. plant science
   d. importance of classifying new plant species

6. The record of plant evolution is the accumulation of ancient plant remains (fossils) in the sediments and sedimentary rocks of the Earth's crust. Most plant remains were deposited in swamp or bog areas where they grew; some were carried by streams to the site of deposition in the sediments of river deltas or lakes. Plant remains may be fossilized only if local conditions prevent their decay. Quick coverage by water, sediments, or ash excludes oxygen and thus preserves the plant tissues for subsequent formation of fossils. Plants that grew in swamps, bogs, or on pond margins and near the sea, were the most likely to be fossilized, whereas plants of inland arid regions were less likely to be preserved.
   —Greulach and Adams, *Plants,* pp. 566–567

   a. sediments
   b. plant fossil formation
   c. local conditions
   d. the earth's crust

7. The gas-diesel engine uses gas such as natural gas or producer gas or sewage gas for fuel. In the true gas diesel, air is compressed in the usual manner, and the gas is injected and ignited by the heat of the compressed air. Such a system requires some means of compressing the gas so it can be injected. Engines of this type which operate satisfactorily are available, but other designs have proven to be more popular.

   –Toboldt, *Diesel*, p. 49

   a. compressing air
   b. gas injection
   c. natural and producer gas
   d. gas-diesel engines

8. The essence of learning by means of a teaching machine lies of course in the material to be learned, arranged in such a form as to be most rapidly mastered. Such a body of arranged material is called a program, and the advantages of a program can be obtained without a machine. The program is not intended as a review or testing device, as in some older forms of testing machines or workbooks; it is intended to do the teaching, that is, to do the sorts of things textbooks and teachers do prior to an examination. Hence a program must present information and must make it possible for the learner to participate by supplying answers that are at first hinted at or prompted before they are overlearned in further use.

   –Hilgard, *Introduction to Psychology*, p. 321

   a. reviewing and testing
   b. learning programs
   c. learning without machines
   d. the role of teachers

9. The term Groups has long been a pivotal concept of sociology. Stated tersely, a group is any number of human beings in reciprocal communication. It may be well to emphasize certain aspects and implications of this short definition which beginning students, as well as some sociologists themselves, frequently overlook or do not appreciate fully. First, a group refers only to persons in communication. Mere physical closeness, if there is not communication, does not make a group. The communication creates the group, not the mere fact of spatial proximity or physical contact. Second, a group may be of any size from two persons, to, theoretically and potentially, the entire population of the world. Third, communication need not be face-to-face or by "word of mouth"; it may be indirect through writing or at long range through such instruments as the telegraph.

   –Cuber, *Sociology*, p. 273

   a. communication in groups
   b. definition of a group
   c. social limitations of a group
   d. size of groups

10. Learning is acquiring new information, new or changed ways of responding, new understanding. The fundamental principles of

learning are few and are not difficult to grasp. Learning, like any other activity, must be initiated and sustained by some driving force or motive. It is purposive — directed toward specific aims or goals. There must be some means of seeing what leads to the goal and what does not: a way of knowing what is right and what is wrong. When errors occur, they must be recognized as errors so that other responses can be substituted. This requires some form of appreciation of what is "right." Whatever is learned is mastered to some degree and the amount of mastery can be increased with additional practice of an appropriate kind. What is learned may be reatined for later use. What has been learned can also help in future learning.

—Meenes, *Studying and Learning*, p. 1

a. motivation for learning
b. errors in learning
c. retaining information
d. principles of learning

EXERCISE 2

Directions: *For each of the following paragraphs, read the paragraph and write the topic in the space provided. Be sure to limit the topic to two or three words.*

1. Radiation is the process by which energy is propagated through space. Radiant energy may be used therapeutically for diagnosis and for treatment of various disease conditions. Treatments dependent upon radiation that the nurse may carry out or assist with in some way include the use of infrared rays, ultraviolet rays, and medical diathermy and treatments with x-ray, radium, and radioactive drugs. Electromagnetic waves are measured in angstrom units (called after a Swedish physicist of that name). An angstrom unit is one ten-millionth of a millimeter. Each type of ray has its own wave length. The electromagnetic spectrum shows the place of each type in relation to all the others.

   —McClain and Gragg, *Scientific Principles of Nursing*, p. 278

   Topic: _____

2. Plants absorb water and mineral salts from the soil; they take in oxygen and carbon dioxide from the atmosphere; they manufacture sugars, starches, fats, proteins, and scores of other substances; they conduct materials from one part of the plant to another; they respire; they grow; they react to the environment in which they live; they reproduce. In short, plants carry on a number of activities; they do work; they have functions. Plant physiology is the area of botany concerned with a study of these activities and functions.

   —Robbins et al., *Botany*, p. 9

   Topic: _____

3. Whenever emotions are aroused, detectable electrical changes take place on the skin. Electrodes attached to the skin (e.g., on the palms of the hands) are connected with a recording galvanometer. The galvanic skin response (GSR) is a sensitive indicator of changes in emotional state. Demonstrations such as the following are commonly used in psychology classes: A male student, with the electrodes attached to his palms, recites the alphabet slowly while thinking of the name of his girl friend. The class tries to judge from the swing of the galvanometer when he has come to her initial. His slight embarrassment or excitement or concern about being detected is commonly revealed through an unusually wide swing of the needle.

   –Hilgard, *Introduction to Psychology*, p. 59

   Topic: _____

4. So-called pressure to conform to the ways of other people is evident to almost everyone, particularly to the young, who in onerous ways experience one or another kind of "control" recurrently. Pressure to conform is no less strong for more mature people, but they, because of their maturity, usually are so thoroughly habituated to the patterns that the pressure is largely unnoticed except under unusual circumstances. Society contains numerous devices to facilitate and assure conformity. Basically there exists a reward and punishment system — one is rewarded for doing the appropriate things and punished for doing the inappropriate things.

   –Cuber, *Sociology*, p. 85

   Topic: _____

5. The structural and functional unit of both animals and plants is the cell. It is the simplest bit of living matter that can exist independently and exhibit all the characteristics of life. The processes of the entire organism are the sum of the coordinated functions of its constituent cells. These cellular units vary considerably in size, shape, and function. Some of the smallest animals have bodies made of a single cell; the body of man, in contrast, is made of countless billions of cells fitted together.

   –Villee et al., *General Zoology*, p. 15

   Topic: _____

6. Many students read too slowly. They continue to read just as they did when in the sixth grade. They move their lips as if pronouncing every word and carry their fingers along the line of print to lead their eyes. It is as if they were reading aloud and had to pronounce each word with care. They have not yet moved to a more skillful level in reading: reading for comprehension rather than for pronunciation. In reading for meaning tracing each word with lips and finger is undesirable as well as unnecessary. Reading seeks the author's thoughts rather than his words. The phrase

rather than the word is the thought unit, and the eyes can learn to take in whole phrases at a glance.

    —Meenes, *Studying and Learning,* pp. 28–29

Topic: _____

7. When you learn a language you learn the sounds used in that language, the basic units of meaning, such as words, and the rules to combine these to form new sentences. The elements and rules constitute the grammar of a language. The grammar, then, is what we know; it represents our linguistic competence. To understand the nature of language we must understand the nature of this internalized, unconscious set of rules which constitutes the grammar.

    —Fromkin and Rodman, *An Introduction to Language,* p. 9

Topic: _____

8. Chinese writing utilizes a system of characters, each of which represents the "meaning" of a word, rather than its sounds. Chinese dictionaries and rhyme books contain tens of thousands of these characters, but to read a newspaper one needs know "only" about five thousand. It is not easy to become a scholar in China! In 1956, the difficulties prompted the government of the People's Republic of China to simplify the characters. They also adopted a spelling system using the Roman alphabet, to be used along with the regular ancient system. It is doubtful whether it will replace the traditional writing, which is an integral part of Chinese culture. In China, writing is an art — calligraphy — and thousands of years of poetry and literature and history are preserved in the old system.

    —Fromkin and Rodman, *An Introduction to Language,* p. 290

Topic: _____

9. Most paper contains a high percentage of wood fibers. Only the more expensive varieties of paper, such as writing paper and blueprint paper, contain appreciable quantities of cotton cellulose fibers. Newsprint, the most abundantly produced form of paper, contains only wood pulp and filler materials. The use of rag fibers improves the strength and other properties of paper. Paper making consists, essentially, of reassembling the fibers of wood or cotton in the form of a continuous sheet by mixing the various types of fibers with large volumes of water, and with appropriate fillers (such as talc, clay, and gypsum) and sizing agents (such as alum and rosin). This mixture is flowed onto a moving belt of fine wire screen. Water drains and is sucked from the fluid and a weak, wet sheet of paper is lifted from the end of the screen. This weak sheet is passed through pressure rolls which reduce the water content to about seventy percent. The paper, perhaps three hundred inches wide and traveling at about two thousand feet per minute, passes over forty steam-heated rolls. These reduce the water content to about eight percent. The paper is then calendered (or polished) and reeled. Paper-making processes differ in many details, but the

process is always basically reassemblage of suspended fibers into thin sheets.
      –Keyser, *Materials Science in Engineering,* p. 370

Topic: _____

10. Perhaps the main characteristic of any photograph is authenticity. Drawings or paintings made from reality or memory are often inaccurate or incomplete; those created entirely from imagination may be totally untrue. But every photograph is an "eyewitness report." It is this quality that makes a photograph "more convincing than a thousand words" and gives it a power of conviction that is not found in any other form of communication. No matter how subjectively the subject may have been seen or how imaginatively treated, the observer is aware that he is looking at an aspect of reality. No matter how strange a rendition may appear, he is aware that the lens cannot "invent" something that wasn't there. Even the most heightened form of perspective distortion, such as produced by extreme closeness or inclusion of an enormous angle of view, is a rendition of reality. That many people object to what they call "unnatural" forms of photographic rendition merely shows that they are not able to "read" such photographs. This difficulty is overcome as one learns more about photography.
      –Feininger, *The Complete Photographer,* p. 14.

Topic: _____

HOW TO FIND THE MAIN IDEA

The main idea of a paragraph tells you what the author wants you to know about the topic. The main idea is usually directly stated by the writer in one or more sentences within the paragraph. The sentence that states this main idea is called the *topic sentence.* The topic sentence tells what the rest of the paragraph is about. In some paragraphs, the main idea is not directly stated in any one sentence. Instead, it is left to the reader to infer, or reason out.

To find the main idea of a paragraph, first decide what the topic of the paragraph is. Then ask yourself these questions: What is the main idea — what is the author trying to say about the topic? Which sentence states the main idea?

Example:
      The Federal Trade Commission has become increasingly interested in false and misleading packaging. Complaints have been filed against many food packagers because they make boxes unnecessarily large to give a false impression of quantity. Cosmetics manufacturers have been accused of using false bottoms in packaging to make a small amount of their product appear to be much more.

In the preceding paragraph, the topic is false packaging. The main idea is that the Federal Trade Commission is becoming increasingly concerned about false or misleading packaging. The author states the main idea in the first sentence, so it is the topic sentence.

WHERE TO FIND THE TOPIC SENTENCE

Although the topic sentence of a paragraph can be located anywhere in the paragraph, there are several positions where it is most likely to be found. Each type of paragraph has been diagramed to help you visualize how it is structured.

In the First Sentence

The most common placement of the topic sentence is first in the paragraph. In this type of paragraph, the author states the main idea at the beginning of the paragraph and then elaborates on it.

Example:
The good listener, in order to achieve the purpose of acquiring information, is careful to follow specific steps to achieve accurate understanding. First, whenever possible the good listener prepares in advance for the speech or lecture he or she is going to attend. He or she studies the topic to be discussed and finds out about the speaker and his or her beliefs. Second, on arriving at the place where the speech is to be given, he or she chooses a seat where seeing, hearing, and remaining alert are easy. Finally, when the speech is over, an effective listener reviews what was said and reacts to and evaluates the ideas expressed.

Usually, in this type of paragraph, the author is employing a deductive thought pattern in which a statement is made at the beginning and then supported throughout the paragraph.

In the Last Sentence

The second most common position of the topic sentence is last in the paragraph. In this type of paragraph, the author leads or builds up to the main idea and then states it in a sentence at the very end.

Example:
Whenever possible, the good listener prepares in advance for the speech or lecture he or she plans to attend. He or she studies the topic to be discussed and finds out about the speaker and his or her beliefs. On arriving at the place where the speech is to be given, he or she chooses a seat where seeing, hearing, and remaining alert are easy. And,

when the speech is over, he or she reviews what was said and reacts to and evaluates the ideas expressed. Thus, an effective listener, in order to achieve the purpose of acquiring information, takes specific steps to achieve accurate understanding.

The thought pattern frequently used in this type of paragraph is inductive. That is, the author provides supporting evidence for the main idea first, and then states it.

In the Middle of the Paragraph

Another common placement of the topic sentence is in the middle of the paragraph. In this case, the author builds up to the main idea, states it in the middle of the paragraph, and then goes on with further elaboration and detail.

Example:
    Whenever possible, the good listener prepares in advance for the speech or lecture he or she plans to attend. He or she studies the topic to be discussed and finds out about the speaker and his or her beliefs. An effective listener, as you are beginning to see, takes specific steps to achieve accurate understanding of the lecture. Furthermore, on arriving at the place where the speech is to be given, he or she chooses a seat where it is easy to see, hear, and remain alert. Finally, when the speech is over, the effective listener reviews what was said and reacts to and evaluates the ideas expressed.

In the First and Last Sentences

Sometimes an author uses two sentences to state the main idea or states the main idea twice in one paragraph. Usually, in this type of paragraph, the writer states the main idea at the beginning of the paragraph, then explains or supports the idea, and finally restates the main idea at the very end.

Example:
    The good listener, in order to achieve the purpose of acquiring information, is careful to follow specific steps to achieve accurate understanding. First, whenever possible the good listener prepares in advance for the speech or lecture he or she is going to attend. He or she studies the topic to be discussed and finds out about the speaker and his or her beliefs. Second, on arriving at the place where the speech is to be given, he or she chooses a seat where seeing, hearing, and remaining alert are easy. Finally, when the speech is over, he or she reviews what was said and reacts to and evaluates the ideas expressed. Effective listening is an active process in which a listener deliberately takes certain actions to ensure that accurate communication has occurred.

EXERCISE 3

Directions: *Read each of the following paragraphs and underline the topic sentence.*

1. In arithmetic, it is never possible to add unlike quantities. For example, we should not add inches and gallons and expect to obtain a sensible answer. Neither should we attempt to add volts, amperes, kilocycles and microfarads, ohms and watts, etc. So it goes through algebra — we can never add quantities unless they are expressed in the same units.

   —Cooke, *Basic Mathematics for Electronics,* p. 68

2. To be able to successfully bridge the gap between ordinary and photographic seeing, a photographer must train himself to see as the camera sees. He must remember that human vision is augmented by other sense impressions: sound, smell, taste, and tactile sensations combine to inform him about the various aspects of his surroundings. If he stands by the ocean, he sees water, sand, and sky; he hears wind and waves; he smells the kelp, tastes the salty spray, and feels the pounding of the surf. But if he takes a photograph trying to record these impressions, he probably will be dismayed that it lacks the feeling of that experience.

   —Feininger, *The Complete Photographer,* p. 14

3. Sedimentary rocks are derived from an earlier generation of rocks and minerals by the geological processes of weathering, transportation, and deposition. Typically, they are hard, cemented deposits formed in an ocean environment, and they contain both primary and secondary minerals. The consolidation of sediments into hard rock results from the accumulation of precipitates that cement loose mineral grains into a continuous mass. Many sedimentary rocks consist almost entirely of precipitated compounds, as for example, limestones formed by lime-secreting organisms in sea water.

   —Hausenbuiller, *Soil Science,* p. 12

4. The skin itself is the largest organ of the body, is composed of epithelial and connective tissue components, and forms a pliable protective covering over the external body surface. It accounts for about 7 percent of the body weight and receives about 30 percent of the left ventricular output of blood. The term protective, as used here, includes not only resistance to bacterial invasion or attack from the outside, but also protection against large changes in the internal environment. Control of body temperature, prevention of excessive water loss, and prevention of excessive loss of organic and inorganic materials are necessary to the maintenance of internal homeostasis and continued normal activity of individual cells. In addition, the skin acts as an important area of storage, receives a variety of stimuli, and synthesizes several important substances used in the overall body economy.

   —Crouch and McClintic, *Human Anatomy and Physiology,* p. 120

5. After you have constructed your speech and written out a full-content outline for it, you are ready to begin your oral practice. The

key-word outline is an excellent aid to memory in such practice. This outline has the same indentation and the same symbols as the full-content outline, but it boils down each statement to a key word, phrase, or brief sentence that can be more easily remembered. By reading a key-word outline through repeatedly from beginning to end, you will be able to fix the ideas of your speech firmly in mind and to recall them readily as you stand before an audience. Of course, to ensure accuracy, you may read specific quotations or figures from note cards.

—Monroe and Ehninger, *Principles and Types of Speech*, pp. 49–50

6. The numbers of small solid objects revolving about the sun that are too small to observe with telescopes are very great indeed, and the number seems to be greater and greater for objects of smaller and smaller size. These tiny astronomical bodies, too small to observe individually as each travels unhindered in its orbit, are called meteoroids. Their presence becomes known only when they collide with the earth, and plunging through the earth's atmosphere, heat with friction until they vaporize. The luminous vapors that are produced look like stars moving quickly across the sky and are popularly known as "shooting stars."

—Abell, *Exploration of the Universe*, p. 252

7. There are basically two types of computers — analog computers and digital computers. Analog computers operate on the principle of a parallel or analog between numbers and physical quantities. For example, a slide rule is an analog device with length representing numbers. Modern analog computers use electronic circuitry to represent physical processes with changes in electric current representing the behavior of the system being studied. Digital computers, on the other hand, are essentially based on counting operations. Most modern computers are digital computers, and it is usually digital computers which are referred to when the word "computer" is used. For this reason, the explanations in the chapters to follow apply only to digital computers.

—Davis, *An Introduction to Computers*, p. 2

8. Nothing is quite so important in establishing personal contact with an audience as the simple device of looking at individuals directly. For this reason, reading a speech or even glancing at notes too frequently reduces this feeling of interpersonal communication and almost invariably detracts from a speaker's effectiveness. Obviously, it is impossible to look at each member of the audience at the same time. Therefore, do as you would in an informal conversation: pick out one person and talk directly to him for a few seconds, looking him in the eye as you do; then shift to someone else. Be careful, moreover, to pick out people in various parts of the audience and to stay with each one long enough to avoid the appearance of simply wagging your head.

—Monroe and Ehninger, *Principles and Types of Speech*, pp. 305–306

9. In their classification, rocks are separated into three major groups of igneous, sedimentary, and metamorphic on the basis of origin, and into a wide range of specific types primarily on the basis of

mineralogy and texture. The mineralogy of a rock depends on the kinds and proportions of different minerals it contains, whereas the texture is a function of the average size of grains or crystals in which these minerals occur. Not only do these two properties provide for fairly easy recognition of major rock types, they indicate the potential weatherability of a rock and the products it is likely to yield under weathering influences.

–Hausenbuiller, *Soil Science*, p. 39

10. The study of mathematics may be likened to the study of a language. In fact, mathematics is a language, the language of number and size. Just as the rules of grammar must be studied in order to master English, so must certain concepts, definitions, rules, terms, and words be learned in the pursuit of mathematical knowledge. These form the vocabulary or structure of the language. The more a language is studied and used, the greater becomes the vocabulary; the more mathematics is studied and applied, the greater becomes its usefulness.

–Cooke, *Basic Mathematics for Electronics*, p. 1

RECOGNIZING DETAILS

The details in a paragraph are those facts and ideas which prove, explain, support, or give examples of the main idea of the paragraph. Once the topic and main idea have been identified, recognizing the supporting details is a relatively simple matter. The more difficult job involved is the selection of the few key, or most important, details which clearly support the main idea.

All details in a paragraph relate to and expand, in some way, the paragraph's main idea, but not all of these details are completely essential to the author's central thought. Some details are just meant to describe; others are meant to provide added, but not essential, information; still others are intended merely to repeat or restate the main idea.

On the other hand, the key supporting details within a paragraph are those statements which carry the primary supporting evidence needed to back up the main idea. To find the key supporting details in a paragraph, ask yourself: What are the main facts the author uses to back up or prove what he said about the topic?

In the following paragraph, the topic sentence is underlined twice; the key supporting details are underlined once. Notice how the underlined details differ, in the type and importance of the information they provide, from the remaining details in the paragraph.

<u>Newspapers are</u> the <u>largest single advertising medium</u> in the <u>nation.</u> They have <u>extensive coverage;</u> hardly a city or town in the country is not served by a local paper or by one from a nearby larger city. For this reason, an <u>advertiser</u> can be <u>highly selective about the markets</u> to which he advertises if he uses them. If he needs a campaign in a limited local area, he can cover just that area by newspapers and not pay for wasted circulation, which he would do if he used a magazine or a large metropolitan daily. Because newspapers are printed

either weekly or daily, the <u>advertiser</u> can <u>take advantage</u> of <u>local opportunities rather quickly</u>; he can advertise in the paper on a few hours notice.

—Buskirk, *Principles of Marketing*, p. 450

All the underlined details give the primary reasons why newspapers are the largest single advertising medium in the nation, while the details in the remainder of the paragraph offer examples or further explanations of newspaper advertising.

EXERCISE 4

Directions: Each exercise below is a statement which could function as the topic sentence of a paragraph. Following each statement are a number of sentences containing details which may relate to the main idea statement. Read each sentence and make a check mark beside those which contain details that can be considered primary support for the main idea statement.

1. *Topic sentence:*

   Licorice is used in tobacco products because it has specific characteristics which cannot be found in any other single ingredient.

   Details:

   _____ a. McAdams & Co. is the largest importer and processor of licorice root.

   _____ b. Licorice blends with tobacco and provides added mildness.

   _____ c. Licorice provides a unique flavor and sweetens many types of tobacco.

   _____ d. The extract of licorice is present in relatively small amounts in most types of pipe tobacco.

   _____ e. Licorice helps tobacco retain the correct amount of moisture during storage.

2. *Topic sentence:*

   Many dramatic physical changes occur during adolescence, between the ages of 13 and 15.

   Details:

   _____ a. Voice changes in boys begin to occur at age 13 or 14.

   _____ b. Facial proportions may change during adolescence.

   _____ c. The forehead tends to become wider, and the mouth widens.

   _____ d. Many teen-agers do not know how to react to these changes.

   _____ e. Primary sex characteristics begin to develop for both boys and girls.

3. *Topic sentence:*

   The development of speech in infants follows a definite sequence or pattern of development.

   Details:

   _____ a. By the time an infant is six months old, he or she can make twelve different speech sounds.

_____ b. Before the age of three months, most infants are unable to produce any recognizable syllables.

_____ c. During the first year, the number of vowel sounds a child can produce is greater than the number of consonant sounds he can make.

_____ d. During the second year, the number of consonant sounds a child can produce increases.

_____ e. Parents often reward the first recognizable word a child produces by smiling or speaking to the child.

4. *Topic sentence:*

The two main motives for attending a play are the desire for recreation and the need for relaxation.

Details:

_____ a. By becoming involved with the actors and their problems, members of the audience temporarily suspend their personal cares and concerns.

_____ b. In America today, the success of a play is judged by its ability to attract a large audience.

_____ c. Almost everyone who attends a play expects to be entertained.

_____ d. Plays allow the audience to release tension, which facilitates relaxation.

_____ e. There is a smaller audience which looks to theater for intellectual stimulation.

5. *Topic sentence:*

In some parts of the world, famine is a constant human condition and exists due to a variety of causes.

Details:

_____ a. In parts of Africa, people are dying of hunger by the tens of thousands.

_____ b. Famine is partly caused by increased population.

_____ c. Advances in medicine have increased life expectancies, keeping more people active for longer periods of time.

_____ d. Agricultural technology has not made substantial advances in increasing the food supply.

_____ e. Due to the growth of cities, populations have become more dense, and agricultural support for these population centers is not available.

6. *Topic sentence:*

The amount of alcohol a person consumes has been found to depend on a number of socioeconomic factors such as age, sex, ethnic background, and occupation.

Details:

_____ a. Some religions prohibit consumption altogether, and most encourage moderation.

_____ b. The lowest proportion of drinkers is found among people with an educational level of below sixth grade.

_____ c. People in a lower socioeconomic level drink more than people in a higher socioeconomic level.

_____ d. In some cultures drinking is common at meals, but these same cultures disapprove of drunkenness.

117

_____ e. Farm owners have the highest proportion of nondrinkers, while professionals and businessmen have the highest proportion of drinkers.

7. *Topic sentence:*
   An individual deals with anxiety in a variety of ways and produces a wide range of responses.
   Details:
   _____ a. Anxiety may manifest itself by such physical symptoms as increased heart activity or labored breathing.
   _____ b. Fear, unlike anxiety, is a response to real or threatened danger.
   _____ c. Psychologically, anxiety often produces a feeling of powerlessness, or lack of direct control over the immediate environment.
   _____ d. Temporary blindness, deafness, or the loss of the sensation of touch are examples of extreme physical responses to anxiety.
   _____ e. Some people cannot cope with anxiety and are unable to control the neurotic behavior associated with anxiety.

8. *Topic sentence:*
   An individual's status or importance within a group affects his behavior in that particular group.
   Details:
   _____ a. High-status individuals frequently arrive late at a social function.
   _____ b. Once a person achieves high status, he attempts to maintain it.
   _____ c. High-status individuals demand more privileges.
   _____ d. Low-status individuals are less resistant to change within the group structure than persons of high status.
   _____ e. There are always fewer high-status members than low-status members in any particular group.

9. *Topic sentence:*
   An oligopoly is a market structure in which only a few companies sell a certain product.
   Details:
   _____ a. The automobile industry is a good example of an oligopoly, although it gives the appearance of being highly competitive.
   _____ b. Breakfast cereal, soap, and cigarette industries, although basic to our economy, operate as oligopolies.
   _____ c. Monopolies refer to market structures in which only one industry produces a particular product.
   _____ d. Monopolies are able to exert more control and fixation of price than oligopolies.
   _____ e. In the oil industry, because there are only a few producers, each producer has a fairly large share of the sales.

10. *Topic sentence:*

    Advertising can be used to expand consumer choice as well as to limit it.

Details:

_____ a. Food stores which typically advertise their "specials" each Wednesday in the local paper are encouraging consumer choice.

_____ b. Department store advertising often makes the consumer aware of new products and styles, as well as of current prices of products.

_____ c. Misleading or excessive advertising is usually rejected by the consuming public.

_____ d. Exaggerated claims made by certain advertisers serve to limit the consumer's actual knowledge and free choice of products.

_____ e. Advertising which provides little or no actual information, but attempts to make the brand name well known, actually restricts consumers' free choice.

EXERCISE 5

Directions: *Read each paragraph below and identify the topic and main idea. Write each in the spaces provided. Then underline the key supporting details.*

1. Alcoholism can be caught and successfully treated long before it reaches final phases. For specific information, one can consult the local Medical Association, the local branch of Alcoholics Anonymous, or the Yale Center of Alcohol Studies. In general, the first step in treatment is to stop the patient's drinking. Next, his personality must be rebuilt to exclude the maladjustive mechanism of drinking, and to include the adjustive mechanism of direct problem-solving. Voluntary associations like Alcoholics Anonymous often can help with the first and second step, and interview therapists with the third step. Thus far, however, no method has been successful in every case.

    –Sperling, *Psychology Made Simple*, p. 179

Topic: _____

Main idea: _____

2. The Spanish-speaking communities in the United States constitute, numerically and culturally, the most important ethnic minority group. Approximately 80 percent of the 5 million Americans of Mexican ancestry live in California, Arizona, New Mexico, Texas, and Colorado. The tenacious preservation by the Mexican-American of his language and culture is little understood by most other Americans. The Mexican-American, like many immigrant Jews to this country, often seeks to obtain what is good and of benefit to him and his family in American society without losing the ethnic identity or the customs and traditions of the old country. Many, but not all, Mexican-Americans preserve their contacts with the people and institutions of old Mexico and take

great pride in the history and culture of their ancestors. In recent years, there has been a great deal of interest among young Mexican-American intellectuals in promoting this sense of identity and pride among Mexican-Americans. The term la raza, for example, means race, but it evokes far more in feelings of brotherhood and comradeship.

–Lugo and Hershey, *Human Development,* p. 57

Topic: _____

Main idea: _____

3. Recent studies show that dreams can be studied objectively as well as subjectively. In a series of experiments at the University of Chicago, two scientists recorded brain waves, body movements, and eye movements made during sleep. Drs. Nathaniel Kleitman and William Dement found that eye movements during sleep are connected with periods of dreaming. In 130 of 160 cases studied, dreams were recalled by subjects awakened after eye movements. Some subjects were awakened five minutes, and some fifteen minutes, after the dream — as shown by the stopping of eye movements — ended. Those awakened after the five minutes could recall far more of the dream than those awakened after fifteen minutes.

–Sperling, *Psychology Made Simple,* p. 158

Topic: _____

Main idea: _____

4. Products purchased mainly for Christmas, such as toys, Christmas-tree lights, and yuletide candles, have a marketing program different from that for products sold uniformly throughout the year. The marketing executive, in order to plan his sales effort successfully, must determine when the consumer wants to buy the product. Timing is of particular importance in promotional activities and can sometimes influence other plans. Special packaging may be called for if the product is purchased for a holiday. Special seasonal pricing may be wise if the item is sold at one time of the year. If a firm's demand occurs only for a short time in the year, it may be impossible for it to maintain its own sales force, thereby creating the need for agents.

–Buskirk, *Principles of Marketing,* p. 109

Topic: _____

Main idea: _____

5. No part of the Earth's surface is exempt from earthquakes, but since the start of systematic recording many large areas have had only occasional shocks of small or moderate intensity. By contrast, several large tracts are subject to frequent shocks, both strong and weak, and are known as seismic belts. The most prominent, aptly called the Circum-Pacific belt, follows the western highlands of South and North America from Cape Horn to Alaska, crosses to Asia, extends southward along the eastern coast and related island

arcs, and loops far to the southeast and south beyond New Zealand. Next in prominence is the broad east-west zone extending through the high mountains of southern Asia and the Mediterranean region to Gibraltar. A third long belt follows the Mid-Atlantic Ridge from Arctic to Antarctic waters, and a fourth runs along the Mid-Indian Ridge to unite with a belt in eastern Africa. Smaller seismic areas include island groups in the Pacific and Atlantic.

—Longwell and Flint, *Introduction to Physical Geology*, p. 402

Topic: _____

Main idea: _____

6. We all know that the sky does not immediately darken when the sun sets. Even after the sun is no longer visible from the ground, the upper atmosphere of the earth can catch some of the rays of the setting sun and scatter them helter-skelter, illuminating the sky. Gases in the earth's atmosphere are dense enough to scatter appreciable sunlight up to altitudes of about 200 mi. The sun must be at least 18° below the horizon for all traces of this postsunset or presunrise sky light (twilight) to be absent. At latitudes near the equator, where the sun rises and sets nearly vertically to the horizon, twilight lasts only a little over 1 hour. However, at far northern and southern latitudes, the sun rises and sets in a much more oblique direction and takes correspondingly longer to reach a point 18° below the horizon, so twilight may last for 2 hours or more. In the far northern countries twilight lasts all night in the summertime. At the North Pole there are 6 weeks of twilight in the late winter before sunrise and again in the early fall after sunset.

—Abell, *Exploration of the Universe*, p. 131

Topic: _____

Main idea: _____

7. The newspaper is still the primary source of news. It has decided advantages over television: it can provide perspective; it has the authority of the printed word; it is constantly at hand, rather than requiring, as television does, presence at stated hours. But newspapers, in too many instances, are not performing their true function, and an improvement in journalism is a prime need. But, even if that betterment is achieved, television has an important role to play. It cannot supplant the newspaper, but, because of its immediacy and its dramatic impact, it can supplement it to a significant degree. Yet television's news performance is far from satisfactory.

—Lineberry, *Mass Communications*, p. 81

Topic: _____

Main idea: _____

8. With all their faults, the media are more responsible today than they were half a century ago. There is less bias in presentation of

news, less venality, broader coverage of national and world affairs, more — but not enough — presentation of complex events in a perspective that makes them meaningful to readers and viewers. Even television, which has been the least conscious of its responsibility as an information medium, is showing some signs of recognizing its obligations. Professor William A. Wood, of Columbia University Graduate School of Journalism, recently estimated that about 30 percent of television and 20 percent of radio stations "have reached the point where they do more than give routine attention to news and show real responsibility and quality in news services."

–Lineberry, *Mass Communications,* pp. 122–123

Topic: _____

Main idea: _____

9. In what important respect does the employment letter differ from other business letters? It differs in that it must first of all pass scrutiny as a letter, whereas other letters succeed better when they are not thought of as letters at all. That is, the regular sales letter focuses attention on the electric razor or the set of books for sale; the collection letter on the balance of $16.23 that is three months overdue; the adjustment letter on the broken lawn mower and how to get it to run again. The reader of these letters is likely not interested in their quality, because he is not interested in the person who wrote them. The employer, however, is interested in the person who wrote the application letter — if the letter succeeds. He actually reads character in the letter; its very correctness and neat appearance will tell him about the writer.

–Williams and Griffin, *Effective Business Communication,* p. 222

Topic: _____

Main idea: _____

10. The rapid rate of innovation during the last two decades has greatly expanded consumer desires for new products. Today many companies are doing the majority of their business in products that were unknown 20 years ago. Before World War II an appliance manufacturer had only relatively few products available for distribution; mechanical refrigerators, washing machines, stoves, and vacuum cleaners were the mainstays of their volume. Today, clothes dryers, automatic washing machines, dishwashers, garbage disposals, electric skillets, rotisseries, television, hi-fi sets, and many other products are standard items in the appliance manufacturers' line.

–Buskirk, *Principles of Marketing,* p. 93

Topic: _____

Main idea: _____

UNSTATED MAIN IDEAS

Occasionally, a writer does not directly state the main idea of a given paragraph in a topic sentence. Instead, he or she leaves it up to the reader to infer, or reason out, what the main idea of the paragraph is. This type of paragraph contains only details or specifics which relate to a given topic and which substantiate an unstated main idea. To read this type of paragraph, start as you would for paragraphs with stated main ideas. Ask yourself the question for finding the topic: What is the one thing the author is discussing throughout the paragraph? Then try to think of a sentence about the topic that all the details included in the paragraph would support.

Read the paragraph in the example below. First identify the topic. Then study the details and think of a general statement that all the details in the paragraph would support or prove.

Example:
Suppose a group of plumbers in a community decide to set standard prices for repair services and agree to quote the same price for the same job. Is this ethical? Suppose a group of automobile dealers agree to abide strictly by the used car blue book prices on trade-ins. Is this ethical? Two meat supply houses serving a large university submit identical bids each month for the meat contract. Is this ethical?

This paragraph describes three specific instances in which there was agreement to fix prices. Clearly, the main idea of the author is whether price collusion is ethical, but that main idea is not directly stated in a sentence anywhere within the passage.

EXERCISE 6

Directions: *In each of these paragraphs, the main idea is* not *directly stated. Read the paragraph, identify the topic, and write it in the space provided. Then write a sentence which expresses the main idea of the passage.*

1. Food supplements are hawked by the myth builders on the basis that methods of food processing and cooking remove or reduce some of the nutrients in our foods, particularly vitamins and minerals. Methods of food processing have been developed to preserve nutritional values, or if necessary, carefully calculated supplements for nutritional improvement as recommended by authorities are added.
   —Fleck, *Introduction to Nutrition*, pp. 402–403

   Topic: _____

   Main idea: _____

   _____

2. Overweight children are frequently rejected by their peer group because they do not do well in sports and because they may be ungainly. A teen-age girl who is overweight, unless she has an

unusual personality, may be ostracized by her peers. She is not asked to dance at parties and may not have dates. The results can be very serious, for these social activities are a normal part of growing up. Both men and women may become the butt of jokes by their friends because of their obese condition. Although they may appear to take it good naturedly, the sting remains.

  —Fleck, *Introduction to Nutrition,* p. 418

Topic: _____

Main idea: _____

_____

3. Traffic is directed by color. Pilot instrument panels, landing strips, road and water crossings are regulated by many colored lights and signs. Factories use colors to distinguish between thoroughfares and work areas. Danger zones are painted in special colors. Lubrication points and removable parts are accentuated by color. Pipes for transporting water, steam, oil, chemicals, and compressed air, are designated by different colors. Electrical wires and resistances are color coded.

  —Gerritsen, *Theory and Practice of Color,* p. 9

Topic: _____

Main idea: _____

_____

4. There can be no doubt that the reaction sought by the after-dinner speaker at a social banquet differs materially from that sought by a legislator urging the adoption of a bill, or that both of these desired responses differ from the response a college professor seeks when he addresses a class. The first speaker wants his audience to enjoy themselves; the second wants them to act, to vote "aye"; the third wants them to understand.

  —Monroe and Ehninger, *Principles and Types of Speech,* p. 115

Topic: _____

Main idea: _____

_____

5. In February 1943 people living in the mountain land 200 miles west of Mexico City were alarmed by frequent earthquakes. Each day for more than a week the number of tremors increased, and on February 19 about 300 were counted. Next day a farmer, Dionisio Pulido, while he worked in his field heard noises like thunder, though the sky was clear. He saw that a crevice had opened in the ground, and from this narrow opening arose a small column of "smoke" — actually vapor and fine dust — with an odor of sulfur. That night strong explosions began at the vent, and coarse rock debris was thrown up, some of it red-hot. At daybreak the vent was

marked by a cone-shaped mound, more than 30 feet high, through which in violent bursts large fragments of rock were hurled high into the air. Successive explosions came only a few seconds apart, and a great cloud of fine rock dust mixed with vapor arose continuously to a great height.

—Longwell and Flint, *Introduction to Physical Geology*, p. 80

Topic: _____

Main idea: _____

_____

6. On the average, babies pronounce recognizable syllables by the third month. As a child matures, his syllables become sharper, cleaner, and more distinct. Cooing and babbling, repeating the same sound over and over again, like "da da da" and "ga ga ga," begin at about this time and continue until about the end of the first year. Early babblings are probably not attempted imitations of adults' speech, but rather sounds the child makes for his own amusement. Toward the end of the first half year, the infant is likely to "talk" to his parents and other familiar people when he is being played with or talked to. Imitation of sounds made by others generally begins after approximately nine months.

—Mussen, *The Psychological Development of the Child*, p. 25

Topic: _____

Main idea: _____

_____

7. The computer can perform any computations that have, in the past, been made by hand or by mechanical calculator. In addition, the stored program used by a computer permits complex problems to be prepared for computer analysis, and the electronic speed of the computations means that problems which could not be solved because of the time required for manual computation can now be solved in minutes by the computer. Not only the time, but also the cost of computation has been dramatically reduced. A popular, large computer system can do computations in one minute that it would take about five years to do manually. Yet the commercial rental cost for using such a system is only about $8 a minute. A man-year of computation, on this basis, costs less than $2.

—Davis, *An Introduction to Computers*, p. 33

Topic: _____

Main idea: _____

_____

8. The basic telephone book is not a good source of lists except for such a purpose as a community fund, but the classified directory frequently is, since it is selective to the extent of grouping names

according to occupation or trade. Some clubs and associations print their memberships, thus supplying somewhat specialized lists, usually with up-to-date addresses. Government records are a fruitful source of mailing lists for certain advertisers. An enterprising bank secured a very large number of savings deposit customers through a mailing piece addressed to newborn children, the names obtainable, of course, from the city clerk's record of birth certificates. Names of newly-weds, automobile owners, and other lists from public records are obtainable if the officials are obliging enough to permit copying them, and many are.

—Williams and Griffin, *Effective Business Communication*, p. 418

Topic: _____

Main idea: _____

_____

9. For some important voices in society, television broadcasting is a part of the institutionalism of education: a method of transmitting knowledge; a device for spreading cultural richness to culturally arid areas; a mechanism for increasing the effectiveness of the school, the library, and the teacher. For the world of business and industry, television broadcasting is an advertising device, capable of moving goods and services from a few central supplying points to the outermost limits of the United States, capable of popularizing brand names of toothpaste, cereals, cigarettes, soaps and beer. For those who regulate broadcasting, television is seen as a user of the radio spectrum — a natural resource — under a federal license requiring operation in the public interest. To those who see this as television's role, any conflict between private and public interest must naturally be resolved in favor of the public.

—Hilliard, *Understanding Television*, p. 11

Topic: _____

Main idea: _____

_____

10. Defined as simply as possible, a glacier is a body of ice, consisting mainly of recrystallized snow, flowing on a land surface. Unlike a stream, a glacier cannot be seen to move; yet measurements show that it is flowing. They show also that long-term changes in its dimensions are closely related to variations of climate; so the study of glaciers has contributed much to what we know of the Earth's recent climatic history. The effects of erosion of bedrock by glaciers and deposits of the eroded material as glacial sediments are characteristic and easily recognizable. Their distribution shows us that in the recent past glaciers have been far more extensive than they are today. At the same time, this evidence has

raised the problem of the cause of the "ice ages" when glaciers were widespread, a problem that is still only partly solved.
    –Longwell and Flint, *Introduction to Physical Geology*, p. 228

Topic: _____

Main idea: _____

_____

EXERCISE 7

Directions: *Turn to the sample textbook chapter included in the Appendix of this text. Beginning with the section headed "Scheduling" on page 344, read each paragraph and identify the topic and main idea. Then place brackets around the topic and underline the sentence that expresses the main idea. Continue reading and marking until you reach the section headed "Evaluating Advertising Effectiveness" on page 347.*

EXERCISE 8

Directions: *Select a three-page section from a textbook that you have been assigned to read. After reading each paragraph, place brackets around the topic and then underline the sentence stating the main idea. If any of the paragraphs have an unstated main idea, write a sentence in the margin which summarizes the main idea. Continue reading and marking until you have completed the three pages.*

SUMMARY

A paragraph is a group of related sentences about a single topic. A paragraph has three essential elements:

1. Topic: the one thing the entire paragraph is about
2. Main Idea: a direct statement or an implied idea about the topic
3. Details: the proof, reasons, or examples which explain or support the paragraph's main idea

A paragraph, then, provides explanation, support, or proof for a main idea (expressed or unexpressed) about a particular topic. A topic sentence expressing the main idea of the paragraph may be located anywhere within the paragraph, but the most common positions for this sentence are first, last, in the middle, or both first and last.

While most paragraphs contain a topic sentence that directly states the main idea of the paragraph, occasionally an author will write a paragraph in which the main idea is not stated in any single sentence. Instead it is left up to you, the reader, to infer, or reason out, the main idea. To find the main idea when it is unstated, ask yourself the following question: What is the one thing (topic) this paragraph is about, and what is the author saying about this thing (main idea)?

11. Understanding Passages

Use this chapter to:

1. *Develop skill in identifying the general subject and central thought of a passage.*

2. *Learn how to recognize supporting ideas.*

3. *Learn to pick out words in a passage that signal a change in topic.*

A *passage* is a group of related paragraphs. Your textbook is made up almost entirely of passages rather than single unrelated paragraphs. Usually passages are separated from one another by the dark print, or boldface, headings within each chapter.

Understanding passages is a critical part of understanding the important ideas contained in your textbooks. It is through groups of passages that an author is able to explain complicated ideas, issues, trends, and causes. It is through passages, rather than single paragraphs, that an author connects and relates ideas to one another.

You will recall from the previous chapter that a paragraph is limited to a single topic and is further limited to expressing one main idea about that topic. By grouping paragraphs together in a passage, a writer is able to present several separate ideas about a particular topic or to discuss several separate, but closely related, ideas about the topic.

Understanding passages involves four steps. First, you have to understand each single paragraph and be able to recognize its topic, main idea, and supporting details. Second, you have to know what one thing the whole passage is about. Third, you have to recognize what the author is saying about that one thing and see how the topic and main idea of each paragraph relate to or support the one thing the passage is about. Finally, you have to recognize what words authors use to connect the single paragraphs in a passage.

FOUR IMPORTANT ELEMENTS OF A PASSAGE

General subject: the one thing the whole passage is about. The topic of each of the paragraphs in the passage must be a part of, or relate to, this general subject.

Central thought: a statement about the general subject in which the author expresses what he or she is trying to communicate about the general subject. Each paragraph in the passage must in some way prove or explain this central thought.

Supporting ideas: the ideas which prove, explain, or support the central thought. Usually, these ideas are the main ideas of each of the single paragraphs within the passage.

Directional words: the words and sentences the author uses to connect ideas and to move from one paragraph to another.

Each of the following examples contains two paragraphs, but only *one* is a passage. It is the one that has the four important elements. Identify the passage.

Example A:

The effective salesperson must consider who the potential buyer is and why he or she might buy the product or service. The "why" here involves more than rational reasons; most consumption is irrational — the choice between most products is an illusory choice, there often being essentially no difference between competing brands.

The leader is able to create different climates in a group: trust or suspicion; acceptance or rejection; optimism or pessimism; and cooperation or competition. "Rugged individualism" has its place; but when people come together in a group, they do so to work together toward common goals. Working together means cooperating: helping each other, sharing ideas and resources, abandoning individual glory for group success.[1]

Example B:

Language, thought, habit, even perception depend upon memory. The psychological present — this moment as we experience it — rests on, incorporates, and is built from a lifetime of accumulated experience. The past lives in the present through memory. Memory is so basic and so essential to thought and action that we sometimes take it for granted. But a total loss of memory would have devastating consequences.

You can improve your memory by improving any of the three functional processes that make up your memory: encoding, storage, or retrieval. Most systems for improving memory concentrate on making the storage process more efficient; however, by improving any of the three processes you will be better able to remember names, dates, shopping lists — even chemical equations, psychological principles, or Balkan geography.[2]

Example C:

Psychological principles can be applied by everyone. You can learn to use scientific psychology to help solve your own problems. There are a number of important advantages of do-it-yourself psychology. One factor is manpower. For most people, the major problem a few generations ago was physical survival: now it is psychological survival. We seem to be tense, alienated, confused. Suicide, addiction, violence, apathy, neurosis — are all problems of the modern world. Psychological problems are accelerating and there are not enough professional psychologists to go around. Non-psychologists must practice psychology if psychology is to be applied to our problems.

A second advantage to do-it-yourself psychology is the factor of closeness. Professional psychologists must always operate after the fact and at a distance. You know your own problem most intimately; other people — even professional psychologists — are on the outside. You experience it; they listen to you talk about it. You know it viscerally; they can know it only verbally. Furthermore, you are there when the problem occurs; a professional psychologist hears about it afterwards. If you are afraid of heights, if you can't concentrate on studying, if you sometimes have difficulty relaxing and going to sleep — you experience these problems more intimately than anyone else can. You are closer to them.[3]

In example A, the two paragraphs are not a passage; they are not about the same general subject. The first paragraph is about effective salesmanship, while the second paragraph is about leadership and group climate. Because the two paragraphs do not have a common general subject, they do not form a passage.

In example B, the two paragraphs do not make up a passage. While both paragraphs have the same general subject — memory — they do not express a central thought about memory. The first paragraph discusses the importance of memory; the second is concerned with the three processes involved in memory.

Example C is a passage. Both paragraphs are about a single general subject — "do-it-yourself" psychology. Each of the paragraphs discusses the advantages of this type of psychology.

The structure of a passage and that of a paragraph are very similar. Both have common elements and similar organizations. Perhaps this diagram will clarify the relationship between the paragraph and the passage.

Passage		*Paragraph*
Subject ⟵	*one thing it is about*	⟶ Topic
Central thought ⟵	*key idea being expressed*	⟶ Main idea
Supporting ideas ⟵	*proof, explanation, support*	⟶ Details

In order to understand a passage, a reader must be able to identify the general subject, central thought, and supporting ideas easily. The following section will present techniques for identifying each.

HOW TO IDENTIFY THE SUBJECT OF A PASSAGE

The subject of a passage is the one thing the whole passage is about. Usually, the subject of a passage can be expressed in two or three words.

To find the subject of a passage, you should ask yourself this question: What is the one thing that is discussed in each of the paragraphs in the passage?

Example:

Many psychologists have noted that women seem to have much stronger needs for friendly social interaction — usually called affiliation needs — than they do for achievement. And women seem to be more interested than men in popularity and the approval of others. The research on fear of success, discussed previously, suggests that some women tend to play down their achievements for fear of intimidating or "putting off" others, especially men. One prominent female psychologist admits she was enraged when her name was published in the university newspaper as having earned an "A" average; she was afraid it would affect her social life.

An interesting experiment arranged things so that women paired with men got higher scores than their male partners on a dynamometer, a device for measuring strength of grip. Most of the women then reduced their efforts, in order to avoid embarrassing the "weakling" males, in spite of the fact that each pair was competing with other pairs on the basis of combined scores.

–Geiwitz, *Looking at Ourselves*, p. 246

In the preceding passage, both paragraphs are concerned with the affiliation needs of women. The first paragraph discusses and explains the general idea of affiliaton needs; the second paragraph reports the results of a particular experiment which demonstrates the affiliation needs. Both paragraphs, therefore, are concerned with the same general subject — affiliation needs.

EXERCISE 1

Directions: *Read each of the following passages. Then underline the best statement of the general subject.*

1. Man's first data processing tools were devices to facilitate counting. Like the lever, one of the earliest machines, the most primitive calculating instruments were completely nonautomatic. Indeed, many of the rudimentary methods used by primitives for counting were simply pebbles, notched sticks, and knotted ropes.

    The abacus was invented independently by the Greeks (the Greek word *abax* means *sand tray*) and the Chinese. This instrument, in various versions, is still used by over half of the world's population, chiefly in the Far East. There are two groups of beads in a typical device: the lower group contains four beads, and the upper group has one. Starting from the 0 position, the number 1 is formed by moving up one of the lower beads. Counting continues by successively moving up a lower bead.

    The counting board, used extensively in medieval Europe, is of great antiquity. It operates on the same principle as the abacus. Small disks are placed on, or between, lines on a board to represent numbers. Each digit position consists of two rows. If a disk is present in the upper row, a 5 is added to the disks in the lower row to produce the desired number.

    –Desmonde, *Computers and Their Uses*, p. 10

    a. early counting tools
    b. the abacus
    c. the counting board
    d. Greek and Chinese systems of counting

2. There is no fixed order in which the problems of philosophy must be studied. Some would insist that the true beginning of philosophy lies (as Rudolf H. Lotze has suggested) in ethics. Others would begin with psychology, or with biology, or with mathematics, or with physics. One of the good ways to begin the study of philosophy proper, however, is to attempt to answer the question: How can one distinguish truth from error? No reliable progress can be made in understanding experience without some means of distinguishing what is true from what is not true. Such a start is both useful and basic.

   The name of the discipline that investigates this and similar questions related to the problem of knowledge is epistemology. It is derived from Greek words meaning theory of knowledge (episteme, logos). Epistemologists are concerned with a number of questions regarding knowledge, including especially that of the criterion or test of knowledge, that of the source of knowlege, and that of the nature of knowledge or of the ways in which our ideas are related to their objects.

   —Brightman, *An Introduction to Philosophy*, p. 49

   a. the order in which to study problems in philosophy
   b. understanding experience
   c. the study of epistemology
   d. the true beginning of philosophy

3. Except for a few periods in their history, the people of England have regularly favored sports and games over systems of formal physical education. Even when formal physical education was included in the school day, the after-school periods were devoted to games. Many of these games were developed in rural settings. The Englishman continued to play after his formal education was complete, and sports clubs arose to supply his need. This pattern is still characteristic of the English culture. The upper classes developed idealistic attitudes of amateurism, which stemmed from social behavior. The English concept of amateurism, promoted in most of England's colonial possessions, is the main source of inspiration for amateur codes in the United States. To this day, it has been difficult to resolve some of the current problems in the light of this definition of amateurism.

   Many English games were brought to this country, and they form the nucleus of our present programs. However, some have been changed to such an extent that very little resemblance can now be noted. Examples are the evolution of football from soccer and rugby and that of baseball from cricket and rounders.

   —Seidel and Resick, *Physical Education*, pp. 24–25

   a. the evolution of football
   b. English concept of and influence on sports
   c. British physical education
   d. upper-class British sports

4. To understand evolution it is necessary to know something about genetics, the science of heredity. Although genetics is a very complicated subject, everyone understands the basic results of heredity. We know, for example, that the result of mating between

cats is kittens, not colts, or little fish. We know that children tend to resemble their parents in physical characteristics; we know that stock breeders can produce cattle with certain desirable characteristics by carefully controlling the multiplying of animals that already possess those characteristics.

Heredity operates in this fashion because of the nature and action of the cells and the chemical substances that compose cells. The nucleus of each of the many cells in the body contains complex structures called chromosomes. These structures occur in pairs in all cells except in the sex cells. The number of chromosome pairs differs from one kind of animal to another; in human beings there are twenty-three pairs.

Each chromosome is divided into many tiny sections called genes, which are causally related to specific physical characteristics and are the actual units of inheritance. Since chromosomes and genes occur in pairs, each individual can have no less than two genes for any given physical characteristic. Actually, very few human characteristics can be shown to result from the action of only a single gene pair; most characteristics are influenced by two or more pairs.

–Schusky and Culbert, *Introducing Culture*, p. 6

a. chromosomes
b. genetics, the biological explanation of heredity
c. sex cells and genes
d. the process of evolution

5. Systems of social inequality exist in all human societies and there are definite behavioral consequences for different positions in a stratified system. Lower-status people view the social environment as hostile and best left alone. They tend to cluster together and informally control a small section of city 'turf,' against social workers, police, and outsiders. They are effectively cut off from the urban environment because they do not read newspapers and seldom watch news programs on television. Most of their information comes from friends. Working-class families tend to be more restricted in their patterns of communication than those of upper- and middle-class status. They tend to choose a residence close to relatives and avoid better employment opportunities when migration to new areas would disrupt family interaction. This results in their preference for certain suburbs and the patronage of familiar commercial areas.

Middle- and upper-status persons exhibit a cosmopolitan mobility. They choose friends throughout the metropolitan area, move across town from "mother" or even across the continent. They have been socialized to consider their social environment as fluid. They are active in organizations and capable of utilizing their political resources of time, money, position, and skill should they desire to influence political decisions.

–Fielding, *Geography as a Social Science*, p. 183

a. communication patterns in lower-status adults
b. city versus metropolitan living patterns
c. employment opportunities as affected by social status
d. differences among lower-, middle-, and upper-class (status) persons

HOW TO FIND THE CENTRAL THOUGHT

The central thought of a passage is the single most important idea that the writer is trying to express in the passage. It is the one idea that is explained, discussed, or supported throughout the passage. The central thought is usually located in the first few lines of the passage. Often, the central thought is expressed in a single sentence at the beginning of the passage.

To find the central thought of a passage, ask yourself this question: What is the one thing the author is trying to say about the general subject?

Example:

Social change is also responsible for recent changes in the roles of the two sexes, particularly in the role of women. In the traditional authoritarian family, the father was the patriarch whose word was law. The mother's role was to keep house, raise the children, and please her husband. But when his work took him away from the home for long periods of time and when she began to work outside the home, she began to demand a bigger share of decision making.

Today, we are seeing the latest developments of this trend in the goals of the women's liberation movement. These goals include total equality of the sexes. Such equality has not yet been attained, certainly not among the majority of married couples. But we can see the difficulties for those who try to ignore the traditional concepts with which they were raised in order to achieve equal partnership in marriage, particularly when a woman in a traditional marriage relationship decides to liberate herself against her husband's wishes.

–Perry and Perry, *Face to Face*, p. 26

In the above passage, the general subject is the role of women in society. The central thought is that the role of women is changing to give women greater equality. The first paragraph describes the change in the family structure from a traditional authoritarian one to one in which women share in decision making. The second paragraph describes the latest developments in women's liberation. Both paragraphs, however, are concerned with a single central thought — the changing role of women.

EXERCISE 2

Directions: *Read each of the following passages. Then write a sentence which clearly states the central thought of the passage.*

1. A contest, or match, and game are not sharply distinguishable today in all circumstances, but they differ in ways significant enough to demand separate treatment. Contest and match may be used interchangeably. One may refer with equal validity to a boxing contest or a boxing match, a wrestling contest or a wrestling match, a chess contest or a chess match, a tennis contest or a tennis match.

One may technically refer to these activities as games when the opposing participants are in fact representing larger collectivities, that is, boxing, tennis, wrestling, and chess are components of the Olympic Games. However, such reference overrides the most salient characteristic of contests or matches — they are in their pure forms individual in both effort and consequence. The participants are opposing individuals who are the sole beneficiaries of participation, goal achievement, or failure.

–Edwards, *Sociology of Sport*, pp. 50–51

Central thought: _____

_____

2.   We all know from experience that a house seen at a distance does not resemble a play house but retains its actual size. A friend standing a block away does not appear to be a midget. Actually, the further away an object is from us, the smaller is the image of the object in the retina of our eyes. The fact that objects do not seem to change in size as the distance increases is known as size constancy.

How do we explain size constancy? Size constancy depends on several factors. Learning plays a very important role. Have you ever seen children on a bridge trying to reach down to pick up the "toy" boats or automobiles? Or a child stretching and reaching for the stars? The explanation that size constancy is based solely on memory of familiar objects does not explain why unfamiliar objects also maintain, although to a lesser degree, size constancy. The size of an unfamiliar object is judged by its relative size to familiar objects around it. If a spaceship from Mars were to land in your city, you could judge its size by comparing the spaceship to the buildings and trees next to it. In other words, size constancy depends on the surroundings as well as on learning. Size constancy would tend to disappear if a strange object landed in a strange desert with no familiar objects around it.

There are other factors that contribute to size constancy. For example, if you were to make left turns in front of a yellow car and a black car, the chances of an accident would be greater while turning in front of a black car. The reason is that a dark object always seems further away than a bright object when both are really equidistant from us.

–Hershey and Lugo, *Living Psychology*, pp. 212–213

Central thought: _____

_____

3.   No one gets much pleasure from large catalogs of facts, however systematically or carefully they may be gathered. Because of our limited capacity for absorbing and retaining knowledge, we are forced to organize it. Only when knowledge is organized can we benefit from it. In science, knowledge is organized into theories. An example of a scientific theory that organizes a multitude of information is Darwin's theory of evolution. Theories also help us make predictions about events which we have not yet observed.

Thus, scientific theorizing helps to enlarge or overcome our limited capacity to handle a multitude of individual facts and is basically no different from everyday selection and categorization. Just as scientific theories are constantly being tested by experiments, for example, so our everyday "theories," our categories, are constantly being tested. When it comes to adapting to the external physical environment, our "theories" generally work quite well. If we happen to be wrong, we are corrected, often in a rather brutal way. We bang our head, get wet, fall over, or break through the ice.

—Werthheimer, *Psychology: A Brief Introduction*, p. 6

Central thought: _____

_____

4. Classification gives significance to unrelated and consequently meaningless facts. It is one of the most fundamental processes carried on by the human mind. When a baby learns to recognize all the various "faces" presented by his mother — smiling, frowning, sad, tired, and laughing — and to distinguish his mother from all other people, he has completed a task in classification.

Without any formal instruction, as one grows up, he reduces all the infinite variety of his environment to groups and subgroups. Any boy will identify a leaf from a tree without hesitation. It is similar to, and different from, millions of other leaves. If it were necessary to consider each leaf as an individual object the mind would be left in absolute confusion. A man would spend his whole life examining leaves.

No matter which way a man turns, he finds the universe divided, classified, and grouped by this natural inclination of the human mind.

—Weinland, *How to Think Straight*, pp. 23–24

Central thought: _____

_____

5. A common defense mechanism is to withdraw from a frustrating or anxiety-arousing situation. Withdrawal may take several forms, one of which is repression. Repression allows a person to withdraw from reality so that conscious experiences of embarrassment, guilt, pain, or other humiliating experiences can be blocked from memory. The last time you went to the dentist, you suffered considerable pain and were uncomfortable for hours. Your next appointment is a week later — but you "forget" to go. You have repressed your knowledge of the next appointment date.

In repression, as distinct from normal forgetting, you actively, although unconsciously, forget certain thoughts or feelings that are specifically painful or self-injurious. Repression is meant to reduce anxiety, whereas normal forgetting is unrelated to anxiety. The similarity between repression and normal forgetting permits the frustrated individual to protect himself from realizing that he does not want to remember certain experiences.

–Silverman, *Psychology*, p. 48

Central thought: _____

_____

HOW TO RECOGNIZE SUPPORTING IDEAS

Supporting ideas are those major facts and ideas which prove, explain, or support the central thought of the passage. Usually, the supporting ideas in a passage are the main ideas of each of the separate paragraphs which make up the passage.

In the passage below, the general subject is group marriage. The central thought is that group marriage is a new concept which is an alternative to monogamous marriage. The supporting ideas are underlined. Notice how each supporting idea explains and tells more about the central thought of the passage.

Group marriage in a communal setting is another alternative to the traditional monogamous marriage that has resulted from the new attitudes toward sex. <u>In a group marriage, men and women, who are presumably attracted to one another, live together and consider themselves and their children to be one family unit.</u> In theory, an open-ended group marriage sounds fine. It negates the very concept of adultery and diminishes jealousy and possessiveness; at least those are the intentions of its practitioners. In reality, the pairing off of some members to the exclusion of others is a frequent occurrence, and jealousy and possessiveness do not disappear.

The fact is that <u>such groups tend to be of short duration.</u> Critics maintain that marriages of this sort fail because their members, claiming to love everyone, end by loving no one. Proclaiming universal love may mask a fear of or unwillingness to accept responsibility. As an example, in one such family there was a three-year-old child who belonged to "everyone," yet when the group disbanded, no one, including the biological mother, wanted to care for the child alone (it could not be established which of the men was the biological father). The members of such groups have been socialized in a thoroughly monogamous society, so it is no wonder that monogamous relationships continually reassert themselves.

–Perry and Perry, *Face to Face*, p. 48

EXERCISE 3

Directions: *Read each passage. Write the general subject and central thought in the space provided. Then underline the supporting ideas in each passage.*

1. In much technical writing, our main purpose is to convey information. In writing concerned with subjects of general interest, our main purpose is usually to express our opinions. This is often true even when we present our writing as a factual account, as a report. A good reporter is always more than a mere reporter. He interprets as well as reports; he reports scenes and events in such a way that they make sense. Directly or indirectly, we learn not only what he has observed but also what he thinks about it. Most of your assignments in college composition will require you to present your opinions — that is, your interpretation of and reaction to what you have observed, experienced, and read.

   Inevitably, many of our opinions are tentative and superficial. We have tentative ideas on many subjects that we have never systematically investigated. Writing a paper forces us to sort out our impressions, to think through problems we had previously slighted or ignored. Writing is instructive because it makes us take stock of our opinions, causing us to reconsider and strengthen them.

   —Guth, *Words and Ideas*, p. 51

   Subject: _____

   Central thought: _____

   _____

2. Until rather recently department store branches in the suburbs could be regarded as simply complementing the downtown, or "parent" stores. It was thought that people were buying only the more standard items in the branch stores and that they would still go downtown for the purchase of style goods. The theory was that only downtown shopping could assure customers, who compete with each other in the effort to be stylishly dressed, that they had succeeded in buying the item that was most suitable for them.

   The development of shopping centers for wealthy patrons is beginning to change this. The Old Orchard shopping center northwest of Chicago is a case in point. In this center Marshall Field has a store that is stocked solely with these high-income consumers in mind. Undoubtedly, a number of its customers feel less need than ever to visit the parent store in the Chicago Loop. Merchandise in Old Orchard is preselected to serve an exclusive clientele, which carries "vicarious search" pretty far. If these consumers went to the downtown store they would find that much of the merchandise displayed there appeals to buyers at lower income levels and is consequently quite outside their range of interest. In fact, department stores may be on their way to becoming local general merchandise chains — without the economies of standardized operations and a single buying staff that characterize established chain operations in the general merchandise field.

   —Alderson and Halbert, *Men, Motives and Markets*, pp. 12–13

   Subject: _____

Central thought: _____

_____

3.   The most recent development in data processing is the electronic computer, which has attracted great interest because of its vastly superior capacity to perform computations and other functions at incredible speeds. This results from the fact that processing in a computer is accomplished by the movement of electrical impulses through the computer's circuitry rather than by the movement of mechanical parts. Through instructions programmed into the computer by means of magnetic tapes, punched paper tapes, or punched cards, thousands of complex operations can be completed in a second.

   Computers are generally able to perform all the manipulative steps in the data processing cycle automatically. However, in spite of the impressive speed with which computers operate, processing is less dramatic than in other systems because there is no visible evidence of what is taking place: the manipulation of data occurs entirely within the computer. Computer operations are usually classified under three headings: input, processing, and output.
   —Arnold, *Introduction to Data Processing,* pp. 9–10

Subject: _____

Central thought: _____

_____

4.   The effect of family disorganization on children is seen as quite significant by Bronfenbrenner. His overarching analysis is that parents are paying less personal attention to their children in America (loving them less), and as a result we are paying the increasingly heavy price of alienated youth. To bolster his case he cites such evidence as the comparatively high infant mortality rate in the United States, which is 14th among industrial nations and which affects black infants two to three times more than it does white infants. This is evidence of national neglect, especially of the poor and black.

   The neglect is much more subtly measurable, however. One study found that the average middle class father spent about 38 seconds a day interacting with his one-year-old infant. And when the parents are with the children, it is more often in passive roles as when the family watches television. The middle class mania for privacy also tends to reduce the parent-child interaction.
   —Schultz, *The Changing Family,* p. 209

Subject: _____

Central thought: _____

_____

5.   A corporation is an association of individuals legally authorized by the state or federal government to carry on certain activities. A

corporation is an artificial entity separate and distinct from the individuals who operate it. Ownership is in the form of shares of stock generally divided among many shareholders. One of the advantages of the corporate form of organization is that stockholders are liable only to the extent of their investment. Another advantage is that the life of the organization is not affected by the death or disability of individual stockholders, or by the transfer of stock to other investors.

The corporation has tremendous growth possibilities through the sale of securities to the general public. This accounts for the fact that most large organizations in the United States are corporations. Large corporations have the resources to hire the most skilled personnel, to build good facilities, and to save money by large-scale purchases.

Corporations have certain disadvantages, however. They are subject to legal restrictions and high taxes. Further, the difficulty of managing a large corporation may lead to inefficiency and red tape.

–Arnold et al., *Introduction to Data Processing*, p. 33

Subject: _____

Central thought: _____

_____

HOW TO RECOGNIZE DIRECTIONAL WORDS

In order to connect ideas to one another within a passage and to indicate direction of thought, authors frequently use a type of word called *directional words* (or signal words). These words signal or clue the reader about what will come next in the passage. Directional words can indicate that a new or different idea will be introduced, that an example will follow, or that the author will present additional information on the same topic.

Read the following sentences, noticing the underlined directional words in each.

<u>To sum up,</u> Aristotle taught that all motions resulted either from the nature of the moving object or from a sustained push or pull.

There is never only a single force in a situation. <u>For example,</u> in walking across the floor, we push against the floor, and the floor in turn pushes against us.

<u>In other words,</u> in an economic sense the family was an almost self-sufficient unit.

In the first sentence, the words *to sum up* tell you that the writer is concluding or summarizing his or her ideas.

In the second group of sentences, the words *for example* clearly tell you that the author is going to give you an example of the statement that there is never only a single force in a situation.

In the third sentence, the words *in other words* suggest that the author is restating or repeating in different language a previously stated idea.

Below are listed many of the most common directional words and an explanation of what type of change or continuation in idea development each suggests. Do not attempt to memorize this list. Instead, try to become familiar with the types of words included and then concentrate on recognizing them as you read.

Types of Directional Words

Time sequence

> *first, second, finally, then, later, next, before, subsequently, presently*
>
> These words indicate that the author is arranging ideas according to the order in which they happened.

Example

> *for instance, for example, in the case of, to illustrate, such as*
>
> A writer uses these words to alert you that he or she is going to explain an idea by giving an example.

Cause-effect

> *because, thus, as a result, therefore, consequently, since, hence*
>
> These words signal that a cause-effect relationship exists. They say that one thing caused another or something happened as a result of something else.

Comparison

> *similarly, likewise, both, as*
>
> To show how two or more things are the same or similar, these words are commonly used.

Contrast

> *however, on the other hand, but, although, nevertheless*
>
> When a writer intends to discuss differences between two or more things or opposite situations, he or she uses these words to notify the reader of the change.

Continuation

> *in addition, also, and, further*
>
> If a writer is planning to continue with the same thought or intends to give additional information about the same topic, he or she often uses these words.

Order of importance

> *first, second, primarily, secondarily*
>
> To show the relative importance of ideas, writers use these words to identify and separate their ideas.

Summary

> *in summary, in conclusion, therefore, again, to repeat, to reiterate, finally, in brief, to sum up*
>
> To signal that he or she plans to summarize or "wrap-up" his or her discussion of a particular topic, a writer frequently uses these words.

EXERCISE 4

Directions: *Read each sentence or group of sentences. Underline any words that function as directional words. In the blank following each sentence, write the type of directional word used.*

1. One of the first things a writer must gain control of is the use of concrete detail. On the other hand, the inclusion of too much detail only tires and confuses the reader. _____

2. In large businesses, clerical jobs are usually very specialized in order to accomplish the work to be done in the most efficient manner. As a result, clerical work is very often routine and highly repetitive. _____

3. In conclusion, it must be emphasized that the steps in a data processing cycle are the core elements into which all data must be analyzed. _____

4. Chimpanzees appear to be capable of abstract thought. For example, they have been observed stacking several boxes on top of one another in order to reach a bunch of bananas. _____

5. Language is a coded series of sounds which conveys conscious thought. In other words, it is a rapid, efficient, and versatile system of communication or signaling. _____

6. Both the amount of stress an individual experiences and the level of aggression he exerts seriously affect his emotional patterns. _____

7. There are clear limitations to population growth and the use of natural resources. First, the food supply could be exhausted due to water, mineral, and soil depletion. _____

8. Unlike the statues of humans, the statues of animals found in Stone Age sites were quite lifelike. _____

9. When a patient enters a mental hospital, he is carefully tested and observed for twenty-four hours. Then a preliminary decision is made concerning medication and treatment. _____

10. One shortcoming of the clinical approach in treating mental illness is that definitions of normal behavior are subjective. Another shortcoming of the approach is that it assumes that when a patient has recovered he will be able to return to his previous environment. _____

EXERCISE 5

Directions: *Read each paragraph and underline the directional word(s). In the blank at the right indicate the type of directional word used.*

1. Ancestor worship is not universal in primitive society. More people believe in the spirits of the

dead and in ghosts than worship them. Ghosts, in fact, are more often feared than worshiped, and any rites associated with them are to drive them away. However, the ghost of the last-deceased household head is sometimes the protector of his family and can thwart the malignant efforts of other ghosts.[4]

_____

2. Tracing books in the card catalog is tiring and time-consuming. It will be even more tiring and time-consuming than usual if you have to return to the catalog repeatedly for information that you failed to record. You should, therefore, work out an efficient system of recording all bibliographical information that you need for your project.[5]

_____

3. Although the term "data processing" is of relatively recent origin, this does not mean that the activity itself is new. On the contrary, there is evidence that the need to process data originated as far back as the beginning of recorded history when man's activities first exceeded his ability to remember the details of his actions. Throughout history commercial and governmental activities have created the need for record keeping of one sort or another.[6]

_____

4. Our attitudes and feelings impel us to action, and, to a large extent, govern our actions. For this reason, the attitudes and opinions of employees, supervisors, and top management should be a major concern of an organization in its efforts to foster cooperation among those groups responsible for production. Attitudes are elusive, fluid, and difficult to interpret. Useful and practical methods have been developed, however, for measuring the attitudes of groups toward specific policies and working conditions, and for the purpose of determining the prevailing level of job satisfaction and areas of content and discontent.[7]

_____

5. Over the years, a body of organization principles has evolved. Some of these principles can be traced back to the earliest records of mankind. For example, in Exodus 18 appears the famous passage in which Moses receives counsel from Jethro, his father-in-law. Jethro is concerned about how Moses can effectively extend his leadership to his followers. He points out that Moses cannot hope to administer justice to all his followers individually. The mass of details would soon overwhelm him. He admonishes Moses first to train ten of his most immediate followers, who in turn would train ten more followers, and so on, until the echelons of organization included all. These deputies would take care of the more routine decisions at each of their levels of organization.[8]

_____

EXERCISE 6

Directions: *Choose a two-page selection from one of your textbooks. Read the selection and list the directional words you find in the first column. In the second column, write the type of directional word used.*

Directional word   *Type*

_____   _____

_____   _____

_____   _____

_____   _____

_____   _____

_____   _____

_____   _____

_____   _____

_____   _____

SUMMARY

A passage is a group of related paragraphs. In textbooks, passages are usually grouped or separated from one another by the dark print, or boldface, headings within each chapter.

Understanding a passage is similar to understanding a paragraph since both contain three similar essential elements. A passage must be concerned with (1) a single general subject. The entire passage must be directed toward expressing (2) a central thought about that general subject. Finally, each separate paragraph within a passage must contain (3) supporting ideas that explain, prove, or give examples of the central thought of the passage. In a paragraph, these three essential features are called topic, main idea, and details.

In addition to the three essential elements, many passages contain a fourth element which helps writers connect their ideas and which aids readers in following the thought pattern or direction of ideas. These words which signal the thought pattern are called directional words.

Part Four
Textbook Reading Skills

Do you think of your textbooks as just something to read? If so, you may not be using them to full advantage. A textbook is much more than a book of chapters, parts of which are assigned by instructors at various times during the semester. Textbooks are actually learning tools or devices. A text is often one of your primary sources of information for a course, and it is a valuable teaching-learning tool when used effectively.

Textbooks are written for the purpose of presenting information about a certain subject that students need to know. Textbook authors, most of whom are college teachers, attempt to present the information in such a way that it can be learned easily by students. They use a variety of methods and include a variety of learning aids, all of them to help students learn the content of their texts. As a student, you want to be aware of these methods and learning aids and know how to use them to make reading and studying easier.

Since the textbook is most often your primary source of information in a college course, you will need to become familiar with techniques for effectively studying and learning textbook material. You will want to know how to learn as you read, and you will want to master the technique of marking a textbook as you read to make reviewing and studying for exams easier.

The textbook chapter in the Appendix of this book (page 335) has been included for purposes of demonstration and practice. It is intended to be only a sample. While it has many similarities to other textbook chapters, do not expect to find every textbook chapter organized or presented exactly like this one. The sample chapter has been included so that you can try out the techniques and suggestions given in this unit. You will notice, also, that the sample chapter is used many times throughout the unit to show how particular techniques are applied or to illustrate particular aspects of effective textbook reading.

12. Textbook Aids to Learning

Use this chapter to:

1. Find out how textbooks can make learning easier.

2. Learn how to take advantage of the various learning aids included in textbooks.

Most college students think of their textbooks as merely chapters of information to be read and learned. What many students do not realize, however, is that textbooks contain not only facts and ideas to be learned but also a structure and guide to learning these facts and ideas.

Think about how your textbook differs from other books and references. What does your textbook contain that other information sources, such as encyclopedias, dictionaries, and library reference materials, do not? How does it differ from such familiar sources of factual information as newspapers, magazines, and nonfiction paperbacks?

Select any nonfiction book you may have read, or just randomly take any book containing factual information from a shelf in the library. Also, choose one of the textbooks you are now using in one of your courses. Use the chart below to make a comparison of the different features contained in each. If either your textbook or the other factual book contains an item listed in the chart, place a check mark in the appropriate column beside that item. Leave the space blank if the item is not included. If you are unsure of what a particular feature, such as a glossary, is, check for the feature among the boldface headings in the section of this chapter entitled "Textbook Aids and How to Use Them."

Feature	Any nonfiction book	Your textbook
Title		
Subtitle		
Author, author's credentials		
Copyright date		
Preface		
Introduction		

Feature	Any nonfiction book	Your textbook
Introduction to students	_____	_____
Table of contents (more than just number of chapters)	_____	_____
Chapter titles	_____	_____
Dark (boldface) and italic headings	_____	_____
Typographical aids (graphs, pictures, charts)	_____	_____
Chapter summary or conclusion	_____	_____
Chapter questions	_____	_____
Vocabulary list	_____	_____
References	_____	_____
Appendix	_____	_____
Index	_____	_____
Glossary	_____	_____

Count up the check marks in the last two columns of the chart. Regardless of what two books you have compared, it is quite probable that you made a significantly higher number of checks in the column for your textbook.

Now that you have seen that textbooks do contain many features not included in other factual books, you will want to know what these extra aids can do to improve your reading and studying efficiency. The following section of this chapter lists several important textbook aids and suggests how you can use each of them more effectively.

TEXTBOOK AIDS AND HOW TO USE THEM

The Title

Try this test: Without looking, jot down the correct title of each textbook you are using this semester. Then check the titles. How many did you get exactly right? Most students do not get more than one or two titles completely correct. This suggests that students may be in the habit of ignoring textbook titles, important aids to learning.

The title of a text is more than a name or convenient label. The title is descriptive. It tells the reader a good deal about the scope and purpose of the text and clues the reader to the organization and level of difficulty of the text. The title *An Introduction to Social Psychology* tells the reader that the text is basic and introductory and that the subject is limited to social psychology. The title *Readings and Perspectives in Early American History* indicates that the text is made up of articles (readings) written by different authors, chosen to give the reader various points of view (perspectives) of early American history. From this title, then, you learned something about the text's organization, about its purposes, and about the subject area it treats.

EXERCISE 1

Directions: *Read each of the five textbook titles. Then decide what, if anything, each tells you about the text's organization, purpose, and subject. Use the outline in the example as a guide.*

Example:

Title: *Conceptual Physics* _____

Organization of the text: organized by concepts or _____

_____ principles _____

Purpose of the text: to present conceptual background for the _____

_____ study of physics _____

Subject of the text: physics _____

1. *Using Psychology*

Organization of the text: _____

_____

Purpose of the text: _____

_____

Subject of the text: _____

2. *The Basics of American Politics*

Organization of the text: _____

_____

Purpose of the text: _____

_____

Subject of the text: _____

3. *Laboratory Studies in General Biology*

   Organization of the text: _____

   _____

   Purpose of the text: _____

   _____

   Subject of the text: _____

4. *Black Insights: Significant Literature by Black Americans*

   Organization of the text: _____

   _____

   Purpose of the text: _____

   _____

   Subject of the text: _____

5. *Foundations and Principles of Health Education*

   Organization of the text: _____

   _____

   Purpose of the text: _____

   _____

   Subject of the text: _____

EXERCISE 2

Directions: *List the titles of all the texts you are using this semester. (If you are taking courses that do not require a text, list the texts that someone you know is using.) After each title, identify what, if anything, each tells you about the text's organization, purpose, and subject.*

1. *Title:* _____

   Organization of the text: _____

   _____

   Purpose of the text: _____

   _____

Subject of the text: _____

_____

2. *Title*:_____

Organization of the text: _____

_____

Purpose of the text: _____

_____

Subject of the text: _____

3. *Title*:_____

Organization of the text: _____

_____

Purpose of the text: _____

_____

Subject of the text: _____

4. *Title*:_____

Organization of the text: _____

_____

Purpose of the text: _____

_____

Subject of the text: _____

Subtitles

Sometimes a subtitle follows the title of a text and further explains or elaborates on the title. Subtitles help the reader in the same way that titles do. They provide information about the text's organization, purpose, and subject area limitations. For a text with the title *Educational Psychology*, the subtitle might be *Theories and Applications for Teachers*. In this example, the subtitle is quite informative. It tells the reader that the text is organized to present theories of educational psychology and practical applications of the theories. The purpose of the text is to present theories and applications useful to teachers. The subject area is educational psychology, but it is limited to those theories in educational psychology which are useful for teachers. Further, you might correctly assume because of the word *applications* that the text is more practical than theoretical — that it deals with theories that teachers can apply in real situations.

EXERCISE 3

Directions: *Read each situation described below. Then underline the title and subtitle of the text that would be most useful in the situation described.*

1. You are interested in locating a textbook on child psychology to loan to your sister, who is trying to understand and cope with the behavior problems of her three-year-old child. Which of the following texts would be most useful to her?
    a. *Face to Face — Individual and Social Problems*
    b. *Readings in Child Development*
    c. *Guidance of the Young Child*

2. Sally is enrolled in a secretarial science program and needs to brush up on her skills in letter writing, punctuation and usage, and sentence structure. Which of the following texts would be most helpful?
    a. *The Secretaries' Handbook — A Practical Guide*
    b. *Business in Contemporary Society*
    c. *The Writer's Guide to Style and Usage*

3. You are in the library trying to locate some information for a term paper on "Drug Use and Abuse in the Seventies." In the card catalog you find the following texts are available. Which do you think would be most helpful?
    a. *Experimental Research on Drug Therapy*
    b. *Drugs in Contemporary Society*
    c. *Drugs — A Clinical Evaluation*

4. In your psychology class today, the instructor discussed instinct and learning in animals and mentioned that experiments are being done with a baby chimpanzee that is being raised by human parents. Researchers are interested to see what animal behaviors and what human behaviors the chimp develops. You decide that you would like to read more about this type of research. Which text might contain further information on the subject?
    a. *Physiological Bases of Human Behavior*
    b. *Animal Behavioral Research*
    c. *The Psychology Experiment — An Introduction*

5. Sam just got a part-time job selling ad space in a local newspaper to area businesses. He realizes that he needs to learn how to approach potential customers and what to say to them. Which of the following texts might be useful to him?
    a. *Executive Action in Marketing*
    b. *Salesmanship*
    c. *Business in Contemporary Society*

The Author(s)

On the title page, the first printed page of the text, you frequently find the name of the author (or authors) and the job title or the name of the college with which the author is affiliated. While you probably will not recognize the author's name, it is useful to be familiar with his or her credentials — that is, his or her qualifications to write the text.

The Copyright Date

Located on the page after the title page, you will find the copyright notice. This contains the date when the book was first published. If you see more than one date, the earliest date indicates when the text was first published, while the others are dates when the text was revised or reprinted.

It is worthwhile to check the copyright to find out how up-to-date your text is. Of course, in some subject areas, a recent publication date is more important than it is in others. A book on Greek philosophy written ten years ago may still be complete and up-to-date, while a ten-year-old text on twentieth-century American history is incomplete and outdated.

When you are locating books in the library to complete an assignment or to write a paper, it is especially important to check the copyright, because in certain fields, a current source of information is necessary. In the sciences, social sciences, and health-related fields, for example, new research, theories, and ideas are developed each year.

EXERCISE 4

Directions: *The following is a list of textbook titles and their copyright dates. Place a check mark beside those you feel are outdated.*

1. ____ *Principles of Behavior Modification* (1980)
2. ____ *Introduction to Data Processing* (1981)
3. ____ *Business Law* (1968)
4. ____ *Business Mathematics* (1974)
5. ____ *Speech Improvement: A Practical Program* (1957)
6. ____ *Logic and Philosophy* (1975)
7. ____ *The History of Music* (1977)
8. ____ *English for Business* (1970)
9. ____ *Economics in American Society* (1982)
10. ____ *Patterns in English History* (1961)

The Preface

The preface is the author's introduction to the text. In some texts this feature may have such a title as "The Introduction" or "To the Student." The preface contains basic information about the text that the author feels you should be aware of before you begin reading.

The preface may contain such information as the following:

1. Why the author wrote the text (his or her purpose in writing)
2. For whom (audience) the book was written

3. The author's major points of emphasis
4. The author's particular slant or focus on the subject
5. How the author organized the book
6. Important references or authorities consulted when writing
7. Suggestions on how to use the text
8. Limitations or weaknesses of the text (subject areas the text does not cover, and so forth)

As you can see, each of the above items is important to know before you use a text. To get a better understanding of the values and importance of a preface, read the sample preface, taken from Russ and Kirkpatrick, *Marketing*,[1] reproduced on pages 155–157. Try to identify and mark the types of information it contains. (Use items 1–8, listed above, for help.)

EXERCISE 5

Directions: *Now that you have read the sample preface, answer the following questions.*

1. Do you expect that the text will be theoretical or practically oriented? Why?

   _____

2. What is the basic organization of the text?

   _____

3. Do you think the study guide would be worth buying? Why?

   _____

4. What features are contained in each chapter to help you learn?

   _____

5. What are the case studies about Levi Strauss intended to show?

   _____

After reading the sample preface, you can no doubt see how important it is to read the preface of any textbook to learn how the author presents information particularly vital in understanding the book's organization and content. If you were to begin reading the text for this psychology book without checking the preface, you would have been confused about several important features of the text. First, you probably would have wondered what the Interludes were and what purpose they served. Second, you would not have clearly understood the function of the Focus sections in relation to the content of individual chapters. Finally, the inclusion of conversations with the author's friend Moon would have seemed out of place and confusing.

Preface

In the 1980s marketers face many challenges, including fast-changing technology, increased foreign competition, shortage of certain resources, and economic conditions marked by inflation and unemployment. Yet the basic concepts of marketing that the professional marketer must know and understand to make the necessary marketing decisions remain the same.

The purpose of this text is to help the marketing student understand the fundamentals of marketing and marketing decision making. With this in mind, we have tried to make the text as readable and concise as possible, focusing on what marketing managers do and why. Because marketing is an "applied science," the text provides many cases and hundreds of examples of marketing in action. In this way the student learns the principles of marketing as they apply to real world situations.

A quick look at the table of contents will show you that this book is comprehensive. Although the elements of the marketing mix dominate, we give prominent coverage to other important subjects such as multinational marketing, industrial marketing, and the marketing of intangibles.

The text begins with an overview of marketing, moves on to specific aspects of marketing strategy, and then comes full circle, placing marketing once again in a broader context. After a discussion in Chapter 1 of what is involved in marketing and how the marketing concept evolved, Part I explains marketing's role in various environments; strategic planning and marketing research are shown to be important tools for coping with these environments. Part II focuses on market segmentation and buyer behavior, both consumer and industrial. Parts III, IV, and V address the important elements of the marketing mix. Pricing and product are treated in the same part because they are inseparable in the real world. Descriptive and strategic aspects of distribution are discussed. In the promotion section a separate chapter is devoted to sales promotion in recognition of its growing importance. Part VI covers two special topics: multinational marketing and the marketing of intangibles. In Part VII we come full circle, returning to another major management task — control — and to marketing's role in society.

vii

Each of the seven parts in the text begins with a short case study that focuses on Levi Strauss and Company. Levi Strauss — or at least its major product, blue jeans — is well known to everyone. More importantly, its successful marketing activities provide helpful illustrations of the basic marketing concepts addressed in this text. Each Levi Strauss case at the beginning of a part provides a glimpse of the topics to be covered, linking them to an identifiable product and company. At the end of each part are three cases to help students tie everything together and apply what they have learned.

Each chapter begins with a short vignette that places the student in the role of a marketing manager. The vignette sets the stage for the chapter discussion, posing questions about what marketing decisions should be made. At the end of the chapter the issues in the vignette are addressed again and solutions are offered — usually the same solutions that the real company arrived at in solving its marketing problems. Each chapter also contains learning objectives, summaries, key terms, review questions, and discussion questions to make the text an effective teaching/learning tool.

In summary, this text will provide the student with excellent and comprehensive coverage of the basics of marketing. Through the extensive use of case material and real world examples, the student can gain an understanding of how decisions are made by the marketing manager.

In addition to the text, there is an accompanying study guide to aid the student in grasping the text information. This guide consists of a review of text material, key terms, review questions, and cases for analysis.

For the instructor, an excellent instructor's manual has been prepared that discusses our philosophy for writing this text and describes what we think are special features and suggestions for teaching the basic course. Additional teaching material is also available for each chapter to aid the instructor in developing class lectures and discussions. For those individuals who adopt the text, a 2000-item test bank is available in printed and computerized form.

Many individuals have worked on this project and we are grateful for their support, patience, and suggestions. Little, Brown has provided excellent editorial support throughout development of the manuscript. We especially appreciate the strong editorial assistance of Al Hockwalt, Madelyn Leopold, Dana Norton, Julia Winston, and Kate Campbell.

A special thanks must go to Geoffrey Colvin of *Fortune* for his assistance on this book.

Over the past few years, many excellent marketing scholars have read and reviewed this manuscript. Their criticisms and suggestions for improvement have been invaluable in rewriting, revising, and shaping this manuscript into its final form. We would like to extend our thanks to the following reviewers: Terry Shimp (University of South Carolina), Gerald Albaum (University of Oregon), R. A. Klages (State University of New York), Jack Denson (Fullerton College), J. Barry Mason (University of Alabama), Richard M. Hill (University of Illinois),

viii / Preface

Edwin A. Giermark (College of DuPage), Paul C. Thistlewaite (West Illinois University), Gary Ford (University of Maryland, College Park), Steve DeVere (Louisiana State), Michael D'Amico (University of Akron), Frank Roberts (California State University, Fullerton), Andreas Falkenberg (University of Oregon), Don Knight (Lansing Community College), Steve Brown (Arizona State University), John Redington (Pennsylvania State University), Bill Locander (University of Houston), Joan Mizis (Florisant Valley Community College), Donald H. Granbois (Indiana University), Michael Mokwa (Arizona State), and John Gwin (Indiana University).

Finally, our colleagues and graduate students here at the university have been a source of ideas and encouragement. Gary Armstrong in particular has worked closely with us on developing certain sections of this text and we owe him a special thank you for his help.

Preface / ix

EXERCISE 6

Directions: *Select one of your textbooks and turn to the preface. Read the preface, and then answer the following questions. If the information is not included in the preface, leave the item blank.*

Title of text: _____

1. Why did the author write the textbook?

    _____

2. For whom was the book written?

    _____

3. What are the author's major points of emphasis?

    _____

4. Describe the author's particular slant or focus on the subject.

    _____

5. How is the text organized?

    _____

6. Did the author use important references or authorities in writing the text?

    _____

7. What suggestions did the author give on how to use the book?

    _____

8. What weaknesses or limitations does the author mention?

    _____

The Table of Contents

The table of contents of a textbook is valuable to read through before beginning to use a text. The table of contents is actually an outline of a book. It lists all the important topics and subtopics. The table of contents also shows the organization of the text and indicates the relationship of the major topics to one another. The relative importance of each topic can also be determined by reading this important textbook feature. By reading the table of contents, you are actually doing a very brief prereading of the entire text.

The table of contents is also useful to refer to before you begin reading any particular chapter. Although chapters are organized as separate parts of a textbook, it is important to recognize that they are parts of a whole — the text itself. Chapters relate and connect to one another. The material covered in any particular chapter is related to the information in the chapters which precede it and follow it. Material in the preceding chapters may give background information, or it may contain descriptions of earlier events, more basic theories, related problems, or early developments. Material in the following chapters may contain further developments, more complex theories, or effects or results.

To understand a particular chapter, it is important to see what the whole chapter is a part of and to note what immediately precedes and follows it. On pages 160–162, the first three pages of the table of contents from Russ and Kirkpatrick, *Marketing,* are reproduced. Read through the pages now. Then go on to Exercise 7.

EXERCISE 7

Directions: *Now that you have read the sample table of contents, answer the following questions in the space provided.*

1.   What feature does this text contain that is intended to make the text practical and interesting?

   _____

2.   Which chapter discusses buyer characteristics?

   _____

3.   List four marketing environments.

   _____

4.   List three characteristics of consumer markets.

   _____

Chapter Titles

Chapter titles are often mistakenly ignored when reading a textbook. Many students, if interrupted while reading a text assignment, cannot recall the name of the chapter they are reading. Chapter titles serve the same function as textbook titles and subtitles. They tell the reader about the topics included in the chapters and provide clues about the organization, purpose, and point of view of the whole text. A chapter title tells you what to expect and starts you thinking about the topics discussed in the chapter before you begin reading. For example, if the title of a chapter is "The Nervous System: An Overview," you know the general topic — the nervous system — and you know that the purpose of the chapter is to provide a general picture, or overview, of the topic. You might expect that the chapter will be introductory and will probably discuss briefly the function, parts, and organization of the nervous system.

Contents

EXERCISE 8

Directions: *Read the title of each text and the topic below it. Then underline the chapter of the text in which you would expect to find a discussion of the topic:*

1.   Text: *Introduction to Anthropology*
       Topic: Development of male and female roles
       Chapters: a. "Discoveries of the First Humans"
                b. "Social Organization and Environment"
                c. "The Riddle of Heredity"

2.   Text: *The American Family*
       Topic: Relationship between teen-ager and parents
       Chapters: a. "The Organization of the American Family"
                b. "The Adolescent Personality"
                c. "Teen-agers and Dating"

3.   Text: *Modern Economics*
       Topic: Leadership and control in large corporations
       Chapters: a. "The Organization of the Modern Corporation"
                b. "Advantages and Disadvantages of the Corporate Form"
                c. "Ownership in the Large Corporation"

4.   Text: *Life Insurance: An Introduction*
       Topic: Use of mortality tables (tables predicting the life span for various groups)
       Chapters: a. "The Measurement of Risk in Life Insurance"
                b. "Fundamental Principles of Policies"
                c. "Legal Concepts in Insurance"

5.   Text: *Photography: A Guide to Basic Principles*
       Topic: How to achieve background and depth in a photograph
       Chapters: a. "Choosing Your Film"
                b. "First Steps for Beginning Photographers"
                c. "Composing a Photograph"

Headings

Interspersed throughout most textbook chapters, as you know, are headings that are distinguished, usually by dark print (**boldface**) or *italics*. These headings have the same purpose as the label on a can of soup — they tell you what the contents are. Boldface and italic headings are labels for what is contained in the different sections of a chapter. They are two- or three-word summaries of what the section or passage is about.

Try to notice and think about the boldface heading before reading a section. Headings make reading easier: they tell you, in advance, what the section is about and what it is you are supposed to know when you finish. If you see the heading "Is memory chemical?" in a chapter on brain functions, you know you are supposed to have the answer to that question — along with the reason why memory is or is not chemical — when you finish the section. When you finish a section with the heading "Two complementary brains" you should know what the two brains are and how they complement each other, or work together.

Graphic Aids

Textbook chapters frequently include various types of graphic aids such as graphs, maps, pictures, and charts. It is tempting to skip over these aids because of the extra time involved in reading and interpreting them. You will find, however, that they are valuable learning aids. Pictures give you a vivid mental image of events. They are also useful memory tools. If you connect certain facts and events with a picture, when you recall the picture, you will also recall the information associated with it.

Maps provide a visual description of the physical location of places. They are much more accurate than words in creating an understanding of position in space or in comparing the locations of two or more countries, cities, or other places. Like pictures, maps can serve as a visual memory aid and facilitate learning.

Graphs and charts are usually comparisons of two or more things and can be used to describe quickly a changing relationship over time. On a graph, for example, you can easily show how much inflation has increased yearly over the past ten years. If, however, you had to write in paragraph form a description of changing rates of inflation, the paragraph would be extremely long and complicated. In addition, the paragraph would not provide a quick overview of the trend or pattern of increase which you could see at one glance on a graph.

How to Read a Graph, Table, or Chart: To read a graph, table, or chart, use the following steps:

1. Read the title to determine what the overall purpose of the graph or chart is.
2. Read the headings on a chart or table or the legend on a graph. The legend is made up of words or numbers written at the sides and bottom of a graph that tell you what units of measurement are used.
3. Determine what two (or more) things are being compared.
4. Study the graph or chart, noticing how the relationship between the two (or more) things changes.
5. Try to make a general statement explaining what the graph or chart shows or what trend or pattern is suggested.

In Figure 12-1,[2] the title "Union Membership as a Percentage of the Labor Force" tells the purpose of the graph: to show changes in the percentage of union membership over many years. Specifically, the graph shows the percentage of membership (see the vertical line) for time periods from 1830 to 1970 (see the horizontal line). The dark, jagged line on the graph shows a sharp increase in union membership from 1900 to 1920 and a peak in membership around 1950.

Now, using the steps listed above, study Figure 12-1. Next, write a

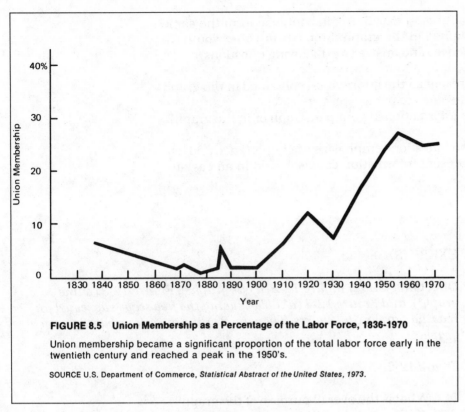

FIGURE 8.5   Union Membership as a Percentage of the Labor Force, 1836-1970

Union membership became a significant proportion of the total labor force early in the twentieth century and reached a peak in the 1950's.

SOURCE U.S. Department of Commerce, *Statistical Abstract of the United States, 1973.*

FIGURE 12-1

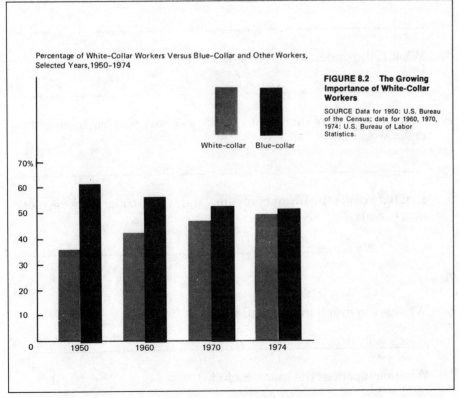

Percentage of White-Collar Workers Versus Blue-Collar and Other Workers, Selected Years, 1950-1974

White-collar   Blue-collar

FIGURE 8.2   The Growing Importance of White-Collar Workers

SOURCE Data for 1950: U.S. Bureau of the Census; data for 1960, 1970, 1974: U.S. Bureau of Labor Statistics.

FIGURE 12-2

165

four- or five-sentence paragraph explaining in sentence form the same information that is contained in the graph. Stop writing after you have written four or five sentences and answer the following questions:

1. Were you able to present all the information contained in the graph in your four- or five-sentence paragraph?
2. Is it easier to locate information in your paragraph or in the graph?

Your answers to these two questions emphasize the importance and use of graphic material: to present information concisely and in an easy-to-read fashion.

EXERCISE 9

Directions: *Study Figure 12-2 (a bar graph[3]), Figure 12-3 (a line graph[4]), and Figure 12-4 (a table[5]), using the five steps suggested for reading graphs and charts. Then answer the questions based on each graph.*

Figure 12-2:

1. What is the overall purpose of the graph?

   _____

2. What two things are being compared?

   _____

3. What is the general trend or pattern of change?

   _____

4. In what year were there nearly twice as many blue-collar as white-collar workers?

   _____

5. In what year is the number of blue- and white-collar workers most nearly equal?

   _____

Figure 12-3:

1. What is the graph intended to show?

   _____

2. What factors does the graph include?

   _____

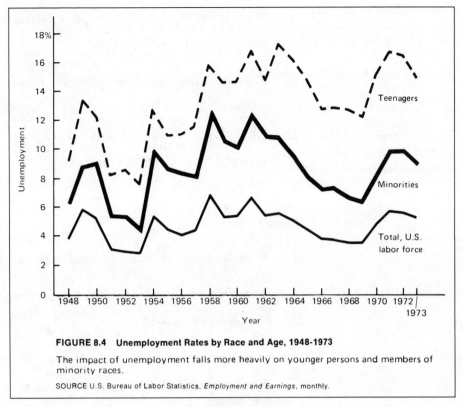

FIGURE 8.4   Unemployment Rates by Race and Age, 1948-1973

The impact of unemployment falls more heavily on younger persons and members of minority races.

SOURCE U.S. Bureau of Labor Statistics, *Employment and Earnings*, monthly.

FIGURE 12-3

Table 6.1   Federal Budget (in millions of dollars).

Year	Receipts	Outlays	Surplus or Deficit
1929	3,862	3,127	734
1939	4,979	8,841	−3,862
1943	23,649	78,533	−54,884
1951	51,646	45,546	6,100
1959	79,249	92,104	−12,855
1968	153,671	178,833	−25,161
1975	280,997	326,092	−45,095
1978*	400,387	462,234	−61,847

Source: *Economic Report of the President*, January 1978.

*1978 figures are estimated.

FIGURE 12-4

3. What is the general trend or pattern that the graph describes?

_____

4. For what group has unemployment been consistently higher?

_____

5. What year was there the greatest difference in unemployment between teen-agers and minorities?

_____

Figure 12-4:

1. What was this table constructed to show?

_____

2. How is it organized?

_____

3. What general trend or pattern can you notice about federal spending?

_____

4. Has the government taken in more money each year than in the previous year?

_____

5. In 1975 how large was the federal deficit?

_____

Chapter Summary or Conclusion

An end-of-chapter summary is useful to read *before* you read a chapter. The summary is a review of the major points covered in the chapter. If you are familiar with the major points that are to be covered in the chapter before you begin reading, the reading of the chapter will be easier. You will be reading with a purpose in mind and will be looking for specific information. Be sure to reread the summary when you finish the chapter. It will provide a good review and will help you tie together, or consolidate, the major points covered in the chapter. Turn to the sample textbook chapter in the Appendix and read the summary on page 357. Notice that it outlines the major points covered in the chapter.

The following end-of-chapter summary is taken from a text on child and adolescent psychology. Read the summary and then identify the general topics and major points that you would expect to be covered in the chapter.

Text: *Child and Adolescent Behavior*
Chapter title: "The Child in the School"
Summary:

The teacher's role in the classroom has been the main emphasis in this chapter. The teacher stimulates and guides the intellectual development of pupils, affects their attitudes and values, and exerts a marked influence on their emotional adjustment through the kind of psychological atmosphere established in the classroom and through differential rewards and punishments.

Many factors relate to academic achievement: intellectual ability, level of maturity, relationship with parents, emotional and personality factors, past success and failure, attitude toward school, the teacher, socioeconomic status, and patterns of interest. Because the primary function of the school is the teaching of academic skills, the extent to which a child learns these skills reflects the effectiveness of the school's endeavor and also bears heavily on the child's concept of himself.

The years spent in school are important ones. Teachers and parents must work together to make certain that for each child these years are fruitful and well used.

—Medinnus and Johnson, *Child and Adolescent Behavior,* p. 472

Now that you have read the chapter summary above, write the topics and major points you would expect to be covered in the chapter.

_____

_____

_____

EXERCISE 10

Directions: *Read each of the following chapter summaries and list the main points presented in each.*

1.   Text: *Psychology of Adolescence*
     Chapter Title: "Social Forces Affecting the Adolescent"
     Summary:

     Changed social and economic conditions have resulted in profound changes in the organization and activities of the community. The increased leisure time of boys and girls has presented a definite challenge to the communities to provide recreational opportunities and better guidance of boys and girls, especially during the adolescent years. Materials have been presented in this chapter showing the activities of adolescents in the community and some of the needs for the community to provide better educational and recreational facilities for boys and girls as they grow through adolescence toward complete maturity.

     A few pieces of lumber, some glue, and nails is not a table. Likewise, a collection of boys, girls, and adults is not a community.

There must be some common interests and needs, mutual confidence and understanding, association and sharing a common lot, if there is to be a true community. Morgan has said in this connection: "In a true community many activities are shared by the same people. This unified living results in deeper social roots and more unified personalities."

The summer camp has come into use as a means for providing for the recreational, health, and educational needs of adolescents. Increased leisure has presented a problem and a challenge. It is important that this time be not wasted, but used as a road to health, efficiency, and morality. Without a purpose or goal, free time may bring the adolescent in contact with vice, crime, and unconventional practices. But if his community offers libraries, museums, school activities, sports, hobby groups, church groups, "Y" settlement houses, playgrounds, movies, and parks, there is less chance that he will divert his energy into undesirable channels.

–Cole and Hall, *Psychology of Adolescence*, p. 37

List the main points here: _____

_____

_____

_____

2. Text: *Oceanography*
Chapter Title: "The History of Oceanography"
Summary:

Initially man explored the surface of the planet to map the distribution of land and water. Exploration was largely completed when Magellan completed his circumnavigation of the globe, in 1522. James Cook greatly improved the charting of distant coasts. The *Challenger* expedition gathered the first comprehensive data about the deep ocean. Subsequent expeditions, equipped with newly developed tools, have added considerably to our knowledge.

–Weyl, *Oceanography*, p. 52

List the main points here: _____

_____

_____

_____

3. Text: *Psychology of Adolescence*
Chapter Title: "Growth in Tissue, Muscle, and Bone"
Summary:

Adolescence is a period of marked growth. In the course of a few years the individual undergoes changes in both size and proportion — changes that take him from a childish to mature level. The rapidity, variety, and force of these developments are alike bewildering, even though they are sometimes exciting and satisfactory. Students vary greatly in both size and maturity during the high school years, and the differences precipitate problems. Both the schoolwork and the personalities of junior high and high school students are affected by the concurrent processes of growth. It is therefore essential that teachers keep in mind the physical background of adolescence so that they may not attribute to other causes those indirect manifestations that are mainly the result of mere growth.

Growth is affected by various factors, of which the most important are nutrition, sex, and family inheritance. Any prolonged deprivation has its retarding effect upon the rate of development.

During the last century, and especially during the last half-century, boys and girls have been growing taller and heavier than their earlier counterparts were at the same ages. These changes are world-wide and are presumably the result of more food, better living conditions, and better medical care.

—Garrison, *Psychology of Adolescence*, p. 342

List the main points here: _____

_____

_____

_____

Chapter Questions

Many texts include discussion or review questions at the end of each chapter. Try to quickly read through these questions *before* you begin the chapter. The questions can serve as a guide to what is important in the chapter and what you should know when you finish the chapter. Along with the chapter summary, the end-of-chapter questions will give you a good idea of what to expect in the chapter. Turn to the sample textbook chapter, pages 357–358, to see examples of both review questions and discussion questions. The review questions cover the factual content of the chapter, while the discussion questions focus your attention on practical applications of its contents.

After reading the chapter, use these questions to test yourself on what you understood and can remember. Review them again when preparing for an exam covering that chapter.

Vocabulary List — New Terminology

Some textbook authors include a list of new terms introduced in the chapter. This list may appear either at the beginning or end of the chapter. In the sample textbook chapter, a list of key terms is presented at the end (see page 357). This list is a useful study aid in preparing for exams. Many instructors include on their exams items which test student mastery of the new terms introduced in their courses, especially in introductory courses. The vocabulary list is a fast way of reviewing. For suggestions on how to learn new terminology, see Part Six, Chapter 20.

References

Some texts include a list of references at the end of each chapter. Other texts may have one complete list of references at the end of the entire text. In this case it may be labeled "Bibliography." References are books or articles to which you can refer to get further information on the topics discussed in the chapter. This reference list is particularly useful when you have to complete an assignment or do a term paper which requires you to locate other information sources. The reference list frequently contains some of the most useful or most authoritative books and articles on a given subject. In some instances, using the reference list can save you hours of time trying to locate adequate sources in the library.

Appendix (Appendices)

The appendix, located at the end of a text, is made up of extra information and materials that the author wanted to include in the text. Frequently these are things that help students learn more about the subject matter, or items that they may need to refer to regularly. In an American history text, the appendix may include a copy of the Constitution, of the Declaration of Independence, a map of the United States, and a list of the terms of office of American presidents. The appendix of a chemistry book might contain an equivalency table of weights and measures, a table of periodic elements, and an answer key to problems at the end of the chapters.

As soon as you buy a text, check to see if it has an appendix, and if so, find out what it contains. Many students waste time and energy searching for information contained right in the text.

Glossary

A glossary is an alphabetical listing of new vocabulary words which are used in the text. The meaning of each word is also included. Located in the back of the text, the glossary serves as a minidictionary. Since the glossary lists only words used in the particular text, it is faster and easier to locate a word in the glossary than in a dictionary. To make it even more convenient to use, take some paper clips and attach them to the first page of the glossary in each of your texts. The paper clips will enable you to turn directly to the glossary without hunting and fumbling.

The glossary is better to use than a regular dictionary. As you know, words have several meanings, and regular dictionaries list all of the most common meanings. To find the meaning of a word in a dictionary, you have to sort through all the meanings until you find one that suits the way the word is used in your text. A glossary, on the other hand, lists only one meaning — and it is the meaning intended by the author of your text. The glossary can save you time and eliminates the chance of selecting a meaning not consistent with the meaning used in the text.

Listed below are both a regular dictionary definition and a glossary definition for a common term used in psychology — *development*. Compare the definitions. You can readily see how much easier and faster it is to locate the meaning in the glossary than in the dictionary entry.

Glossary entry:
> **development** the sequence of physical, behavioral, and mental changes that take place in a maturing organism.[6]

Dictionary entry:
> **de·vel·op·ment** (di-'vel-əp-mənt), n. (Fr. développement < développer), 1. a developing or being developed (in all senses of the verb). 2. a step or stage in growth, advancement, etc.; hence, 3. an event or happening. 4. a thing that is developed; result of developing. 5. in music, a) the elaboration of a theme by rhythmic, harmonic, or melodic changes. b) the middle part of the sonata form. Also spelled developement.[7]

In the dictionary, you have to sort through five different meanings, and even then you do not get a specific definition of the term as used in the field of psychology. The glossary entry, on the other hand, gives a clear and concise definition of the term as it is used by the author.

The glossary can serve as a useful study aid, particularly at the end of a course when you have completed the text. The glossary is actually a list of words for which you should have learned the meanings. The easiest way to check whether you have learned these new terms is to go through each column of the glossary, covering up the meanings with an index card or folded sheet of paper. Read each word and try to give a definition for it. You might write the definition or just make up the definition mentally. Then uncover the meaning and see if you were correct. Keep track of those you miss and study them later.

Index

At the end of the text you will find an index — an alphabetical listing of topics covered in the book. When you purchase a text, take a quick look at the index to see how it's organized. Some indexes contain both main and subtopics arranged together in a single, alphabetical sequence. Other indexes may have the main topics arranged alphabetically with the subtopics that relate to a particular topic arranged in alphabetical sequence under each. These are indexes with multiple alphabetical sequences. The following are examples of each type.

Single alphabet sequence (topics only)
> safety 361, 768
> schedules 547
> schizophrenia 218–225
> science 21–30[8]

Multiple alphabetical sequences (topics and subtopics)
> Schader-Singer experiment, 252–254, 510
> schedules, reinforcement, 136–140
> schizophrenia, 82, 436–437
> > chemistry of, 426–428
> > and environment, 428–430
> > functional psychosis, 422–430
> > and heredity, 424–426

EXERCISE 11

Directions: *Check each of your textbooks to see what learning/study aids each contains. Use the following chart to evaluate each text. Unless otherwise indicated in the chart, place a check mark in the appropriate box if the particular learning aid is contained in each of the texts.*

Learning/ Study aid	Textbook	Textbook	Textbook	Textbook	Textbook
Title	☐	☐	☐	☐	☐
Subtitle	☐	☐	☐	☐	☐
Author(s)	☐	☐	☐	☐	☐
Copyright	☐	☐	☐	☐	☐
Preface	☐	☐	☐	☐	☐
Table of contents	☐	☐	☐	☐	☐
Chapter titles	☐	☐	☐	☐	☐
Dark print headings	☐	☐	☐	☐	☐
Graphic aids (list type included)	☐	☐	☐	☐	☐
Chapter summary	☐	☐	☐	☐	☐
Chapter questions	☐	☐	☐	☐	☐
Vocabulary list	☐	☐	☐	☐	☐
Appendix (list what is contained)	☐	☐	☐	☐	☐
Glossary	☐	☐	☐	☐	☐
Index (list type)	☐	☐	☐	☐	☐

SUMMARY

While textbooks are important sources of information, they are also valuable learning aids. Textbooks contain many features which are included for the sole purpose of helping you read, study, and learn the content of the text. At the beginning of the text, the title, subtitle, author's name and credentials, and copyright all provide a perspective on the nature and type of text. The preface, introduction, and table of contents provide more specific information about the scope and focus of the text. The preface and introduction describe the text and include specific information about the intended audience as well as the purposes and limitations of the text. The table of contents serves as an outline of the text, showing the relationship and relative importance of topics covered in the text.

Within each chapter there also are particular aids to ensure understanding and retention. The chapter title and chapter introduction both provide an overall perspective on the chapter content. The boldface headings serve as labels or titles which summarize the content of each section. Within each chapter, graphic aids, such as maps, graphs, charts, and pictures, assist the reader by visually emphasizing important concepts and ideas. At the end of each chapter, the chapter summary, chapter questions, and vocabulary list provide an outline of important information and terminology presented in the chapter.

At the end of the text, the index, glossary, list of references, and appendix aid the reader by organizing information presented in the text or by presenting valuable additional information. The index provides for rapid location of specific information; the glossary functions as a mini-dictionary, listing all important terminology introduced in the text. The references recommend sources of further information for many of the topics discussed in the text. The appendix contains additional or supplementary information which is frequently useful to the reader proceeding through the text.

13. Reading-Study Systems

Use this chapter to:

1. *Cut down your study time.*
2. *Find out how to learn as you read.*

Does reading textbook assignments take you a long time? And do you have to spend a lot of time studying and reviewing what you have read in order to remember it? Even after you have spent considerable time and effort reviewing and studying, are you still dissatisfied with the amount of information you remembered or how well you scored on an exam covering the material you studied? If so, you may need to learn a new way to read and study textbook assignments. One very efficient way is to use a reading-study system.

WHAT IS A READING-STUDY SYSTEM?

A reading-study system is a step-by-step procedure for reading a textbook chapter that will help you learn as you read. Using such a system will increase your understanding, help you concentrate, and increase the amount of material you are able to remember. Essentially, it is a way to study and review while you are reading.

LEARNING A READING-STUDY SYSTEM

You already have learned some of the techniques that are used in reading-study systems. All you have to do now is to put these techniques into a step-by-step system. There are many names given to reading-study systems and, although these systems are different in some ways, all have several key techniques in common. In this chapter, an overview of reading-study systems currently in use will be presented, and then the most widely used system — the SQ3R method — will be discussed in detail and compared with other systems.

READING-STUDY SYSTEMS

Over the past fifty years, reading researchers have carefully studied the most efficient ways to study as you read. As a result of their research, numerous reading-study systems have been developed. Some of the most popular and widely used systems and the steps in each are given in the table that follows.

Reading-Study Systems

Name	Steps
SQ3R	Survey-Question-Read-Recite-Review[1]
SQ4R	Survey-Question-Read-Recite-"Rite"-Review[2]
POINT	Purpose-Overview-Interpret-Note-Test[3]
OK4R	Overview-Key Ideas-Read-Recite-Review-Reflect[4]
PQRST	Preview-Question-Read-Summarize-Test[5]
RSVP	Review-Study-Verbalize-Preview[6]
EARTH	Explore-Ask-Read-Tell-Harvest[7]
OARWET	Overview-Ask-Read-Write-Evaluate-Test[8]
PANORAMA	Purpose-Adaptability-Need to Question-Overview-Read-Annotate-Memorize-Assess[9]

How the Reading-Study Systems Are Alike

As can be seen in the table, all these systems call for the use of similar techniques. They all involve several steps prior to reading and several review or checking procedures after reading. The steps that they all have in common are discussed below.

Looking the Material Over First (preview, overview, survey): Although the various systems use different terms for it, all suggest a step in which you become familiar with, or look over, material before reading it. You learned specific techniques for this step in Chapter 7, "Prereading."

Establishing a Purpose (question, ask, purpose): Again using different words to describe it, all reading-study systems include a step in which you decide what you are going to look for or what you are going to find out as you read. In some systems, this step involves forming a question to be answered; in others, it involves predicting what the reading material will contain.

Reading (read, interpret): When using any of the reading-study systems, the reading step is never simply "covering" or looking at information. Instead, it is an active search for information or for answers to questions.

Immediate Recall Check (recite, summarize, verbalize): All the systems suggest some way of testing recall immediately after reading. This is an important step because if you cannot remember information immediately after reading it, there is little chance you will recall it later.

This step also forces you to state ideas in your own words, which should show you how completely you understand what you have read.

Long-term Recall Check (review, test, assess): All reading-study systems contain at least one step in which you check your recall of material already learned, from time to time. Since memory fades very rapidly, it is important to review frequently what you have learned to be sure you retain it. Also, as was more fully explained in Chapter 6, reviewing immediately following reading is a highly effective way of ensuring long-term recall.

READING-STUDY SYSTEMS DO WORK

Many reading-study systems, or their parts, have been tested scientifically. Research has been done to see if students benefit from using a reading-study system. The result of research studies overwhelmingly suggest that students who are taught to use a reading-study system understand and remember what they read much better than students who have not been taught to use such a system.

One research study was designed to test the effectiveness of the SQ3R reading-study system.[*] The reading rate and comprehension level of a group of college students were measured before and after learning and using the SQ3R system. After students learned the SQ3R method, the average reading rate increased by 22 percent; the comprehension level increased by 10 percent.

If you consider for a moment how people learn, it becomes clear why reading-study systems are effective. One major way to learn is through repetition. Consider the way you learned the multiplication tables. Through repeated practice and drills, you learned $2 \times 2 = 4$, $5 \times 6 = 30$, $8 \times 9 = 72$, and so forth. The key was repetition. Reading-study systems provide some of the repetition necessary to ensure learning. If you look again at the table, you will see that each step, in whatever system you consider, provides four or five repetitions of each main idea in the assignment. Compared with the usual once-through approach to reading textbook assignments which provide one chance to learn, reading-study systems provide numerous repetitions and increase the amount learned.

Reading-study systems have many psychological advantages over ordinary reading. First, prereading gives you a mental organization or structure — you know what to expect. Second, you always feel that you are looking for something specific rather than wandering aimlessly through a printed page. Third, when you find the information you're looking for, it is rewarding; you feel you have accomplished something. And, if you can remember the information in the immediate and long-term recall checks, it is even more rewarding.

All of the reading-study systems listed in the table present an organized approach to the reading-learning process, and all are effective in increasing the amount of material you can take in as you read. To help you get started using reading-study systems, one of them — the SQ3R method — will be presented in detail in the next section.

---

[*] Francis P. Robinson, *Effective Study,* Harper & Row, 1941, p. 30.

THE SQ3R READING-STUDY SYSTEM

The SQ3R system has been in use for many years. Since it was developed by Robinson in the 1940s, it has been included in numerous texts on the reading-study process, in many college courses on how to read and study, and in commercial reading-efficiency courses offered to businesspeople and professionals.

The Steps in the SQ3R System

S — Survey: Try to become familiar with the organization and general content of the material you are to read. To do this:

1. Read the title.
2. Read the lead-in or introduction. (If it is extremely long, read just the first paragraph.)
3. Read each boldface heading and the first sentence following each heading.
4. Read titles of any maps, charts, or graphs; read the last paragraph or summary.
5. Read through the end-of-chapter questions.
6. After you have surveyed the material, you should know generally what it is about and how it is organized.

See Part Two, Chapter 7, "Prereading," for a more detailed explanation of how to survey.

Q — Question: Try to form questions that you can answer as you read. The easiest way to do this is to turn each boldface heading into a question. (Part Two, Chapter 8, "Establishing a Purpose for Reading," discusses this step in depth.)

R — Read: Read the materials, section by section. As you read, look for the answer to the question you formed from the heading of that section.

R — Recite: After you finish each section — stop. Check to see if you can answer your question for the section. If you cannot, look back and find the answer. Then check your recall again. Be sure to complete this step after you read each section.

R — Review: When you have finished the whole reading assignment, go back to each heading; recall your question and try to answer it. If you can't recall the answer, be sure to look back and find the answer. Then test yourself again.

DEMONSTRATION OF SQ3R

Two pages from a textbook are reproduced on pages 181 and 182. The pages are taken from the same basic marketing text used throughout this book. Try out the SQ3R method on these sample pages. As you work through the method, follow the specific suggestions for each step given below.

Step 1: S — Survey

To survey the sample, you should read only the shaded material. You will notice that this includes the three headings. The first heading, because it is larger size print, is a heading for an entire section. The paragraph following it is introductory and tells what the section will be about. The second and third headings are actually subheadings and introduce particular parts of the section. By checking these shaded areas, you will have read the parts which are likely to contain the main points on the sample pages. Do you have a general idea of what the pages are about?

Step 2: Q — Question

Next, form questions about what the pages will probably tell you. Use the boldface headings to construct your questions. After you form your own questions, compare them with the questions given here:

1. How is advertising managed?
2. What are the objectives of ads?
3. What media are used in advertising?
4. What strategies are used?

Step 3: R — Read

Now read the pages, part by part, being sure to look for the answers to your questions as you read. Stop at the end of each part and go to step 4. If you are underlining your text, underline the words that help answer your question.

Step 4: R — Recite

Complete this step after you finish reading the material under each heading. Look back at the heading and recall the question you formed. Then without looking, test yourself to see if you can remember the answer to your question. If you cannot remember, look back and reread until you find the answer. Then, look away, and try to answer your question again. Be sure to use your own words rather than attempting to memorize or recall the exact words of the writer.

Step 5: R — Review

After you have finished reading the entire section, review it. Go back to each heading and recall the question you asked. Then, without looking, test yourself to see if you can still recall the answer. Check the information below the heading to see if you were correct. If you do not remember the answer to your question, reread the information until you find the answer. Then test yourself again. Continue in this manner,

Colony's offering was a consumer product, advertising would be a very important part of its promotional mix. And so it faced some big questions: What should its ads say? Should they name competitors? Where should the ads appear? And how much should be spent on running them? [1]

Say the word "advertising" in a crowd and the reactions are likely to be many, strong, and varied. Children may know it as the short but entertaining interruptions in their Saturday morning television shows. Shoppers know that it tells them when and where products are for sale or on sale. Owners of radio or television stations, magazines, or newspapers think of advertising as the source of most of their revenues. Government regulators and consumer advocates consider it the source of — and occasionally the solution to — many of their problems. A firm's financial managers may view advertising as a questionable investment, while the same firm's marketing managers are sure that it is one of the most important weapons in their competitive arsenal.

A list of differing viewpoints could be endless. Yet few would disagree that advertising is an economic force and social institution that affects the lives of everyone.

Advertising is an important element in the promotional programs of most retailers and manufacturers, even though they may spend four or five times as much money for personal selling. Not surprisingly, advertising is more important in certain lines of business, like soap, drugs, and food, than in such others as insurance, construction, and mining. When launching a new brand a manufacturer may budget $30 million, or even more, for its advertising. Advertising revenues in the United States were expected to exceed $60 billion in 1981, about half of the world's total.

Before discussing the management of advertising, the institutions within the industry, and how advertising should be created, we begin with a definition. **Advertising** is *any paid form of nonpersonal, promotional presentation of ideas or products by a sponsor whose identity is known.* Advertising is transmitted in mass communication media, not by individual salespeople. Because the advertiser pays for advertising he controls it.

The Management of Advertising

As we have said before the management of just about anything in business, advertising included, is a process of setting goals, then developing strategies for achieving those goals and controlling the process through continual evaluation. Our first question, then, is: What are advertising's goals?

[1] John Revett, "Wineries Adopting New Market Tact," *Advertising Age,* April 20, 1981, p. 1.

Objectives of Ads

Firms advertise for a purpose, and each advertisement has a specific objective. The purpose of most advertising is to sell a product, a service, a company, even an idea. It is to inform, persuade, and remind; to affect attitudes and behavior. It is to help the seller realize a greater profit than if it had not advertised.

The clearer and more specific the objective is, the more effectively the ad can be created and transmitted, and the more satisfactorily the ad's effects can be evaluated later. Different types of advertisements may have different objectives, as the following list demonstrates.

1. To encourage consumers to put their savings in a savings and loan association by showing how savings grow.
2. To tell retailers that they will increase their earnings on Blue Lustre carpet cleaner because it is to be advertised on CBS.
3. To offer consumers a fifteen-cents-off coupon (attached to the ad) on a purchase of Tang.
4. To maintain or improve buyers' goodwill and loyalty toward the advertising firm. Lilly has run full-page ads the copy of which says only, "For four generations, we've been making medicines as if people's lives depended on them."
5. To help customers (an important "public") use a service more economically. AT&T's headline, "20 ways to save money on your phone bill" is an example.
6. To announce to consumers that new Fruit Helper from Betty Crocker, the General Mills trade character, turns a can of fruit into a terrific dessert.
7. The headline of a department store (Gimbel's) ad in the *New York Times* read "Save 20% to 40% on every Oriental rug in our stock."

Figure 19-1 shows ads that illustrate other specific objectives.

In short, advertising objectives are diverse. It stands to reason that different advertisers will have different goals, but these goals all have a common element: they involve changing the attitudes and behavior of some audience, usually buyers. And just as all advertising goals have a common element, all strategies for achieving the goals have something in common as well. They all deal with the question, how should advertising messages be sent to the target audience?

Media Strategy

Advertising media surround us nearly every moment of our lives. We are all familiar with most popular ones: newspapers, magazines, television, radio, outdoor locations, and transportation vehicles like buses and subways. The trend today is toward creating even more advertising media. Movie theaters now show a few minutes of ads before the feature. Cars are painted and transformed into traveling billboards.

To the marketing manager each advertising medium is a means for conveying a message to the target audience.

Advertising / 419

182

testing your recall of the answer to each of your questions, until you have reviewed both complete pages.

To be most successful in using the SQ3R method, do not skip any of the steps. As you can see, each step depends on one or more of the previous steps. If you leave out any steps, you will limit the method's effectiveness.

EXERCISE 1

Directions: *Turn to the sample textbook chapter included in the Appendix of this text (p. 335). Read the chapter using the SQ3R method. The following SQ3R worksheet will help you get started. Fill in the required information as you go through each step.*

SQ3R Worksheet

S — *Survey:* Read the title of the chapter, the introduction, each boldface heading, and the summary, and look at any pictures or graphs included.

    1. What is the chapter about?

    _____

    2. What major topics are included?

    _____

Q — *Question 1:* Turn the first heading into a question.

    _____

R — *Read:* Read the material following the first heading, looking for the answer to your question.

R — *Recite:* Reread the heading and recall the question you asked. Briefly answer this question in your own words without looking at the section. Check to see if you are correct.

    _____

    _____

Q — *Question 2:* Turn the second heading into a question.

    _____

R — *Read:* Read the material following the second heading, looking for the answer to your question.

R — *Recite:* Briefly answer the question.

_____

_____

Q — *Question 3:* Turn the third heading into a question.

_____

R — *Read:* Read the material following the third heading, looking for the answer to your question.

R — *Recite:* Briefly answer the question.

_____

_____

Continue using the question, read, and recite steps until you have finished each part of the chapter. Then complete the review step.

R — *Review:* Look over the total chapter by rereading the headings. Try to answer the question you made from each heading.

Answer to Question 1:

_____

_____

Answer to Question 2:

_____

_____

Answer to Question 3:

_____

_____

Check to see that your answers are correct.

EXERCISE 2

Directions: *Select a chapter from one of your textbooks. Choose a chapter that has been assigned by one of your instructors or one that you expect will be assigned soon. Read the chapter, using the SQ3R reading-study system. Use the following SQ3R worksheet to get started.*

SQ3R Worksheet

S — *Survey:*   Read the title of the chapter, the introduction, each boldface heading, and the summary, and look at any pictures or graphs included.

1. What is the chapter about?

   _____

2. What major topics are included?

   _____

Q — *Question 1:*   Turn the first heading into a question.

   _____

R — *Read:*   Read the material following the first heading, looking for the answer to your question.

R — *Recite:*   Reread the heading and recall the question you asked. Briefly answer this question in your own words without looking at the section. Check to see if you are correct.

   _____

   _____

Q — *Question 2:*   Turn the second heading into a question.

   _____

R — *Read:*   Read the material following the second heading, looking for the answer to your question.

R — *Recite:*   Briefly answer the question.

   _____

   _____

Q — *Question 3:*   Turn the third heading into a question.

   _____

R — *Read:*   Read the material following the third heading, looking for the answer to your question.

R — *Recite:*   Briefly answer the question.

   _____

   _____

Continue using the question, read, and recite steps until you have finished each part of the chapter. Then complete the review step.

R — *Review:*   Look over the total chapter by rereading the headings. Try to answer the question you made from each heading.

Answer to Question 1:

_____

_____

Answer to Question 2:

_____

_____

Answer to Question 3:

_____

_____

Check to see that your answers are correct.

SUMMARY

In many college courses, textbooks are the primary source of information. Frequently, they serve as the foundation upon which the instructor organizes and builds the course. To learn the information presented in a text, it is necessary to do more than simply read the material as it is assigned. The information must be reviewed and studied, then transferred to your permanent, or long-term, memory. This chapter presented several systems for learning and reviewing as you read.

The most common reading-study system is SQ3R; it provides a step-by-step procedure to follow in reading a textbook chapter. The steps are:

Survey: Quickly become familiar with the overall content and organization of the material before beginning to read.
Question: Use the boldface headings to develop specific questions which you will attempt to answer as you read.
Read: Read in an active, searching manner, looking for answers to the questions you developed.
Recite: Test yourself regularly by stopping and trying to recall the content of the section that you just finished reading. Check to see if you can answer the questions you developed in the

Question step. Go back and reread for information you cannot recall.

Review: When finished reading the entire chapter, test yourself again by trying to recall the content of each section that you read by answering the question you developed for each section.

14. Textbook Underlining and Marking

Use this chapter to:

Learn how to make study and review easier by underlining and marking textbooks as you read.

As you have already discovered, most college courses have lengthy and time-consuming reading assignments. Just completing reading assignments is a big job. Have you begun to wonder how you will ever go back over all those textbook chapters when it is time for an exam?

THE PROBLEM OF TEXTBOOK REVIEW

Let's suppose that it takes you at least four hours to read carefully a forty-page chapter for one of your courses. Assume that your text has ten chapters of approximately forty pages each. It would take a total of 40 hours, then, to read completely through the text once. Suppose that your instructor is giving a final exam which will cover the entire text. If the only thing you did to prepare for the final was to reread the whole text, it would take close to another 40 hours to study for the exam; but one additional reading is no guarantee that you'll pass the exam anyway.

There is a technique you could have used to review and study the chapters of your text adequately at exam time. You could have underlined and marked important ideas and facts as you were first reading the chapters. Then, when you were ready to review, you would have had to read and study only what you marked. If you had marked or underlined 15 to 20 percent of the chapter material, you would have cut down your rereading time by 80 to 85 percent, or 32 hours! Of course, to prepare effectively for the exam, it would have been necessary to review in other ways besides rereading, but you would have had time left in which to use these other ways.

HOW TO UNDERLINE TEXTBOOKS

To learn how to underline textbooks effectively, start with the following guidelines:

1. Read first; then underline. As you are beginning to develop skill in underlining, it is better, at first, to read a paragraph or section first, and then *go back* and underline what is important to remember and

review. Later, when you've had more practice underlining, you may be able to underline while you read.

2. Read the boldface headings. Headings are labels, or overall topics, for what is contained in that section. Use the headings to form some questions which you expect to be answered in the section.

3. After you have read the section, go back and underline the parts which answer your questions. These will be parts of sentences that express the main ideas, or most important thoughts, in the section. In reading and underlining the following section, you could form a question like the one suggested and then underline as shown:

Question to Ask: How can office sound be controlled?

OFFICE SOUND CONTROL

This element of the office environment has become increasingly important because of the greater mechanization of office work. With machinery has come much more noise and also the fatiguing side effects resulting from too much sound. <u>Office noise</u> should either be <u>absorbed or isolated</u> (<u>unless,</u> of course, it <u>can be eliminated by installing quieter equipment</u>). Sound can be absorbed by proper materials used in ceilings, side walls, and floor coverings; it can be isolated by a complete physical separation of the noisy area from the rest of the office or by installation of specially designed hoods over noisy equipment. The use of room dividers — such as partitions, file cabinets, or bookcases — will also help by breaking up the sound patterns.

In some cases, <u>office noise</u> may be successfully <u>counteracted by playing music</u> over a public address system. Surprisingly, music that is loud enough to be audible in a noisy office is just as soothing as soft music played in a quiet office. The sole restriction on this office morale booster applies to the kind of music used; it should not be too rhythmical or too recently popular. Light classical selections or hit tunes of a few years back are ideal. Management should avoid selections which might promote informal glee-clubbing or solos on company time.

—Rausch, *Principles of Office Administration,* p. 86

4. As you identify and underline main ideas, look for important facts that explain or support the main idea and underline them too.

5. When underlining main ideas and details, do not underline complete sentences. Underline only enough so that you can see what is important and so that your underlining makes sense when you reread. Notice how only key words and phrases are underlined in the following:

A <u>brand name</u> in itself can be <u>good or bad</u>; it can help or hinder sales. There are several <u>essential factors</u> which must be considered in <u>choosing</u> a <u>brand name.</u> First, a good brand name should be <u>easy to pronounce</u> and remember. In general, people do not like to be embarrassed by attempting to pronounce a word which they find difficult to say correctly. Second, a good brand name should be <u>short.</u> Short words are easy to remember and have many sales-promotion advantages. For example, *it* can be printed in larger letters in a given amount of space. Third, a brand name should give the <u>right connotation to the buyer</u>; that is, it should form the right images in his mind.

    —Buskirk, *Principles of Marketing*, p. 228

ASPECTS OF EFFECTIVE UNDERLINING

For your underlining to be effective and useful to you as you study and review, it *must* follow four specific guidelines: (1) the right amount of information must be underlined; (2) the underlining must be regular and consistent; (3) it must be accurate; and (4) it must clearly reflect the content of the passage. Suggestions for and examples of each of these guidelines are given below.

Underlining the Right Amount

Students frequently make the mistake of underlining either too much or too little. If you underline too much, it will take you too long to reread when studying. If you underline too little, you won't be able to get any meaning from your underlining as you review it. To get an idea of each mistake, study the passages below.

Too Much Underlining:
    Because a <u>brand name is property</u>, <u>firms</u> must <u>take positive action</u> to <u>protect</u> it and <u>enhance</u> its <u>value</u>. The first <u>step</u> is to <u>obtain legal ownership</u> and <u>exclusive right</u> to use the <u>brand name</u> on a <u>product</u>. The <u>Lanham Act of 1947</u> allows a <u>manufacturer to protect his brand name by recording it in a principal register</u>. This registration does provide the firm with <u>certain legal advantages</u>. For example, <u>registration stipulates</u> that <u>after the name</u> is used <u>for five years</u>, the <u>firm has the incontestable right</u> to use it <u>permanently</u>.[1]

Too Little Underlining:
    Because a <u>brand name</u> is <u>property</u>, firms must take positive action to protect it and enhance its value. The first step is to obtain <u>legal ownership</u> and exclusive right to use the brand name on a product. The <u>Lanham Act</u> of 1947 allows a manufacturer to protect his brand name by recording it in a principal register. This <u>registration</u> does provide the firm with certain legal advantages. For example, registration stipulates that after the name is used for five years, the firm has the <u>incontestable right</u> to use it permanently.

Effective Underlining:
    Because a <u>brand name is property</u>, firms must take positive action to <u>protect it</u> and <u>enhance its value</u>. The first step is to <u>obtain legal ownership</u> and exclusive right to use the brand name on a product. The <u>Lanham Act of 1947</u> allows a

manufacturer to <u>protect his brand name</u> by <u>recording it</u> in a <u>principal register</u>. This registration does provide the firm with certain <u>legal advantages</u>. For example, registration stipulates that after the <u>name is used</u> for <u>five years</u>, the firm has the incontestable <u>right to use it permanently</u>.

Almost all of the first passage is underlined. To underline nearly all of a passage is as ineffective as not underlining at all because it does not sort out or distinguish important from unimportant information. In the second passage, only the main point of the paragraph is underlined, but very sketchily — not enough detail is included. The underlining in the third passage is effective; it identifies the main idea of the paragraph and includes sufficient details to make the main idea clear and understandable.

As a general rule of thumb, try to underline no more than one-quarter to one-third of each page. This figure will vary, of course, depending on the type of material you are reading. Here is another example of effective underlining. Notice that approximately one-third of each paragraph is underlined.

THE FLIGHT TO SUBURBIA

The problems of the inner city are not the only problems plaguing our large cities. <u>Cities</u> are constantly <u>short of the funds necessary to provide</u> those <u>basic services that make a city livable</u>: maintenance of streets, transportation systems, police, fire, sanitation, and schools. Again, a vicious circle is operative. Because the <u>greatest source of funds is tax revenue</u>, our <u>cities</u> have <u>had to increase taxes</u> and enact new taxes to continue to serve increasing numbers of residents. <u>High taxes</u>, in turn, have spurred many <u>people to flee to the outskirts of cities</u>, outside city jurisdiction. For a while, suburbanites were able to avoid paying city taxes while continuing to avail themselves of many city services. The cities have been <u>doubly burdened</u> as a result: they have had to <u>provide as many services</u> as before, but now they have a much <u>smaller</u> and <u>poorer population</u> from whom <u>to collect taxes</u>.

As the suburbs grew, their <u>image as "bedroom communities"</u> dependent on the central city <u>rapidly changed</u>. Industry and commerce followed the population into the suburbs, so that now a major portion of new jobs, industrial plants, retail outlets, and entertainment facilities are located in suburbs. <u>Suburbs have become self-contained, self-sufficient communities</u>, virtually independent of the cities around which they grew up. The result is that the <u>suburbs now are faced</u> with <u>many of the same problems besetting the cities</u>. In fact, established <u>suburbs</u> are <u>suffering</u> the <u>same fate as the big cities</u>. Just as the suburbs prevented the growth of cities during the fifties and sixties, so now, in the seventies, the <u>growth of many suburbs is blocked by adjoining, newer surburbs</u>.

—Perry and Perry, *Face to Face*, pp. 251–252

EXERCISE 1

Directions: *Look at the set of passages below. Identify the passage which has too much underlining, the passage with too little underlining, and the passage with the most effective underlining. Write the answer on the line following each passage.*

1.   One of the unique characteristics of the American marketing scene is the <u>widespread use</u> of <u>installment</u> and <u>open-book credit</u>. This is a relatively <u>recent development</u> which is centered largely in this country. Although it got its start in the 1930s, it blossomed into full <u>maturity in the post-World War II years</u>. Though installment credit <u>started</u> in the fields of <u>automobiles</u> and <u>appliances</u> where the large initial purchase price almost excluded the average consumer if forced to pay cash, it has <u>now spread to</u> the point where people are buying just <u>about everything</u> on installment plans. The <u>current rage</u> is for the <u>revolving charge accounts</u> whereby <u>nominally priced merchandise</u> can be purchased on credit.[2]

_____

2.   One of the <u>unique characteristics</u> of the American marketing scene is the widespread use of installment and <u>open-book credit</u>. This is a relatively <u>recent development</u> which is centered largely in this country. Although it got its start in the 1930s, it blossomed into full maturity in the post-World War II years. Though installment credit started in the fields of <u>automobiles</u> and <u>appliances</u> where the large initial purchase price almost excluded the average consumer if forced <u>to pay cash</u>, it has now spread to the point where people are buying just about everything on installment plans. The current rage is for the <u>revolving charge accounts</u> whereby nominally priced merchandise can be purchased on credit.

_____

3.   One of the <u>unique characteristics</u> of the American <u>marketing scene</u> is the <u>widespread</u> use of <u>installment</u> and <u>open-book credit</u>. This is a relatively <u>recent development</u> which is <u>centered largely</u> in this <u>country</u>. Although it got its <u>start in the 1930s</u>, it blossomed into <u>full maturity in the post-World War II years</u>. Though installment <u>credit started</u> in the fields of automobiles and <u>appliances</u> where the <u>large initial purchase price almost excluded</u> the average consumer if forced to <u>pay cash</u>, it has now spread to the <u>point where</u> people are buying <u>just</u> about <u>everything on</u> <u>installment plans</u>. The <u>current rage</u> is for the <u>revolving charge accounts</u> whereby <u>nominally priced merchandise</u> can be <u>purchased on credit</u>.

_____

Develop a Regular and Consistent System of Underlining

As you develop your textbook underlining skills, you should focus on this second guideline: develop a system for what type of information you will underline and how you will mark it. First, decide what type of information you want to mark. Before marking anything, decide whether you will mark only main ideas or whether you will mark main ideas and details. You should also decide whether you will underline or mark definitions of new terminology and, if so, how you will distinguish them from other information marked in the paragraph. Second, it is important to use consistently whatever system and type of underlining you decide upon so that you will know what your underlining means when you review it. If you sometimes mark details and main ideas and other times underline only main ideas, you will find that, at review time, you are unsure of what passages are marked in what way, and you will be forced to reread a great deal of material.

You may decide to develop a system for separating main ideas from details, major points from supporting information. When you review underlining done this way, you will immediately know what is *the most important point* of a paragraph or section, and you will not get bogged down in the details, unless you need to. One such system uses double underlining for main points and single underlining for details. Another system might be to enclose the main points in brackets and use single underlining for the supporting details. A third choice may be to underline both main ideas and details with a single line but to place a check mark (√) or asterisk (*) in the margin next to the main idea.

Each of the following paragraphs has been underlined using one of the suggested systems. You will notice that the paragraphs vary in the type of information marked in each.

Version 1:

Another climatic characteristic of deserts is the great range of temperature from day to night. This difference between day temperatures and night temperatures is known as the daily, or diurnal, range. Deserts hold the world's record for the highest daily range of temperature. During the day, the skies may be sunny and clear. The air may be extremely hot. The highest temperatures on the earth's surface have been recorded in low-latitude deserts. Azizia, located south of Tripoli in the Sahara, once experienced a temperature of 136.4 degrees Fahrenheit. Death Valley in our own country has recorded a temperature almost as high.[3]

Version 2:

Another [climatic characteristic] of [deserts] is the [great] [range of temperature] from [day to night]. This difference between day temperatures and night temperatures is known as the daily, or diurnal, range. Deserts hold the world's record for the highest daily range of temperature. During the day, the skies may be sunny and clear. The air may be extremely hot. The highest temperatures on the earth's surface have been recorded in low-latitude deserts. Azizia, located south of Tripoli in the Sahara, once

experienced a temperature of 136.4 degrees Fahrenheit.
Death Valley in our own country has recorded a temperature
almost as high.

*
*
Version 3:

 Another <u>climatic characteristic</u> of deserts is the <u>great
range of temperature</u> from <u>day to night</u>. <u>This difference</u>
between day temperatures and night temperatures is <u>known
as the daily</u>, or <u>diurnal, range</u>. <u>Deserts hold</u> the <u>world's record</u>
for the <u>highest daily range of temperature</u>. During the day,
the skies may be sunny and clear. The air may be extremely
hot. The highest temperatures on the earth's surface have
been recorded in low-latitude deserts. Azizia, located south of
Tripoli in the Sahara, once experienced a temperature of
136.4 degrees Fahrenheit. Death Valley in our own country
has recorded a temperature almost as high.

EXERCISE 2

Directions: *Read each paragraph or passage and then underline
the* main idea *and* important details *in each. You may want to try
out various systems of underlining as you work through this
exercise.*

1.   Australia was first used as a penal colony. Portuguese explorers
sighted Australia in the sixteenth century. After looking briefly at
the north coast, however, they decided that the new land had no
possibilities for settlement. Soon after, the Dutch also sighted
Australia but discarded it in favor of the East Indies.

 It was Captain James Cook who convinced the British that
Australia held possibilities for development. In 1770, Captain Cook
explored the previously unknown east coast of Australia. He put in
at Botany Bay, near present-day Sydney, and later brought back to
England favorable reports of what he had seen. The period
coincided with the beginning of the Industrial Revolution, which
left many Englishmen uprooted from their usual way of life and
forced them deeply in debt. At that time people were often placed
in prison for failing to pay their debts, and England's jails were
overcrowded. Remembering the report of Captain Cook, the
British in 1778 sent a shipload of prisoners to serve their sentences
in Australia. For the next 80 years, Australia continued to receive
the English prisoners.

 –Kohn and Drummond, *The World Today,* pp. 518–519

2.   The great mountains of the world have always presented a special
challenge to the explorer. They have faced him with a set of
difficulties that he has found nowhere else.

 The greatest of these difficulties is produced by altitude itself,
by the fact that as one goes higher and higher above sea level
reduced air pressure makes it more difficult to breathe. Men who
first climbed the slopes of the world's mountains were not fully

aware of this danger. All they knew was that as they went higher they found it increasingly difficult to breathe, so it was not unnatural to suppose that the snow-covered summits of the world could not support human life.

The snow itself presented other problems, for its consistency varied from one season to the next. Men did not know whether they would find it hard and frozen, or so soft that they would sink into it up to their thighs. Then there were the glaciers — huge rivers of ice — many miles long and hundreds of yards across, which in some places offered the easiest approaches into the mountain recesses. But the glaciers were split by huge fissures, called crevasses, hundreds of feet deep and in which a man could be lost forever.

—Clark, *Explorers of the World*, p. 218

3. Crowd behavior is learned. Crowd emotionality can be interpreted in terms of heightened suggestibility, that is, the tendency of an individual in a crowd to respond uncritically to the stimuli provided by the other members. The individual learns early to make almost automatic responses to the wishes of others, particularly those in authority and those he greatly respects. From infancy on, he is so dependent upon the judgment of others for direction in his own affairs that he comes to lean heavily on the opinions of others. Moreover, he learns to value highly the esteem in which other persons hold him, and consequently he courts their favor by confirming to their ways and wishes. For these reasons, among others, when he finds himself in a congenial crowd of persons, all of whom are excited, it is natural that he, too, should become excited.

The effect of suggestion is to produce a partial dissociation of consciousness. When we are critical about a matter, we give it close attention, and our whole interest is centered upon it. But when a suggestion is made by someone who we esteem, our attention is divided between the issue at hand and the person who made the suggestion. The more awesome the source of the suggestion, the greater the degree of dissociation and the greater the amount of automatic behavior.

—Ogburn and Nimkoff, *Sociology,* p. 154

4. In terms of employment and income Switzerland is primarily an industrial country, despite the fame of its picturesque resorts and Alpine dairy farms. Swiss industry is based on the country's two major industrial resources — hydroelectric power and the skill of Swiss workers. Most raw materials as well as supplemental fuels are imported. The country's industries are specialized along lines that minimize Switzerland's lack of bulky raw materials, while making full use of its power resources and traditions of workmanship that date back to handicraft days before the industrial revolution. The major products are (1) metal goods, including·machinery (much of it designed to order) and, of course, the famous Swiss watches, (2) chemicals, especially pharmaceuticals, and (3) textiles, generally of very high quality and with a large component of synthetic yarns and fabrics, plus

cotton, wool, and silk. In recent years chemicals and aluminum products have been gaining in importance.

—Wheeler et al., *Regional Geography of the World*, pp. 204–205

5.   An inference, as we shall use the term, is a statement about the unknown made on the basis of the known. We may infer from the material and cut of a woman's clothes her wealth or social position; we may infer from the character of the ruins the origin of the fire that destroyed the building; we may infer from a man's calloused hands the nature of his occupation; we may infer from a senator's vote on an armaments bill his attitude toward Russia; we may infer from the structure of the land the path of a prehistoric glacier; we may infer from a halo on an unexposed photographic plate that it has been in the vicinity of radioactive materials; we may infer from the sound of an engine the condition of its connecting rods. Inferences may be carelessly or carefully made. They may be made on the basis of a broad background of previous experience with the subject matter, or no experience at all. For example, the inferences a good mechanic can make about the internal condition of a motor by listening to it are often startlingly accurate, while the inferences made by an amateur (if he tries to make any) may be entirely wrong. But the common characteristic of inferences is that they are statements about matters which are not directly known, statements made on the basis of what has been observed.

—Hayakawa, *Language in Thought and Action*, p. 41

Underline Accurately

A third guideline for marking textbooks is to be sure that the information that you underline accurately conveys the thought of a paragraph or passage. In a rush, students often overlook the second half of the main idea expressed in a paragraph, miss a crucial qualifying statement, or mistake an example or contrasting idea for the main idea. Read the paragraph in the example below and evaluate the accuracy of the underlining.

Example:

It has long been established that the American legal court system is an open and fair system. Those suspected to be guilty of a criminal offense are given a jury trial in which a group of impartially selected citizens are asked to determine, based upon evidence presented, the guilt or innocence of the person on trial. In actuality, however, this system of jury trial is fair to everyone except the jurors involved. Citizens are expected and, in many instances, required to sit on a jury. They have little or no choice as to the time, place, or any other circumstances surrounding their participation. Additionally, they are expected to leave their job and accept jury duty pay for each day spent in court in place of their regular on-the-job salary. The jury must remain on duty until the case is decided.

In the paragraph above, the underlining indicates that the main idea of the paragraph is that the legal system which operates in American courts is open and fair. The paragraph starts out by saying that the legal system has long been established as fair but then goes on to say (in the third sentence) that the system is actually unfair to one particular group — the jury. In this case, the student who did the underlining missed the real main statement of the paragraph by mistaking the introductory contrasting statement for the main idea.

Make Your Underlining Understandable for Review

As you underline, keep this fourth guideline in mind: be certain that your underlining clearly reflects the content of the passage so that you will be able to reread and review it easily. Try to underline enough information in each passage so that it expresses an idea. Try to string phrases together so that the passage reads smoothly when you review it.

Read these two versions of underlining of the same passage. Which underlining is easier to reread?

Version 1:

After the best application of communication principles has been determined and the correct facilities are selected to be installed, <u>workers must be trained</u> in the <u>proper use</u> of <u>communication equipment</u> or <u>services</u>. Of course the <u>actual techniques</u> of use <u>will vary substantially, depending upon</u> the <u>equipment involved</u>; however, it is possible to discern <u>basic patterns</u> of good communication practice which apply <u>universally</u> to all systems or services.[4]

Version 2:

After the best application of communication principles has been determined and the correct facilities are selected to be installed, <u>workers</u> must be <u>trained</u> in the proper use of <u>communication equipment</u> or <u>services</u>. Of course the <u>actual techniques</u> of use will vary <u>substantially</u>, depending upon the <u>equipment involved</u>; however, it is possible to discern <u>basic patterns</u> of good communication practice which apply universally to all systems or services.

A good way to check to see if your underlining is understandable for review is to reread only your underlining. If parts are unclear right after you read it, you can be sure it will be more confusing when you reread it a week or a month later. Be sure to fix ineffectual underlining in one paragraph before you continue with the next paragraph. You may find it useful, at first, to use a pencil for underlining. Then, when the underlining in a passage needs revising, you can accomplish this easily by erasing.

TESTING YOUR UNDERLINING

As you are learning underlining techniques, it is important to check to be certain that your underlining is effective and will be usable for review purposes. To test the effectiveness of your underlining, take any passage that you have underlined in exercise 2 and reread only the underlining. Then ask yourself the following questions:

1. Have I underlined the right amount or do I have too much or too little information underlined?
2. Have I used a regular and consistent system for underlining?
3. Does my underlining accurately reflect the meaning of the passage?
4. As I reread my underlining, is it easy to follow the train of thought or does the passage seem like a list of unconnected words?

EXERCISE 3

Directions: *Turn to the sample chapter which is included in the Appendix of this text (p. 335). You may already have read this sample chapter as part of an exercise in a previous chapter. Now read (or reread) the sample chapter and underline the main ideas and important details. When you have finished, test your underlining. Use the four questions for testing your underlining given above. Make any changes that will make your underlining more consistent, accurate, or understandable.*

EXERCISE 4

Directions: *Select a three-to-four-page selection from one of your textbooks. Read the selection and underline the main idea, the important details, and key terminology that is introduced. When you have finished, test your underlining, again using the four questions, and make any changes that will improve your underlining.*

MARKING A TEXTBOOK

As you were underlining paragraphs and passages in the earlier part of this chapter, you may have realized that underlining alone is not sufficient, in many cases, to separate main ideas from details and both of these from new terminology. You may have seen that underlining does not easily show the relative importance of ideas or indicate the relationship of facts and ideas. Therefore, it is often necessary to mark, as well as underline, selections that you are reading. Marking may involve such things as the following:

1. Writing summary words or phrases in the margin
2. Circling words for which you don't know the meaning
3. Marking definitions
4. Numbering lists of ideas, causes, reasons, and so forth
5. Placing asterisks next to important passages
6. Putting question marks next to confusing passages
7. Marking notes to yourself like "check w/ instructor," "reread," or "good test item"
8. Drawing arrows to show relationships
9. Drawing summary charts or diagrams

Two versions of the same paragraph are presented below. The first version contains only underlining, while in the second, both underlining and marking are used. Which version more easily conveys the meaning of the passage?

Version 1:

Diplomacy is steeped in formality and etiquette, much of which dates back to antiquity. This is seen in the classification of diplomats agreed upon by the Congress of Vienna in 1816 and supplemented from time to time. At present there are five classes: the first includes ambassadors, legates (envoys of the Pope chosen from the cardinals for special assignments), and nuncios (envoys of the Pope assigned to permanent posts and chosen from outside the rank of cardinals); the second class consists of envoys extraordinary, ministers plenipotentiary, and apostolic internuncios (envoys of the Pope next in rank to nuncios); in the third class are ministers resident; in the fourth, chargés d'affaires; and in the fifth, a group known as diplomatic agents. Envoys rank within each class according to the date of arrival at their post. The one in the highest rank with the most seniority at a given post is known as the doyen, or dean, of the diplomatic corps. Envoys of the various classes perform practically the same functions and enjoy the same rights and privileges; the chief difference is a matter of prestige.[5]

—Ferguson and McHenry, *Elements of American Government*

Version 2:

Diplomacy is steeped in formality and etiquette, much of which dates back to antiquity. This is seen in the classification of diplomats agreed upon by the Congress of Vienna in 1816 and supplemented from time to time. At present there are five classes: the first includes ambassadors, ① legates (envoys of the Pope chosen from the cardinals for special assignments), and nuncios (envoys of the Pope assigned to permanent posts and chosen from outside the rank of cardinals); the second class consists of envoys ② extraordinary, ministers plenipotentiary, and apostolic internuncios (envoys of the Pope next in rank to nuncios); in ③ the third class are ministers resident; in the fourth, chargés ④ d'affaires; and in the fifth, a group known as diplomatic ⑤ agents. Envoys rank within each class according to the date of arrival at their post. The one in the highest rank with the most seniority at a given post is known as the doyen, or dean, of the diplomatic corps. Envoys of various classes perform practically the same functions and enjoy the same rights and privileges; the chief difference is a matter of prestige.

As you can see, in version 2 the five classes of diplomats are easy to identify. Marking the numbers of the classes makes them immediately noticeable and distinguishes them from the remainder of the passage.

Using Summary Words

Writing summary words or phrases in the margin is one of the most valuable types of textbook marking. It involves pulling together ideas and summarizing them in your own words. This summarizing process forces you to think and evaluate as you read and makes remembering easier. Writing summary phrases is also a good test of your understanding. If you cannot state the main idea of a section in your own words, you probably do not understand it clearly. This realization can serve as an early warning signal that you may not be able to handle a test question on that section.

To illustrate effective marking of summary phrases, the following sample passage has been included. First, read through the passage. Then look at the marginal summary clues.

Sample Passage Marked with Summary Clues:

types of money
  Let us list the main kinds of money in daily use: small coins, paper currency, and check-account bank deposit money.

1. coins
  First, there are coins we use for small change: copper pennies, nickel five-cent pieces, and silver dimes, quarters, half dollars and (in the Far West) dollars. These constitute our so-called "fractional currency." Children think them important, but in total they do not add up to very much — in fact, to less than one-thirteenth of the community's cash. Because the metal in all these coins is worth far less than their face value, they are termed "token money." These coins are valued far beyond their metallic worth only because they can be readily converted into other money — 20 nickels to the dollar, and so forth.

2. paper currency
  Far more important is the second kind of money: paper currency. Most of us know little more about a one-dollar or five-dollar bill than that each is inscribed with the picture of some American statesman, that each contains the signature of one or another government official, and — most important of all — that each bears a number showing its face value.

  There is also a third category of what economists call money. This is so-called "demand deposits" — made up of bank deposits subject to checking on demand.

3. bank deposits - checking
  If I have $1,000 in my checking account at the Cambridge Trust Company, that deposit can be regarded as money. Why? Because I can pay for purchases with checks drawn on it. The deposit is like any other medium of exchange, and, being payable on demand, it serves as a "standard value," or "unit of account," in the same sense as $1,000 worth of silver quarters; i.e., both the deposit and the quarters are convertible into standard money or cash at fixed terms, dollar for dollar and penny for penny.
  –Samuelson, *Economics,* pp. 272–273, 274

Summary clues are most effectively used in passages which contain long and complicated ideas. In these cases it is simpler to write a summary phrase in the margin than to underline a long or complicated statement of the main idea and supporting details.

To write a summary clue, try to think of a word or phrase which accurately states in brief form a particular idea presented in the passage. Summary words should "trigger" your memory of the content of the passage.

EXERCISE 5

Directions: *Read each of the following textbook selections. Then, mark, as well as underline, important information contained in the passage.*

1. More than four-fifths of the states derive revenues from property taxes, although the proceeds account for only a small proportion of total receipts. States prefer, as a general rule, to leave this revenue source to local governments.

   For tax purposes, property falls into three categories. Real property consists chiefly of land and buildings. Tangible property includes such items as furniture, livestock, machinery, autos, jewelry, and inventory. Intangibles include such assets as bank deposits, cash value of life insurance policies, mortgages, stocks, and bonds. Practices vary widely in those states which tax property. Some tax all categories, others tax but one or two.
   –Ferguson and McHenry, *The American System of Government,* p. 780

2. Property used here as a synonym for ownership is the right to use and dispose of an animal or thing for a legitimate end without the interference of any other person. In the category of property insurance is included every form that has for its purpose the protection of persons against loss arising from the ownership or use of property, as above defined.

   There are two general classifications of property insurance. The first undertakes to indemnify the insured in the event of loss growing out of damages to, or destruction of, his own property. The second form undertakes to pay damages for which the insured is legally liable, the consequence of negligent acts that result in injuries to third parties. The first of these is known as "direct loss insurance," the second form is known as "liability insurance."
   –Magee and Bickelhaupt, *General Insurance,* pp. 33–34

3. The middle-class family has more children than upper-class but less than lower-class families. In the middle-class family the children "belong" to both parents, in contrast to the upper class where they belong to the kinship and are important as links in the historical family. The family unit for the child consists of his parents, himself, and his brothers and sisters. Next in importance are the grandparents, especially if they live in the same community and are seen often or if the children are left in the care of the grandparents when their parents go to some social affair or are on a vacation. The tie to uncles, aunts, and cousins is less marked, and these relatives may be almost unknown if they live at a distance and are not visited. It is not uncommon for the middle-class child not to know the names of even first cousins if personal contacts have been allowed to lapse. This narrowing of the family circle to parents and children — and perhaps grandparents — restricts emotional ties to a small group and consequently tends to intensify them. The fact that children are relatively few in number and that the parents and especially the mother assumes personal care of the children also adds to the intensity. Children often are taken by the parents on all vacation trips, and it is not unusual for

the child never to have spent a night separated from the parents
from infancy to the time of college entrance or marriage.
–Cavan, *The American Family*, pp. 126–127

USING SYMBOLS

While each person marks a text somewhat differently, it is important that you develop a consistent set of abbreviations and symbols that
you can write rapidly and reread later without confusion. You might
want to start to use the following list of symbols and develop your own
variations as you become more skilled in textbook marking.

Symbol	Meaning
ex	example
def	definition
✳	important passage
T	good test question
??	confusing
C	check later
RR	reread later
sum	summary statement

IS UNDERLINING AN EFFECTIVE MEANS OF PREPARATION FOR STUDY?

In a study conducted by Willmore,* a group of college students were
each taught four study techniques: underlining, outlining, SQ3R, and
reading. The students then applied each of the four techniques to four
different chapters in a college text. Tests were given on each chapter.
Students scored significantly higher on the test when they used underlining as a study technique than when using any of the other three
methods.

WHY UNDERLINING AND MARKING WORK

Underlining and marking are effective ways to prepare for study for
several very important reasons. First, the process of underlining forces
you to sift through what you have read to identify important information.
This sifting or sorting helps you keep your mind on what you are doing.
Second, underlining and marking keep you physically active while you
are reading. The physical activity helps to direct or focus your concentration on what you are reading. Third, when you are underlining you are
forced to weigh and evaluate what you read. In other words, you must
think about and react to what you are reading in order to decide whether

* D. J. Willmore, "A Comparison of Four Methods of Studying a College Textbook."
Unpublished doctoral dissertation, University of Minnesota, 1966.

to underline it. Fourth, underlining helps you to see the organization of facts and ideas as well as their connections and relationships to one another because you are forced to look for these things in order to mark and underline effectively. Finally, underlining demonstrates to you whether you have understood a passage you have just read. If you have difficulty underlining, or your underlining is not helpful or meaningful after you have finished reading, you will know that you did not understand the passage.

SUMMARY

Reading textbook chapters is a long and time-consuming process. As you read, you encounter a considerable amount of information that you know you will need to study and review for your next exam or quiz. To be able to locate this information quickly when you study, it is necessary to underline and mark important information as you read. Without a system of underlining and marking, it would be necessary to reread an entire chapter in order to review it effectively. This chapter offers step-by-step instructions for underlining and marking textbooks.

After offering some general suggestions to follow in underlining, four specific guidelines for effective underlining are given. These include: (1) underline the right amount; (2) develop a regular and consistent system of underlining; (3) underline accurately; and (4) make your underlining understandable for review. A system for marking as well as underlining is discussed. Marking involves the use of marginal notes, summary words, and symbols that can make a passage easier to review.

Part Five
Classroom
Performance Skills

The average college student spends between 15 and 18 hours in class each week. Attending class, then, represents a significant portion of a student's weekly schedule. Since such a large amount of time is spent in class each week, it is important to use this time effectively. While attending class, you can actually be doing things to help you learn, make studying easier, and earn better grades. Among the most important classroom skills are notetaking, test taking, and participating in class discussions.

Taking notes on class lectures is extremely valuable. Class lecture notes are an important source of information and are excellent study aids. Chapter 15 ("Notetaking Techniques") will show you how to take good notes and suggest how you can use them effectively to study.

Participation in classroom discussions is expected by many college instructors. While you may be reluctant at first to become involved, you will find taking part in discussions an excellent way of keeping yourself interested, learning while in class, and showing the instructor that you are interested and involved. Chapter 16 ("Participating in Class Discussions") will present information on how to prepare for discussions, how to get involved, and how to study for or learn from discussion classes.

Besides the time spent in class each week, students are expected to spend time outside class. One important out-of-class activity is preparation for exams. And, of course, it is how thoroughly you prepared and studied which largely determines how well you perform on quizzes and exams. Chapter 17 ("Studying for and Taking Exams") will discuss how to study for exams and will also present some tips on how to do well on an exam while you are taking it.

Another activity that requires considerable time and effort outside class is writing papers. Some instructors require brief essays, reports, or reaction papers, while others require a research paper. Chapter 18 ("Preparing Written Assignments and Research Papers") offers specific suggestions for writing all types of papers and outlines a step-by-step procedure for researching and writing research papers.

15. Notetaking Techniques

Use this chapter to:

1.   Find out what information to write down and what to skip during a lecture.

2.   Learn how to take notes so that they are easy to study later.

WHY NOTETAKING IS IMPORTANT

As you are sitting in a class in which the instructor lectures, it is easy just to sit back and listen, especially if the instructor and/or the subject are interesting and exciting. At the time information is presented, it may seem that you will always be able to remember it. Unfortunately, memory fades quickly, and a lecture that is vivid in your memory today will be only vaguely familiar several weeks later. Since instructors do expect you to remember and apply facts and ideas presented in each lecture throughout the semester, it is necessary to take notes as lectures are given. A set of good lecture notes is a valuable study aid and will make it easier to get good grades in a course.

PREPARING FOR A LECTURE CLASS

Before you attend a lecture class, it is important to become familiar with the main topic of the lecture and to be aware of some of the important subtopics and related areas.

You will find understanding the lecture simpler and notetaking easier if you have some idea of what the lecture is about. If your instructor assigns a textbook chapter which is related to the lecture, try to read the assignment before attending. If you are unable to read the entire chapter before class, at least preread the chapter to become generally familiar with the topics it covers. If no reading assignment is given in advance, check your course outline to determine the topic of the lecture. Then preread the sections of your text which pertain to the topic.

HOW TO TAKE LECTURE NOTES

A good set of lecture notes must accomplish three things. First, and most important, your notes must serve as a record or summary of the main points of the lecture. Second, they must include enough details and examples so that you can recall the information completely several weeks later. Finally, your notes must, in some way, show the relative importance of ideas presented and reflect the organization of the lecture.

Recording Main Ideas

The main ideas of a lecture are the points on which your instructor emphasizes and elaborates. They are the major ideas which the details, explanations, examples, and general discussion support. Frequently, instructors give many clues to what is important in a lecture. Discussed under the following headings are a few ways speakers show what is important.

Change in Voice: Some lecturers change the tone and/or pitch of their voices when they are trying to emphasize major points. A speaker's voice may get louder or softer or higher or lower as he or she presents important ideas.

Change in Rate of Speech: Speakers may slow down as they discuss important concepts. Sometimes a speaker goes so slowly that he or she seems to be dictating information: if a speaker giving a definition pauses slightly between each word or phrase, it is a way of telling you the definition is important and that you should write it down.

Listing or Numbering Points: A lecturer may directly state that there are "three important causes" or "four significant effects" or "five possible situations" as he or she begins discussing a particular topic. These expressions are major clues to the importance of the material. Frequently, a speaker further identifies or emphasizes the separate, particular facts or ideas which make up the "three causes" or "four effects" with such words as *first, second,* and *finally,* or *one effect, a second effect, another effect,* and *a final effect.*

Writing on the Chalkboard: Some lecturers write key words or even outlines of major ideas on the chalkboard as they speak. While not all important ideas are recorded on the chalkboard, you can be sure that if an instructor does take the time to write a word or phrase on the chalkboard, it is most certainly important.

Use of Audiovisuals: Some instructors emphasize important ideas, clarify relationships, or diagram processes or procedures by using audiovisual aids. Commonly used are overhead projectors that project on a screen previously prepared material or material the instructor draws or writes. Also, an instructor may use movies, filmstrips, videotapes, or photographs to emphasize or describe important ideas and concepts.

Direct Announcement: Occasionally, an instructor will announce straightforwardly that a particular concept or idea is especially important. He or she may begin by saying, "Particularly important to remember as you study is. . . ." or "One important fact that you must keep in mind is. . . ." The instructor may even hint that such information would make a good exam question. Be sure to mark hints like these in your notes. Emphasize these items with an asterisk or write "possible exam?" in the margin.

Nonverbal Clues: Many speakers give as many nonverbal as verbal clues to what is important. Often lecturers provide clues to what they feel is important through their movements and actions as well as their words. Some lecturers walk toward their audience as they make a major point. Others may use hand gestures, pound the table, or pace back and forth as they present key ideas. While each speaker is different, most speakers use some type of nonverbal clues.

EXERCISE 1

Directions: *Select one of your instructors and analyze his or her lecture style. Attend one lecture, and, as you take notes, try to be particularly aware of how he or she lets you know what is important. After the lecture, try to analyze your instructor, using the following questions:*

1. Did the instructor change his or her voice? When? How?

_____

2. Did his or her rate of speech vary? When?

_____

3. Did the instructor list or number important points?

_____

4. Did the instructor use the chalkboard?

_____

5. Did he or she directly state what was important?

_____

6. What nonverbal clues did the instructor give?

_____

Recording Details and Examples

A difficult part of taking notes is deciding how much detail to include with the main ideas. Obviously, you cannot write down everything, since lecturers usually speak at the rate of 125 words per minute. Even if you could take shorthand, it would be nearly impossible to record everything the lecturer says. As a result, you have to be selective and record only particularly important details. As a rule of thumb, record a brief phrase which summarizes each major supporting detail. Try to write down a phrase for each detail that directly explains or clarifies each major point.

If an instructor gives you several examples of a particular law, situation, or problem, be sure to write down in summary form at least one example. Record more than one if you have time. While at the time of the lecture it may seem that you completely understand what is being discussed, you will find that a few weeks later you really do need the example to help you recall the lecture.

Recording the Organization of the Lecture

As you write down the main ideas and important details of a lecture, try to organize or arrange your notes so that you can easily see how the lecture was organized. By recording the organization of the lecture, you will be able to determine the relative importance of ideas, and you will know what to pay most attention to as you study and review for an exam.

There is a simple way to show a lecture's organization: use indentation. Retain a regular margin on your paper. Start your notes on the most important of the topics at the left margin. For less important main ideas, indent your notes slightly. For major details, indent slightly further. Indent even further for examples and other details. The rule of thumb to follow is this: the less important the idea, the more it should be indented. Your notes might be organized like this:

```
Major topic
    Main Idea
        detail
        detail
            example
    Main Idea
        detail
        detail
        detail
Major topic
    Main Idea
        detail
            example
```

Notice that the sample looks like an outline but is missing all the roman numerals (I., II., III.), capital letters (A., B., C.), and arabic numerals (1., 2., 3.) that are usually contained in an outline. Also notice, however, that this system of notetaking does accomplish the same major goal as an outline — it separates important information from less important information. This indentation system, like an outline, shows at a glance how important a particular fact or idea is. If the organization of a lecture is obvious, you may wish to use a number or letter system in addition to indenting.

The notes in Figures 15-1 and 15-2 show that effective lecture notes should have a record of main ideas, important details, and examples, and that they should reflect the lecture's organization. Both sets of notes were taken on the same lecture. One set of notes is thorough and effective; the other is sketchy and does not focus on key ideas. Read through and evaluate each set of notes.

I. Social Stratification

Soc. 106
9/16

    Def's
        Soc. Strat. - hierarchy of ranks that exist in
               society
        Status - criteria to find position in soc.
           - depends partly on roles
           2 types
             1. ascribed status - handed down, inherited
               ex.: titles, race, wealth, ethnic background
             2. achieved status - things you control
               ex.: education, jobs

II. Social Mobility
    Def. - how indiv. moves in hierarchy
       - amt. of movement depends on society

    2 Types
        1. caste - ex.: India - no mobility -
           you inherit class + status

        2. open - large amt. of achieved status -
           great mobility - ex.: U.S.A.

FIGURE 15-1

Social Stratification

    Social stratification - defined as the ranks that exist in society - the position that any person has - ascribed status - it is handed down - example: titles. A second kind is achieved - it is the kind you decide for yourself.
    Social stratification is important in understanding societies.

    How a person moves up and down + changes his social status is called mobility. Some societies have a lot of mobility. Others don't have any - example is India.

    There are 2 kinds of movement.
        1. Caste system is when everybody is assigned a class and they must stay there without any chance to change.
        2. Open - people can move from one to another. This is true in the United States.

FIGURE 15-2

Tips for Making Notetaking Easier

If you record main ideas, details, and examples, using the indentation system to show the lecture's organization, you will take adequate notes. However, there are some tips you can follow to make notetaking easier, to make your notes more complete, and to make study and review easier.

Use Ink: Pencil tends to smear and is harder to read.

Use a Standard-sized Notebook and Paper: Paper smaller than 8½" x 11" doesn't allow you to write as much on a page, and it is more difficult to see the overall organization of a lecture if you have to flip through a lot of pages.

Keep a Separate Notebook or Section for Each Course: You need to have the notes for each course together so that you can review them easily.

Date Your Notes: For easy reference later, be sure to date your notes. Your instructor may announce that an exam will cover everything presented after October 5. If your notes are not dated, you will not know where to begin to study.

Leave Blank Spaces: To make your notes more readable and to make it easier to see the organization of ideas, leave plenty of blank space. If you know you missed a detail or definition, leave additional blank space. You can fill it in later by checking with a friend of referring to your text.

Mark Assignments: Occasionally, an instructor will announce an assignment or test date in the middle of a lecture. Of course you will jot it down, but be sure to mark "Assignment" or "Test Date" in the margin so that you can find it easily and transfer it to your assignment notebook.

Mark Ideas That Are Unclear: If an instructor presents a fact or idea which is unclear to you or one which you do not understand, put a question mark in the margin. Later, ask your instructor or another student about this idea.

Sit in the Front of the Classroom: Especially in large lecture halls, it is to your advantage to sit near the front. In the front you will be able to see and hear the instructor — you can maintain eye contact and observe his or her facial expressions and nonverbal clues. If you sit in the back, you may become bored, and it is easy to be distracted by all the people in front of you. Because of the people seated between you and the instructor, a feeling of distance is created. You may feel that the instructor really is not talking to you.

Don't Plan to Recopy Your Notes: Some students take each day's notes in a hasty, careless way and then recopy them in the evening. These students feel that recopying helps them to review the information and think it is a good way to study. Actually, recopying often becomes a mechanical process which takes a lot of time but very little thought. The time spent in recopying can be better spent in reviewing the notes in a manner that will be suggested later in this chapter.

Avoid Tape-Recording Lectures: As a maximum effort to get complete and accurate notes, some students resort to tape-recording each lecture. After the lecture, they play back the tape and take notes on it, starting and stopping the tape as needed. This is a tremendously time-consuming technique and very inefficient in terms of the time spent relative to the amount of learning that occurs. In using the tape system, a student has to spend at least an additional hour in playback for every hour spent in class just to complete his or her notes.

Use Abbreviations: To save time, try to use abbreviations instead of writing out long or frequently used words. If you are taking a course in psychology, you would not want to write out *p-s-y-c-h-o-l-o-g-y* each time the word is used. It would be much faster to use the abbreviation *psy*. Try to develop your own abbreviations which are appropriate for the subject areas you are studying. The abbreviations below were devised by a student in business management. They will give you an idea of the possibilities and choices you have. Notice that both common words and specialized words are abbreviated.

Common words	Abbreviation	Specialized words	Abbreviation
and	+	organization	org.
with	w/	management	man.
compare, comparison	comp.	data bank	D.B.
		structure	str.
important	imp't	evaluation	eval.
advantage	adv.	management by objective	MBO
introduction	intro.		
continued	cont'd.	management information system	MIS
		organizational development	OD
		communication simulation	comm./sim.

As you start to use abbreviations, be sure to begin gradually. It is easy to overuse abbreviations and end up with a set of notes that are almost meaningless.

EXERCISE 2

Directions: *Select one set of lecture notes from a class you recently attended. Reread your notes and look for words or phrases you could have abbreviated. Write some of these words in the space provided.*

Word   Abbreviation

_____   _____

_____   _____

Word	Abbreviation
_____	_____
_____	_____
_____	_____
_____	_____
_____	_____
_____	_____

HOW TO EDIT YOUR NOTES

After you have taken a set of lecture notes, do not assume that they are accurate and complete. Most students find that they missed some information and were unable to record as many complete details or examples as they would have liked. Even very experienced notetakers are faced with these problems. Fortunately, the solution is simple. Do not plan on taking a final and complete set of notes during the lecture. Instead, record just enough during the lecture to help you remember a main idea, detail, or example. Leave plenty of blank space; then, if possible, sit down immediately after the lecture and review your notes. Fill in missing information. Expand, or make more complete, any details or examples that are not fully explained. This process is called editing. It is essentially a process of correcting, revising, and adding to your notes to make them more complete and accurate. Editing notes for a one-hour lecture should take no more than five or ten minutes.

If you are unable to edit your notes immediately after a lecture, it is critical that you edit them that evening. The longer the time lapse between the notetaking and the editing, the less effective the editing becomes. Also, the greater the time lapse, the more the facts and examples you will be unable to recall and fill in.

The sample set of lecture notes in Figure 15-3 has been edited. The

Anxiety + Defense Mechanisms   Page 602
                                                  10/12

I. Anxiety generalized
      def gen fear or worry
    Levels
        1. moderate - productive
            athletes - higher level of phys. functioning
            test-taking - certain am't helps - keeps you alert
        2. Extreme - uncomfortable   ex.: nauseous,
                    extremely nervous, hands shaking.
                  - can be reduced by defense mechanism

II. Defense Mech
  def - uncon^scious devices to protect self and /or keep self
       under control
     ex.: student who is hostile toward teacher
          explains it to himself by saying that "the
                                              teacher hates me"
Types of Def. Mechanism
  1. Repression - to drive out of consciousness
     ex.: student - math instructor   student forgets
          to keep app't with math instructor because
          he's afraid he will be told he is failing the
          course!
                    to anxiety
  2. Regression - reaction^ by going back to less
       mature behavior
     ex.: college student applying for job but
          doesn't get it - pouts + says the
          interviewer cheated + hired son of
          his best friend.

FIGURE 15-3

notes taken during the lecture are in black writing; the additions and changes made during editing are in lighter writing. Read through the notes, noticing the types of information added during editing.

HOW TO STUDY YOUR NOTES

Taking and editing good lecture notes is only part of what must be done to learn from your instructors' lectures. You also have to learn and review the notes in order to do well on an exam. To study lecture notes, try to apply the same principles that you use in learning material in your textbooks. (1) Do not try to learn your notes by reading them over and over. Rereading is not an efficient review technique because it takes too much time relative to the amount you learn. (2) As in reading textbook assignments, identify what is important. You must sort out what you will learn and study from all the rest of the information which you have written in your notes. (3) Have a way to check yourself — a way to decide if you have learned the necessary information. In studying textbooks, you use the "Recite" step of the SQ3R method to check your recall of what you have read. And you can use facts cards or summary sheets to test your recall further. For studying lecture notes, there is a system which uses similar techniques of study; it is called the Recall Clue System.

The Recall Clue System

The Recall Clue System helps make the review and study of lecture notes easier and more effective. You will notice that it is very similar to the summary word technique suggested in Chapter 13. To use the Recall Clue System, follow these steps:

1.   Leave an extra 2″ margin at the left side of each page of notes.
2.   This margin stays blank while you are taking notes.

3. After you have edited your notes, fill in the left margin with words and phrases which very briefly summarize the notes.

The recall clues should be words that will trigger your memory and help you recall the complete information in your notes. These clues function as memory tags. They help you pull out, or retrieve, from your memory any information which is labeled with these tags. When you are trying to recall information on an exam, the memory or recall clue from your notes will work automatically to help you remember necessary information. Figure 15-4 shows a sample of notes in which the Recall Clue System has been used.

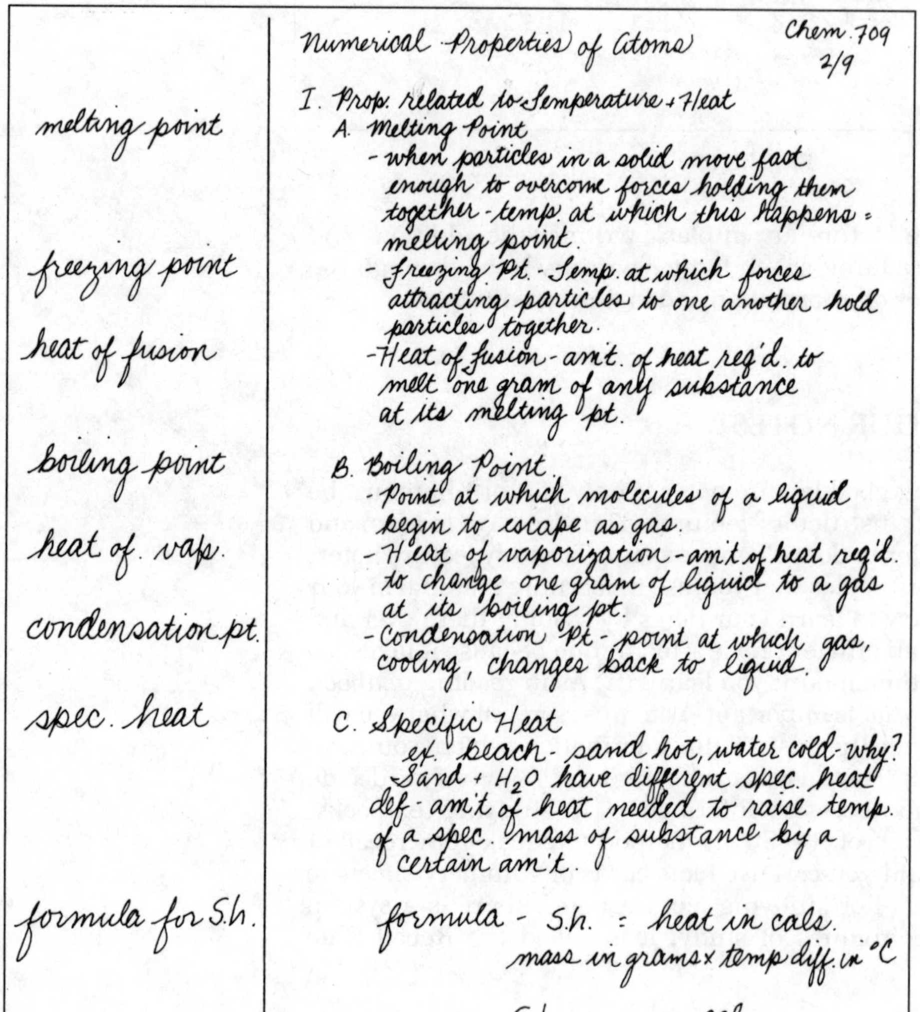

	Numerical Properties of Atoms — Chem. 709, 2/9
melting point	I. Prop. related to Temperature + Heat A. Melting Point - when particles in a solid move fast enough to overcome forces holding them together - temp. at which this happens = melting point.
freezing point	- Freezing Pt. - Temp. at which forces attracting particles to one another hold particles together.
heat of fusion	- Heat of fusion - am't. of heat req'd. to melt one gram of any substance at its melting pt.
boiling point	B. Boiling Point - Point at which molecules of a liquid begin to escape as gas.
heat of. vap.	- Heat of vaporization - am't of heat req'd. to change one gram of liquid to a gas at its boiling pt.
condensation pt.	- Condensation Pt. - point at which gas, cooling, changes back to liquid.
spec. heat	C. Specific Heat ex. beach - sand hot, water cold - why? Sand + H_2O have different spec. heat def - am't of heat needed to raise temp. of a spec. mass of substance by a certain am't.
formula for S.h.	formula - $S.h. = \frac{\text{heat in cals.}}{\text{mass in grams} \times \text{temp diff. in } ^\circ C}$ $S.h. = \frac{cal}{g \times ^\circ C}$

FIGURE 15-4

A variation on the Recall Clue System that students have found effective is to write questions rather than summary words and phrases in the margin. (See Figure 15-5.) The questions, then, trigger your memory and enable you to recall the information that answers your

	Advertising
	- Widely used in our economy.
	- Promotes competition; encourages open system
What is Advertising?	definition - presentation of a product/service to broad segment of the population.
What are its Characteristics?	Characteristics
	1. non-personal - uses media rather than person-to-person contact.
	2. paid for by seller
	3. intended to influence the consumer.
What is the Ultimate Objective?	Objectives
	Ultimate objective - to sell product or service
What is the Immediate Objective?	Immediate objectives
	1. to inform - make consumer aware ex. new product available
	2. to persuade - stress value, advantages of product. ex. results of market research
	3. to reinforce - happens after 1 and 2. - consumers need to be reminded about prod./service - even if they use it. - often done through slogans and jingles.

FIGURE 15-5

question. The use of questions enables you to test yourself, thereby allowing you to simulate an exam situation.

Using the Recall Clue System

To study your notes using the Recall Clue System, cover up the notes with a sheet of paper, exposing only the recall clues in the left margin. Then read the first recall clue and try to remember the information in the portion of the notes beside it. Then slide the paper down and check that portion to see if you remembered all the important facts. If you remembered only part of the information, cover up that portion of your notes and again check your recall. Continue checking until you are satisfied that you can remember all the important facts. Then move on to the next recall clue on the page, following the same testing-checking procedure.

To get into the habit of using the Recall Clue System, mark off with a ruler the 2″ column on the next several blank pages in each of your notebooks. Then, when you open your notebook at the beginning of a class, you will be reminded to use the system.

EXERCISE 3

Directions: *Read the sample set of notes in Figure 15-6. Fill in the recall clues or formulate questions that would help you study and learn the notes.*

I. Psychoanalytic theory - created by Sigmund Freud

    A. free association - major diagnostic techniques in psychoanalysis; patient reports whatever comes to mind / holds nothing back.

    B. repression - psych. process of driving ideas out of consciousness

    C. suppression - conscious of an idea, but won't tell anyone about it.

    D. trauma - particularly disturbing event; most psych. disturbances traceable to a trauma.

    E. interp. of dreams - dreams - fantasies which person believes to be true/have profound influence on personality devlpmt.

F. Id - power system of personality providing energy.
   1. pleasure principle - all unpleasent events should be avoided.
     a. primary process - normal logic does not operate.
      ex. bizarre dreams, hallucinations

G. Ego - strategist of personality / concerned w/ what a person CAN do.
   1. reality principle - distinction between real + unreal rather than dist. between pleasure + pain. Satisfies id in a realistic manner.
     a. secondary process - rational, logical, critical.

H. Superego - "good versus bad", rewards and punishments.
   1. conscience - critical, punitive aspect of superego.

FIGURE 15-6

EXERCISE 4

Directions: *For each course that you are taking this semester, use the Recall Clue System for at least one week; be sure to review your notes several times, using the recall clues. At the end of that week, evaluate how well the system works for you.*

1. What advantages does it have?

    _____

2. Did it help you remember facts and ideas?

    _____

3. Are there any disadvantages?

    _____

SUMMARY

Since many college instructors expect you to remember and apply facts and ideas presented in their class lectures, it is necessary to take good lecture notes, to edit them properly, and to develop a system for studying them effectively.

Effective lecture notes should accomplish three things. First, good notes should serve as a summary of the main points of the lecture. Well-taken lecture notes serve as a valuable and important study material. Second, lecture notes should include enough details and examples so that you can completely understand and recall the information several weeks later. Third, the notes should show the relative importance of ideas and reflect the organization of the lecture. The chapter provided specific suggestions on how to accomplish each of these goals and offered numerous tips on making notetaking easier.

After taking a set of lecture notes, it is necessary to correct, revise, fill in missing or additional information, and expand your notes to make them more complete. This process of editing your notes results in clearer, more accurate notes from which to study.

Effective study of lecture notes follows many of the same principles and procedures which are used for studying textbook chapters. The Recall Clue System is a way of making study and review easier and more effective. A 2″ margin at the left of each page of notes is left blank during notetaking. Then, later, as you reread your notes, you write in the left margin words and phrases which very briefly summarize the notes to the right. These phrases, or recall clues, trigger your memory and help you to recall information in the notes.

16. Participating in Class Discussions

Use this chapter to:

1. *Help you prepare for class discussions.*
2. *Learn how to participate in class discussions.*

While many instructors prefer the lecture method as a means of conducting a class, others prefer to handle the class more informally, using a discussion, or student-participation, approach. The instructor's choice of the lecture or discussion method is not a matter of simple preference. Rather, instructors determine how they will conduct their class on the basis of such things as class size, type of material to be taught, and type of learning that is to occur. If, for example, it is an instructor's purpose to encourage his students to react to, evaluate, and think critically about various controversial issues, then a discussion class is more appropriate. If, on the other hand, the instructor's main goal is to present a base of factual information, then the lecture format is more efficient. In Chapter 14, you read of techniques and suggestions for handling lecture classes. The purpose of this chapter is to give you some ideas on how to deal with discussion, or class-participation, situations.

Class-discussion courses differ from lecture classes in several ways. First, the amount of advance preparation differs greatly. Second, your involvement in each class is of a different level and type. Finally, the manner in which you review and study for class-discussion courses is different from techniques used for study and review in lecture classes.

PREPARING FOR CLASS DISCUSSIONS

Preparing for a class discussion demands much more time and effort than does getting ready to attend a lecture class. In fact, in a lecture course, most of your work comes after the classes, editing your notes and using the Recall Clue System to review them. Just the opposite is true for discussion courses. Most of your work is done before you go to class. Considerable time must be spent in reading, evaluating, and making notes. Below are a few suggestions to help you get ready for a discussion class.

Reading the Assignment

Usually a class discussion is about a particular topic (issue, problem). Frequently instructors give textbook or library reading assignments that are intended to give you some background information. The reading assignments are also intended to start you thinking about a topic, show you different points of view about an issue, or indicate some aspects of a problem.

The first step in preparing for a discussion class is to read carefully the material assigned. Do not just skim through it as you might for a lecture class. Instead, read the assignment with the purpose of learning all the material. Use the SQ3R method to help you learn, and mark and underline important ideas as you read.

Review: Making Notes for Discussion

After you have read the assignment, review it with the purpose of identifying and jotting down the following:

1.   Ideas, concepts, or points of view you do not understand. Keep a list of these; you can use the list as a guide to form questions during class.
2.   Ideas and points with which you disagree or strongly agree. By jotting these down you will have some ideas to start with if your instructor asks you to react to the topic.
3.   Good and poor examples. Note any examples which you think are particularly good or particularly poor. These will also be helpful to you in reacting to the topic.
4.   Strong arguments and weak arguments. As you read, try to follow the line of reasoning, and evaluate any arguments presented. Make notes on your evaluations; the notes will remind you of points you may want to make during the discussion.

Go to Class with Specific Ideas and Questions

When you go to class, have in mind specific comments you could make and questions you could ask. With these in mind, at least you will know there is something you can say — and you know you will not draw a blank if called upon.

GETTING INVOLVED IN CLASS DISCUSSIONS

Discussion classes require greater, more active involvement and participation than do lecture classes. In lecture classes, your main concern is to listen carefully and to record notes accurately and completely. In discussion classes, your responsibility is much greater. Not only do you have to take notes, but you also have to participate in the discussion. The problem many students experience in getting involved in discussions is that they do not know what to say or when to say it. Here are a few instances when it may be appropriate to speak. Say something when:

1.   You can ask a serious, thoughtful question.
2.   Someone asks a question that you can answer.
3.   You have a comment or suggestion to make on what has already been said.

4. You can supply additional information that will clarify the topic under discussion.
5. You can correct an error or clarify a misunderstanding.

To get further involved in the discussion, try the following suggestions:

1. Even if you are reluctant to speak before a group, try to say something early in the discussion; the longer you wait, the more difficult it becomes. Also, the longer you wait, the greater the chance that someone else will say what you were planning to say.
2. Make your comments brief and to the point. It is probably a mistake to say too much rather than too little. If your instructor feels you should say more, she or he will probably ask you to explain or elaborate further.
3. Try to avoid getting involved in direct exchanges or disagreements with any specific members of the class. Always speak to the group, not individuals; and be sure that your comments relate to and involve the entire class.
4. When you feel it is appropriate to introduce a new idea, clue your listeners that you are changing topics or introducing a new idea. You might say something like: "Another related question is . . ." or "Another point to consider is . . . ."
5. When you think of comments or ideas that you want to make as the discussion is going on, jot them down. Then, when you get a chance to speak, you will have your notes to refer to. Notes help you organize and present your ideas in a clear and organized fashion.
6. Try to keep an open mind throughout the discussion. Leave personal dislikes, attitudes toward other members of the group, and your own biases and prejudices outside.
7. Organize your remarks. First, connect what you plan to say with what has already been said. Then state your idea as clearly as possible. Next, develop or explain your idea.
8. Watch the group as you speak. When making a point or offering a comment, watch both your instructor and others in the class. Their responses will show whether they understand you or need further information, whether they agree or disagree, and whether they are interested or uninterested. Then, based on their responses, decide whether you made your point effectively or whether you need to explain further or defend your argument more carefully.

NOTETAKING DURING DISCUSSIONS

While most of your energy in a class discussion is taken up by following and participating in the discussion, it is important to take summary notes while the discussion is going on. Your notes should not be as detailed as they would be for a lecture class; write down only the key topics discussed and the important concepts and ideas brought into the discussion.

Editing the notes you take in discussion classes is extremely important. Because you have so little time and mental energy to devote to notetaking during the discussion, it is very important to fill in and complete your notes at a later time. Since discussions frequently change direction and focus as they go on, it is particularly important to edit your notes to reflect these changes. Be sure to fill in any information of this type as you edit your notes. A once-through review of your notes as you edit them will tie together and give you an overview of the entire discussion and help keep it in your memory.

REVIEWING AND STUDYING FOR DISCUSSION CLASSES

Just as preparing for and participating in discussion classes are different from preparing for and participating in lecture classes, so does the review-study process for discussion classes require slightly different techniques from those used for lecture classes. Fortunately, since more work is done prior to attending a discussion class, less is required after it. To review and study for a discussion class, be sure to:

1. Review your notes; use the Recall Clue System to check your recall of important information.
2. Review any reading assignment given prior to the class discussion. You may want to reread the assignment. Given the new ideas and perspectives introduced in class, you will probably find new ways of approaching and viewing the information presented in the assignment. As you review, be sure to mark and underline any information that you now realize is particularly important or has direct bearing upon the discussion.
3. Try to anticipate possible test or exam questions based on your notes, the reading assignment, and your recall of the discussion. Most likely, your instructor will give you either essay or short-answer questions on exams. Objective questions (true-false, multiple-choice, or matching) would be rather difficult to construct because there is no clear base of factual information. Essay or short-answer questions lend themselves more readily to the concerns, purposes, and goals your instructor most likely has for a discussion course. Basically, you would use the same techniques for preparing for and taking essay and short-answer exams that you learned in the previous chapter. Pay particular attention to topics for which your instructor allowed the most discussion time and those with which your instructor seemed to get most involved.

EXERCISE

Directions: *Review the sample chapter in the Appendix. Assume that you have been assigned this chapter as preparation for a discussion class. What notes would you make and what questions would you be ready to ask as you prepared for a class discussion? Record each in the space provided.*

Notes: _____

_____

_____

_____

Questions: _____

_____

_____

_____

SUMMARY

Although many instructors prefer the lecture method as a means of conducting classes, others prefer to organize their classes more informally, using a discussion, or student-participation, approach. In a discussion class, your responsibilities and level of participation differ significantly from your participation and responsibilities in a lecture class. Advance preparation is usually required for the discussion class; your involvement and participation during class is of a different level and type; review-study procedures for a discussion class are somewhat different.

A substantial amount of advance preparation is required before attending each discussion class. Preparation often includes the careful reading of an assignment and the development of notes for discussion. The notes may include specific comments, ideas, and questions you could contribute to the discussion. During the class, you are expected to get involved, to participate in the discussion. As the discussion is going on, it is important to take summary notes which can be expanded during a later editing process.

As you review and study after a class discussion, first review your notes and check your recall of the information by using the Recall Clue System suggested for taking lecture notes. Then, review and mark any reading assignment you completed prior to the discussion. Finally, try to anticipate test or exam questions that could be based on your notes, the reading assignment, and your recall of the discussion.

17. Studying for and Taking Exams

Use this chapter to:

1. *Decide the best way to study for an exam.*

2. *Find out what you can do to improve your ability to take tests.*

Tests, quizzes, and examinations are an important part of most college courses. They are important to students because they, in part, determine grades. Tests are also important as learning experiences. Daily or weekly quizzes force you to keep up with reading assignments and attend class regularly. Also, it is through preparing for and taking exams that a student consolidates, or ties together, concepts and facts learned in a course. Finally, it is through the review and study involved in preparing for an exam that information is learned or stored in your memory.

Your ability to take exams will probably make a great deal of difference in how well you do in your courses and what grades you earn. Have you noticed a student in your class who doesn't seem to work very hard but always seems to do well on the exams? How does he do it? Probably he is not extremely intelligent and he probably does not spend all his time studying. Most likely, the student is highly skilled in preparing for and taking exams. He has learned various ways to get ready for exams. He also knows the tips and tricks to use while taking the exam to gain a few extra points.

PREPARING FOR EXAMS

Studying is the single most important thing you can do to increase your chance of passing an exam. When exam papers are returned, have you ever overhead a comment like this: "I spent at least ten hours studying, I went over everything, and I still failed the exam!" Students frequently complain that they spend large amounts of time studying and do not get the grades they deserve. Perhaps the problem is that they do not use their time effectively. They do not study the material in the best way. The most important factors in preparing for exams are: *when* you study, *what* you study, *where* you study, and *how* you study. It is also important to realize that your approach to study depends on the type of exam you are taking.

If you are using the techniques for learning as you read (see Part Four, Chapter 13), you are avoiding one of the most serious traps students fall into in preparing for exams. Many students make the mistake of waiting to study until an exam is scheduled. These students may read textbook assignments as they are given, but they hurry through them, planning to study them carefully later. Some students do the same with their lecture notes — they take them but do not edit them, review them, or use the Recall Clue System suggested in the previous chapter.

The reading-study systems and the Recall Clue System are ways to study as you go. When an exam is scheduled, if you are using these systems, you will only have to *review* what you have already learned, not just start to learn the material.

WHEN TO REVIEW

The timing of your review sessions is crucial to achieving good test results. Plan your review sessions using the following suggestions:

1. Schedule several review sessions well in advance of the exam. Start a week in advance. Set aside specific times for review each day and incorporate them into your weekly schedule. If you are having difficulty with a particular subject, it might be especially useful to study with one or two students from the same class.
2. Spend time organizing your review. Make a list of all the chapters, notes, and teacher handouts that need to be reviewed. Divide the material up, planning what you will review during each session.
3. Reserve time the night before the exam for a last, once-through review. Do not review new material during this session. Instead, use the time to go through again the most difficult material, checking your recall of important facts, or to do a last review of information for possible essay questions.

WHAT TO REVIEW

In preparing for an exam, be sure to review every major source of information — textbook chapters and lecture notes as well as sources sometimes overlooked by students, including old exams and quizzes, teacher handouts, course outlines, and outside assignments.

Textbook Chapters

All chapters assigned during the period covered by the exam or relating to the topics covered in the exam must be reviewed in preparation for an exam. Review of textbook chapters should be a fairly easy task if you have kept up with weekly assignments, used SQ3R, the study-as-you-read system, and marked and underlined each assignment.

Lecture Notes

In addition to textbook chapters, all lecture notes that pertain to the exam must be reviewed. This, too, is an easy task if you have been using the notetaking and editing system suggested in the preceding chapter.

Previous Exams and Quizzes

Be sure to keep all old tests and quizzes from each course. These are valuable sources of review for the longer, more comprehensive exams which cover some of the same material covered on the tests and quizzes. While most instructors do not repeat exactly the same test questions, the old quizzes do have a practical use. They serve as a list of facts, terms, and ideas that are important. Review the quizzes to be certain you still remember the information. The comprehensive exam will probably test your recall of some of the same information through different types of questions. Pay particular attention to any items that you got wrong. If they were troublesome to you before, be sure the confusion has been cleared up.

Teacher Handouts

Instructors frequently hand out duplicated sheets of information. These may be summary outlines, lists of terms, sample problems, maps and charts, or explanations of difficult concepts. Any material that an instructor takes the time to prepare specially for distribution to students is bound to be important. As you receive these sheets throughout a course, date them and label the lecture topic to which they correspond. Keep them in one place — in a separate folder or in the front of your notebook — so that you can refer to them easily.

Course Outlines

At the beginning of a course, instructors often distribute outlines which tell what the course is about. They usually list the major topics to be covered. It is these topics, then, which the instructor feels are important to the course. The outlines may contain clues to what the instructor feels is important enough to ask in an essay question.

Other instructors, in addition to listing topics, are much more specific and list objectives to be covered for each topic. Check each objective and see if you can accomplish it. If one of the objectives is to learn the laws of motion, you should be sure you have learned the laws and can explain each in your own words.

Outside-of-Class Assignments

Assignments may be problems to solve, library research, written reaction or evaluation, or a lecture or movie to attend. If an instructor gives an assignment to be completed outside of class, the topic or area of the assignment is probably quite important. Due to the limited number of assignments that she or he can give in a particular course, it is likely that the instructor chooses only the ones she or he feels are most valuable. Therefore, you should keep your notes on assignments and returned assignments together for easy review before exams.

HOW TO REVIEW

The methods and procedures you use to review depend on the type of exam you are preparing for. You would study differently for a multiple-choice test than you would for an essay exam.

Exams can be divided into two basic types — objective and essay. Objective tests are short-answer tests in which you choose one or more answers from among several that are given. Multiple-choice, true-false, matching, and fill-in-the-blank are all types of objective tests. In each of these, the questions are constructed so that the answers you choose are clearly either right or wrong; scoring is completely objective, or free from judgment.

Essay tests are those which require you to write answers to questions in your own words. You have to recall information, organize it, and present it in acceptable written form. This is a completely different task from choosing one answer out of those given. Because taking an essay exam is much different from taking an objective test, you have to use different methods to prepare and review for each.

When studying for a particular exam or test, be certain to find out whether it will be objective or essay or a combination of both. If your instructor does not tell you the type of exam when he announces the exam date, ask either during or after class. Most instructors are willing to tell students what type of exam will be given — sometimes they simply forget to mention it when announcing the exam. If an instructor chooses not to tell you, do not be concerned; at least you have shown that you are concerned and interested and are thinking ahead about the exam.

Be certain that you know exactly what material the exam will cover. Usually, your instructor will either announce the topics to be covered in the exam or give the dates or weeks in the course that the exam will cover.

Another important and practical part of studying for an exam is finding out what your instructor expects of you and how he or she will evaluate your exam. Some instructors expect you only to recall text and lecture material; others expect you to agree with their views on a particular subject; still others encourage you to think, discuss, recall, and disagree with the ideas and information they have presented. In grading exams, some instructors award partial credit, even on short-answer questions; others do not. If you learn that an instructor awards partial credit, be sure to write a response even though you know it is not completely correct, so that you may earn partial credit.

Reviewing for Objective Tests

Objective tests usually require you to recognize the right answer. On a multiple-choice test, for example, you have to pick out the correct answer from among the choices given. In true-false tests, you have to recognize the true and false statements. In matching tests, you have to recognize which two items go together. Your goal, then, in reviewing for objective tests, is to become so familiar with the course material that you can recognize or pick out the right answers.

The First Step: Identify what information is to be reviewed. In your textbook use the boldface headings along with the SQ3R reading-study method to identify information to be reviewed. Your textbook marking and underlining in each chapter will confirm your identification of important material. Also use all textbook aids—such as summaries, end-of-chapter questions, and vocabulary lists—to determine what to study. The marginal recall clues in your class lecture notes serve as a list of important topics, facts, and concepts to review.

The Second Step: Test yourself — check to be sure you have learned all the necessary facts and ideas. By testing yourself before the instructor tests you, you are preparing in a very realistic way for the exam. If you were entering a marathon race, you would prepare yourself for the race by running, not by — let's say — playing golf. The same is true for test-taking. To prepare for a test, practice taking tests, tests that you give yourself. Do not prepare by simply rereading chapters or staring at page after page of notes.

The Third Step: Use the learning and study aids that you have been preparing as the course has been going on. In your text, the most valuable learning aid is your underlining and marking. In your lecture notes, you also have a ready-to-use learning aid — the marginal recall clues you have written as you reviewed and edited each day's notes.

Using Your Underlining and Marking: Your underlining can be used in several ways for review. First, just reread your underlining in each chapter to remember the chapter content. Second, read the bold-face headings in the chapter, and form a question for each as you did for the Q step of SQ3R. Try to answer your question; then check your underlining to see if you were correct. Finally, review any special markings you may have included. If, for example, you marked new or important definitions with a particular symbol, go through the chapter once just noting these terms and checking your recall of their meanings.

Using the Recall Clues in Your Lecture Notes: Go back through each set of lecture notes and check your recall of each by using the marginal recall clue system. Test yourself by asking yourself questions and trying to recall the answer. Mark in red pen things you are still having difficulty remembering.

Index Cards and Study Sheets

When reviewing for an objective exam, you can use an organized, easy-to-study system to gather the information that has to be learned. Two such systems are presented here — the index card system and the study sheet system.

The Index Card System: The index card system is an effective way of organizing information. Using 3″ x 5″ index cards, or just small sheets of paper, write part of the information on the front of the card, the remainder on the back: to review the dates of important events, write the date on the front, the event on the back; to review vocabulary, put each term on the front of one card, each definition on the back. See the sample index cards shown in Figure 17-1. They were made by a student preparing for an objective exam on the sample chapter in the Appendix.

To study each of these cards, you would look at the front and try to

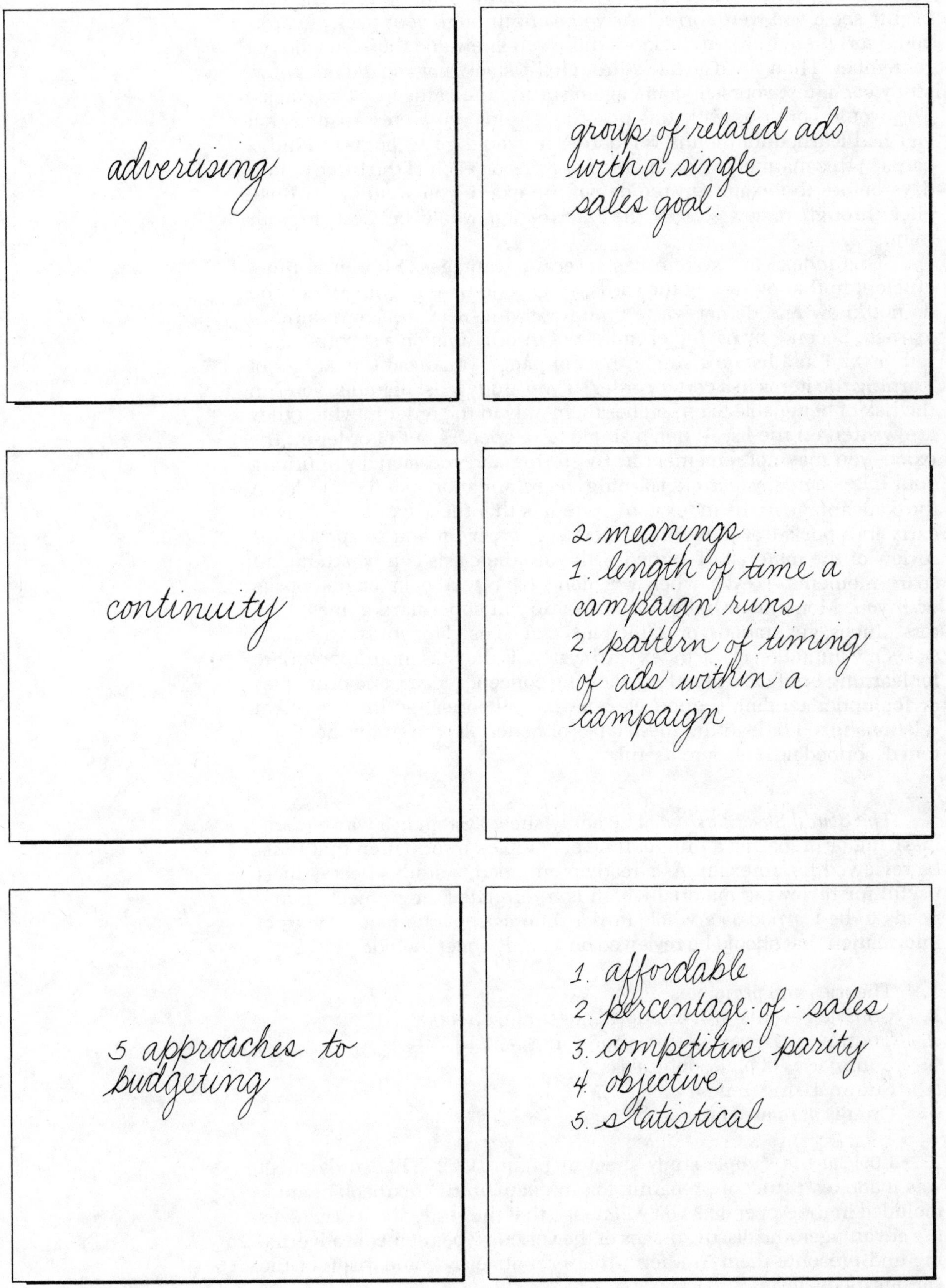

advertising

group of related ads
with a single
sales goal.

continuity

2 meanings
1. length of time a
campaign runs
2. pattern of timing
of ads within a
campaign

5 approaches to
budgeting

1. affordable
2. percentage of sales
3. competitive parity
4. objective
5. statistical

FIGURE 17-1

remember what is written on the back. Then you would turn the card over to see if you were correct. As you went through your pack of cards, you'd sort them into two stacks — those you knew and those you did not remember. Then you'd go back through the stack that you did not know, study each, test yourself again, again sorting the cards into two stacks. You would continue with this procedure until you were satisfied that you had learned all the information. You would go through the index cards in this manner two or three times a day on each of the three or four days before the exam. On the day of the exam, you would do a final, once-through review so that the information would be fresh in your mind.

This index card system has several advantages. First, it is time-efficient in that by sorting the cards, you spend time learning what you do not know and do not waste time reviewing what you have already learned. Second, by having each item of information on a separate card rather than in a list on a single sheet of paper, you avoid the danger of learning the items in a certain order. If you study a list of items, you run the risk of being able to remember them only in the order in which they are written on the list. When a single item appears out of order on the exam, you may not remember it. By sorting and occasionally shuffling your index cards, you avoid learning the information in a fixed order. A third advantage of the index card system is that these cards are easy to carry in a pocket or purse. It is therefore easier for you to space your review of the material. If carried with you, the cards can be studied in spare moments — even when you don't have textbooks or notebooks with you. Moments usually wasted waiting in supermarket lines, doctors' offices, gas stations, or traffic jams can be used for study.

One limitation of the index card system is that it is more appropriate for learning brief facts than for reviewing concepts, ideas, and principles or for understanding sequences of events, theories, and cause-effect relationships. For learning these types of materials, the study sheet system described next is more useful.

The Study Sheet System: The study sheet system is a way of summarizing or preparing a mini-outline of complex information that must be reviewed for an exam. As already mentioned, a study sheet is most useful for reviewing material which is interrelated, or connected, and needs to be learned as a whole rather than as separate facts. Types of information that should be reviewed on a study sheet include:

1. Theories and principles
2. Complex events with multiple causes and effects
3. Controversial issues — pros and cons
4. Summaries of philosophical issues
5. Summarizing trends
6. Groups of related facts

Look at the sample study sheet in Figure 17-2. This study sheet was made by a student preparing for an exam on the textbook chapter included in the Appendix. You will notice that the study sheet organizes the advantages and disadvantages of the various types of media advertising and presents them in a form that permits easy comparison of the various media forms.

To prepare a study sheet, first select the information to be learned.

Media

Media form	_Advantages_	_Disadvantages_
1. Newspapers	- widely read - regional flexibility - offer use of inserts	- little buyer selectivity
2. Magazines	- better appearance than newspapers - longer life - people do re-read.	- advance commitment required - may have to buy entire national circulation.
3. TV	- reaches 95% of households - can produce favorable product images - can choose stations to carry the ad.	- commercial clutter (must compete with other ads)
4. Radio	- inexpensive - can afford high level of repetition - geographic selectivity - can change ads frequently and easily.	- short lived (can't "re-read") - people don't "listen" to the ads.
5. Outdoor Advertising	- large amount of repetition - low cost per exposure.	- copy must be short

FIGURE 17-2

Then outline the information, using as few words as possible. Group together important points, facts, and ideas which relate to each topic.

To learn the information on a study sheet, first read through it several times. Then, take the first topic in your outline, write it on a blank sheet of paper, and see if you can fill in the information under that topic on your study sheet. If you cannot recall all the information, keep on testing yourself until you have learned it. Continue in this way with each topic.

Reviewing for Essay Exams

Essay exams demand complete recall. Starting with a blank sheet of paper, you are required to retrieve from your memory all the information that answers a question. Then you must organize that information and express your ideas about it in acceptable written form.

To review for an essay exam, first identify topics that may be included on the exam. Then learn and organize enough information about the topics so that you are ready to write your ideas about each of them.

How to Select Topics to Study: By choosing topics to study, you are really attempting to predict what questions will be included on the exam. There are several sources in which you can choose topics. First, you can use the major boldface headings in your textbook to identify important topics or subtopics. End-of-chapter discussion questions and recall clues written in the margin of your lecture notes may also suggest topics. And don't forget to check the course outline distributed by your instructor at the beginning of the course. Frequently this outline contains a list of major topics covered in the course.

How to Study the Topics Selected: Once you have made your choices, identify what aspects of the topics you should review. Perhaps the best source of information is your instructor. He or she has probably been consciously or unconsciously giving clues all semester about what the most important topics are. Train yourself to watch and listen for these clues. Specifically, look for your instructor's approach, focus, and emphasis with respect to the subject matter: Does your history instructor emphasize causes and dates of events? Is he or she more concerned with the historical importance and long lasting-effects of events? Is your ecology instructor concerned with specific changes that a pollutant produces or its more general environmental effects?

After you have identified the aspects of each topic that you should study, prepare a study sheet on each. Include all the information you would want to remember if you were going to write an essay on each topic. As you prepare these study sheets, organize the information so that you could write a clear, concise essay on every topic. You might organize the causes of a particular historical event in the order of their importance or in chronological order. By organizing the information, you will be able to remember it more easily when you are taking the exam. After your study sheets are prepared, study each one, trying to recall the major subtopics you included. Also, test yourself to see if you can recall the specific facts under each subtopic.

To make remembering easier, and to ensure that you will write an organized essay answer, try the key word system for keeping in mind the items you want to include in your essay answer. The key word system is a way of remembering information by summarizing each idea with a

234

newspapers	cost
magazines	regional/geographic flexibility
T.V.	appearance
radio	repetition
	audience reached
	competition
outdoor advertising	preparation time

FIGURE 17-3

single word or phrase. You can memorize each key word or phrase in a particular order. Together, these words and phrases form a mini-outline of the ideas or topics you want to include in the essay. You might test the effectiveness of your key word outline and your ability to recall it by formulating your own exam questions and then writing complete or outline-form answers to the questions. When you are actually taking the exam, write the key word mini-outline for each question on scrap paper or on the back of the exam paper before you start to write your answer. The outline will be an easy-to-follow guide of all the major points to include in your essay.

The sample study sheet in Figure 17-2 was made by a student preparing for an essay exam in business marketing. The textbook chapter in the Appendix was part of the information on which the exam would be based. Among the topics which this student chose to review was advertising media. She was predicting that her instructor might include a question on the advantages and disadvantages of various media for advertising. From her study sheet, the student made the key word lists shown in Figure 17-3. The list on the left shows the various advertising media. The list on the right records some of the features or variables that are used to assess the value of a particular advertising form. By learning these two lists, the student will be well prepared to discuss the advantages and/or disadvantages of any or all of the media.

TAKING EXAMS

There are many things you can do to raise your grade in an exam. First, there are some general techniques and suggestions to follow when taking any exam. Second, there are particular tricks and approaches to use depending on whether the exam is objective or essay.

General Suggestions for Taking Exams

Here are a few suggestions to help you approach any exam in an organized, systematic way.

Take Necessary Materials: When going to any exam, be sure to take along any possible material you might be asked or allowed to use.

Be sure you have an extra pen, and take a pencil in case you need to make a drawing or diagram. Take paper — you may need it for scrap or to write essay answers. Take along anything you have been allowed to use regularly throughout the semester. You might consider taking a pocket calculator, ruler, conversion charts, or dictionary. If you are not sure whether you are allowed to use them, ask the instructor.

Get There on Time — Do Not Arrive Too Early: It is, of course, important to arrive at the exam room on time or a few minutes early. Arrive in time to get a seat and get organized before the instructor arrives. If you are late, you may miss important directions, and you will feel rushed and nervous as you begin the exam. However, if you arrive too early (10–15 minutes ahead), you run the risk of becoming confused and nervous by listening to panic-stricken students questioning each other, trading last-minute memory tricks, and worrying about how difficult the exam will be.

Sit in the Front of the Room: If you have a choice, the most practical place to sit in an exam room is at the front. There, you often receive the test first and get a few minutes head start. There, also, you are sure to hear directions and corrections and can easily read any changes written on the chalkboard. Finally, it is easier to concentrate and avoid distractions at the front of the room. At the back, you can see and sometimes cannot avoid such distractions as someone dropping the papers, someone cheating, or the person in front of you who is already two pages ahead of you on the exam.

Preread the Exam: Before you start to answer any of the questions, quickly page through the exam, noticing the directions, the length, the type of questions, and the general topics covered. Prereading is useful because it gives you an overview of and perspective on the whole exam. Prereading also helps eliminate the panic you may feel if you just start right in with the first few questions and find that you are unsure of the answers.

Plan Your Time: After prereading the exam, you will know the number and types of questions included. The next thing to do is roughly estimate how much time you should spend on each part of the exam. The number of points each section is worth (the point distribution) should be your guide. If, for example, one part of an exam has 20 multiple-choice questions worth 1 point each and another part has 2 essays worth 40 points each, you should spend much more time answering the essay questions than working through the multiple-choice items. If the point distribution is not indicated on the test booklet, you may want to ask the instructor what it is.

As you plan your time, be sure to allow approximately a minute or two to preread the exam. Also allow 3 to 4 minutes at the end of the exam to read through what you have done, answering questions you didn't answer and making any corrections or changes that are necessary.

In order to keep track of time, always wear a watch. Many classrooms do not have wall clocks, or you may be sitting in a position in the room where it is not convenient to look at the clock regularly.

If you were taking an exam with the question and point distribution shown below, how would you divide your time? Assume the total exam time allowed is 60 minutes. You probably should divide your time as indicated.

Type of question	Number of questions	Total points
Multiple-choice	25 questions	25 points
True-False	20 questions	20 points
Essays	2 questions	55 points

Division of time

Prereading	1–2 minutes
Multiple-choice	15 minutes
True-False	10 minutes
Essays	30 minutes
Review	3–4 minutes

Because the essays are worth twice as many points as either of the other two parts of the exam, it is necessary to spend twice as much time on the essay portion of the exam.

EXERCISE 1

Directions: *For each of the exams described below, estimate approximately how you would divide your time.*

1. Time limit: 75 minutes

Type of question	Number of questions	Total points
Multiple-choice	20 questions	40 points
Matching	10 questions	10 points
Essay	2 questions	50 points

How would you divide your time?

Prereading _____ minutes

Multiple-choice _____ minutes

Matching _____ minutes

Essay _____ minutes

Review _____ minutes

2. Time limit: 40 minutes

Type of question	Number of questions	Total points
True-False	15 questions	30 points
Fill-in-the-blanks	10 questions	30 points
Short-answer	10 questions	40 points

How would you divide your time?

Prereading   —— minutes

True-False   —— minutes

Fill-in-the-blanks   —— minutes

Short-answer   —— minutes

Review   —— minutes

3.   Time limit: 15 minutes (quiz)

Type of question	Number of questions	Total points
Short-answer	10 questions	20 points

How would you divide your time?

Prereading   —— minutes

Short-answer   —— minutes

Review   —— minutes

Hints for Taking Objective Exams

When taking objective exams — usually multiple-choice, true-false, or matching — if you keep in mind the several hints below, they may give you a few more points.

Read the Directions: Before answering any questions, read the directions. Often, an instructor may want the correct answer marked in a particular way (underlined rather than circled). The directions may contain crucial information that you must be aware of in order to answer the questions correctly. If you did not read directions like those below, and you assumed the test questions were of the usual type, you could lose a considerable number of points.

True-False Test Directions: Read each statement. If the statement is true, mark a *T* in the blank to the left of the item. If the statement is false, add and/or subtract words that will make the statement correct.
Multiple-Choice Test Directions: Circle all the choices that correctly complete each statement.

Without reading the directions for the true-false test, you would not know you have to correct statements which are incorrect. Without reading the directions for the multiple-choice test, you would not know that you are to choose more than one answer.

Leave Nothing Blank: Before turning in your exam, check through it to be sure you have answered every question. If you have no idea about the correct answer to a question — guess; you might be right! On a true-false test, your chances of being correct are 50 percent; on a four-choice multiple-choice question, your odds are 25 percent. In other words, if you guess on two true-false questions, you are likely to get one right, and your chances of guessing the correct answer to such a multiple-choice question are one in four.

Students frequently turn in tests with some items unanswered because they leave difficult questions blank, planning to return to them later. Then, in the rush to finish everything, they forget to go back to them. The best way to avoid this problem is to choose immediately what look like the best answers and then mark the question numbers with an X or check mark so that, if you have time at the end of the exam, you can give them further thought. If you run out of time, at least you will have attempted an answer.

Look for Clues: If you encounter a difficult question, choose what seems to be the best answer, mark the question so that you can return to it, and keep the item in mind as you go through the rest of the exam. Sometimes you will see some piece of information later in the exam that brings back your memory of a particular fact or idea. At other times you may notice a piece of information that, if true, contradicts (or proves false) an answer you had already chosen.

Hints for Taking True-False Tests

When taking a true-false test, be sure to read each question carefully. Often there is just one word that makes a statement true or false. Consider for a moment an oversimplified example. Read these two statements:

1. All cats are white.
2. Some cats are white.

Of course, the first statement is false, whereas the second is true. In each statement, only one word determined whether the statement was true or false. While the words and statements are much more complicated on college true-false exams, you will find that one word often determines whether a statement is true or false.

Examples:
1. *All* paragraphs must have a stated main idea.
2. Spelling, punctuation, and handwriting *always* affect the grade given to an essay answer.
3. When taking notes of a lecture, try to write down *everything* the speaker says.

In each of the above examples, the word in italics modifies — or limits — the truth of each statement. When reading a true-false question, look carefully for any limiting words. Among the most common are: *all, some, none, never, always, usually, frequently, most of the time.* To overlook these words may mean the difference of several points on an exam.

EXERCISE 2

Directions: *The following true-false test is based on content presented in the sample chapter in the Appendix of this text. Read each item. Then find and underline the single word which, if changed or deleted, could change the truth or falsity of the statement. In the space provided at the right, indicate whether the statement is true or false by marking* T *for True and* F *for False.*

1. There is no "typical" advertiser. ____

2. The most important element of an ad is the promise it makes. ____

3. Advertisers differ only slightly in the amounts and types of advertising they do. ____

4. Advertising is always evaluated according to how well it communicated to potential buyers. ____

5. The term "continuity" sometimes refers to the timing of advertising within a campaign. ____

6. One disadvantage of advertising in newspapers is that there is little buyer selectivity. ____

7. All advertisements have specific objectives. ____

8. Individual salespeople in a company often are expected to transmit a firm's advertising to the public. ____

9. Budgeting is usually independent from the ad schedule. ____

10. Television is the most widely used advertising for national advertisers. ____

Hints for Taking Matching Tests

In taking a matching test, you are asked to match items in one column with those in a second column. Answer the easiest question first. Cross off choices as you use them unless items may be used more than once. Reason out, as best you can, the remaining items. Be sure to guess, even wildly, for items that you have no idea about.

Hints for Taking Multiple-Choice Exams

First, read the directions carefully to find out whether you are to select the single best answer or all possible answers. In most cases, you are asked to choose the *one best* answer.

A multiple-choice item is made up of a stem and, usually, four or more choices which, when read with the stem, form a statement or complete idea.

Example:
Los Angeles is located in   ←*Stem*
   a. California ⎫
   b. Arizona   ⎬ *Choices*
   c. Nevada
   d. Oregon   ⎭

Los Angeles is located in California (the combination of the stem and the correct choice) forms a true statement. All other combinations make false statements.

This information about the construction of a multiple-choice test should provide you with a strategy for reading multiple-choice questions:

Read the stem and then combine it with each of the choices
to form a statement or sentence. If the statement is false,
eliminate and cross out that choice.

Be sure to read all choices *first,* testing out all the choices in this manner. Do not stop with the second or third choice, even if you are sure that you have found the correct answer. Remember, on most multiple-choice tests your job is to pick the *best* answer, and the last choice may be a better answer than the first three.

Most multiple-choice exams offer at least four choices. In most cases you are directed to choose the one best correct answer. The three remaining choices are known as *distractors,* items that are intended to divert your attention from the correct answers. They are plausible but incorrect. Distractor items often follow this pattern: One item is close to being correct; one is obviously incorrect if you are at all informed about the topic; one item is the opposite of the correct answer or somewhat off the topic.

Some multiple-choice tests include choices that are combinations of previously listed choices. Read the test item in the example below.

Example:
Among the causes of slow reading are
   a. lack of comprehension
   b. reading word-by-word rather than in phrases
   c. poorly developed vocabulary
   d. making too few fixations per line
   e. a and b
   f. a, b, and c
   g. a, b, c, and d

While the addition of choices that are combinations of the previous choices tends to make things confusing, the same procedure suggested above applies. Treat each choice, when combined with the stem, as a true or false statement. As you consider each choice, mark it true or false. If you find more than one true statement, then select the choice which contains the letters of all the true statements you identified.

While nothing can replace recognizing the correct answer as a result of careful study and preparation, you will no doubt encounter questions that you cannot answer. In these situations it is always wise to guess (unless the instructor uses a scoring system in which there is a penalty for guessing). However, rather than making a random guess, use the following suggestions to make an educated guess.

Use Logic and Common Sense: Even if you are unfamiliar with the subject matter, it is sometimes possible to reason out the correct answer. The following item is taken from a history exam on Japanese-American relations after World War II.

Example:
Prejudice and discrimination are
   a. harmful to our society because they waste our economic, political, and social resources
   b. helpful because they ensure us against attack from within
   c. harmful because they create negative images of the United States in foreign countries
   d. helpful because they keep the majority pure and united against minorities

Through logic and common sense, it is possible to eliminate choices b and c. Prejudice and discrimination are seldom, if ever, regarded as positive, desirable, or "helpful," since they are inconsistent with democratic ideals. Having narrowed your answer down to two choices, a or c, you can see that a offers the stronger, more substantial reason why prejudice and discrimination are harmful. What other countries think of the United States is not as serious as a waste of economic, political, and social resources.

Study Items That Are Very Similar: When two choices seem very close and you cannot decide between them, stop and examine each. First, try to express each in your own words. Then, analyze how they differ. Often this process will lead you to a recognition of the correct answer.

Look for Level of Qualifying Words: As is true in true-false tests, the presence of certain qualifying words is important. Since many statements, ideas, principles, and rules have exceptions, you should be careful in selecting items that contain such words as *best, always, all, no, entirely, completely,* all of which suggest that something is always true without exception, and of statements containing such words as *none, never, worst,* suggesting things that are never true without exception. Items containing words that provide for some level of exception, or qualification, are more likely to be correct. Here are a few examples: *often, usually, most, less seldom, few more, most.*

In the following item notice the use of the italicized qualifying words:

Example:
In most societies
   a. values are highly consistent
   b. people *often* believe and act on values which are contradictory
   c. *all* legitimate organizations support the values of the majority
   d. values of equality *never* exist alongside prejudice and discrimination

In this question, items c and d contain the words *all* and *never,* suggesting that those statements are true without exception. Thus, if you did not know the answer to this question based on content, you could eliminate items c and d on the basis of the level of qualifiers.

Hints for Taking Essay Exams

Essay questions are usually graded on two counts — what you say and how you say it. It is not enough, then, simply to include the correct information. The information must be presented in a logical, organized way which demonstrates that you have an understanding of the subject you are writing about. There can be as much as one whole letter-grade difference between a well-written and poorly written essay, although both contain the same basic information. Here are a few hints for getting as many points as possible on essay questions:

Read the Directions First: The directions may tell you how many essays to answer, how to structure your answer, or specify a minimum or maximum length for your answer.

Read the Question Carefully: The question usually includes three valuable pieces of information. First, the question tells you the topic(s) you are to write about. Second, it also contains a limiting word which restricts and directs your answer. Finally, the question contains a key word or phrase which tells you how to organize and present answers. Read the essay question in this example:

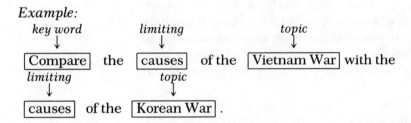

Example:

key word   limiting   topic

Compare   the   causes   of the   Vietnam War   with the

limiting   topic

causes   of the   Korean War .

In this example you have two topics — the Vietnam War and the Korean War. The question also contains a limiting word which restricts your discussion to these topics and tells you what to include in your answer. In the sample question, the limiting word is *causes*. It tells you to limit your answer to a discussion of events that started, or caused, each war. Do not include information about events of the war or its effects. The key word in the sample question is *compare*. It means you should consider the similarities, and possibly the differences, in the causes of the two wars. When directed to compare, you already have some clues as to how your answer should be written. One possibility is to discuss the causes of one war and then the causes of the other and finally to make an overall statement about their similarities. Another choice is to discuss one type of cause for each of the wars, and then go on to discuss another type of cause for each. For instance, you could discuss the economic causes of each, then the political causes of each.

There are several common key words and phrases used in essay questions. They are listed below along with the usual meaning of each:

Discuss: Consider all important aspects, characteristics, or main points about the topic. Give as much information as possible.

Compare: Discuss how items are the same; mention all important similarities. Include details and examples. Some instructors use the word *compare* more generally, and intend that you should discuss both similarities and differences.

Contrast: Discuss the differences between the items mentioned in the question. Show how the items differ by including details and examples.

Define: Give a clear meaning of the term along with some detail to indicate that you really understand it. A good definition should show the limits or restrictions of the term as well as how it differs from similar things in its class.

Explain: When explaining a concept, trend, or idea, you are expected to describe and include sufficient detail to demonstrate that you understand and have thought about the idea. Be as specific as possible, including examples, illustrations, and reasons.

Trace: In paragraph form, describe the development or progress of the particular trend, usually in chronological order.

Evaluate: React to the topic or problem in a logical way, applying theories and principles you have learned in the course. If available, include opinions of authorities as well as your own reactions. Be sure to include reasons and the background information used in forming your evaluation.

Summarize: Cover the major points in brief form. When an instructor asks you to summarize, a detailed explanation of each point is usually not expected. However, be sure to write in complete sentences using a paragraph format.

Describe: When you are asked to describe something, you are usually expected to tell what something looks or feels like, or how something happened, in a manner that would enable the reader to create a mental picture of the object or event.

EXERCISE 3

Directions: *Read each of the following essay questions. In each question, underline the topic, circle the limiting word, and place a box around the key word.*

1. Discuss the long-term effects of the trend toward a smaller, more self-contained family structure.
2. Trace the development of monopolies in the late nineteenth and early twentieth centuries in America.
3. Explain one effect of the Industrial Revolution upon each of three of the following:
   a. transportation
   b. capitalism
   c. socialism
   d. population growth
   e. scientific research
4. Discuss the reasons why, although tropical plants have very large leaves and most desert plants have very small leaves, cactus grows equally well in both habitats.
5. Describe the events leading up to the War of 1812.
6. Compare and contrast the purposes and procedures in textbook marking and lecture notetaking.
7. Briefly describe a complete approach to reading and studying a textbook chapter that will enable you to handle a test on that material successfully.

8. List four factors that influence memory or recall ability, and explain how each can be used to make study more efficient.
9. Summarize the techniques a speaker or lecturer may use to emphasize the important concepts and ideas in his lecture.
10. Explain the value and purpose of the prereading technique, and list the steps involved in prereading a textbook chapter.

Organize Your Answer: As mentioned before, a well-written, organized essay often gets a higher grade than its opposite. Read each of these examples and notice how they differ. Each essay was written in response to this question on a psychology final exam: *Describe the stages involved in the memory process.*

Example 1:

Memory is important to everybody's life. Memory has special ways to help you get a better recollection of things and ideas. Psychologists believe that memory has three stages: encoding, storage, and retrieval.

In the encoding stage, you are putting facts and ideas into a code, usually words, and filing them away in your memory. Encoding involves preparing information for storage in memory.

The second stage of memory is storage. It is the stage that most people call memory. It involves keeping information so that it is accessible for use later in time. How well information is stored can be affected by old information already stored and newer information that is added later.

The third step in memory is retrieval, which means the ability to get back information that is in storage. There are two types of retrieval — recognition and recall. In recognition, you have to be able to identify the correct information from several choices. In recall, you have to pull information directly from your memory without any help or clues. When you write an essay test, you are using the recall type of retrieval.

Example 2:

Memory is very complicated in how it works. It involves remembering things that are stored in your mind and being able to pull them out when you want to remember them. When you pull information out of your memory it is called retrieval. How well you can remember something is affected by how you keep the information in your mind and how you put it in. When keeping, or storing, information you have to realize that this information will be affected by old information already in your memory. Putting information in your memory is called encoding, and it means that you store facts and ideas in word form in your memory. Information stored in your memory can also be influenced by information that you add to your memory later.

There are two ways you can retrieve information. You can either recognize it or recall it. When you recognize information you are able to spot the correct information among other information. When you recall information you have to pull information out of your head. Recall is what you have to do when you write an essay exam.

While these two essays contain practically the same information, the first will probably receive a higher grade. In this essay, it is easy to see that the writer knows that there are three stages in the memory process and knows how to explain each. The writer opens the essay by stating that there are three stages and then devotes one paragraph to each of the three stages.

In the second essay it is not easy to find out what the stages of memory are. The paragraphs are not organized according to stages in the memory process. The writer does not write about one stage at a time in a logical order. Retrieval is mentioned first; then storage and retrieval are discussed further. At the end, the writer returns to the topic of retrieval and gives further information.

Before you start to write, stop and think about what information you will include in your answer and how you will arrange it. Make a mini-outline of all the things you want to include in the answer. Here you may draw upon the word lists you studied while preparing for the exam. Once you have a word outline, rearrange it in the most effective order. You may want to put major topics and important ideas first and less important points toward the end. Or you may decide to organize your answer chronologically, discussing events early in time near the beginning of the essay and mentioning more recent events near the end. The topic you are discussing will largely determine the order of presentation.

Write Answers in Correct Form: Be sure to write your answers in complete sentences and to include only one major point in each paragraph. Each paragraph should have a main idea, usually expressed in one sentence. The remainder of the paragraph should explain, prove, or support the main idea you state. A frequent criticism instructors make of student essay answers is the failure to explain fully or to support ideas. By following the rule of thumb of only one major idea per paragraph, you will avoid this danger and will force yourself to explain your major points.

Your first paragraph should contain a general statement of what the entire essay is about. You might begin an essay to answer a question which asks you to discuss the practical applications of Newton's three laws of motion by writing: "There are many practical applications to Newton's laws of motion." Then you should proceed to name each of the three laws and its practical applications, devoting one paragraph to each law. If you have time, your final paragraph may be a summary or review of the major points you covered in the essay.

Make Your Answers Readable: Because there is a certain amount of judgment and personal reaction involved as an instructor reads your answer, it is to your advantage to make your paper as easy to read as possible. It is annoying to an instructor to try to read poor handwriting and carelessly written answers. Try these hints:

1. Use pen — it is easier to read and does not smear.
2. Use 8½″ × 11″ paper if paper is not provided. Reading a handful of small sheets is sometimes difficult and confusing.
3. Number your pages and put your name on each sheet.
4. Use clean, unwrinkled paper.
5. Do not scratch out sentences you want to leave out — just draw a single line through each and write *omit* in the margin.
6. If the paper is thin or ink runs, write on only one side of the paper.

7. Leave plenty of space between questions. Leave a 1"–2" margin at each side. The instructor will need space to write in comments.

Proofread Your Answers: After you have written the essay, read through it twice. Before rereading your essay the first time, read the question again. Then check to see that you have included all necessary facts and information and that you have adequately explained each fact. Add anything you feel improves your answer. Then reread the essay a second time, checking and correcting all the mechanical aspects of your writing. Check for hard-to-read words, spelling errors, and punctuation errors. Again, make all necessary corrections.

If You Run Out of Time: Despite careful planning of exam time, it may happen that you run out of time before you can finish writing one of the essays. If this happens, try to jot down the major ideas which you would discuss fully if you had time. Often, your instructor will give you partial credit for this type of response, especially if you mention that you ran out of time.

If You Don't Know the Answer: Despite careful preparation, you may not know or cannot remember a particular answer. If this should happen, do not leave a blank page; write something. Attempt to answer the question — you may even hit upon some partially correct information. However, the main reason for writing something is to give the instructor a chance to give you at least a few points for trying. If you leave a completely blank page, your instructor has no choice but to give you zero points. And usually when you lose full credit on any one essay, you have automatically eliminated your chances of getting a high passing grade.

SUMMARY

Tests, exams, and quizzes are an important part of most college courses, because they, in part, determine grades. This chapter provided specific suggestions on how to prepare for exams and offered practical techniques on how to take various types of exams.

In preparing for an exam, the essential task is to review what you have already learned. It is important to review all major sources of information, including textbook assignments, lecture notes, previous exams and quizzes, teacher handouts, course outlines, and out-of-class assignments. The timing of your review and the manner in which you review also influence how well you perform on the exam.

Specific techniques are suggested for reviewing both objective tests and essay exams. For objective tests, effective review involves the careful identification of information to be reviewed in such sources as textbook underlining and lecture notes. Self-testing and organization of the information in an easy-to-study index card system or study sheet system are important parts of the review process. In preparing for an essay exam, it is suggested that you identify topics that may become questions in the exam, and then collect and organize sufficient information on each topic.

When taking any type of exam, try to approach it in an organized, systematic way. This involves taking necessary equipment, arriving on time, deliberately choosing a seat in a nondistracting section of the room, prereading the exam, and planning the time you will devote to various sections of the exam. In taking any type of objective exam, be sure to read the directions carefully, leave nothing blank, and look for clues that will help you recall the information. Specific suggestions are included for taking true-false, matching, and multiple-choice exams. When taking an essay exam, it is important to read the question carefully to determine exactly what type of response your instructor wants. Essay answers should be carefully organized and written in an easy-to-read form.

18. Preparing Written Assignments and Research Papers

Use this chapter to:

1. *Learn how to prepare common types of written assignments.*
2. *Develop a step-by-step procedure for writing research papers.*

Do you have difficulty getting started on writing assignments? When you start writing do you feel like you have nothing to say? Have you ever worked hard on a paper and still not received a grade that was worth all the time and effort you put in? If you answered "yes" to any of these questions, your response is typical of many college students. Many students find writing to be a difficult, often frustrating, task. In fact, many professional writers experience the same difficulty generating ideas and getting started. One purpose of this chapter is to offer some practical suggestions for getting started on and successfully completing the most common types of writing assignments. Another is to provide specific step-by-step procedures for organizing and writing a research paper.

WHY WRITTEN ASSIGNMENTS ARE GIVEN

If you are going to put in all the effort that is required to complete a writing assignment, it often helps to understand why instructors assign them. You know that instructors use papers as a means of evaluating your learning and awarding grades. More important, however, writing assignments are a means of helping you learn. Putting your ideas on paper forces you to think your ideas through, draw them together, and examine how they relate to one another. If you can put important concepts and ideas from the course into your own words, you will retain them longer and begin to put them to use more readily. Often, once you have recorded your ideas, you will find that you need additional information or that you need to read what others have written about the topic. Instructors, then, may assign a paper for the purpose of encouraging you to learn more about a particular topic.

How to Take Advantage of Written Assignments

Most students, if given their choice, would rather take an exam than write a paper. Actually, written assignments have several advantages over exams. In fact, you might think of a paper as a golden opportunity to demonstrate what you know. An exam is usually a one-time-only, you-know-it-or-you-don't pressured situation. A written assignment allows you unlimited time, unlimited references, and the opportunity to ask for help from friends or from your instructor. When a paper is assigned, then, think of it as an opportunity to work in an open-ended, nonpressured way. Relax, take your time, and prove what you know.

TYPES OF WRITTEN ASSIGNMENTS

There are several types of writing that an instructor may assign to you. The most common types are listed here along with a brief description of what is usually expected for each.

Essay Exams

Although essay exams aren't papers, they do constitute a major portion of assigned writing in some courses. The most important thing to remember in writing essay exams is to answer each question *clearly* and *specifically*. Take the time to figure out what the instructor is asking for; then, write your essay in direct response to the question (see Chapter 17 for more information on studying for and taking essay exams).

Essays or Compositions

Many instructors give assignments that require you to present or discuss your own ideas on a particular topic. Often this type of assignment is simply called a paper. A philosophy instructor may ask you, for instance, to "write a paper explaining your views on abortion." Usually, the instructor specifies the topic or the general subject area to write about. An exception may occur in English composition classes, when you are allowed to select a topic but the instructor specifies *how* you are to write or organize your paper. Often, too, the instructor suggests a particular length, either in number of words or pages.

When a paper of this type is given, listen carefully as the instructor announces and discusses the assignment. At that time, the instructor will often indicate what is expected. Jot down the instructor's exact wording of the assignment so that you can refer to it before you begin writing. Also jot down any examples he or she may give. You might find them useful as a starting point for generating ideas.

If the assignment is unclear or you feel you do not understand what is expected, do not hesitate to check with others in the class or to ask the instructor after class. It is your responsibility to let your instructor know if you do not understand what you are to do. If you decide to speak with your instructor, try to ask specific questions rather than simply saying you do not understand the assignment. By asking specific questions, you are more likely to get specific information that will help you to complete the assignment.

If you are required to write about a topic that you know little or nothing about, it is worthwhile to spend an hour or so in the library reading about the topic. Once you have learned a little about the topic, you will feel more confident writing about it.

Factual Reports

Another type of writing assignment commonly used in college courses is the report. When you write a report you are expected to present factual information on a particular topic. For example, in a chemistry course a summary or description of a laboratory experiment might be considered a report. Or in psychology class you may be asked to observe the behavior of a particular group of people and report your observations. In sociology, you might be asked to do a survey and report your findings. Most often, your instructor will suggest, or perhaps require, that you follow a particular format. The length will often be dictated by the nature of the assignment. Here are a few specific guidelines for writing reports:

1. Be thorough. Include all important details.
2. Be concise. Express your ideas clearly and in the briefest possible way.
3. Be accurate. Because you are reporting facts or observations, be certain that the information you include is correct.
4. Avoid flowery language, creative or humorous touches.
5. If you do not have sufficient information, be sure to check reference books to acquire what you need. Do not hesitate to use the library if your text does not contain the information you need.
6. If no format is suggested by your instructor, devise a logical format with headings or subheadings before you begin writing.
7. Do not include reactions, opinions, or interpretation of your topic unless your instructor has indicated that you should do so.

Reaction Papers

Unlike a report, a reaction paper should present your personal opinion or reaction to a particular topic. You may be asked to react to something you've read, such as a poem or short story or to describe your feelings about a film, lecture, play, recording, or demonstration. The length of a reaction paper may vary, but it is usually a one- or two-page paper. To write reaction papers effectively, use the following suggestions:

1. Think before you write. Decide what your reactions really are. You may need to review or reread the material (if you are reacting to something you have read) or any notes that you may have.
2. Be sure to state and briefly describe what your reaction paper is about.
3. Organize or group your reactions in some way. Don't just write reactions as they occur to you.
4. As a means of getting started and of collecting ideas, discuss the topic with a friend.

Research Papers

The research paper is the longest and most time-consuming type of writing assignment. Because of the amount of work it requires, the research paper is usually weighted heavily in determining your final course grade. A research paper or "term paper" involves locating new information and ideas about a particular topic and organizing them into written form. The first step is to research the topic in the library, locating and reading appropriate books, periodicals, and reference sources. As you read, you should record, in note form, information you may want to include in your paper. Then, once you've collected sufficient information, organize your information and write the paper. (Specific suggestions for writing and researching this type of paper will be presented later in the chapter.)

GENERAL SUGGESTIONS FOR WRITING PAPERS

When they begin working on a paper, many students just pick up a pen and start writing the paper. This is not usually the best way to begin. Actually, in writing, as in reading, there are certain things you can do *before* you begin writing the paper as well as *after* you have written the paper that can help ensure that you have produced an acceptable, well-written product. The steps, or stages, that most good writers go through in writing a paper are prewriting, organizing, writing, revising, and proofreading.

Prewriting

You might think of prewriting as a process similar to prereading. When prereading (see Chapter 7) you are, in a sense, getting ready to read, focusing your attention on the material and anticipating the content and organization. When you write, you also need to get ready by making some decisions about the purposes, overall organization, and content of what you will write. Here are a few suggestions for how to get off to a good start:

Get Organized: As is true for reading and study, when and where you write is important. Choose a time of day when you can concentrate and a place free of distractions. Have plenty of paper, pens, pencils, and a dictionary available. Begin by reviewing what your assignment is. Re-read either your instructor's statement of the assignment, if presented in writing, or your notes on the assignment if it was given orally. As you review look for clues about what specifically is expected.

Once you are familiar with the nature and scope of the assignment, try to establish a time schedule for its completion. Never try to complete a paper in one evening. You need time to let the paper rest; this allows you to come back to it later to reconsider what you've written in a different perspective and with a critical eye.

Choose a Manageable Topic: In many cases, except for research papers, the topic is defined by your instructor or by the nature of the assignment. In the event that you do have a choice, use the following guidelines:

1. Choose a topic that interests you. You will find that it is much easier to maintain a high level of concentration and motivation if the topic is genuinely interesting. Also, ideas will flow more easily if you are involved with your topic.

2. Choose a topic you know something about. If you do not know very much about a topic, it is very difficult, in some cases almost impossible, to write about it. So, unless you are prepared to learn about a topic before writing about it, avoid topics that you know little about.

3. Choose a topic that can be handled effectively in the length of paper you are writing. For example, you could not do a good job of discussing the general topic "Religions of the World" in a three-page paper. There are many religions in the world, and each has its own set of beliefs, rituals, and codes for living. It would be impossible to discuss each in the length of paper assigned. A much better, more manageable, topic would be something like "Changing Trends in Catholicism in the Twentieth Century." This topic is more specific than "Religions of the World" and is a manageable part of that broader topic. Techniques for narrowing a subject to a workable topic will be discussed in a later section of this chapter.

Develop Ideas about the Topic: Once you have chosen a topic, the next step is to generate or develop ideas about your topic. If you have trouble, as many students do, in finding something to say, you might try a technique called free writing. Figure 18-1 shows a portion of free

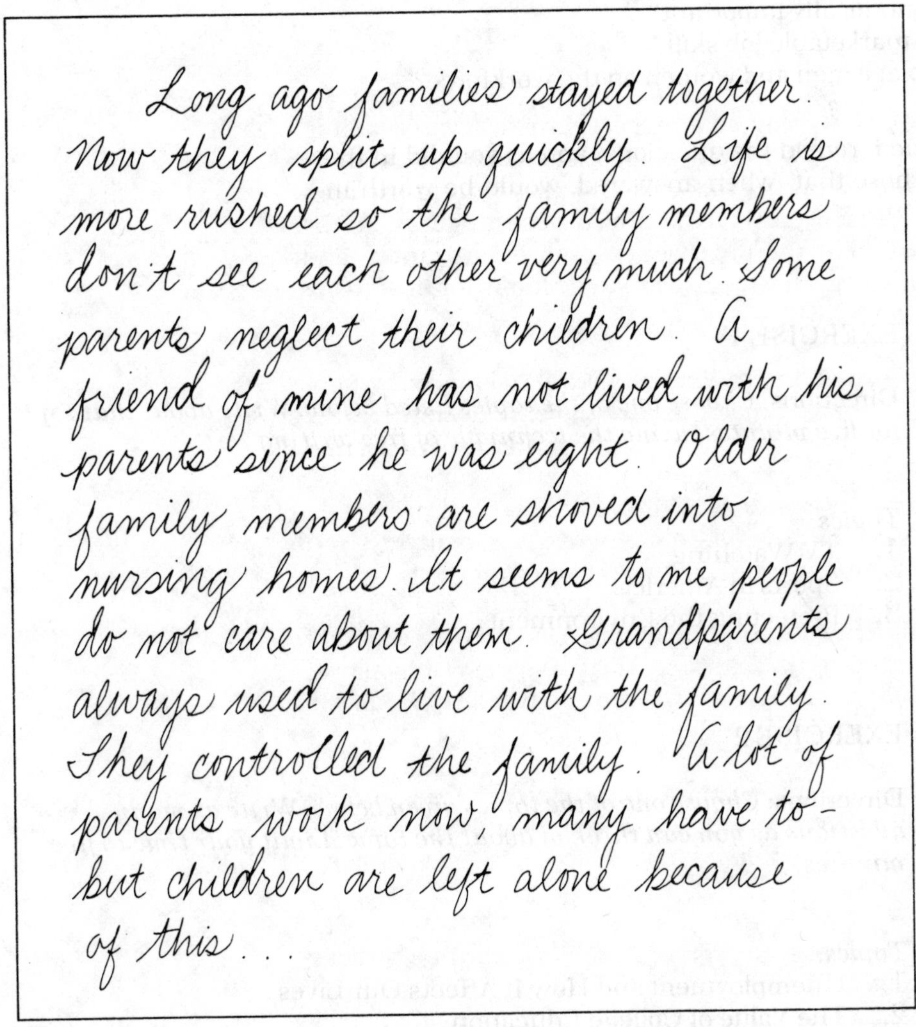

> Long ago families stayed together. Now they split up quickly. Life is more rushed so the family members don't see each other very much. Some parents neglect their children. A friend of mine has not lived with his parents since he was eight. Older family members are shoved into nursing homes. It seems to me people do not care about them. Grandparents always used to live with the family. They controlled the family. A lot of parents work now, many have to—but children are left alone because of this . . .

FIGURE 18-1

writing on the topic of the changing American family. It works like this: Take a piece of paper and just start writing anything that comes into your mind about the topic. Do not be concerned about whether you are writing in complete sentences or whether the ideas make sense or connect to one another. You might think of free writing as a type of "brainstorming," or thinking of a variety of ideas on a topic. Keep writing continuously for a set period of time, four to five minutes or so. If you cannot think of an idea about the topic, write whatever else comes to mind.

When you've finished, reread what you have written. You'll be surprised at the number of different ideas that you've thought of. Then, underline or rewrite those ideas that seem worth including in your paper. An alternative technique to generate ideas is to take five minutes or so and write down all the questions you can think of on your topic. For instance, you might write the following questions about the topic of the role of computers in our daily lives:

1. How do computers affect our lives?
2. Have computers changed our way of life?
3. Who allows computers to influence us?
4. Do computers invade our right to privacy?
5. Are computers economically important?
6. Is computer skill a marketable job skill?
7. Can computers replace men and women on the workforce?

When you've finished, reread the questions, and as you did in free writing, try to identify those that, when answered, would be worth including in your paper.

EXERCISE 1

Directions: *Choose one of the topics listed below. Write about that topic for five minutes, using the technique of free writing.*

Topics:
1. TV Watching
2. Sports in America
3. Protecting the Environment

EXERCISE 2

Directions: *Choose one of the topics given below. Write as many questions as you can think of about the topic. Limit your time to five minutes.*

Topics:
1. Unemployment and How It Affects Our Lives
2. The Value of College Education
3. Soap Operas

Organizing and Outlining

Once you have identified some ideas to include in your paper, the next step is to organize them. This involves arranging the ideas in an order that will result in an understandable and well-written paper. The most effective way to organize your ideas is to make an outline. An outline will help you see the relationship of ideas to one another. To accomplish this use the following steps:

1. Quickly list the ideas in the order in which you wrote them.
2. Read through the list looking for ideas that are similar or those that should follow one another.
3. Rewrite your outline, trying to group ideas together so that they are listed in a logical order (an order that would be a sensible one for discussing your topic).

Writing a Draft

Now that you have oganized your ideas, you are ready to begin writing a first draft of your paper. Here are a few suggestions:

1. Always plan on revising and recopying your paper. Never plan on your first draft being your final copy.
2. As you begin, only be concerned with getting your ideas down on paper. Do not be concerned with exact word choice or with correct punctuation. You can check and correct those details later.
3. Use your outline as a guide. Discuss the ideas in the order in which they appear in the outline.
4. Be sure to explain each idea completely. A common fault instructors find with student papers is that they do not include enough detail. Try to include, where appropriate, examples, reasons, descriptions, or other supporting information.
5. Do not hesitate to make changes as you think of them.

Revising

Revision is the step that can make a good paper a better one or an unacceptable paper acceptable. Revision involves rereading, rewriting, and making changes to improve both the content and organization of your paper. Here are a few suggestions to follow:

1. Do not revise as soon as you have finished writing. Instead, try to arrange for a lapse of time between writing and revision. The lapse of time gives you the distance and objectivity that you do not have immediately upon completing your draft.
2. If you have trouble finding anything wrong with your paper, ask a friend to read and criticize it. Also, ask him or her to summarize what your paper said. This will allow you to see if you have expressed your ideas clearly and accurately.
3. To evaluate your own paper, try asking yourself the following questions:

a. Are the ideas clearly expressed?

b. Do the ideas tie together to form a unified piece of writing?

c. Is each major idea supported with facts and details?

Proofreading

Once you have prepared the final copy of your paper, be sure to read it to detect any errors in spelling, punctuation, grammar, and usage. At this point, try to ignore the idea flow and simply check each sentence to be sure that it does not contain errors. To locate spelling errors, try reading the paper backward, word for word. To locate sentence structure errors, read the paper backward, sentence by sentence. If your paper is typewritten, also check for typographical errors such as omitted words or sentences and transposed letters.

Although you may not think it is fair, your paper's physical appearance and grammatical correctness will actually influence its grade. It pays to make sure that your work is error free. After all, it would be unfortunate to spend a great deal of time and effort on a research paper only to have it downgraded because you did not take a few minutes to proofread and make final corrections.

WRITING RESEARCH PAPERS

In assigning a research paper, your instructor is really asking you to learn about a topic and then to organize and to summarize what you have learned. You are expected to learn on your own, using whatever resources and references are available. Completing a research paper, then, involves much more than just writing. It involves topic selection, locating appropriate sources of information, reading, taking notes, and organizing the information. In fact, writing is actually the final step in the process of acquiring and organizing information on a particular topic.

The purpose of this portion of the chapter is to offer general guidelines for completing a successful research paper. After providing some general tips for getting started, the section will present a step-by-step procedure for collecting information and writing the paper.

Tips for Getting Started

The first college research paper you do is always the most difficult. The reason for this is that you are learning *how* to do the paper while doing it. Once you have mastered the techniques for your first research paper, later ones will be much easier and less time consuming. Here are a few tips to help you get started:

1. Find out how important the research paper is by finding out how heavily the paper counts in your final course grade. This information will help you to determine how much time and effort you should put into the paper.

2. Get an early start. Even if the paper is not due until the end of the semester, start working on the paper as soon as possible. Starting

early may enable you to produce a good rather than a just barely acceptable paper. Also, if you have not done a research paper before, you will need time to become familiar with the process.

There are several other advantages to starting early. You will find books and references readily available in the library, while if you wait until everyone is working on their papers, popular sources will be in use or checked out by other students. Also, starting early gives you time to acquire information you may need from other libraries through interlibrary loan services. Finally, an early start allows you the time to think, to organize, and even to make mistakes and have time to correct them.

3. Ask your instructor for advice. If you experience difficulty, ask your instructor for help with a particular problem. Often, through their experience with the subject matter, instructors are able to suggest alternate approaches to the topic, recommend a particular reference, or suggest a different organization. However, do not go to see your instructor until you've wrestled with the problem yourself and find yourself at a standstill. When you do see your instructor, take your notes, outlines, and rough drafts.

STEPS IN WRITING A RESEARCH PAPER

In paging through the remainder of this chapter, you might think that writing a research paper is a very complicated process. You will see that eleven steps are shown and that they appear to be fairly detailed. However, if you follow each step, you will discover that you are carefully led through a fairly routine process of focusing your paper, collecting information, and writing the paper. The steps are:

1. Narrow your topic.
2. Determine the purpose of the paper.
3. Locate appropriate sources of information.
4. Refine the topic through further reading.
5. Write a tentative thesis statement.
6. Collect information.
7. Form an outline.
8. Write a first draft.
9. Revise the draft.
10. Prepare the final copy.
11. Prepare the bibliography.

Step 1: Narrow Your Topic

Choosing and narrowing your topic is critical to producing a good paper. If you begin with an unmanageable topic, regardless of how hard you work, you will be unable to produce an acceptable paper. Also, your task can be made much easier if you choose a manageable topic — one for which information is readily accessible and understandable. Some instructors might require that you select a topic within a specific subject area; others may accept any topic that pertains to the course. In either case choice is involved.

The most important consideration in selecting a topic is to choose one that is neither too broad nor too narrow. If you choose a topic that is too broad, it will be impossible for you to cover all its aspects adequately. On the other hand, if it is too specific, you may have difficulty finding enough to write about. For most students, the tendency is to select a topic that is too general.

Suppose you are taking a course in ecology and the environment and you've been assigned a fifteen-page research paper. Your instructor will allow you to choose any topic related to the course of study. You have always been interested in environmental pollution and decide to do your research paper on this subject. Because there are many causes of pollution, many types of pollution, many effects of pollution, both immediate and long-term, you realize that the topic of environmental pollution is much too broad. To narrow or limit this topic you might choose one type of pollution — such as water pollution — and then decide to research the causes or the effects. Or you might decide to limit your topic to a study of the different types of chemicals that pollute the air.

Often it is necessary to narrow your topic two or three times. The process of narrowing a topic might be diagramed as shown here:

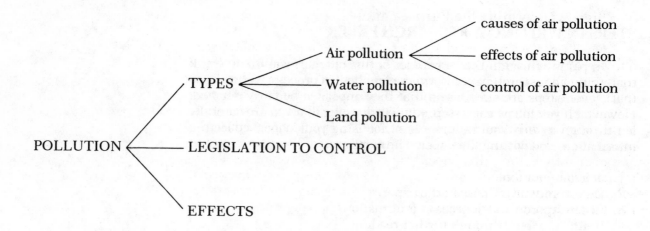

Once you have a subject area or a broad topic in mind, try to think of ways your topic could be subdivided. Often, it is necessary to acquire some general background about the subject. For ideas to start with, check the card catalog in the library under your subject and read the subject headings that immediately follow it to see how the subject is divided. Also check an encyclopedia to see how the subject is divided. Then, skim quickly through to learn a little about the topic. Depending on your subject, you may also wish to consult other texts in the subject area to get a brief overview of the field. Make a list of possible topics. As an alternate approach, make a list of questions that might be asked about the subject. Each of your questions suggests a possible division of your subject. Often, it may be necessary to further limit these divisions.

EXERCISE 3

Directions: *Assume that one of your instructors has assigned a research paper on one of the following subjects. Choose one and narrow it to a topic that is manageable in a ten- to twenty-page paper. If necessary check the card catalog, an encyclopedia entry, or various texts in the field. Use an outline like the one shown below.*

Subjects:
1. Clothing styles and fashion
2. Test tube babies
3. Sports
4. Death
5. Pornography

Subject

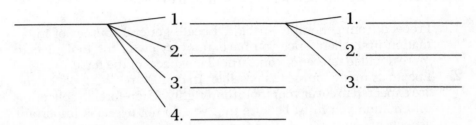

Step 2: Determine the Purpose of the Paper

Once you have narrowed your topic, the next step is to decide the purpose of your paper. You should decide whether you want to prove something about your topic, inform others about it, or explain or analyze it. In some cases, your purpose may have already been defined by your instructor when he or she assigned the research paper. However, most of the time you will need to decide how you will approach your topic. To determine your approach, ask yourself this question: What do I want to accomplish by writing this paper? Whatever you determine as an approach will affect directly how you proceed from this point. The type of sources you consult, the amount of reading you do, and the thesis statement that you state and develop are each shaped by your purpose.

Step 3: Locate Appropriate Sources of Information

Your campus library, its librarians, and its reference materials are the keys to locating appropriate sources of information on your topic. If you have not used the library on your campus, take a half hour or so to visit the library just to become acquainted with its organization and the services it offers. Do not try to begin researching your topic until you know what is available in your library and how to use it. Be sure to find out:

1. how the card catalog is organized
2. how the books are arranged on the shelves
3. where the reference section is located
4. whether there is a reference librarian available
5. whether there is a photocopy machine
6. where periodicals (journals and magazines) are located
7. the procedure for checking out books and periodicals
8. whether your library participates in an interlibrary loan system
9. if a floor plan of the library is available

If you feel lost in the library or find that you are unfamiliar with many of the reference materials, check to see what assistance the library has to offer. Some libraries offer one- to two-hour workshops on library usage and research skills; others have pamphlets, brochures, or video-tapes that provide basic information on using the campus library. If none of these services is available, ask the reference librarian for assistance. After all, a reference librarian's prime responsibility is to assist students in using the library.

Rules of Thumb for Locating Sources: Once you are generally familiar with the library, then you are ready to begin locating sources of information. There are several rules of thumb to follow:

1. Proceed from general to specific. Locate general sources of information first; then, once you have an overview of the topic, locate more detailed references on particular aspects of the topic.

2. Locate as many sources as possible. In doing a research paper you are expected to cover your topic thoroughly. Therefore, in collecting information you must be sure that you do not overlook important aspects of your topic. By locating and checking as many references as possible you can be certain that you have covered the topic completely. Once you have read several sources, it is possible to skim additional sources, checking to see what new information is provided.

3. Record all sources used. Many students waste valuable time by failing to keep a complete record of all references used. An important part of any research paper is the bibliography, or list of all the references you use to write the paper (see Step 11, p. 266). To prepare this bibliography in the easiest way possible, just write down each source as you use it. If you forget to do this, you will have to spend additional time later checking back and trying to locate each source you used.

   The easiest way to record bibliographical information is to use a separate 3 x 5 index card for each source. Later you will see that the cards enable you to alphabetize your references easily. To avoid wasting time recopying or rewriting information, record it in the exact form in which it should appear in the bibliography.

4. Ask for assistance. If you are having difficulty locating information or if you are not certain that you have exhausted all possible sources, ask the reference librarian for assistance. Most librarians are ready and willing to guide serious students in their research.

Using the Card Catalog: The key to every library is the card catalog. It is an easy-to-use record of all the books and periodicals that the library owns. Two, three, or more separate cards are filed for each book in the library. Each book may be listed by author, by title, and by subject(s) covered. The card briefly describes what the book covers and contains a call number that you can use to locate the book on the shelf. The card catalog, then, is one of the first places to start in researching a topic.

Using Reference Materials: In addition to its holdings of books and periodicals, libraries have a reference section that contains general references, sources that cannot be checked out. Among the most common reference materials are encyclopedias, dictionaries, periodical indexes, almanacs, biographical dictionaries, atlases, and statistical handbooks.

Also, many libraries contain a reserve section in which instructors "reserve," or place on restricted use, important, useful sources that many students wish to use. The reference librarian is available to assist you in using these sources.

Step 4: Refine the Topic Through Further Reading

To become familiar with the range and scope of your topic, and to acquire background information, it is useful to read or skim several general sources of information. Your purpose, at this point, is to learn enough about your topic to be able to refine the direction, or focus, of your paper. Again, a good starting point is the encyclopedia. The entry will provide you with an overview of your topic and may suggest directions for further limiting your topic. Other useful sources include textbooks on the general subject of which your topic is part, or books written on the subject.

Since your purpose is to get an overview of the topic, do not try to read everything. You might read parts of the material and skip others. Do not try to take notes on your reading yet. Instead, just jot down on index cards references that would be useful for later, more thorough reading. Also, jot down any ideas that might come to mind about how to approach, to further limit, or to organize your topic. Continue sampling general sources until you find that most of what you are reading is no longer new and that you have already read it in another source.

Step 5: Write a Tentative Thesis Statement

A thesis statement is a one-sentence statement of what your whole paper is about. It states the idea you will develop throughout the paper. You might think of a thesis statement as similar to the topic sentence of a paragraph or the central thought of a passage. Each states, in a general way, what the entire paragraph or passage is about. Similarly, the thesis statement indicates to your reader what your paper will be about.

Here are a few examples of thesis statements that could be written for the topic of effects of air pollution:

Examples:

1. Air pollution has had a dramatic effect on the lives of twentieth-century Americans.
2. Air pollution has been the primary cause of numerous health-related problems for Americans.
3. Public concern over the long-range effects of air pollution has forced industrial reform.

Notice that each specifically states what the writer intends to show about air pollution and its effects.

Since, at this point, you have done only preliminary reading and research, your thesis statement is only tentative. You should plan on changing, revising, or narrowing this statement as you proceed through the remaining steps. Right now your thesis statement should express the idea *you think* your paper will explain or discuss. In a sense, the thesis statement further narrows your topic, by limiting your paper to a specific focus or approach.

EXERCISE 4

Directions: *Assume that each of the following is the topic of a research paper. For each, write a thesis statement that suggests a direction of development or focus for the topic.*

1. *Topic:* Cigarette Smoking and Health
    Thesis Statement: _____

    _____

2. *Topic:* The Progress of the Women's Liberation Movement
    Thesis Statement: _____

    _____

3. *Topic:* The Draft for Women
    Thesis Statement: _____

    _____

4. *Topic:* Choosing a Career
    Thesis Statement: _____

    _____

5. *Topic:* Gay Liberation
    Thesis Statement: _____

    _____

Step 6: Collect Information: Reading and Notetaking

Now that you have written a tentative thesis statement, the next step is to collect and record the information that supports your thesis.

Reading Reference Material: In reading reference material your purpose for reading is clearly defined: you are looking for facts and ideas that will help you prove, explain, or support your thesis statement. However, reading reference sources is a very different type of reading than you are required to do in textbooks. In textbooks you are reading for retention and recall of most of the information presented. When reading reference material, on the other hand, not all information is useful or important. Also, you are not trying to remember everything you read; instead, when you find a useful piece of information, you can write it down for later reference.

Prereading is a valuable skill in identifying sources that may contain information on your topic. Once you've located a book in the card catalog and then found it on the library shelves, take a few minutes to preview it to determine if it contains useful information before you check it out. You can save yourself valuable time and can avoid carrying home armloads of books by prereading to select only appropriate, usable sources.

Because high retention is not required when reading reference material, you can afford to skim, scan, and skip large portions of material (see Chapter 24 for skimming and scanning techniques). In fact, trying to read everything, regardless of whether you use it in your paper, would be an extremely inefficient use of time.

Taking Notes: The manner and form in which you take notes largely determines whether writing the paper will be a relatively simple or extremely difficult, time-consuming task. The next two steps, developing an outline and writing the paper, require that the information you collect be in a form that can be rearranged or placed in a specific order.

One effective way to take notes is to use index cards; the 5 x 8- or 4 x 6-inch sizes are best. Some students prefer to use separate full sheets of paper. Use a separate card or sheet of paper for each different subtopic, or different aspect of your topic. Record the author's last name and the pages you used in the upper right corner. In the upper left corner write the subtopic that the notes are concerned with. Be sure to write only on one side of the cards. A sample notetaking card or sheet might look like this:

Violence - how it's learned   Barlow p. 125-6

    violence learned through imitation + modelling.

      - experiments by Bandura show that children

pick up behavior patterns of adults they know or respect.

    ex. Child views film of woman beating/kicking a doll/

        then child is given similar doll.

        Child performs similar violent behavior

        as woman.

    - patterns may be learned from watching adults

      on. T.V.

patterns are retained through life + generalized to other situations

reward + punishment play imp't role in this type of learning.

Here are a few suggestions for taking good research notes:

1.   Record the information in your own words, instead of copying the author's words. By recording the author's wording, you run the risk of using the author's wording in your paper, perhaps without realizing that you have done so. Whenever you use an author's words instead of your own, you are required to give the author credit by indicating the author and source from which the material was taken. The same rule applies when you use someone's idea, theory, or argument that is not common knowledge. Failure to give credit is known as plagiarism and means that you have borrowed someone

else's words and ideas without acknowledging them. Plagiarism is a serious error, and many institutions penalize students who either knowingly or unknowingly plagiarize.

2. Try to summarize and condense information. You will find that it is impossible to record all the information you find, so whenever possible try to state the facts and ideas as concisely and as briefly as possible.

3. Record information only once. As you continue reading, eventually you will find the same information appearing and reappearing in various sources. If you have already made a note once, do not spend time writing it again. Occasionally, you may need to check back through your notes to see what you've already recorded. You might, however, want to note the fact that there is common agreement in a number of sources about the information.

4. Record useful quotes. If you find a statement that strongly supports your thesis, you may want to include it as a quotation in your paper. Copy it down exactly and place it in quotes in your notes, with its source.

Step 7: Form an Outline

Once you are satisfied that you have collected sufficient information, take a few moments to reread and organize your note cards. Try to group them together by subtopic. You may find some subtopics that overlap and others that can be grouped together under a more general subtopic. Remember to change the subtopic written in the upper left corner of the card for any cards that you reclassify.

Next, sort your cards in separate piles according to subtopic. Then, with each pack of cards or sheets laid out in front of you, try to arrange them in some logical order or sequence. You might arrange your subtopics chronologically, in order of importance, or by cause-effect. Often your purpose for writing, your thesis statement, or the content of the paper will dictate the order or arrangement. In fact, you can use the organizational patterns you learned to identify in reading paragraphs as a means of organizing your paper. Arrange them in a manner that supports your thesis statement. Once you've done this, you have a tentative outline. To record this arrangement, list the subtopics in order. Now that you can see how the ideas relate to one another, reread your outline and revise it. Check each subtopic to be sure that it directly supports your thesis statement.

Step 8: Write a First Draft

Using your outline as a guide and your note cards to provide the specific facts and information, start writing the first draft of your paper. Your paper should have a brief introduction of one or two paragraphs, a body, and a conclusion or summary. In the introduction you should lead up to and state the thesis of the paper. Before stating it, you might lead up to it by supplying necessary background information or by providing a context.

The body, which comprises most of the paper, should explain and discuss the thesis statement. Each idea should be directly related to and support the thesis statement. Finally, in the conclusion or summary you should draw together the ideas you presented and bring the paper to a close. That is, in the last several paragraphs, try to review the major points you presented and connect them, once again, to the thesis statement.

Step 9: Revise the Draft

Once you have written a first draft, the next step is to reread, evaluate, and revise it. As with any other type of paper, revision is a critical step and can make a difference in the grade you earn.

When revising your paper ask yourself the following questions:

1. Does each paragraph directly support the thesis statement?
2. Are the ideas expressed clearly and concisely?
3. Are the major points connected to one another as well as to the thesis statement?
4. Are there sufficient explanation and support for the thesis statement?

After you have reread your paper and made changes, ask someone else to read your paper. Then ask the person to identify the thesis statement and to summarize the supporting information. If he or she is unable to do so or does so incorrectly, then you may not have communicated your message effectively.

Some students find it necessary to go through more than one revision, especially if their first draft is weak or poorly organized. Also, on occasion, you may find that you need additional information; then it is necessary to go back to the research stage to check new sources. Do not be discouraged by these additional steps; remember, the first few times you write a research paper, you are learning *how* to do the assignment. Therefore some extra time and effort may be required, initially.

Step 10: Prepare the Final Copy

Once you are satisfied that you have made sufficient revision to produce a well-done research paper, then you are ready to prepare the final copy for submission. It is generally agreed that a typewritten copy is strongly desirable. Some instructors require typewritten copy; most prefer it to handwritten papers. If you have poor, illegible handwriting, your instructor may become annoyed while reading the paper and may unconsciously react to your paper negatively or critically. A typewritten copy, on the other hand, presents a neat appearance and suggests that you care enough about your work to present it in the best possible form.

An important part of preparing a final copy, regardless of whether it is handwritten or typed, is proofreading. Once you have prepared the final copy, be sure to take the time to read it through and correct spelling, punctuation, and grammar. If you are weak in one or more of these areas and cannot easily recognize your own errors, ask a friend to proofread your paper and point out or mark the errors.

Step 11: Prepare the Bibliography

The final steps to completing a research paper are to prepare a list, or bibliography, of all the sources that you used to write the paper, and to prepare any endnotes necessary. Endnotes list in consecutive order the sources from which you have taken quotations or which contained unique or specialized information particular to a certain source. Endnotes are called footnotes if placed at the bottom of each page rather than in a consecutive list at the end of the paper. You will need to consult a handbook to determine the specialized format endnotes require.

As mentioned earlier, if you kept careful records as you collected your information, preparing a bibliography is a relatively simple task. In the bibliography you simply list alphabetically the sources you consulted. Also, you must use a consistent form for listing the information. Depending on your instructor, as well as the subject area with which you are working, different formats may be expected. Although each format requires basically the same information, arrangement of information as well as punctuation may vary. Some instructors may specify a particular format, while others may accept any standard, consistent format. If your instructor prefers a particular format, by all means use it.

It is well worth the initial cost to purchase a handbook or style guide that explains a particular format. Among the most commonly used books and handbooks that explain how to do a bibliography as well as how to handle many of the other stylistic features of research papers are:

1. *The MLA Handbook for Writers of Research Papers, Theses, and Dissertations* (New York: Modern Language Association, 1977).
2. Turabian, Kate L. *A Manual for Writers*, 3rd ed. (Chicago: University of Chicago Press, 1973).
3. Turabian , Kate L. *Student's Guide for Writing College Papers*, 3rd ed. (Chicago: University of Chicago Press, 1976).

SUMMARY

Written assignments and research papers are an important part of many college courses. There are several types of writing that instructors commonly assign: essay exams, essays or compositions, factual reports, reaction papers, and research papers. Writing a good paper involves much more than picking up a pen and starting to write. The steps involved in writing any type of paper are prewriting, organizing, writing, revising, and proofreading. Writing a research paper is a process of acquiring and organizing information on a particular topic. It involves selecting an appropriate topic, locating useful sources of information, reading, taking notes, and organizing information. This chapter presented some tips for getting started and then outlined a step-by-step approach for completing a research paper. The steps are as follows:

1. Narrow your topic.
2. Determine the purpose of the paper.
3. Locate appropriate sources of information.

4. Refine the topic through further reading.
5. Write a tentative thesis statement.
6. Collect information.
7. Form an outline.
8. Write a first draft.
9. Revise the draft.
10. Prepare the final copy.
11. Prepare the bibliography.

Part Six
Vocabulary Development

Vocabulary development is crucial to the development of effective and efficient reading. By *vocabulary* is meant "the ability to recognize individual words and to associate meaning with the particular combination of letters that form a word."

Words are symbols: they are groups of letters that stand for, or represent, either a physical object or an idea. The word *table* can call to our minds a physical reality — an object with a flat plane surface, usually supported by means of four perpendicular legs, and commonly used for holding objects or for eating dinner. The word *love,* on the other hand, does not represent a physical object; it symbolizes the feeling of one person toward another. The combination of the letters *t-a-b-l-e* or *l-o-v-e* has no real meaning in itself; it is only when the combination of letters is associated with a particular object or idea that it becomes meaningful. Take, for example, *hoglag;* you can read it, you can pronounce it, but it has no meaning for you. You have not built up any associations between this combination of letters and a physical object or idea. The major task involved in building vocabulary, then, is to increase the number of associations you can make between words (combinations of letters) and the physical objects or ideas they stand for.

The number of word-meaning associations you have acquired defines your vocabulary level. Adult vocabulary levels vary greatly — some adults are functionally illiterate; others have attained an amazing mastery of words and their meanings. The average adult knows the meanings of thousands of words. Since you, as a college student, are well above the educational level of most adults, you should strive to develop your vocabulary well beyond an average adult level.

There are a number of methods you can use to develop your vocabulary. Some methods employ a word analysis approach; they require you to learn or memorize hundreds of prefixes, roots, and suffixes, and involve extensive drill. These methods require the time-consuming completion of many practice exercises. Other methods approach vocabulary through a list-learning process. Words to be learned are listed along with their meanings, and you complete drills to help you learn the words. A major problem with this approach is that the words included in the lists may be either words you already know or words you have no practical need to know.

The methods presented in this part of the text are limited to those with the most practical, immediately beneficial approaches. Chapter 19 presents an extremely quick and practical method of figuring out the meaning of an unknown word in a sentence, paragraph, or passage. By using the words around an unknown word, called its **context,** it is often possible to determine the meaning of the word. The chapter will focus on specific techniques for effectively using clues in the context to derive word meanings.

Chapter 20 will be concerned with methods of learning and remembering new terms and definitions presented in textbooks and lectures. As you have already realized, each subject area has its own specialized, or technical, vocabulary. You could say each subject has a language of its own. Some common words take on a very specialized meaning in each of these languages, and many new technical words are introduced. The chapter will discuss approaches to handling these new terms.

Finally, Chapter 21 will focus on a systematic approach to increasing both your general and technical vocabulary. As you no doubt have discovered many times, looking up a word in a dictionary or even using the word in an essay you are writing in no way guarantees that the word will become a usable part of your speaking or writing vocabulary. Often you forget the word soon after you use it in speaking or writing. The chapter will present techniques for using new words and developing long-term recall of their meanings.

19. Effective Use of Context

Use this chapter to:

1. *Learn techniques to figure out the meaning of a word from the words around it.*

2. *Learn the types of clues that can suggest the meaning of a particular word in a sentence, paragraph, passage, and so forth.*

What should you do when you are reading a passage and you come to a word you don't know? If your instructor were asking this question, you might reply, "I'd look the word up in the dictionary." And as you were saying this, you would know that you really don't often take the time to check the dictionary, but you were giving an answer you thought your instructor would want to hear and would agree with.

Actually, looking up a word in a dictionary is not the first thing to do when you meet a word you don't know. In fact, a dictionary is your last resort, something to turn to when all else fails. Instead, it is best to try to figure out the meaning of the word from the words around it in a sentence, paragraph, or passage that you are reading. Very often, among these surrounding words are various types of clues that make it possible to reason out the meaning of the unknown word. The words around an unknown word which contain clues to its meaning are referred to as the *context*. The clues themselves are called *context clues*. There are four basic types of context clues that you can use in determining word meaning in textbook material: *definition*, *example-illustration*, *contrast*, and *logic of the passage*.

DEFINITION CONTEXT CLUES

The most obvious type of context clue is a direct statement of the meaning of a new term by an author. Usually this occurs in textbook writing when the author is aware that the word is new to the reader and takes the time to give an accurate definition of the term. In the first chapter of a chemistry book, the term *chemical reaction* is defined:

> A chemical reaction is an interaction involving different atoms, in which chemical bonds are formed, or broken, or both.[1]

Some writers signal you directly that they are presenting a definition with expressions such as "Mass is. . . ." or "Anthropology can be defined as. . . ." However, other writers are less direct and obvious when they include a definition. Parentheses may be used to give a definition, partial definition, or synonym of a word, as in the following sentence:

> Scientists measure temperature with two scales: the Celsius (or centigrade) scale (C), and the Kelvin (or thermodynamic) scale (K).[2]

Or an author may employ the parenthetical use of commas or dashes to include a brief definition or synonym within the sentence:

> To begin with, he (Mendel) needed true-breeding plants, plants that showed little variation from generation to generation.[3]

> *or*

> The importance of bipedalism — two-leggedness — cannot be overestimated.[4]

Finally, an author may simply insert a synonym directly within the sentence:

> Another central issue, that of the right of a state to withdraw or secede from the Union, was simply avoided.[5]

EXERCISE 1

Directions: *In each sentence, locate the part of the sentence which gives a definition or synonym of the underlined word. Underline this portion of the sentence.*

1. A democracy is a form of government in which the people effectively participate.[6]
2. The amount of heat that it takes to melt one gram of any substance at its melting point is called the heat of fusion.[7]
3. Linoleic acid is an essentially fatty acid necessary for growth and skin integrity in infants.[8]
4. When a gas is cooled, it condenses (changes to a liquid) at its condensation point.[9]
5. But neither a monkey nor an ape has thumbs long enough or flexible enough to be completely opposable, able to reach comfortably to the tips of all the other fingers as is required for our delicate yet strong precision grip.[10]

EXAMPLE-ILLUSTRATION CONTEXT CLUES

Authors frequently explain their ideas and concepts by giving specific concrete examples or illustrations. Many times, when an example is given which illustrates, or explains, a new term, you can figure out the meaning of the term from the example. Suppose, for instance, that you frequently confuse the terms *fiction* and *nonfiction* and you are given the following assignment by your instructor: *Select any nonfiction book and write a critical review; you can choose from a wide range of books such as an autobiography, sports, "how-to" manuals, commentaries on historical periods, or current consumer-awareness paperbacks.* From the examples given, you can easily see that *nonfiction* refers to books that are factual, or true.

Writers sometimes give you an advance warning or signal that they are going to present an example or illustration. Phrases that signal an example or illustration to follow include: *for example, for instance, to illustrate, such as, included are,* and so on.

Examples:
1. Some everyday, common <u>solutions</u> include gasoline, antifreeze, soda water, seawater, vodka, and ammonia.
2. Specifically, management of a New York bank developed a strategic plan to increase its customers by making them see banks as offering a large variety of services rather than just a few <u>specialized services</u> (cashing checks, putting money into savings accounts, and making loans).[11]

EXERCISE 2

Directions: *Read each sentence and write a definition or synonym for each underlined word. Use the illustration-example context clue to help you determine word meanings.*

1. Since then a near <u>symbiotic</u> relationship has developed between the player and the fan in the stands watching him — that phrase "I just die when the Chiefs (or the Rams, or the Mets or whatever)" . . . the fan's forefinger raised to denote that his team (and he) are Number One, the "we did it, we did it," and the self-satisfied smiles on the faces of the people coming down the stadium ramps after their teams have won.[12]

   _____

2. The play contained a variety of <u>morbid</u> events: the death of a young child, the suicide of her mother, and the murder of an older sister.

   _____

3. Psychological disturbances are sometimes traceable to a particular <u>trauma</u> in childhood. For example, the death of a parent may produce long-range psychological effects.

   _____

4. To <u>substantiate</u> his theory, Watson offered experimental evidence, case study reports, testimony of patients, and a log of observational notes.

   _____

5. There are many <u>phobias</u> that can seriously influence human behavior; the two most common are claustrophobia (fear of confined spaces) and acrophobia (fear of heights).

    _____

6. <u>Homogeneous</u> groups, such as classes of all boys, or social organizations of high IQ people, or country clubs of wealthy families, have particular roles and functions.

    _____

CONTRAST CONTEXT CLUES

It is sometimes possible to figure out the meaning of an unknown word from a word or phrase in the context which has an opposite meaning. To use a simple example, in the sentence "Sam was thin, but George was obese," a contrasting or opposite description is set up between George and Sam. The word *but* signals that an opposite or contrasting idea is to follow. By knowing the meaning of *thin* and knowing that George is the opposite of thin, you figure out that *obese* means "not thin," or *fat*.

Most often when an opposite or contrasting meaning is given, there is a signal word or phrase in the sentence which indicates a change in the direction of the thought. Most commonly used are these signal words or phrases: *on the other hand, however, while, but, nevertheless, on the contrary.*

Example:
The Federalists, from their <u>pessimistic</u> viewpoint, believed the Constitution could protect them by its procedures, while the more positive Anti-Federalists thought of the Constitution as the natural rights due to all people.

In the above example, if you did not know the meaning of the word *pessimistic,* you could figure it out because a word appears later in the sentence which gives you a clue. The sentence is about the beliefs of two groups, the Federalists and the Anti-Federalists. The prefix *anti-* tells you that they hold opposite or differing views. If the Federalists are described as "pessimistic" and their views are opposite those of the Anti-Federalists, who are described as "more positive," you realize that *pessimistic* means "the opposite of positive," or *negative.*

Here is another example:

Most members of Western society marry only one person at a time, but in other cultures <u>polygamy</u> is common and acceptable.

In this sentence, by the contrast established between Western society and other cultures, you can infer that *polygamy* refers to the practice of marriage to more than one person at a time.

274

EXERCISE 3

Directions: *Read each sentence and write a definition or synonym for each underlined word. Use the contrast context clue to help you determine the meaning of the word.*

1. The philosopher was <u>vehement</u> in his objections to the new grading system, while the more practical historian, on the other hand, expressed his views calmly and quietly.

   _____

2. The mayor was very <u>dogmatic</u> about governmental policy, while the assistant mayor was more lenient and flexible in his interpretations.

   _____

3. Instead of evaluating each possible solution when it was first proposed, the committee decided it would <u>defer</u> judgment until all possible solutions had been proposed.

   _____

4. The <u>tenacious</u> islanders responded reluctantly to the government compromise on land settlement, whereas the immigrants agreed immediately to the government offer.

   _____

5. Cultures vary in the types of behavior which are considered socially acceptable. In one culture, a man may be <u>ostracized</u> for having more than one wife, while in other cultures, a man with many wives is an admired and respected part of the group.

   _____

CONTEXT CLUES IN THE LOGIC OF THE PASSAGE

One of the most common ways in which context provides clues about the meaning of an unknown word is through logic or general reasoning about the content of a sentence, or about the relationship of ideas within a sentence. Suppose that before you read the following sentence you did not know the meaning of the word *empirical*.

Some of the questions now before us are <u>empirical</u> issues that require evidence directly bearing on the question.[13]

From the way *empirical* is used in the sentence, you know that an empirical issue is one that requires direct evidence, and from that information you can infer or reason that *empirical* has something to do with proof or supporting facts.

Now suppose that you did not know the meaning of the term *cul-de-sac* before reading the following sentence:

A group of animals hunting together can sometimes maneuver the hunted animal into a <u>cul-de-sac</u>: out onto a peak of high land, into a swamp or river, or into a gully from which it cannot escape.[14]

From the mention of the places into which a hunted animal can be maneuvered — a gully, a peak, or a swamp — you realize that the hunters have cornered the animal and that *cul-de-sac* means a blind alley or a situation from which there is no escape.

EXERCISE 4

Directions: *Read each of the following sentences and write a synonym or definition for each underlined word or term. Look for logic of the passage context clues to help you figure out the meaning of each.*

1. The creation of a unified organization resulted in <u>lobbying activities</u> at state and national levels that increased pressure to obtain legislation favorable to the mentally retarded.[15]

    _____

2. The two philosophical theories were <u>incompatible</u>: one acknowledged the existence of free will; the other denied it.

    _____

3. When the judge pronounced the sentence, the convicted criminal shouted <u>execrations</u> at the jury.

    _____

4. The police officer was <u>exonerated</u> by a police review panel of any possible misconduct or involvement in a case of police bribery.

    _____

5. The editor would not allow the paper to go to press until certain passages were <u>expunged</u> from an article naming individuals involved in a political scandal.

    _____

EXERCISE 5

Directions: *Each of the following sentences contains an underlined word or term whose meaning can be determined from the context. Underline the part of the sentence that contains the clue to the meaning of the underlined words. Then in the blank below identify what type of context clue you used.*

1. <u>Separation of powers</u> is the principle that the powers of government should be separated and put in the care of different parts of the government.[16]

   _____

2. Samples of moon rock have been analyzed by <u>uranium dating</u> and found to be about 4.6 billion years old, or about the same age as the earth.[17]

   _____

3. Like horses, human beings have a variety of <u>gaits</u>; they amble, stride, jog, and sprint.[18]

   _____

4. In the past, <u>malapportionment</u> (large differences in the populations of congressional districts) was common in many areas of the country.[19]

   _____

5. Tremendous <u>variability</u> characterizes the treatment of the mentally retarded during the medieval era, ranging from treatment as innocents to being tolerated as fools to persecution as witches.[20]

   _____

6. In the olfactory sense (smell), <u>adaptation</u> occurs very rapidly. On entering a room, you may notice an odor, but in a very short time, your awareness disappears.[21]

   _____

SUMMARY

One of the easiest and most practical ways of determining the meaning of an unknown word is to study carefully how the word is used in the sentence, paragraph, or passage in which it is found. The context — the words around an unknown word — frequently contains various types of clues that help you figure out the meaning of the unknown word. There are four basic types of context clues that are useful in determining the meanings of words in factual material. These types of clues are named and described in this list:

Definition: A brief definition or a synonym of an unknown word may be included in the sentence in which the word is used.
Example-illustration: Writers may explain their words and ideas by giving specific, concrete examples of them. It is sometimes possible,

when an example is given to illustrate or explain a new term or concept, to figure out the meaning of an unknown word from the example.

Contrast: The meaning of an unknown word can sometimes be determined from a word or phrase in the context which has the opposite meaning.

Logic of the passage: The meaning of an unknown word can sometimes by determined through reasoning or applying logic to the content of the sentence or paragraph.

20. Learning New Terminology

Use this chapter to:

1.   Find out what words are important to learn in a course.

2.   Learn the best way to learn new terminology introduced in a course.

Define the following words: *group, class, drive, self, role*. No doubt you were able to give an accurate definition of each, but do you know the specialized meanings these words have in the field of sociology? Now, define the following terms: *megalopolis, monogamous, mechanization, ecosystem, oligopoly*. Were you able to give precise definitions of these words? Probably not. These terms are words which are special or particular to the field of sociology and related sciences. The new terminology (words) in any subject area can be divided into two categories: (1) common, everyday words which take on a very particular or specific meaning for the subject area, and (2) technical words which are used only in the subject area.

RECOGNIZING SPECIALIZED TERMINOLOGY

As you have already realized, new terminology is introduced in each course you are taking — both common and technical words which have specialized meanings in the particular course. Each subject area can be said to have a language of its own — its own set of specialized words which makes it possible to describe and discuss accurately topics, principles and concepts, problems, and occurrences related to the subject area.

One of the first tasks facing both a college instructor and a textbook author is the necessity of introducing and teaching the specialized language of a course. This task is especially important in introductory, first-semester courses in which a student studies or encounters the subject area for the first time. In an introduction to psychology course, for instance, you often start by learning the meaning of *psychology* itself — what the study is devoted to, what it encompasses, how it approaches situations, events, and problems. From that point you move on to learn related terms: *behavior, observations, hypothesis, experiment, variables, subjects*, and so forth.

Often the first few class lectures in a course are introductory. They are devoted to acquainting students with the nature and scope of the subject area and to introducing students to the specialized language. Check your notes for the first few classes of any course you are now taking. How many new or specialized terms were introduced?

The first few chapters within a textbook are introductory too. They are written to familiarize students with the subject of study and acquaint them with the specialized language of the subject. In one particular economics textbook, a total of 34 new terms were introduced in the first two chapters (40 pages). In the first two chapters (28 pages) of a chemistry book, 56 specialized words were introduced. A sample of the words introduced in each text is given below. From these lists you can see that some of the words are words of common, everyday usage which take on a specialized meaning; others are technical terms used only in the subject area.

New terms:
Economics text

capital
ownership
opportunity cost
distribution
productive contribution
durable goods
economic system
barter
commodity money

New terms:
Chemistry text

matter
element
halogen
isotope
allotropic form
nonmetal
group (family)
burning
toxicity

EXERCISE 1

Directions: *Turn to the chapter on advertising contained in the Appendix. Without referring to the list of key terms at the end of the chapter, identify as many new terms as you can and record them in the spaces provided below.*

New specialized vocabulary:

_____

_____

_____

EXERCISE 2

Directions: *Select any two textbooks you are currently using. In each, turn to the first chapter and check to see how many specialized terms are introduced. List the total number of terms. Then list several examples.*

Textbook 1 _____   Textbook 2 _____
            (title)   (title)

Total specialized words _____   Total specialized words _____

Examples of specialized words:

1. _____
2. _____
3. _____
4. _____
5. _____

Examples of specialized words:

1. _____
2. _____
3. _____
4. _____
5. _____

Recognition of specialized terminology is only the first step in learning the language of a course. More important is the development of a systematic way of identifying, marking, recording, and learning the specialized terms. Since new terminology is introduced in both class lectures and course textbooks, it is necessary to develop a procedure for handling the specialized terms in each.

SPECIALIZED TERMINOLOGY IN CLASS LECTURES

Throughout the semester, but more so in the first few weeks of class, instructors devote considerable time during their lectures to presenting the language of the subject carefully and explicitly. It is important, then, to record accurately each new term for later review and study. Lecturers give you clues as to what terms and definitions are important to record. Some instructors make a habit of writing new words on the chalkboard, both as a means of emphasis and as a way to helping you recognize them and their correct spellings. If you see *and* hear a word, it is easier to remember than if you just hear it pronounced. Other instructors may emphasize important new terms and definitions by slowing down, almost dictating slowly so that you can write the terms down. Still other instructors may repeat a word and its definition several times or define a new term in several different ways.

As a part of your notetaking system, develop a consistent way of separating new terms and definitions from other facts and ideas. You might circle or draw a box around each new term; or as you edit your notes (make revisions, changes, additions to your notes after taking them), underline each new term in red; or mark "def." in the margin each time a definition is included. The particular mark or symbol you use is a matter of preference; the important thing is to find some way to identify definitions for further study. In addition, as part of your editing process, check each definition to be sure that it is complete and readable. Also, if you were not able to record any explanation or examples of new terms, add them as you edit. If the definitions you recorded are unclear, check with a friend or with your instructor. The last step in handling new terminology presented in class lectures is to organize the terms into a system for efficient study. One such system will be suggested later in this chapter.

SPECIALIZED TERMINOLOGY IN TEXTBOOKS

Textbook authors use various means to emphasize new terminology as they introduce it. In some texts, new vocabulary is printed in italics, boldface type, or colored print. Other texts indicate new terms in the margin of each page. Still the most common means of emphasis, however, is a "New Terminology List" or "Vocabulary List" at the beginning or end of each chapter.

As already demonstrated, textbook chapters (especially introductory chapters) are heavily loaded with new specialized vocabulary. While you are reading and underlining important facts and ideas, you should also mark new terminology. It is of prime importance to consistently mark and separate definitions from other chapter content. (The particular mark or symbol you use is your choice.)

Occasionally in textbooks you may meet a new term which is not defined or for which the definition is unclear. In this case, check the glossary at the back of the text for a thorough explanation of the meaning of the word. Make a note of the meaning in the text margin.

The glossary, a comprehensive list of terms introduced throughout the text, is an aid that can help you learn new terminology. At the end of the course, when you have covered all or most of the chapters, the glossary is one way of reviewing terminology. Use the glossary to test yourself: read an entry, cover up the meaning and try to remember it, then check to see if you were correct. As you are progressing through a course, however, the glossary is not an adequate study aid. A more organized, systematic approach to learning unfamiliar new terms is needed.

LEARNING NEW TERMINOLOGY: VOCABULARY CARD SYSTEM

Once you have identified and marked new terminology, both in your lecture notes and in your textbook, the next step is to organize the words for study and review. One of the most efficient and practical ways to accomplish this is the vocabulary card system. Use a 3″ x 5″ index card for each new term. Record the word on the front and the meaning on the back. If the word is particularly difficult, you might also include a guide to its pronunciation. Underneath the correct spelling of the word, indicate in syllables how the word sounds. For the word *eutrophication* (a term used in chemistry meaning "overnourishment"), you could indicate its pronunciation as "you-tro-fi-kay'-shun." On the back of the card, along with the meaning, you may want to include an example to help you remember the term more easily. A sample vocabulary card, front and back, is shown in Figure 20-1.

Use these cards for study, review, and for testing yourself. Go through your pack of cards once, looking at the front and trying to recall the meaning on the back. Then, reverse the procedure: look at the meanings and see if you can recall the terms. As you go through the pack in this way, sort the cards into two piles: words you know and words you don't know. Then, the next time you review the cards, use only cards in the "don't know" pile for review. This sorting procedure will help you avoid wasting time reviewing words you have already learned. Continue to review the cards until you are satisfied that you have learned each

Front of Card

conglomerate

con -glom'-er-it

Back of Card

def.: an organization comprising two or more companies that produce unrelated products.

ex.: Nichols Company owns a shoe factory, vineyards in France, soft drink factories, and Sara Jane pastry company.

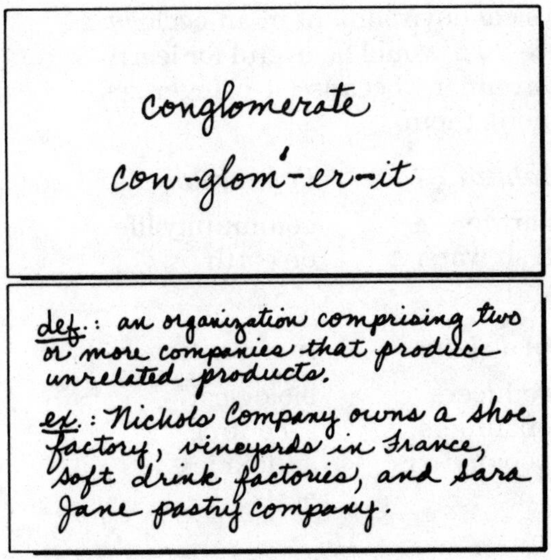

FIGURE 20-1

new term. To prevent forgetting, it will be necessary to review the entire pack of cards periodically.

EXERCISE 3

Directions: *Select two or three sets of notes on a particular topic from any course you are taking. Prepare a set of vocabulary cards for the new terms introduced. Review and study the cards.*

EXERCISE 4

Directions: *Select one chapter from any of the textbooks you are currently using. Prepare a vocabulary card for each new term introduced in the chapter. Review and study the cards.*

LEARNING NEW TERMINOLOGY: ORGANIZATIONAL DIAGRAMS

A second procedure to use in learning new terminology employs several of the major principles of memory — organization, categorization, and meaningfulness. You will recall that information which is meaningful is easier to remember than information which is not meaningful. Facts that are related and that are part of some larger idea or structure are easier to remember than isolated facts. A chart, diagram, or sequence list of new terms can be a useful aid to learning. A learning aid like this will help you see connections and relationships among terms. If you had to learn the anatomical names of each major bone in the upper body, you could draw a sketch of the human body and label the bones. Then you could study the terminology either by covering up each name on your diagram and trying to recall it, or by drawing a new diagram and labeling each bone from memory.

Suppose you are studying the physical environment in an ecology course. A diagram like the one in Figure 20-2 would be useful for learning terms related to the physical environment because it categorizes such terms and shows relationships among them.

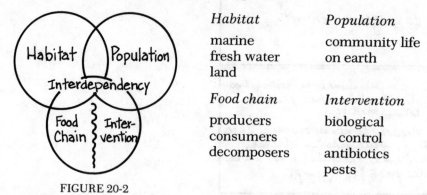

Habitat

marine
fresh water
land

Population

community life
on earth

Food chain

producers
consumers
decomposers

Intervention

biological
    control
antibiotics
pests

FIGURE 20-2

The principle of categorizing, or grouping and labeling similar items, applies to developing vocabulary. To learn the names and characteristics of the elements in a chemistry course, you could group them by families as they are grouped on the periodic table of elements: the carbon family, the oxygen family, the nitrogen family. Categorizing the elements by families to which they belong will make learning easier and more meaningful because elements in the same family have similar characteristics. Figure 20-3 was constructed to categorize the various

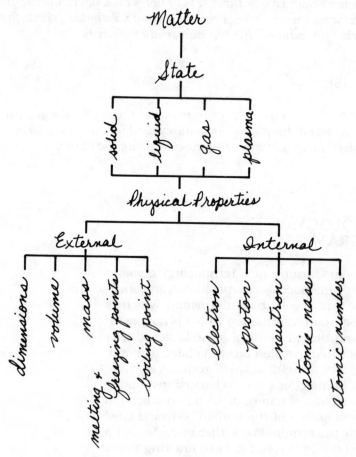

FIGURE 20-3

states and physical properties of matter. The diagram makes it easy to visualize the classification of matter and to understand the various characteristics, both external and internal, by which matter is described.

SUMMARY

Each subject area has a language, or terminology, of its own — a set of specialized words which makes it possible to accurately describe and discuss the topics, principles and concepts, problems, and occurrences within that field. These specialized words are introduced and used regularly by your instructors in class lectures and by the authors of your textbooks. To be successful in any course, it is necessary to develop a system of identifying, marking, recording, and learning these terms as you encounter them in both lectures and textbooks.

It is important to include new words introduced in class lectures in your notes and to distinguish them from other facts and ideas. In textbook chapters, new words should be marked in a distinctive way to help you rapidly locate them for review.

After identifying new terminology presented in both lectures and textbooks, the words need to be organized for study and review. Index cards are used in one system for organizing new terminology: each new term is recorded on the front of a card, its meaning on the back. The correct pronunciation and/or an example may also be included on the card. A second system for learning specialized terminology emphasizes principles of memory — organization and categorization. It consists of the development of an overview or structure that helps you see the connection and relationship of terms to one another. Most often used in this system are charts, diagrams, or sequence lists.

21. Organizational Approaches to Developing General Vocabulary

Use this chapter to:

1. *Become more aware of your various vocabulary levels.*

2. *Learn how to improve your vocabulary.*

As you discovered in the previous chapter, learning specialized terminology is an important part of mastering the subject matter in any college course. As you proceed through college, successfully completing more and more courses, your specialized vocabulary in your field of study will become extensive. But what about your general, everyday, nonspecialized vocabulary? Will it also increase? Will it increase as much as your specialized vocabulary? Will it remain unchanged? What can you do to improve it? It is the intent of this chapter to focus on techniques for developing your general vocabulary.

WHAT IS YOUR VOCABULARY LEVEL?

Actually, you have more than one vocabulary level; you have at least four vocabulary levels. This is because you have four different vocabularies — a *reading vocabulary*, a *listening vocabulary*, a *writing vocabulary*, and a *speaking vocabulary*. There are words you understand as you read but do not use in your own writing. Similarly, there are words you understand as you listen to an instructor use them in a lecture but do not ordinarily use in your own speech. And then there are words you recognize when you read them which may not be part of your speaking vocabulary.

While there is a basic core of words that must be part of each of your vocabularies, you will find that many words are found in one or two of your vocabularies, but not in all four. And it is not necessary that each of your vocabularies be identical. There are words in your speaking vocabulary, for instance, that are not appropriate for use in writing and would not be needed in reading factual materials. Many slang words and informal expressions are not used in writing. Expressions like *Aw, come on!* or *What a dope!* are seldom used in factual writing. And there are words, expressions, and sentence patterns used in writing that would sound out of place in speech and would not be part of your speaking or listening vocabulary either.

EXERCISE 1

Directions: *To emphasize the various types of vocabularies that you have, complete the following tasks:*

1. Write ten words that you use in your everyday speech but do not use in your writing.

   _____

   _____

2. Check any page or two in one of your textbooks. Write ten words for which you know the meaning but do not use in your own daily speech or writing.

   _____

   _____

3. As you attend a lecture for one of your courses, pay particular attention to the words the instructor uses. As you listen, jot down five words which he or she used that you know the meaning of but do not use in your own speech or writing. Try to avoid selecting specialized or technical words which pertain directly to the topic of the lecture. Then write them in the space provided.

   _____

Of your four vocabularies, which do you think is the largest and most fully developed? Most likely it is either your reading vocabulary or your listening vocabulary. You probably can understand the meaning of many more words than you normally use in your own speaking or writing. And which vocabulary do you think is growing most rapidly because of your college courses? Again, it is either your reading or listening vocabulary. By listening to your instructors and reading your textbooks, you are constantly adding new words and expressions to these vocabularies.

Through listening and reading, you are meeting many new words, but you are probably aware that you do not learn and remember each new word you meet. Words that your instructor uses frequently and that are repeated often in textbooks are learned more or less automatically. You do not have to make a conscious effort to learn these; you pick them up without trying. But words used only once or twice after learning them are often forgotten. An important task, then, in developing your overall vocabulary is to make a conscious effort to learn as many of the words you meet each day as possible and to use them frequently.

As previously mentioned, your listening and reading vocabularies are developing most rapidly. Your writing and speaking vocabularies are expanding less rapidly. This can be explained by the fact that, on a daily basis, you do less speaking and writing than reading or listening. A second important task, then, in improving your overall vocabulary is to use in your speaking and writing the new words you learn by listening and reading.

The approach for expanding your reading vocabulary is slightly different from techniques used for developing your listening vocabulary. Similarly, ways to expand your writing vocabulary differ from methods used for developing your speaking vocabulary.

DEVELOPING YOUR READING VOCABULARY

As you read a page in a textbook, you probably meet at least one word for which you do not know the exact meaning. Meeting the unknown word doesn't stop your reading; usually you can figure out enough of the meaning from the context (the way it is used with the words around it in the sentence, paragraph, or passage). Unless this word is repeated several more times in the same chapter, you probably will not remember the meaning you derived from the context. Rather, you will place the word in a separate category (a "gray area") along with many other words already there. All these are familiar — you know you have seen them before — but you do not remember their meanings.

Some direct action is needed to help you remember words like these so that they will not slip into the "gray area." The first thing to do is mark such a word; underline it, circle it, or place a box around it. Then continue reading. Do not interrupt your train of thought while reading to learn the new word. Instead, after you have finished reading, return to all the words you marked, learn their meanings, and begin to make these words a permanent part of your reading vocabulary by using them in your speaking and writing.

When you return to a word you've marked, first reread the sentence in which it appears. Rereading the context will help you to recall the meaning you derived. Next, check the meaning of the word in a dictionary. (Be sure to keep a dictionary handy so that it is convenient to check word meanings.) Note the various other meanings for the word as well as the meaning which is appropriate for the sentence in which you read the word. Next, record the word and its meaning on a "New Word" list or on an index card. Try to use the word in a sentence. Then, think of several situations in which you could use the word in speaking. Try to recall if you have ever heard anyone use the word in speech.

Using the new word in writing and speaking and recalling the use of the word in someone else's speech are all forms of rehearsal, or practice, that help you transfer the word from your immediate, short-term memory to your long-term memory. Periodic review of the word will also be necessary in order to prevent its loss from your long-term memory. In addition to reviewing and testing yourself on your "New Word" list or index cards, also try to incorporate the words into your speech or writing.

To help you get started using new words, it is helpful to realize that, at the college level, many new words do not represent brand new concepts. They are more accurate and more descriptive replacements, or substitutes, for simpler, more basic words and expressions that you already know and use. The list below contains several examples:

dichotomy: division into two contradictory parts
    A clear <u>dichotomy</u> exists within the political party.
articulate: able to speak clearly and concisely
    The lawyer was bright and <u>articulate</u>.
facilitate: to help along, make easier
    Exercise <u>facilitates</u> weight loss.
transpose: to change or switch the order
    The typist <u>transposed</u> several words in the title.
paraphrase: to say in other words
    The instructor <u>paraphrased</u> the president's announcement.

alienate: to cause to become unfriendly or indifferent
The speaker <u>alienated</u> most women in the audience.

EXERCISE 2

Directions: *Select a three-page passage from one of your textbooks that you have been assigned to read. As you read, mark all the words that you recognize but cannot accurately define. When you have finished reading, transfer the words onto a sheet of paper or onto index cards. Check a dictionary to determine the exact meaning as it is used in context and then write a sentence using each word.*

DEVELOPING YOUR LISTENING VOCABULARY

As you are listening to an instructor lecture, you should be alert for three types of words. First, listen for new specialized or technical words which relate specifically to the subject matter the instructor is presenting. These words should be recorded in your lecture notes for that class. Techniques for learning these terms are discussed in the previous chapter. Second, be alert for general, everyday words the instructor uses which are unfamiliar to you. Third, listen for general words which are vaguely familiar to you but are not part of your own speaking vocabulary. Jot these words in the left margin of your notes. Writing these words is a form of rehearsal that will help transfer them to your long-term memory.

Later, after the lecture, return to the words you wrote in the left margin. Check the dictionary meanings if necessary. Then transfer each word to either a "New Word" list or an index card. Study and review each word by anticipating uses of the word and testing yourself on recall of meaning.

EXERCISE 3

Directions: *Attend a portion of a college lecture or listen to a speech on TV. As you listen, concentrate on the words used by the lecturer. Try to identify words in each of the following categories and then write some examples of each.*

Technical/ specialized words	Everyday unfamiliar words	Familiar words you don't use
_____	_____	_____
_____	_____	_____
_____	_____	_____
_____	_____	_____
_____	_____	_____

DEVELOPING YOUR WRITING VOCABULARY

When you write, your primary purpose is to express and communicate ideas. Therefore, your first concern in writing should be to express your ideas clearly so that they can be understood by the reader. When writing a paragraph, do not be concerned initially with using newly acquired vocabulary or with choosing the most accurate or descriptive words. First, organize your ideas and try to express them as clearly as possible. Then, after you are satisfied that you have written what you want to say and that it is organized and understandable, reread what you have written with the intent of revising or changing various words to make your meaning more precise or descriptive. Especially look for groups of words whose meaning might be more concisely expressed by a single word. Also, note any sentence which you feel does not communicate your meaning in the best possible way. Could you replace a word with another, more accurate word? Or could you add a word which makes a description more vivid? Below are listed several examples in which choosing other words contributed to clearer, more descriptive writing.

Examples:

1. Revising a paper ~~helps you to get across~~ **expresses** your ideas more clearly.

2. When editing your lecture notes, you should ~~put in bits and pieces~~ **add information** that ~~were~~ **was** left out and take out ~~stuff~~ **points** that ~~is~~ **are** not important.

3. The SQ3R method helps me to ~~keep my mind~~ **concentrate** on what I am reading.

One of the most difficult parts of developing your writing vocabulary is finding the right word. One obvious source is the dictionary; however, a thesaurus is easier to use. It is written for the specific purpose of grouping words together that are similar in meaning. This book is a valuable reference and is useful in locating a precise or accurate word or phrase to fit your intended meaning.

Suppose you are searching for a more precise term for the expression *looked over* in the following sentence:

My instructor looked over my essay exam.

The thesaurus lists the following synonyms:

VERBS 12. see, behold, observe, view, witness, perceive, discern, spy, espy, descry, **sight**, have in sight, make out, spot [coll.], twig [coll.], discover, notice, distinguish, recognize, ken [dial.], **catch sight of,** get a load of [slang, U.S.], take in, look on *or* upon, cast the eyes on *or* upon, **set** *or* **lay eyes on, clap eyes on** [coll.]; pipe, lamp, nail, peg [all slang]; **glimpse,** get *or* catch a glimpse of; see at a glance, see with half an eye; see with one's own eyes.

13. **look, peer,** direct the eyes, turn *or* bend the eyes, lift up the eyes; **peek, peep,** pry, take a peep *or* peek; play at peekaboo *or* bopeep; get an eyeful [coll., U.S.].

14. **look at,** take a look at, take a gander at [slang, U.S.], have a looksee [slang, U.S.], look on *or* upon, gaze at *or* upon; **watch, observe,** pipe [slang], **view, regard**; keep in sight *or* view, hold in view; look after, follow; spy upon.

15. **scrutinize, survey, eye, ogle,** contemplate, look over, give the eye [slang], give the once-over *or* double-O [slang, U.S.]; examine, **inspect 484.31;** size up

[coll.], take one's measure [slang].

16. **gaze,** gloat, fix ∼, fasten *or* rivet the eyes upon, keep the eyes upon; eye, ogle; **stare,** look [coll.], goggle, **gape, gawk** [coll.], gaup *or* gawp [dial.], gaze open-mouthed; crane, crane the neck; rubber, **rubberneck,** gander [all slang, U.S.]; look straight in the eye, look full in the face, hold one's eye *or* gaze, stare down; strain the eyes.

17. **glare, glower,** look daggers.

18. **glance, glimpse,** glint, cast a glance, glance at *or* upon, take a glance at, take a slant *or* squint at [slang].

19. **look askance** *or* **askant,** give a sidelong look, cut one's eye [slang], glime [dial.]; squint, look asquint; cock the eye; **look down one's nose** [coll.].

20. **leer,** leer the eye, look leeringly, give a leering look.

21. **look away, avert the eyes;** look another way, break one's eyes away, stop looking, turn away from, turn the back upon; drop one's eyes *or* gaze, cast one's eyes down; avoid one's gaze, cut eyes [coll.].

Right away you can identify a number of words that are more specific than the phrase *looked over*. The next step, then, is to choose a word from the entry that most closely suggests the meaning you want to convey. The easiest way to do this is to "test out" or substitute various choices in your sentence to see which one is most appropriate; check the dictionary if you are not sure of a word's exact meaning.

Many students misuse the thesaurus by choosing words that do not fit the context. *Be sure to use words only when you are familiar with all their shades of meaning.* Remember, a misused word is often a more serious error than a wordy or imprecise expression.

The most widely used thesaurus was originally compiled by Roget and is known today as *Roget's Thesaurus;* it is readily available in an inexpensive paperback edition.

EXERCISE 4

Directions: *Replace the underlined word or phrase in each sentence with a more descriptive word or phrase. Use a thesaurus to locate your replacement.*

1. When Sara learned that her sister had committed a crime, she was sad.
2. Compared to earlier chapters, the last two chapters in my chemistry text are hard.
3. The instructor spent the entire class talking about the causes of inflation and deflation.
4. The main character in the film was a thin, talkative British soldier.
5. We went to see the film that won the Academy Award for the best picture; it was great!

EXERCISE 5

Directions: *Write a paragraph on one of the topics suggested below. Before you write, organize your ideas; then try to express them clearly. After you have finished, reread your writing and make any word changes that make your meaning more precise or descriptive.*

Topics:
1. First impressions that count
2. What can go wrong in a job interview
3. What the college should change

_____

_____

_____

_____

_____

DEVELOPING YOUR SPEAKING VOCABULARY

Your speaking vocabulary is probably the most difficult of your vocabularies to change and expand. Speech is most often spontaneous; you have little time to plan, organize, or revise what you say. When someone asks you a question, there is very little time in which to plan and choose the most suitable words to use in your response. Especially when you are under pressure or nervous about speaking before a group, words never seem to come out exactly as you would like.

One useful way to improve the level and sophistication of your speech is to practice what you might say in situations in which you know you will have to say something. If, for example, you are going to ask a question in class or you want to contribute to a class discussion, take a moment to plan out what you are going to ask or say. Replace any words which sound awkward or unclear with other words. If you are planning to go to an instructor's office to ask for help, try to imagine what you will say. What is the best or clearest way to say it? This process of anticipation, or practice, will allow you to begin to develop your speaking vocabulary.

SUMMARY

This chapter focused on the nature of and techniques for improving your general, everyday, nonspecialized vocabulary. In assessing your general vocabulary, it is necessary to realize that you do not have a single vocabulary level. You have at least four: a reading vocabulary, a listening vocabulary, a writing vocabulary, and a speaking vocabulary. While a basic core of words makes up part of each of these vocabularies, you will find that the size and content of each vocabulary vary significantly.

Summary

The chapter presented suggestions for improving each of the four types of vocabulary. To develop your reading vocabulary, it was suggested that you concentrate on words which are familiar but whose precise meanings you don't know. As you read, mark these words; then return to them for analysis, study, and review. Systems for remembering new words were suggested — "New Word" lists and vocabulary cards.

Procedures for developing your listening vocabulary follow the same pattern as those for improving your reading vocabulary. As you listen to an instructor speak, make note of both specialized and general vocabulary with which you are unfamiliar. Later, after the lecture, study and review each word using the procedures suggested.

Your writing vocabulary is best developed through a process of revising and rewriting your own work. After you have organized and expressed your ideas as clearly as possible, reread your writing for the purpose of choosing words which are more precise or more descriptive than those you first choose. A thesaurus is a useful reference for locating a precise word to suit your meaning.

Developing your speaking vocabulary requires a deliberate attempt to concentrate on using clearer, more expressive language. Your speaking vocabulary can be improved by practicing, or anticipating, what you might say and the most suitable words for saying it in particular situations.

Part Seven
Reading Efficiency
Techniques

Most adults, including college students, are inefficient readers: they do not make the best possible use of their reading time, and they do not apply skills that would enable them to read faster. They read all types of material at the same rate, and they are always careful to read everything. Many adults have the capacity to read twice as fast as they usually read.

The purpose of this part of the book is to discuss situations in which you could read faster and to present techniques that will enable you to do so. Chapter 22 discusses the variables which affect how fast you read and then suggests reading rates for four different categories of reading. The chapter gives you an opportunity to measure your own reading rate for each category.

Chapter 23 is concerned with the physical aspects of the reading process and shows how eye movement is related to reading rate. The chapter also offers specific suggestions on how to improve your reading efficiency through control of eye-movement patterns.

Chapter 24 considers situations in which it is not necessary to read everything and offers specific techniques for selective reading. The chapter suggests a procedure for *skimming* — getting an overview, or general picture, of an article — and a procedure for *scanning* — rapidly looking through material to locate a particular piece of information.

22. What Is Your Reading Rate?

Use this chapter to:

1. *Find out how fast you read and how your rate compares to that of other college students.*

2. *Find out if you read everything at the same rate.*

Reading rate, the speed at which you read, is measured in words per minute (wpm). Do you read 100 wpm, 200 wpm, 300 wpm, 400 wpm? At what rate should you be reading? Are you a fast reader or a slow reader? The answer to these questions: you should be able to read at 100, 200, 300, and 400 wpm; you should be both a fast and a slow reader. Though these answers may seem strange or even contradictory, they are correct. Your reading rate should change in different situations and with different types of reading material. There are a number of variables which determine what your reading rate should be on any particular printed page. The purpose of this chapter is to present these variables which affect reading rate and to show you how to adjust, or vary, your reading rate to deal with them.

VARIABLES THAT INFLUENCE READING RATE

There are literally hundreds of variables that influence how fast you read. Many of these variables also affect your *comprehension* (how well you understand) of what you read. Variables that influence both reading rate and comprehension can be divided into two general categories: writer (or text) variables and reader variables. *Writer-text variables* are the features of the printed material that influence how easy or difficult it is to read. The characteristics of a person which determine or affect rate and comprehension are called *reader variables.*

Writer-Text Variables

The way writers write, the words they use, how they put words together, how clearly they can express ideas all contribute to how easy it is to read a passage and how fast it can be read. Try the following experiment. First, read each of the following passages:

EXPERIMENT

Passage 1:
   It always takes something called *force* to set anything in motion. Force is the push or pull on an object. When you walk, run, skate, ride a

bicycle, hammer nails, throw a ball, or turn the pages of this book, you are using force. Even if you push against a wall and it does not move, you are still using force. You just are not using enough force to move the wall. It takes more force to move something heavy than to move something light.

Scientists say that work is done only when a force actually moves an object. When you push as hard as you can against a wall, are you doing work? You might think so, but a scientist would say that you are not. Since the wall you push against does not move, you are not doing any work.

–Barnard et al., *Science for Tomorrow's World*, pp. 28–29.

Passage 2:

In popular language the word *work* is used to denote any form of physical or mental effort. In physics and engineering, however, the term *work* is employed in a technical sense only. If physical translational work is to be accomplished, two things are necessary: a force must act on a body and the body must move in such a way that its displacement has a component parallel to the direction in which the force is acting. As an example, consider the work done on an object which a person lifts through a vertical height and then carries as he walks horizontally, keeping the object at the same height. Technically, work is done on the object only during the lifting process when the lifting force, which acts vertically, moves through a vertical distance. During the walking process, the force necessary to support the object at a given height acts vertically while the displacement, being horizontal, has no vertical component, and no work is accomplished by the force supporting the object.

–Morgan, *Introduction to University Physics*, pp. 183–184

Which passage seemed easier? The passages are approximately the same length, but they differ greatly in many other features — primarily features that contribute to difficulty. Passage 1 is written at a fourth-grade level, while passage 2 is at a college level of difficulty.

Look again at each passage; what features of the writing make passage 1 easier or passage 2 more difficult? Try to list below as many differences as you can.

Passage 1   Passage 2

_____   _____

_____   _____

_____   _____

_____   _____

_____

In these two passages, there were a great many differences. Some of the obvious differences were:

1. Passage 1 uses short, relatively simple sentences. The words are short, the vocabulary is easy. The passage contains clear examples, and the terms are clearly defined.
2. In passage 2, the sentences are longer and more complex. The words are longer and are more difficult. The explanation of *work* is more detailed and complicated, and words with specialized, technical meanings are used.

Linguists, people who study language, could list many other differences between the two passages. Very technical or subtle features of language, called linguistic variables, have been found to affect how easy a passage is to understand. Linguistic variables include such things as the total number of syllables, the number of times a word is repeated, and the arrangement of words within a sentence. Actually, any one of these linguistic variables can affect how difficult a passage will be to read. However, there are some variables which have a greater effect than others and are more useful to note; these are sentence length, vocabulary difficulty, and the sophistication of the concepts being discussed.

Sentence Length: A passage with very long sentences can make reading more difficult and will force you to read more slowly. Try reading the following paragraph; notice how the length of the sentences seems to hold you back and slow you down.

The relatively low probability of criminal sanctions being imposed, and the relatively high probability that they will be mild when they are imposed, is enjoyed not only by corporate offenders who violate regulatory laws, but also by those who steal from their employers, by those who defraud the public, and by those who violate public trust while holding political office. Compared to the "traditional" criminal — the robber, burglar, heroin pusher, rapist — the occupational criminal generally faces little in the way of organized efforts to enforce the law, and when exposed, is ignored, handled informally and unofficially, ordered to "cease and desist," forced to pay a nominal fee, or placed on probation.
—Barlow, *Introduction to Criminology*, p. 258

Vocabulary: A passage with difficult or unfamiliar vocabulary can have the same effect — understanding becomes difficult or impossible, and your rate of reading is extremely slow. Try the following:

The liberal-cynical criminologist is skeptical about the perfectability of crime control efforts, and locates criminogenic forces in the basic structure and institutions of society, but he still retains a belief in the continued viability of American society in its present form. In radical criminology such a belief is absent. . . . More moderate radical criminologists shade into the newer brand of liberal-cynical criminology, but still view crime and the criminal as manifestations of the exploitative character of monopoly capitalism. . . .
—Barlow, *Introduction to Criminology*, p. 28

The preceding examples have focused on two of the more mechanical aspects of writing, aspects that have to do with the words themselves and how they are arranged.

Ideas and Concepts: In addition to these mechanical features of language, there is a third entire set of writer variables which affect difficulty — those that have to do with the ideas and concepts presented in a passage. An article, though written in fairly simple language, may discuss complicated ideas or may follow a sophisticated line of reasoning. In the sample below, you will notice that, although the language used is relatively simple, a difficult concept is being discussed.

> This interrelationship between electricity and magnetism, Einstein stated, was a consequence of the more profound interrelationship between space and time. Just as the forces between electrical charges are affected by motion, the very measurements of space and time are also affected by motion. All measurements of space and time depend on relative motion — for example, the length of a rocket ship poised on its launching platform and the tick of clocks within are found to be different when the same ship is moving at high speeds. It has always been common sense that we change our position in space when we move — but Einstein flouted common sense and stated that in moving we also change our rate of proceeding into the future — time itself is altered. Einstein went on to show that a consequence of the interrelationship between space and time is an interrelationship between mass and energy, given by the famous equation, $E = mc^2$.
>
> —Hewitt, *Conceptual Physics,* p. 563

While you can do nothing to change the features of writing that affect difficulty, you can change how you approach the writing. You can deliberately slow down if you encounter a passage with long, complicated sentences or an article which presents difficult concepts or complicated arguments. Or you can deliberately speed up when you find a passage with simple, unsophisticated vocabulary. In other words, you can *adjust* your rate to the characteristics of the reading material.

Learning to adjust your rate according to style and content will require a conscious effort at first. If you are now in the habit of reading everything at the same pace, as most college students are, then you will need to force yourself to make an assessment of the particular reading material before deciding how fast you can read it. When you use the technique of prereading, you are only a small step away from adjusting your rate. By prereading, you are familiarizing yourself with the overall content and organization of the material. You may also include, as part of your prereading, a step in which you pay particular attention to the overall difficulty of the material. In the prereading process, you will sample enough of the actual writing to be able to assess the level of complexity of both the language and the content.

Deciding how much to speed up or slow down for a particular article is a matter of judgment. You will find through experience that you will be able to judge how much you can afford to alter your speed. It is not important to know precisely how much to increase your speed. Rather, the important thing is to develop the skill of *flexibility* — the ability to change your speed in response to the nature of the material.

Reader Variables

A second set of variables which influence how fast you can read and how well you can comprehend is related to you, the reader. Here is only a partial list of the many things about your reading ability that affect reading speed.

Your Vocabulary Level: If your general reading vocabulary level is high, you will not encounter many words that you do not know, and your speed will be unaffected. On the other hand, if your reading vocabulary is weak and you meet several unknown words in every paragraph, you will find that you lose speed as you pause to look for context clues to the meaning. Even if you decide to skip over an unknown word, making the decision to skip it will affect your speed and will interrupt the flow of ideas as you read.

Your Comprehension Ability: Your level of skill in understanding sentences and paragraphs will affect your rate. If you have trouble locating the core parts of a sentence or cannot identify the topic, main idea, and details of a paragraph, then your rate will suffer as you spend time looking for these things.

Your Physical State: How you feel physically affects both rate and comprehension. If you are extremely tired, or just recovering from the flu, you will not be able to perform at your peak level. Concentration may become a problem, or you may not be able to force yourself to stay awake. If you are hungry, or if the room is extremely hot or cold, your reading performance may also be affected.

Your State of Mind: Just as your physical state can affect your reading rate, so can your mental or emotional state. If you are depressed or worried, you may not be able to concentrate easily; if you are excited or anxious about something, your mental state may not be conducive to effective reading.

Your Interest in the Material: Your interest in what you are reading may influence how fast and with what degree of comprehension you read. If you are reading about a topic that interests you a lot, you are likely to read faster and with more understanding than if you are reading about a subject in which you have little or no interest.

Your Background Knowledge: The amount of knowledge you have of a topic partially determines how well you will be able to read about it. Suppose you were assigned to read a passage taken from the middle of an introductory botany textbook. If you had completed a course in botany, the passage would probably be understandable and easy enough to read. On the other hand, if you had never studied botany, the passage would be extremely difficult and confusing; it would be necessary to read very slowly, and you might have to stop to look up unfamiliar terms and concepts.

ADJUSTING YOUR RATE TO YOUR PURPOSE

The purpose for reading is an important factor related to both rate and comprehension and involving both the nature of the material and the reader's approach to the material. If you are reading a magazine article for enjoyment, your purpose is different from when you are reading a textbook chapter to prepare for an exam. If you are paging through the newspaper, your purpose differs from your purpose when you are reading a poem for your English literature class.

Your reading rate is determined by your purpose for reading. There are four basic types of reading of printed material, ranging from an extremely slow analysis to an extremely rapid overview of the material. Each type is related to a specific kind of material, a definite purpose, and is done at a certain speed. These are summarized in the chart below.

Type of reading	Range of speed	Purpose in reading	Types of material
Analytical	Under 100 wpm	Detailed comprehension: analyze, evaluate, critique	Poetry, argumentative writing
Study-reading	150–250 wpm	High comprehension and high recall	Textbooks, library research
Casual reading	250–400 wpm	Moderate comprehension of main ideas, entertainment, enjoyment, general information	Novels, newspapers, magazines
Accelerated reading	Faster than casual reading	Overview of material, rapid location of a specific fact	Reference material, magazines, novels, nonfiction

A PROCEDURE FOR ADJUSTING YOUR RATE

The previous sections in this chapter discussed variables that affect reading rate. These sections were included to make you aware of the complexity of reading rate and to indicate that improving your reading rate is an involved process. Now that you are familiar with these variables, you can begin to adjust your own reading rate according to your needs and purposes. Here is a step-by-step procedure you can follow that will help you build the habit of varying your reading rate. In this procedure, you must complete the following steps before you begin reading.

1. Choose a time and place for reading that will help rather than hinder your concentration. Choose a time when you are alert and your state of mind is conducive to study.
2. Preread the material. As you preread, assess the difficulty of both the writing style and the content. Are there a lot of difficult words? Are the sentences long and complicated? How factual is the material? How much background information do you have on the subject?
3. Define your overall purpose for reading. Your purpose will determine the level of comprehension and the degree of retention that you require. Are you reading for enjoyment, looking up facts, or reading a text chapter to prepare for an exam?
4. Decide what rate would be appropriate for reading this particular material.
5. After you've finished the first page of the reading material, stop and evaluate. Are you understanding and remembering what you are reading? Can you summarize the ideas in your own words?

MEASURING YOUR READING RATE

You now realize that the type of material you read and how you approach it determine, in part, your reading rate. Although measuring reading rate is complex, most students want some idea of whether they are fast or slow readers, or at least an indication of whether they are above or below average. It is possible to measure reading rate if a particular type of material is used and the reader has a particular purpose in mind.

If you refer back to the chart on page 302, you can see that the rate for each type of reading can be measured. Before beginning to measure your rate for each type, you will need to know how to figure out words per minute, the unit of measurement used in computing reading rate.

How to Compute Words per Minute

1. After you have chosen a passage in a book or article, count the total number of words in any three lines. Divide the total by 3. Round it off to the nearest whole number. This will give the average number of words per line.
2. Count the number of lines in the article or book (or on one page if it is longer than one page). Multiply the number of words per line by the total number of lines. This will give you a fairly accurate estimate of the total number of words.
3. As you read, time yourself using a watch with a second hand. Record both minutes and seconds of your starting time (4:20 18). Start reading when the second hand of the clock reaches twelve. Record your finishing time. Subtract your starting time from your finishing time.
4. Divide the total reading time into the total number of words. To do this, round off the number of seconds to the nearest quarter of a minute and then divide. For example, if your total reading time was 3 minutes and 12 seconds, round it off to 3¼ or 3.25 minutes and then divide. Your answer will be your words-per-minute score.

Example:

Total number of words on 3 lines: 23
Divide by 3 and round off: 23 ÷ 3 = 7⅔ = 8
Number of lines in article: 120
Multiply number of words per line by number of lines:
8 × 120 = 960 (total words)

$$
\begin{array}{rl}
\text{Subtract finishing time} & 1{:}13\ 22 \\
\text{from starting time} & \underline{1{:}05} \\
& 8 \text{ minutes 22 seconds}
\end{array}
$$

Round off to nearest ¼ minute: 8½ minutes
Divide time into total number of words:

960 ÷ 8.5 = 112 + a fraction (your reading rate)

Measuring Your Analytical Reading Rate

1. Select a poem or a passage from a complicated essay in an English textbook, or choose an extremely complicated description of a process from another of your texts, or pick a discussion of a controversial issue which you plan to analyze carefully. (A poem — William Wordsworth's "Lucy Gray" — has been included below to use for this purpose.)

2. Count the number of words, read the material, time yourself, and compute your words-per-minute score. Record your wpm in the chart on page 307.

3. Check your comprehension; could you now write a paper analyzing and reacting to what you read?

Lucy Gray
OR SOLITUDE

by William Wordsworth

Oft I had heard of Lucy Gray:
And, when I crossed the wild,
I chanced to see at break of day
The solitary child.

No mate, no comrade Lucy knew;
She dwelt on a wide moor,
—The sweetest thing that ever grew
Beside a human door!

You yet may spy the fawn at play,
The hare upon the green;
But the sweet face of Lucy Gray
Will never more be seen.

"Tonight will be a stormy night —
You to the town must go;
And take a lantern, Child, to light
Your mother through the snow."

"That, Father! will I gladly do:
'Tis scarcely afternoon —
The minster clock has just struck two,
And yonder is the moon!"

At this the Father raised his hook,
And snapped a faggot band;
He plied his work — and Lucy took
The lantern in her hand.

Not blither is the mountain roe;
With many a wanton stroke
Her feet disperse the powdery snow,
That rises up like smoke.

The storm came on before its time;
She wandered up and down;
And many a hill did Lucy climb,
But never reached the town.

The wretched parents all that night
Went shouting far and wide;
But there was neither sound nor sight
To serve them for a guide.

At daybreak on a hill they stood
That overlooked the moor;
And thence they saw the bridge of wood,
A furlong from their door.

They wept — and, turning homeward, cried,
"In heaven we all shall meet";
—When in the snow the mother spied
The print of Lucy's feet.

Then downwards from the steep hill's edge
They tracked the footmarks small;
And through the broken hawthorn hedge,
And by the long stone wall;

And then an open field they crossed:
The marks were still the same;
They tracked them on, nor ever lost;
And to the bridge they came.

They followed from the snowy bank
Those footmarks, one by one,
Into the middle of the plank;
And further there were none!

—Yet some maintain that to this day
She is a living child;
That you may see sweet Lucy Gray
Upon the lonesome wild.

O'er rough and smooth she trips along,
And never looks behind;
And sings a solitary song
That whistles in the wind.

Measuring Your Study-Reading Rate

Choose a selection from one of your textbooks which you have not read but expect will be assigned. Assume that you will have to pass an exam on the material later in the course. Then follow steps 2 and 3 given on page 304.

Measuring Your Casual Reading Rate

Choose a selection of several pages from a novel you are reading or select several pages from a magazine article that interests you. Read it only for enjoyment or general information. Then compute your wpm, and record them in the chart. (A sample magazine article has been included here to use in measuring your casual reading rate.)

Sexes

Army Husband

If Mom's a G.I., who baby-sits?

It was Purple Hearts and flowers from the start. He was in the Air Force; she was in the Army. They fell in love while they were studying broadcasting and journalism, respectively, at the Defense Information School in Indianapolis. And then they carried on a long-distance romance between New Mexico's Holloman Airbase, where he was assigned to a supply unit, and Fort Lee, Va., where she worked as an Army journalist. Personnel officers at both bases assured them that he would have no difficulty transferring to a supply unit in Fort Lee, so Private First Class Richard Venema, then 21, and Sergeant Elayne Chalifour, then 19, decided to join forces. In 1977 they got married.

Then the military began behaving according to tradition. Richard was told he could not transfer to Fort Lee after all; the supply units were incompatible. He was unable to get a job anywhere near Fort Lee, nor could Elayne transfer to New Mexico. Richard even tried to transfer to the Army—to no avail. Exasperated by months of snafus, Richard resigned from the Air Force and joined Elayne at Fort Lee. There he eventually found a job as a salesman in a department store. No sooner had he done so than the Army transferred her to West Berlin on an "unaccompanied tour," with no accommodation for a spouse. Richard went along anyway; this time he settled for work as a handyman. Soon there was a new complication on the domestic front. "The baby

was planned," says Richard. "The situation after Stephen's birth was not."

The couple's tactical problem: Who would guard the home front, with Momma in the front lines? Obviously Poppa, since in these days of deflated dollars Yanks in Germany can no longer easily afford such amenities as full-time baby sitters. So Richard dutifully quit his job once more. In increasingly liberated America, househusbands are becoming an accepted part of life. But in the macho world of the military, Richard is an unassimilable anomaly: as far as his military neighbors were concerned, he might as well have bartered away Pentagon secrets. Explains Richard: "The husbands won't talk to me, because I do 'womanly' things and they work." And their wives are no more sympathetic, barely acknowledging his presence when he does the family wash in the basement laundry of the military apartment complex where the Venemas live. Nor is life any easier at the PX; every time Richard goes there he seems to have to explain to yet another puzzled clerk that his wife is the soldier, he the dependent. Grousing does not help: "Nobody listens to me because nobody has to listen to me."

Difficult as their plight may seem, the Venemas are soldiering on. But they may not do battle much longer. Elayne's tour of duty is up in 1980, and she will re-enlist only if the Army assigns her to a U.S. city, where Richard can pursue his dream of becoming a disc jockey. Meanwhile, he continues to care for their five-month-old son during the day and take business courses at night. Undaunted, the couple is considering a second child. ∎

TIME, APRIL 16, 1979

Measuring Your Accelerated Reading Rate

Your accelerated reading rate cannot really be accurately or fairly computed in terms of words per minute. When you are reading to locate a particular fact, for example, you are not really reading or comprehending everything. Instead you are searching, reading certain parts, skipping over others. Or if you are reading to get an overview of an article, you read selectively — you read only key parts of the article and skip the remainder. However, accelerated reading should be extremely fast, much higher than in casual reading situations. Techniques and procedures for accelerated reading will be presented in Chapter 24.

Type of reading	Average speed	Your speed
Analytical	Below 100 wpm	_____
Study-reading	150–250 wpm	_____
Casual reading	250–400 wpm	_____
Accelerated	Faster than casual reading	_____

INTERPRETING YOUR RESULTS

If your reading rate was below average for one or more of the types of reading, but not below average for all, or if your rate was nearly the same each time, this suggests that you do not vary your speed according to purpose and type of material.

If your rates were below the range indicated for each type of reading, this suggests that you are a slow reader. Within the reading process, a slow reading rate is more often a symptom than a cause. A slow rate is to reading as chills and fever are to a cold. The chills and fever are not the cause of the cold; rather they are symptoms that let you know you have a cold. Similarly, a slow reading rate usually suggests that something else is wrong. Usually the problem is comprehension — you are having difficulty understanding what you read. If your reading rate is slow, do not simply try to read faster. Instead work on the cause — comprehension skills. Focus on developing the comprehension skills presented in Part Three of this text.

SUMMARY

The chapter addressed the question of reading rate and its measurement. Reading rate is influenced by many variables, which fall into two basic categories — writer variables and reader variables.

Writer variables refer to all the features of written language which influence the level of difficulty of the material. Among the most important writer variables are sentence length, difficulty of vocabulary, and complexity of ideas. Each of these variables definitely affects the rate at which you read a given piece of material. While you can do nothing to alter the writer's style, you can alter your approach to the reading of the material. You can deliberately slow down or speed up according to the type of material you are reading.

Reader variables refer to those characteristics, skills, and habits that affect reading rate which you, the reader, have developed. Among the most important variables are your vocabulary level, your level of comprehension, your physical and mental state, your interest in the material, and your familiarity with the subject.

While both writer and reader variables directly influence your rate, a third major factor should determine how fast you read — your purpose for reading. Depending on the amount and type of information you must retain, your reading rate should fluctuate widely. Your reading rate is determined by the type of reading and your purpose for reading as follows:

Analytical reading: reading for detailed comprehension, analysis, and evaluation (below 100 wpm)

Study-reading: reading for a high level of comprehension and recall (150–250 wpm)

Casual reading: reading for main ideas, general information, or enjoyment (250–400 wpm)

Accelerated reading: reading for an overview of the material or to locate specific information rapidly (faster than casual reading)

23. Eye Movement and Physical Aspects of Reading

Use this chapter to:

1. *Learn how your eyes function in the reading process.*

2. *Learn to control or alter your eye movement to become a more efficient reader.*

Reading is both a physical and a mental, or cognitive, process. As you read, your eyes first converge or focus upon groupings of symbols — letters or words. The visual image of these symbols is transferred to the brain, and meaning is associated with them; for instance, your eyes see the letters *c-a-t* and transfer them to your brain, which connects the word spelled by the letters *c-a-t* with what it represents — an animal that looks like a cat.

Next, your eyes progress to the next word, and the same symbol-meaning association process takes place. The manner and efficiency with which your eyes move across the line affect your reading rate and influence your level of comprehension. The purpose of this chapter is to describe the physical process of reading and to relate it to the improvement of reading rate and comprehension.

VISUAL PROBLEMS

Before being concerned with the nature of eye movement in the reading process, it is first necessary to determine that your vision is adequate to read effectively and that there are no visual problems standing in the way of your efficient reading. You have no doubt heard of farsightedness and nearsightedness — two common visual defects. Farsightedness, the ability to see at distances but not close at hand, is the defect that most commonly affects reading. Fortunately, there are many symptoms which can alert you to the problem of farsightedness.

On the checklist below is a series of symptoms of visual problems. Make a check mark in the yes column if any symptoms describe what occurs when you read for a reasonable length of time. For some of the items, you may want to ask a friend to observe you while you read.

If you checked the yes column for three or more of the items in the checklist, you probably should have your eyes examined. Do not rely upon a clinic that tests your vision with a wall chart alone. The wall chart will indicate if you have problems with distance viewing but may not reveal problems of close vision.

Visual Problems Checklist	Yes	No
1. Do you frequently lose your place while reading?	☐	☐
2. Do you hold the book you are reading closer to your body than other people do?	☐	☐
3. Do you frown, squint, or blink frequently while you read?	☐	☐
4. Do your eyes become irritated if you read for long periods of time?	☐	☐
5. Are your eyes red or puffy when you finish reading?	☐	☐
6. Do you rub or scratch your eyes as you read?	☐	☐
7. Do lights of particular brightness bother you?	☐	☐
8. Do you get frequent headaches while you read?	☐	☐
9. Do you often get a stiff neck or backache after reading?	☐	☐
10. Do you sometimes read with one eye closed?	☐	☐

EYE-MOVEMENT PATTERNS

Your eyes are intricate and complicated instruments. They have the capacity to recognize visual symbols rapidly and transmit them in the form of signals to the brain. The initial stage of word recognition is a physical, fairly mechanical process, and training and practice can improve the efficiency of this process. Before beginning specific practice techniques, it is important to understand what occurs as your eyes move across a line of print.

Left-to-Right Movement

First of all, your eyes are already well trained to move from left to right across the page. Watching small children try to read, you may notice that the left-to-right progression is not an automatic response. It is a learned behavior. The children may scan a line of print from right to left, or they may pick out words at any point in the line. Although left-to-right movement is well learned at this point in your life, the speed with which your eyes move is variable and can be increased.

Fixations

As your eyes move across a line of print, they move and stop, move and stop. While your eyes are moving from one word to another, they see nothing and transmit nothing to your brain. When your eyes stop, they see a group of letters and send a signal to your brain. Each stop that your eyes make is called a *fixation*.

Your eyes make a certain number of stops, or fixations, on each line of print. The number of fixations your eyes make can be counted and used as an indication of how efficiently you read. The average reader spends about 6 percent of reading time on eye movement and 94 percent of the time in making fixations.

A reader's eye movement across a line of print might look like this, with the words and word parts between each set of slashes (/ — /) representing a fixation:

/ Philhar / monic / Hall in / New / York / City / was / designed / by / archi / tects. /

On this line of print, the reader made eleven fixations. Notice that the fixations included material of varying length. One fixation included two small words, another only a single word, others only parts of words. The amount of time your eyes spend on each fixation also varies. Research studies show, however, that good readers spend less time on each fixation than do poor readers.

Eye Span

Your eyes fixate on a group of letters or words. The number of letters or words that your eyes see in one fixation is called your *eye span*. Your eye span may range from several letters to several words and is affected by the content and difficulty of what you are reading. One technique to improve your rate is to try to widen your eye span — to see more in each fixation. Later in this chapter, specific suggestions are included for widening eye span.

Regression

As your eyes move across a line, fixating on groups of letters or words, they normally proceed from left to right. Occasionally your eyes will, instead of moving to the next word, move backward, or regress, to a previous word on the same line or to a word in a line already read. In the line below, each fixation is numbered to show a reader's regression pat-

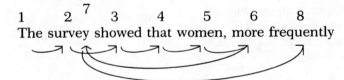

Notice that the reader progressed from left to right up to the sixth fixation. Then, instead of proceeding on to the next word, the reader regressed to a previous word (7), reread it, and then went back to where he or she left off (8). This habit, known as regression, is usually unnecessary and slows you down.

By regressing to words you have already read you are scrambling the sentence order, and this could result in a loss of meaning. Read the following sentence, which is written as it would be read by a student who made two regressions in the sentence. Then compare it with the correct sentence.

Order as read by the student:
The mockingbird is noted for its ability noted to mimic mockingbird other birds.

Correct sentence order:
   The mockingbird is noted for its ability to mimic other birds.

Notice how difficult and confusing the first sentence is. Regression always creates this kind of difficulty and confusion.

Regression may occur when readers feel they are not getting the meaning, that they have missed something or misread a word. Readers then go backward and reread a certain word or phrase. Often the regression is unnecessary. When you are reading a sentence, the meaning is not supposed to be complete until the sentence has been read all the way through. To regress in midsentence, before the meaning has been fully expressed, is often unnecessary. For many students regression has become a habit which occurs automatically and which they are not aware of.

Return Sweep

When your eyes reach the end of the line, they must return to the left side of the page in order to begin reading the next line. This return motion is called the *return sweep*. The speed with which your eyes make this return sweep can vary and affects your overall reading efficiency.

EYE-MOVEMENT PRACTICE

To get a better understanding of the movement patterns your eyes make, choose another person to work with and try the three experiments under the following headings. First, sit so that you and the other person are facing each other. Then choose from a textbook any page you have not already read.

Experiment 1: Observing Eye Movements
   Holding the book so that the other person can see your eyes, start reading any paragraph. Have the person watch your eyes closely. Your eye movements, both fixations and return sweeps, will be visible to the other person.

Experiment 2: Counting Fixations
   As you read, have the other person count the number of fixations you make on each line. By counting the number of words per line and dividing the total by the number of fixations, you will be able to figure out your average eye span.

Experiment 3: Regressions
   As you read, deliberately move your eye backward to a previous word on the line. Have the other person tell you when you regress. This deliberate regression will demonstrate how regression looks. Next, start reading a new paragraph; try to choose one that is long and complicated. As you read, ask the other person to note whether you are making any regressions.

IMPROVING YOUR READING EFFICIENCY

Now that you are familiar with the physical aspects of eye movement, you can begin to apply various techniques to improve your reading efficiency. Most important to the improvement of rate and comprehension are reducing regression and widening your eye span.

Reducing Regression

While even very good readers occasionally make regressions, your reading rate and comprehension will improve if you can reduce the number of regressions that you make. There are various machines and mechanical devices which can be used to reduce regression. However, you can easily accomplish the same results by trying the following techniques:

1. Be conscious of the tendency to regress, and force yourself to continue reading. Do not allow yourself to regress until you have finished a sentence. Then, if the meaning is still unclear, reread the entire sentence.

2. If you frequently regress to a word or phrase on a previous line, you might try sliding a 5″ x 8″ index card down the page as you read. Use the card to cover up the lines you have finished reading. This technique will help break the habit of regression because when you look back, the line will be covered up. If you look back enough times and find nothing to look at, eventually you will stop looking back.

3. To force yourself continually forward, try guiding your eye movement using a pen or your finger. Move your finger across each line at a speed with which your eyes can keep pace. The forward motion of your finger or pen will guide your eye and force it along in a left-to-right pattern.

Increasing Your Eye Span

You probably found out from the three eye-movement experiments you tried earlier that your eye span is a single word per fixation. This span is typical for many adult readers. Many good readers are able to see more than a single word in a fixation; they are able to expand their eye span to two or even three words per fixation. Seeing more than one word at a time improves reading rate because you make fewer fixations per line. Perhaps more important, seeing groups of words can increase your understanding. If you analyze language and study how it is put together, you see that words depend on each other and that words have real meaning only when connected with other words. The words *the, as, an, when, where, how, of, in* carry little meaning by themselves, but when they are with other words, they do contribute to the meaning of a phrase or sentence: *the* pen, *as* many, *an* apple, *when* he failed, *where* she went, *how* you know, *of* course, and *in* the room.

Ideally, you should try to read together any words that belong together. Try to see, in one fixation, two words that belong together. This technique is known as *phrase reading*. To understand what phrase reading is like, read through the following paragraph. It has already been divided into phrases, or groupings of words that go together.

The electronic computer / is the / latest tool / developed by man / to aid / him / in processing data. / For business / or government / agencies / dealing with / great numbers / of records, / none of the previously mentioned / data processing / methods / is fast enough. / It is / almost impossible / to describe / a computer's / many uses. / The computer / helped land men / on the moon! / It is used / for arranging / class schedules, / sorting and / routing mail, / assisting doctors / in diagnosing / and controlling diseases, / printing this book, / navigating ships, / verifying income / tax returns, / keeping airline reservations / in order.
—Meehan et al., *Clerical Office Procedures*, p. 111

Now, to see if you can read in phrases, divide those in the following passage with slashes. The first line has been done for you.

The system / of handling / outgoing mail, / like the system of handling incoming mail, depends upon the size and the type of business in which you are employed. In a small office a mail clerk usually is responsible for all the details connected with outgoing mail. In a large office the mail is collected from each department several times throughout the day by a messenger or a mail clerk and taken to the mailing department where it is sealed and stacked near the postage meter, which is a machine that automatically prints the amount of postage, the postmark, and the mailing date on the envelope.
—Meehan et al., *Clerical Office Procedures*, pp. 150–151

Once you are able to recognize a group of words that belong together, the next step is to try to build your eye span to see such groups of words in one fixation. Do not use your textbooks to experiment with phrase reading. They are written at a level which is too difficult, and you cannot afford to lose comprehension as you experiment with this new technique. Instead, practice phrase reading with a newspaper or magazine article which is fairly easy but interesting to read.

EXERCISE 1

Directions: *Select an interesting article from a magazine or newspaper which you will enjoy reading. The article will be used to practice phrase reading. Before you begin reading it, divide the first three sentences into phrases, using slash marks. Similarly, divide the first sentence of every third paragraph into phrases. Now read the article, concentrating on reading in phrases. The first three marked sentences will get you started reading in phrases, and the others will serve as reminders in case you fall back into word-by-word reading. Practice reading the passage several times.*

SUMMARY

Reading is both a physical and a mental process. The purpose of this chapter was to describe the physical process of reading and to relate it to reading rate and comprehension improvement. First, it is important to be certain that visual problems are not interfering with the physical aspects of the reading process. A checklist for identifying possible visual problems was included in the chapter.

The eye-movement process involved in reading is described. At the most basic level, your eyes are trained to move from left to right across the lines on a page. As they move across a line of print, they move and stop, making a series of pauses, or fixations. The number of letters and/or words your eyes see when they stop is known as your eye span. Occasionally, as your eyes move across a line, they return to a word already read instead of moving on to the next word or phrase. This backward movement, known as regression, results in loss of meaning and slows down your reading rate. To improve your reading efficiency, suggestions are offered for reducing the number of regressions that you make. The technique of phrase reading is presented as a means of increasing eye span and reducing the number of fixations per line.

24. When Not to Read Everything

Use this chapter to:

1. *Learn to adjust your rate to what you are reading and your purpose for reading it.*

2. *Learn techniques for skimming and scanning.*

Can you think of any situation in which it would not be necessary to read every word on a printed page? Consider the telephone directory. Have you ever read all the words on any page of it? The answer is obvious; each time you look up a phone number, you read selectively, picking out only the information which you need and skipping everything else. Think of other types of printed material which you read the same way. List them below:

_____ _____

_____ _____

_____ _____

_____ _____

Your responses probably included such things as bus schedules, TV program listings, theater schedules, want ads, and dictionaries.

There are many types of printed material which do not require thorough, beginning-to-end, careful reading. It is the intent of this chapter to discuss situations in which you can afford to skip material as well as types of material in which it is not necessary to read everything. The chapter will also present a systematic approach to help you decide what to read and what to skip.

WHEN DON'T YOU HAVE TO READ EVERYTHING?

Before beginning to think about the situations in which it is appropriate to read selectively, it is first necessary to recognize and accept the notion that there is nothing sacred about the printed word. Many students erroneously think that anything that appears in print must be true, valuable, and worth reading. Actually, the importance and value of printed information are affected by whether you need to learn it, whether it has any importance and relevance to you, and whether you can use it in a practical way. Depending upon the particular material and your purpose for reading it, it is appropriate many times to read some parts and skip over others.

First and most common of situations in which you can afford to skip information are those in which you are not attempting to maintain a high level of comprehension (80 percent or above) and an equally high level of recall. If you are not trying to remember a major portion of the facts and details, then you might concentrate on reading only main ideas. This method of reading only main ideas is called *skimming*. Specific techniques for skimming will be presented later in the chapter.

A second situation in which you clearly need to skip over material is when you are searching for one particular fact or piece of information. If you are looking up the date of a historical event in your history text, you would skip over everything in the chapter except the exact passage which contains the information. This technique of skipping everything except the specific information for which you are looking is called *scanning*. Practice in scanning techniques is included later in the chapter.

A third common situation in which you may decide it is appropriate to skip information is when you have a high level of familiarity with the content of the material you are reading. Suppose that you are taking Chemistry I this semester and that you have already completed a year of high school chemistry. Chemistry was your favorite subject, you were interested in it, and you did extremely well in the high school course. Now, in your college chemistry course, you find that the first few chapters of your text are very basic and that you are already familiar with the material. In this situation, you could afford to skip such things as basic definitions and explanations and examples of principles that you already know. Do not, however, decide to skip the entire chapter or even large sections within it; there just may be some new information included. Check each paragraph to be sure that there is nothing new to you. You may find that more exact and detailed definitions are given or that a new approach is taken toward a particular topic.

Finally, you can afford to skip over material which contains information which does not fulfill your purpose in reading. Suppose, in making an assignment in your physics text, your instructor told you to concentrate on theories, laws, and principles presented in the chapter. As you begin reading the chapter, you find that the first topic discussed is Newton's law of motion, but the chapter also contains a biographical sketch of Newton giving detailed information about his life. Since your purpose in reading the chapter is to focus on theories, laws, and principles, it would be appropriate to skip over much of the biographical information.

TYPES OF MATERIAL TO SKIP

Just as there are situations when it is appropriate to skip over information, there are also various types and styles of writing in which it is possible to skip information. Some writers include many examples of a particular concept or principle. If, after reading two or three examples, you are sure that you understand the idea being explained, just quickly glance at the remaining examples. Unless they present a new aspect or different point of view, skip over them.

Other writers feel the need to provide detailed background information before leading into a discussion of the intended topic. If a chapter starts out by summarizing information that was covered in a chapter you just read last week, it would not be necessary to read this information again carefully unless you feel you need to review.

EXERCISE 1

Directions: *Each of the items below suggests a reading situation and describes the material to be read. After reading each item, decide whether the reader should:*
a. *read the material completely.*
b. *read parts, skip other parts.*
c. *skip most of the material.*

1. You are reading a textbook chapter in anthropology and you _____ know you will be quizzed on it next week. Your instructor's quizzes are usually detailed and thorough. How should you read the chapter?

2. Your history instructor assigned each student to read a _____ historical novel for the purpose of getting a realistic picture of what life was like and how people lived during a certain period in history. As you are reading, you come to a detailed two-page description of the type of gowns southern women wore to a particular party. How should you read these two pages?

3. You are doing research for a sociology term paper on the _____ world population explosion. You are looking for information and statistics on recent population trends. You have located several books from the 1940s on the topic of population growth in the United States. How would you read these books?

4. Your nursing instructor has just returned a test on a chapter _____ describing the nursing process. She indicated that the class's overall performance on this test was poor and suggested that the chapter be reviewed. You received a grade of 79 on the test. How should this chapter be reread?

5. Your biology professor has assigned a number of brief _____ outside readings along with the chapters in your regular textbook. He has put them on reserve in the college library for the use of all his classes. This is the only place they can be used. He did not say whether you would be tested on them. How would you read them?

6. You have just attended English class where your instructor _____ discussed Milton's *Paradise Lost*. During his discussion he made numerous references to Dante's *Inferno*. You have never read this second work but think it is important to know something about it. How would you read it?

SKIMMING TECHNIQUES

As you know, the term *skimming* refers to the process of reading only main ideas within a passage and simply glancing at the remainder of the material. Skimming is most commonly used to get an overall picture of an article, to become generally familiar with the topics and ideas presented, or to get the gist of a particular article. Usually, skimming is an end in itself; that is, skimming is all that you intend to do with the article. You do not intend to read it more completely later. You are willing to settle for an overview of the article, giving up a major portion of the details.

At this point, you may be thinking that skimming seems similar to the technique of prereading. If so, you are correct. Prereading is actually a form of skimming. To be more precise, there are three forms of skimming: *preread skimming*, *skim-reading*, and *review skimming*. Preread skimming assumes that you plan to read the entire article or chapter and that you are prereading as a means of getting ready to read. Skim-reading refers to situations in which skimming is the only coverage you plan to give the material. Review skimming assumes you have already read the material and are going back over it as a means of study and review.

Prereading has already been discussed in Part Two, Chapter 7. Methods of review after reading are part of the reading-study systems, such as SQ3R, discussed in Part Four, Chapter 13. Therefore, this chapter will focus on skim-reading techniques.

DEMONSTRATION OF SKIMMING

The sample passage on pages 320–321 has been included to demonstrate what should occur in the skimming process. Only the parts of the passage which should be read while skimming have been retained; all other parts of the passage have been deleted.

The passage is taken from a sociology text on courtship and marriage. It appears at the end of a chapter which discusses masculine and feminine roles and conflicts. The article is included, not as a part of the chapter, but as an additional reading selected to give a perspective on or interpretation of the topic discussed in the chapter itself. Since the article is not factual and not part of the text itself, skimming it for main ideas is appropriate.

HOW TO SKIM-READ

Your purpose in skimming is to get an overall impression of the content of a reading selection. The technique of skimming involves selecting and reading those parts of the selection which contain the most important ideas and merely glancing at the rest of the material. Below is a step-by-step procedure to follow in skimming for main ideas.

1. Read the title. If it is an article, check the author, publication date, and source.
2. Read the introduction. If it is very long, read only the first paragraph completely. Read the first sentence of every other paragraph. Usually this sentence will be a statement of the main idea of that paragraph.
3. Read any headings and subheadings. The headings, when taken together, form an outline of the main topics covered in the material.
4. Notice any pictures, charts, or graphs included; they are usually included to emphasize important ideas, concepts, or trends.
5. If you do not get enough information from the headings or if you

It's Really the Men Who Need Liberating

Mary Calderone

. . . I am particularly concerned about the hostility now fermenting between men and women. Just when men and women have the opportunity to mean more to each other than ever before, and when the world, the society and that entity known as the family need them *together*, they are exploding apart.

Men and women are deeply uneasy with and about each other; they circle each other **warily**, fencing and **feinting**; their visual contacts are sidewise, not direct; they are mistaking bodily for interpersonal intimacy. There is **little trust** between them.

One reason for this may be that women have come so far, so fast. In the span of my own lifetime, women have achieved rights and freedoms undreamed of in the previous century: rights of franchise, of **property ownership,** of guardianship of children; freedoms in education, professions, occupations, recreation, movement, **dress,** behavior. Imagine that at 15 I was wearing long black stockings for swimming, and felt daring when I rolled them below the knees!

By contrast, in this same period, males, who have always had the rights, have achieved far fewer freedoms. Only recently have they begun to emerge from their age-old stereotyped grooves of earning, governing and fighting, and from their compulsively **fixed patterns** of masculinity in dressing, professions, recreation and life-style. That these were grooves and patterns they had themselves designed made them no less confining, but it did make breaking out of them all the more fearful a process. As men have begun to emerge from these **stereotypes,** doubtfully and hesitantly, they have found that in leaving the security of their old shells, they are that much more exposed and vulnerable to the incomparably more secure and liberated females.

A few years ago at a meeting of about 100 professionals in counseling and family life, I asked the men to sit in the rear and listen while the **women gave** me a series of adjectives on the theme **"What I would like to see men become 20 years from now."** For a half hour the women discussed the qualities they desired, then they faced the men. At first, the men were **defensive** about adjectives they termed predominantly "feminine," such as tender, gentle, empathetic, nurturing, artistic. But the women convinced them that these were desirable qualities that would enhance men's own evolution as individuals. By the time the meeting ended the men admitted that the women had listed qualities that they would like to have had but felt they were "not permitted" to develop. Not permitted by whom? Today I would answer, **by the norms of the society as a whole that have been set primarily by the males themselves in a kind of self-fulfilling process of entrapment.**

This is why I would like to propose to women that for women to choose to strike out at men at this moment is not only unwise and counterproductive, but inhumane and therefore self-defeating. Granted the justice of so many of the

Adapted by permission of the author from Mary Calderone. "It's Really the Men Who Need Liberating." Guest Editorial, *Life* 69 (4 September 1970). Dr. Calderone is cofounder and president of SIECUS, the Sex Information and Education Council of the U.S.

Demonstration of Skimming

claims made by women against their own subjugation and exploitation by males over the centuries and in the present, the bald fact is that hostility and vengefulness of half a population against the other half is never what is needed at any moment in history, but most especially in this one.

What *is* needed, then, in the relationships of the sexes to each other? I would say primarily a joint realization from the very earliest years that participation in all life processes relates to being human rather than to being sexual. Therefore it is not so much competitiveness or aggressiveness or submission or exploitation of either sex by the other that is at issue, as the opportunities each one of us, being human, can find to enjoy and be enjoyed by, help and be helped by, stimulate and be stimulated by members of the sex that is not ours as well as of the one that is.

Women simply cannot run this world alone. But then, neither can men! Together they can do it, and much, much better than it is being run at present. Together, both as individuals and as the two sexual collectivities, they can help and support each other in the free choices to be made as *both* sexes find out that love and sex, jobs and families, work and play, world concerns and self concerns are not mutually exclusive. They are points in the life continuum that deserve and can receive different emphases at different epochs or moments in that life—without being at the expense of either man or woman.

"His" and "Hers" should not divide the world, which is *ours*. There is no need for any lifelong choice of a role or an occupation. Either sex should be free to come and go across frontiers that exist only as we ourselves choose to establish them. . . .

Freedom to choose what and how to be, as male or female—by knowing what the choices are and balancing one's own good, one's partner's or associate's good and the common good—this is what each sex should make possible *for* the other sex, not wrest violently *from* the other sex. Women will have to make the first gestures on behalf of men's liberation, for at this moment men are still entrapped in their own centuries-old power play. But women can afford such generosity, for women have forged ahead of men at other, deeper levels. The obligation is on us, as women, to ease the way for men to those deeper levels of relationships where power is powerless and the truest satisfactions as human beings are to be found.

Then the power questions won't matter at all, nor even exist anymore.

are working with material which does not have headings, read the first sentence of each paragraph.

6. Glance at the remainder of the paragraph.
   a. Notice any italicized or boldface words or phrases. These are key terms used throughout the selection.
   b. Look for any lists of ideas within the text of the material. The author may use numerals, such as (1), (2), (3), in the list or may include such signal words as *first, second, one major cause, another cause*.
   c. Look for unusual or striking features of the paragraph. You may notice a series of dates, many capitalized words, or several large-figure numbers.
7. Read the summary or last paragraph.

EXERCISE 2

Directions: *Skim each of the following selections. Then summarize each article in the space provided.*

Selection 1: "To Lie or Not to Lie? — The Doctor's Dilemma"

_____

_____

_____

Selection 2: "Aging and Death"

_____

_____

_____

Selection 3: "A Good Word for Bad Words"

_____

_____

_____

1. TO LIE OR NOT TO LIE? — THE DOCTOR'S DILEMMA

Sissela Bok

Should doctors ever lie to benefit their patients — to speed recovery or to conceal the approach of death? In medicine as in law, government, and other lines of work, the requirements of honesty often seem dwarfed by greater needs: the need to shelter from brutal news or to uphold a promise of secrecy; to expose corruption or to promote the public interest.

What should doctors say, for example, to a 46-year-old man coming for a routine physical checkup just before going on vacation with his family who, though he feels in perfect health, is found to have a form of cancer that will cause him to die within six months? Is it best to tell him the truth? If he asks, should the doctors deny that he is ill, or minimize the gravity of the prognosis? Should they at least conceal the truth until after the family vacation?

Doctors confront such choices often and urgently. At times, they see important reasons to lie for the patient's own sake; in their eyes, such lies differ sharply from self-serving ones.

Studies show that most doctors sincerely believe that the seriously ill do not want to know the truth about their condition, and that informing them risks destroying their hope, so that they may recover more slowly, or deteriorate faster, perhaps even commit suicide. As one physician wrote: "Ours is a profession which traditionally has been guided by a precept that transcends the virtue of uttering the truth for truth's sake, and that is 'as far as possible do no harm.' "

Armed with such a precept, a number of doctors may slip into deceptive practices that they assume will "do no harm" and may well help their patients. They may prescribe innumerable placebos, sound more encouraging than the facts warrant, and distort grave news, especially to the incurably ill and the dying.

But the illusory nature of the benefits such deception is meant to bestow is now coming to be documented. Studies show that, contrary to the belief of many physicians, an overwhelming majority of patients do want to be told the truth, even about grave illness, and feel betrayed when they learn that they have been misled. We are also learning that truthful information, humanely conveyed, helps patients cope with illness: helps them tolerate pain better, need less medication, and even recover faster after surgery.

Not only do lies not provide the "help" hoped for by advocates of benevolent deception; they invade the autonomy of patients and render them unable to make informed choices concerning their own health, including the choice of whether to *be* a patient in the first place. We are becoming increasingly aware of all that can befall patients in the course of their illness when information is denied or distorted.

Dying patients especially — who are easiest to mislead and most often kept in the dark — can then not make decisions about the end of life: about whether or not to enter a hospital, or to have surgery; about where and with whom to spend their remaining time; about how to bring their affairs to a close and take leave.

Lies also do harm to those who tell them: harm to their integrity and, in the long run, to their credibility. Lies hurt their colleagues as well. The suspicion of deceit undercuts the work of the many doctors who are scrupulously honest with their patients; it contributes to the spiral of litigation and of "defensive medicine," and thus it injures, in turn, the entire medical profession.

Sharp conflicts are now arising. Patients are learning to

press for answers. Patients' bills of rights require that they be informed about their condition and about alternatives for treatment. Many doctors go to great lengths to provide such information. Yet even in hospitals with the most eloquent bill of rights, believers in benevolent deception continue their age-old practices. Colleagues may disapprove but refrain from remonstrating. Nurses may bitterly resent having to take part, day after day, in deceiving patients, but feel powerless to take a stand.

There is urgent need to debate this issue openly. Not only in medicine, but in other professions as well, practitioners may find themselves repeatedly in straits where serious consequences seem avoidable only through deception. Yet the public has every reason to be wary of professional deception, for such practices are peculiarly likely to become ingrained, to spread, and to erode trust. Neither in medicine, nor in law, government, or the social sciences can there be comfort in the old saw, "What you don't know can't hurt you."

2. AGING AND DEATH

James Geiwitz

> Grow old along with me!
> The best is yet to be,
> The last of life, for which
>   the first was made.
> —Robert Browning

Aging and death are two subjects that are generally avoided in conversation. When they come up, an uneasy atmosphere develops. Growing old generally elicits bad jokes at best, and death is discussed in euphemisms — "passed away," "kicked the bucket," "the late ———."

Why do Americans have such strong negative reactions to growing old and to dying? Perhaps the fear of death is understandable, since what happens next is totally unknown, and uncertainty is always a little frightening. But why do millions of Americans dye their hair, have "face-lifts" and other cosmetic surgery, and otherwise spend so much time, energy, and money on the effort to keep looking young?

Aging: Psychological Aspects

Some of the reasons the American culture is so youth-oriented have to do with its rapidly changing, super-industrial status. In some cultures, particularly in the past, the wisdom of the "elders" was highly valued. They had experience: They knew what was likely to happen and what to do in a variety of situations. In our culture, the elders know about things that no longer exist. Often they are bewildered about events. Old people are no longer respected for their wisdom; they are "out of date."

Ironically, it is the super-industrial cultures that have the most old people. Advances in medical science have doubled the percentage of United States citizens over the age of 65 in this century alone. At the same time, our society has pressed to make earlier retirements possible and, in some industries, required.

Retirement means an abrupt change in habits. For some people, it is an unhappy switch from an active, productive life into what feels like uselessness. The daily routine of a job disappears, leaving the retired person plenty of spare time — but for what? Some people are unable to seek out new friends and activities. These men and women, disabled by the physical ailments of old age or restricted by the loss of income that comes with retirement, may be forced to leave their homes and move in with their children or go to a nursing home. No longer able to direct their own lives, they become dependent on other people. They may feel that all their choices have been taken away: What they eat, whom they see, where they go may all be decided for them. Sources of stimulation often become fewer. A person may spend day after day within the same room or rooms, with only brief periods of human contact. Even in a family situation the elderly person may be ignored much of the time. However, there are increasing numbers of social help agencies that can work to alleviate these problems, and a loving family can sometimes find new activities or jobs that will give the aging relative a sense of being a valuable part of the household.

It is important to realize that the changes we face at retirement *can* be dealt with, just like changes at any other time of life. For many people, retirement is an opportunity, a chance to do things they never had time to do before. As you might expect, people who adjusted well to life before retirement are the best adjusted after retirement. But in both youth and age, adjustment is an active process. The people who are happiest in retirement are those who seek out new activities, like gardening and volunteer social work, to replace the ones no longer available to them. They also seek out social companions who share their interests, instead of sitting in sullen isolation, lamenting the deaths of friends and how no one visits them anymore. They may even join the Gray Panthers, a radical political organization for old people that lobbies for the rights and benefits of the elderly: improved bus services, tax reforms, new health laws.

Aging: Biological Aspects

Biologically, aging may be defined as a decline in the ability of the body to avoid or fight off the effects of accidents, disease, and other types of stress. Thus, most people die of a disease, not "natural causes." There is good evidence that each of us has an alloted time in life that can be shortened by disease or accident, but not lengthened. Medical science has increased the *average* lifespan in many countries by saving the lives of infants and young people, but it has had little effect among the very old. For example, if all cancer (a prime killer of the elderly) were eliminated, the average lifespan would increase by only 1.5 years.

It is very difficult to distinguish between "pure" aging and the effects of various chronic diseases that often come with age. These diseases include arthritis — inflammation of the joints, causing pain and decreased dexterity and mobility — and arteriosclerosis — hardening and thickening of the arteries. Arthritis makes it hard for the victim to move around and to do certain things. Arteriosclerosis causes increased blood pressure, which may cause headaches and generally poor circulation. Poor circulation, in turn, makes adjustment to cooler temperatures more difficult; and poor blood circulation to the brain may result in some problems in processing information.

A classic study of *healthy* men between the ages of 65 and 91 compared their physical and mental abilities to those of another group of men, average age 21. The older men proved as fit as the younger men on a number of variables. Measures of blood flow to the brain and oxygen consumption during exercise did not differ between groups. The older subjects were superior in non-timed tests of intelligence, such as vocabulary, and poorer in tests requiring speed or involving reaction time. The reaction-time tests showed the most marked results. By and large, however, there were very few differences between the healthy old men and healthy young men. This indicates the validity of a definition of aging as increasing susceptibility to diseases, diseases which cause many of the symptoms we often incorrectly attribute to aging itself.

Of course, many physical changes are directly related to aging. Hair may become gray (or disappear altogether); the skin wrinkles; the senses become less acute and the bones more brittle, making accidents more likely and more serious. There is some evidence that pain becomes less painful, so not all changes are for the worse. And contrary to popular myth, people up to and even over 80 years old are capable of enjoying sexual intercourse — and many do.

Death and Dying

Death and dying are sad, depressing subjects to most of us. No matter how prepared we are, or however strongly we may believe in a life after death, the loss of a close friend or relative is painful. The bereaved — those who have lost a loved one to death — are often faced with serious problems of adjustment, including coping with loneliness, sorrow, and the simple tasks of day-to-day living. There is a funeral, a will to be read and executed, expressions of sympathy to be accepted and responded to. These institutionalized aspects of the mourning period may help, as Freud once suggested, to spread the grief over several days. But soon they are over, and then comes the crying, the depression, the difficulty in sleeping, concentrating, and remembering, the lack of appetite for food and for life — the most common symptoms in a study of over 100 people who had lost a husband or wife.

During the period of bereavement, which often lasts a year or two, grief at least slightly affects the person's ability to function. For someone who has lost a spouse, the probability of a fatal illness, accident, or suicide is slightly higher during this period; these symptoms may be related to others, such as heavy drinking.

But what is death like for the person who is dying? From interviews with over 200 dying patients, one psychiatrist identified five attitudes experienced by these patients, often but not always in sequence (Kübler-Ross, 1970). *Denial* is usually the first stage. The patient says, in effect, "No! Not me!" Patients even choose to ignore obvious symptoms instead of openly confronting their own fears. This stage is followed by *anger:* The patient demands, "Why me? Why now?"

In the third stage, called *bargaining,* the patient seeks for a pardon or at least a postponement. Often he or she tries to make a bargain, secretly or openly, with God or "fate" or even Satan. One woman's bargain was "If I can only be allowed to live to see my son marry. . . ." She managed to get the hospital staff to teach her self-hypnosis to control the pain so that she could attend her son's wedding.

The fourth stage is *depression,* which develops as the patient realizes the loss of everything and everybody he or she loves is close at hand. This "preparatory" sorrow is probably necessary for the final stage, *acceptance.* In this fifth and last stage, the patient usually weans himself away from the world, desiring less and less contact with an increasingly small number of close friends. Acceptance was perhaps best expressed by Stewart Alsop, the noted journalist, just before he died: "A dying man needs to die as a sleepy man needs to sleep, and there comes a time when it is wrong, as well as useless, to resist."

One of the most important points brought out in Kübler-Ross's studies is the dying person's need to talk about his or her fears and feelings about death. In fact, Kübler-Ross believes that if we were more open in thinking and talking about our deaths throughout our lives, we would live fuller lives and die with much less trauma and struggle. Death is, after all, one of the inescapable facts of human experience, and should be allowed to take a less fearsome and more accepted position in our daily lives.

3. A GOOD WORD FOR BAD WORDS

Time Magazine

Zurich, Switzerland's largest city, installed an obscenity hot line in the late '70s. Subscribers to the service received a code name and a secret telephone number. At any hour of the day or night, for about a dollar a minute, they could talk to four men and four women who cheerfully listened to obscenities. That service reflects well enough the changing nature of profanity. It is not socially approved — an approved profanity is no profanity at all — but more and more tolerated and even encouraged. Movies and greeting cards are filthier than ever. Graffiti are the subject of scholarly tomes, and many forms of therapy goad patients into relieving their frustration by letting loose expletives. As all scholars know, many successful men are prominent cursers, from George Washington to Dodger

Manager Tommy Lasorda, who unfurled 144 obscenities in a brief pep talk to his team last year [1980].

All to the good, says Psychologist Chaytor Mason, who thinks it is time that cursing got the (expletive deleted) credit it deserves. Like most theorists of swearing, Mason regards foul language as a valuable safety valve that helps society function without too much frustration. Mason, a professor at the University of Southern California's Institute of Safety and Systems Management, has found that people under hypnosis never swear (no stress, no swearing) and that in patients suffering from depression, a barrage of profanity is often a sign of recovery. "Profanity is the essence of the human being," he says. "Like scratching, it releases tension, and like sex, it's one of those very personal, satisfying acts."

Among grandiose claims for gutter language, Mason's may rank only third. The silver medal goes to one William Dwight Whitney, a 19th century Yale philologist who thought that human speech evolved out of primitive cursing — the angry yawps and yelps of early man. The gold medal winner is Sigmund Freud, who once suggested that cursing was the beginning of civilization. "The first human being who hurled a curse instead of a weapon against his adversary," Freud once remarked, "was the founder of civilization."

Not all cussing is so glorious, of course. Mason thinks the movies are overdoing it nowadays because "it sells." Obsessive profanity can be a sign of schizophrenia, he says, especially if a person has always been excessively restrained. Conformists in dead-end jobs often use harsh swear words. "Moderates who use milder words a small amount of the time usually are, on the whole, pretty happy."

But too little swearing is as bad as too much, he says. Used judiciously, four-letter words can salvage self-esteem and save one's ego from extermination. "The person using them," says the professor, "is proving that at least he has a mastery over something, if only his own mouth. He is verbally hitting below the belt. It's a way of feeling powerful when one feels helpless. Show me a person who never swears, and I'll show you a person who is unduly afraid of people. There are times when we all have to get down and get earthy."

Women, for example, are swearing more and fainting less: "Historically, men never permitted or taught women to swear, so when they became upset, their blood pressure would drop and they'd faint." Swearing even has a role to play in romance. A man or women might swear early in a relationship as a test of affection. And during sexual intercourse, says Mason, "a woman may want her partner to talk dirty so she can temporarily become another person who is emotionally unrestrained."

Children almost automatically go through a swearing period, he says, using the magic words as a form of pre-adult swagger or to test the limits of their freedom at home. Though parents may bridle, Mason thinks they should actually guide their young in swearing, telling them which words are appropriate and where to use them. Reason: if parents swear but children are not allowed to, the lesson is that parents teach a code they do not live by. As a result, children often give up confiding in parents and start leading the familiar double life of angel at home and delinquent elsewhere.

Mason thinks World War II was the great watershed in American cursing. In 1939 Clark Gable's line in *Gone With the Wind,* "Frankly, my dear, I don't give a damn," had the nation gasping. But the wartime draft taught millions of youngsters, and later their friends and families, the foul and aggressive language of the barracks. Now, says Mason, damn and hell are virtually useless as swearwords. Even fouler and more powerful expressions too are losing their ability to shock. He suggests, rather lamely, that Americans will rise to the challenge by inventing new shocking expressions to meet a national need.

Not so, says Reinhold Aman, an admitted sewer mouth who edits *Maledicta,* a scholarly magazine about insults and swearing. Aman thinks Americans have nearly used up their patrimony of high-shock expressions and will not be able to create new ones. His suggestion: restore the florid insults and curses long common in rural America and also start using foreign expressions. "Europe, Asia and Africa make up an inexhaustible reservoir of foul language with tremendous shock value," he says, offering several unprintable examples. For those who cannot bring themselves to use the "dirty dozen" or so foul expressions left to most Americans, he suggests his own training regimen. Since most U.S. dirty words stress *f, sh, k, p, t, s* and *x* sounds, make up harmless combinations, such as "shexing" and "oh fex." This, he reasons, will let off steam, puzzle many and offend none.

Aman agrees with Mason that there is no point in trying to stop swearing. One sign that they are correct is the fate of Curseaholics Anonymous, an anti-swearing group founded in Cambridge, Mass., last June. Its 24-hour hot line was so swamped with foulmouthed calls from offended swearers that the group disbanded in July.

SCANNING TECHNIQUES

Scanning is a method of selective reading which is used when you are searching for a particular fact or the answer to a question. Scanning can best be described as a looking rather than a reading process. As you look for the information you need, you ignore everything else. When you finish scanning a page, the only thing you should know is whether it contained the information you were looking for. You should *not* be able to recall topics, main ideas, or details presented on the page. You already use the technique of scanning daily: you regularly scan telephone books, TV listings, and indexes. The purpose of this section is to help you develop a rapid, efficient approach to the scanning process.

Use the following step-by-step procedure to become more skilled in rapidly locating specific information:

1. State in your mind specifically what information you are looking for. Phrase it in question form if possible.

2. Try to anticipate how the answer will appear and what clues you might use to help you locate the answer. If you are scanning to find the distance between two cities, you might expect either digits or numbers written out as words. Also, a unit of measurement, probably miles or kilometers, will appear after the number.

3. Determine the organization of the material; it is your most important clue to where to begin looking for information. Especially when you are looking up information contained in charts and tables, the organization of the information is crucial to rapid scanning.

4. Use headings and any other aids that will help you identify which sections might contain the information you are looking for.

5. Selectively read and skip through likely sections of the passage, keeping in mind the specific question you formed and your expectations of how the answer might appear. Move your eyes down the page in a systematic way. While there are various eye-movement patterns, such as the "arrow pattern" (straight down the middle of the page) or the "A pattern" (zigzagging down the page), it is best to use a pattern that seems comfortable and easy for you.

6. When you reach the fact you are looking for, you will find that the word or phrase will stand out, and you will notice it immediately.

7. When you have found the needed information, carefully read the sentences in which it appears in order to confirm that you have located the correct information.

EXERCISE 3

Directions: *Scan each paragraph or passage below to locate the answer to the question stated at the beginning of each.*

1. *Question:* How much does a cubic foot of water expand when it changes into ice?

   Passage: In general, when a liquid freezes, it contracts, for molecules vibrate less vigorously in the solid than in the liquid state and so can be closer to one another. But when we remember that ice floats and pitchers of water are often cracked by freezing, we conclude that water is a liquid that expands on freezing. In fact, a cubic foot of water becomes 1.09 cubic feet of ice. Cast iron is another substance that expands a little in solidifying. It is therefore adapted to making castings, for in this way every detail of the mold is sharply reproduced. Allowance has, of course, to be made for shrinkage of the solid in cooling. For making good type, a metal which expands a little on solidifying is needed; hence an alloy of lead, antimony, and copper, which has this property, is used.

   —Black and Little, *An Introductory Course in College Physics*, pp. 288–289

2. *Question:* What instrument is used to measure the velocity of the wind?

   Passage: In weather reports, a wind is named according to the direction from which it blows. Thus, a "northeaster" is a wind blowing from the northeast direction. The weather vane is the most familiar instrument for indicating the direction from which the wind is coming. At airfields the direction is indicated by a wind cone, or by a large triangular-shaped wind indicator which points into the wind. It is outlined with lights and can be seen easily by day or night. The velocity of the wind is measured by an anemometer, which consists of 3 or 4 metallic cups attached to a metal frame that in turn is mounted on a vertical shaft so as to spin around according to the velocity of the wind.

–Black and Little, *An Introductory Course in College Physics*, pp. 288–289

3. *Question:* How does the efficiency of the phototube compare with the solar cell?

    Passage: Our sun constantly radiates enormous quantities of heat and light energy to the earth. Numerous, and, so far, fairly unsuccessful attempts have been made to harness these energies. The phototube is able to convert the light to electrical energy. But it is able to deliver as power only about 0.5 percent of the light energy it receives.

    The scientists at the Bell Telephone Laboratories have developed a solar cell that is about 20 times as efficient as the phototube. It consists of a thin wafer of silicon to which has been added a minute amount of arsenic. An extremely thin layer of silicon containing a trace of boron is deposited on one surface of the wafer. Leads connected to the wafer and layer complete the cell.

    –Marcus, *Basic Electricity*, p. 258

4. *Question:* In what two respects does the skull structure of men and apes differ?

    Passage: In many ways the skull offers some of the most important contrasts between apes and men. It becomes particularly important when we know that most of our data on prehistoric men are confined to the skull alone, since this part of the human skeleton is most likely to survive the ravages of time. There are two main respects in which differences of skull structure between men and apes are most marked — the shape and capacity of the brain case and the proportions of the face.

    Man's brain case is largest in capacity, averaging 1,450 cc. (= cubic centimeters) as compared to averages of 500 cc. for the gorilla, 404 for the chimpanzee, 395 for the orang, and 128 for the gibbon. In other words, the skull of man has roughly three times the capacity of that of the largest-brained ape. Even more important is the fact that man's skull is highly developed in the frontal region, his forehead extending almost vertically upward for a considerable

distance. In all apes this region is little developed, the head sloping sharply backward from the brow ridges.
—Beals and Hoijer, *An Introduction to Anthropology,*
pp. 49–50

5. *Question:* What is monopoly power?

   Passage: Without pure competition, no longer can we say that the price is a true reflection of society's demand for and cost of the product. If one buyer or seller gets large enough to influence the total demand or total supply for a product, he can then influence the price of the product. He can restrict his output and keep the price high and make big profits. This power to restrict output and hold up the price (as you probably already know) is called market power, or monopoly power.
   —Bowden, *Economics: The Science of Common Sense,*
   p. 76

6. *Question:* What was the most famous opera house of the eighteenth century?

   Passage: In the eighteenth century, every ambitious young composer hoped for the day when he would conquer the musical and fashionable world with an opera. In order to achieve this aim it was necessary to compose a serious opera or a comic opera to an Italian libretto. Italian had long been the international language of opera, the La Scala Opera House in Milan was regarded as the greatest in the world, and Italian composers had shown the world how to compose in a manner congenial to singers and audiences alike. The Italian style of singing, called *bel canto,* was indeed the basis for almost all vocal melodic composition. But *bel canto,* however beautiful in design and execution, often seemed to show little respect for the sense of words.
   —Young, *A Concise History of Music,* p. 530

7. *Question:* What is meant by the speed of a camera lens?

   Passage: The most important part of the camera is the lens. The best quality of your picture is limited by the capability of your lens, and the price of most cameras reflects the quality of the lens. The lens "sees" the same subject you see in your view-finder and then projects the subject onto your film.

   No doubt you have heard of slow and fast lenses — or the "speed" of lenses. Speed in this case means the ability of a lens to collect and transmit light rays. This speed is obtained by complicated optical design and grinding, which we will not discuss here.
   —Bauer, *Outdoor Photography,* pp. 11–12

8. *Question:* What did the Greek astronomer Hipparchos categorize?

   Passage: Naked-eye astronomy could distinguish the planets from the fixed stars. It could speculate about a comet if there was one in the sky. It could also determine that some stars had a color that was quite different from the norm — for example, the star the Greeks called Antares because it had the same color as the planet they called Ares (Mars). And naked-eye astronomy could tell quite easily that some stars were brighter than others. In about 150 B.C., the Greek astronomer Hipparchos of Nicea decided to categorize the brightnesses, to establish a *schema*. The brightest stars in the sky were stars of the "first magnitude," the ones that were slightly less bright were of "second magnitude," and so on until he came to the dimmest stars, which were barely visible, and these he called the stars of the "sixth magnitude." This is as far as naked-eye astronomy could go in classifying stars. Until the astronomer's eye was aided by instruments which would have seemed incredible to Hipparchos, nothing else could be done except to determine as exactly as possible the positions of the stars relative to one another.

–Bonestell and Ley, *Beyond the Solar System,* pp. 31–32

SUMMARY

Many adults feel that it is important to read every word on a printed page. This mistaken notion is often responsible for a slow, inflexible rate of reading. Actually, there are many types of material which do not require a thorough, beginning-to-end, careful reading. There are also many situations in which reading everything is not necessary — situations in which selective reading (reading some parts and skipping others) is more appropriate. It is effective to read selectively in situations in which you need only main ideas, you are looking for a specific fact or answer to a question, you are highly familiar with the content of the material, or the material contains information which does not relate to your purpose for reading. Finally, there are certain types of material and styles of writing in which it is possible to skip information.

In situations where it is appropriate to read selectively, the techniques of skimming and scanning are useful. Skimming is a process of reading only main ideas and simply glancing at the remainder of the material. There are three basic types of skimming: preread skimming, skim-reading, and review skimming. The type of skimming used depends on the reader's purpose. Scanning is a method of selective reading which is used when searching for a particular fact or answer to a question.

Appendix

SAMPLE TEXTBOOK CHAPTER

19

Advertising

After reading this chapter you should be able to:
- Tell what advertising is and discuss how both consumers and producers benefit from it.
- Explain how advertising is planned, budgeted, controlled, and evaluated.
- Outline the way advertisers organize.
- Describe what advertising agencies do, how they work, and how they are compensated for their services.
- Discuss the creative side of advertising.

When Americans began to increase their wine consumption rather dramatically sometime during the seventies, competition among wine makers, especially California wine makers, began to intensify. E. & J. Gallo was the perennial leader in the wine market. In 1978, Taylor Wines, owned by Coca-Cola, began running ads on television that cited competing wines by name while claiming that Taylor tasted better. Such direct comparative advertising was previously unheard of in the wine business, but it worked so well for Taylor — moving it into fourth place in the market — that other wine makers soon followed Taylor's lead. The fancy gloves were off, and wine companies were competing like the makers of any other consumer product.

In this tough environment, Colony Wines, owned by Heublein's United Vintners subsidiary, wanted to improve its performance. Since

417

Colony's offering was a consumer product, advertising would be a very important part of its promotional mix. And so it faced some big questions: What should its ads say? Should they name competitors? Where should the ads appear? And how much should be spent on running them? [1]

Say the word "advertising" in a crowd and the reactions are likely to be many, strong, and varied. Children may know it as the short but entertaining interruptions in their Saturday morning television shows. Shoppers know that it tells them when and where products are for sale or on sale. Owners of radio or television stations, magazines, or newspapers think of advertising as the source of most of their revenues. Government regulators and consumer advocates consider it the source of — and occasionally the solution to — many of their problems. A firm's financial managers may view advertising as a questionable investment, while the same firm's marketing managers are sure that it is one of the most important weapons in their competitive arsenal.

A list of differing viewpoints could be endless. Yet few would disagree that advertising is an economic force and social institution that affects the lives of everyone.

Advertising is an important element in the promotional programs of most retailers and manufacturers, even though they may spend four or five times as much money for personal selling. Not surprisingly, advertising is more important in certain lines of business, like soap, drugs, and food, than in such others as insurance, construction, and mining. When launching a new brand a manufacturer may budget $30 million, or even more, for its advertising. Advertising revenues in the United States were expected to exceed $60 billion in 1981, about half of the world's total.

Before discussing the management of advertising, the institutions within the industry, and how advertising should be created, we begin with a definition. **Advertising** is *any paid form of nonpersonal, promotional presentation of ideas or products by a sponsor whose identity is known.* Advertising is transmitted in mass communication media, not by individual salespeople. Because the advertiser pays for advertising he controls it.

The Management of Advertising

As we have said before the management of just about anything in business, advertising included, is a process of setting goals, then developing strategies for achieving those goals and controlling the process through continual evaluation. Our first question, then, is: What are advertising's goals?

[1] John Revett, "Wineries Adopting New Market Tact," *Advertising Age,* April 20, 1981, p. 1.

418 / Chapter 19

Objectives of Ads

Firms advertise for a purpose, and each advertisement has a specific objective. The purpose of most advertising is to sell a product, a service, a company, even an idea. It is to inform, persuade, and remind; to affect attitudes and behavior. It is to help the seller realize a greater profit than if it had not advertised.

The clearer and more specific the objective is, the more effectively the ad can be created and transmitted, and the more satisfactorily the ad's effects can be evaluated later. Different types of advertisements may have different objectives, as the following list demonstrates.

1. To encourage consumers to put their savings in a savings and loan association by showing how savings grow.
2. To tell retailers that they will increase their earnings on Blue Lustre carpet cleaner because it is to be advertised on CBS.
3. To offer consumers a fifteen-cents-off coupon (attached to the ad) on a purchase of Tang.
4. To maintain or improve buyers' goodwill and loyalty toward the advertising firm. Lilly has run full-page ads the copy of which says only, "For four generations, we've been making medicines as if people's lives depended on them."
5. To help customers (an important "public") use a service more economically. AT&T's headline, "20 ways to save money on your phone bill" is an example.
6. To announce to consumers that new Fruit Helper from Betty Crocker, the General Mills trade character, turns a can of fruit into a terrific dessert.
7. The headline of a department store (Gimbel's) ad in the *New York Times* read "Save 20% to 40% on every Oriental rug in our stock."

Figure 19-1 shows ads that illustrate other specific objectives.

In short, advertising objectives are diverse. It stands to reason that different advertisers will have different goals, but these goals all have a common element: they involve changing the attitudes and behavior of some audience, usually buyers. And just as all advertising goals have a common element, all strategies for achieving the goals have something in common as well. They all deal with the question, how should advertising messages be sent to the target audience?

Media Strategy

Advertising media surround us nearly every moment of our lives. We are all familiar with most popular ones: newspapers, magazines, television, radio, outdoor locations, and transportation vehicles like buses and subways. The trend today is toward creating even more advertising media. Movie theaters now show a few minutes of ads before the feature. Cars are painted and transformed into traveling billboards.

To the marketing manager each advertising medium is a means for conveying a message to the target audience.

Advertising / 419

Figure 19-1 Each of these ads has a specific objective or objectives. With the ad pictured above, American Airlines hopes to improve employee morale and motivation and to encourage buyers to fly American. The Ford ad (top right) is intended to build an international image for the car and to inform buyers of specific product attributes. Maintaining and enhancing corporate image is the objective of Frank B. Hall's ad (bottom right).

420 / Chapter 19

341

Media Choices. Table 19-1 shows 1965, 1975, and 1980 spending on the major media choices available to advertisers, and tells how much was placed by national and local advertisers. Media choices are complex decisions: they depend on the objectives of the ads, the size of the advertising budget, the audience targeted, and so on. Some factors that media planners consider as they make media choices are discussed below.

Newspapers are significant in the lives of most consumers: more than three-fourths of the adult population reads a daily newspaper. Newspapers are the main shopping guides for most consumers. Because they offer current information (ads or news stories) their physical life is short.

Newspapers give manufacturers almost complete regional flexibility. A manufacturer can advertise in Philadelphia but not Baltimore — in New York but not Boston; it can place a newspaper advertisement in just those markets that need it. Some large newspapers offer geographical selectivity within the areas they serve. For example, an advertiser can buy the whole circulation of the *New York Times* or *Sunday News* or choose to focus only on residents of New York City, Long Island, or the New Jersey, New York, or Connecticut suburbs. Newspapers offer

Table 19-1 United States advertising expenditures on major media (in millions of dollars)

Medium	1965	1975	1980
Newspapers	$4,426	$8,442	$15,615
National	784	1,221	2,335
Local	3,642	7,221	13,280
Magazines	1,903	2,458	5,055
Consumer	1,161	1,465	3,225
Business and farm publications	742	993	1,830
Television	2,515	5,263	11,330
Network	1,237	2,306	5,105
Spot	892	1,623	3,260
Local	386	1,334	2,965
Radio	917	1,980	3,690
Network	60	83	185
Spot	275	436	750
Local	582	1,461	2,755
Outdoor	180	335	610
Direct Mail	2,324	4,181	7,655
All Other	2,985	5,571	10,795
Total	$15,250	$28,230	$54,750

SOURCE: Prepared for *Advertising Age* by Robert J. Coen, McCann-Erickson, *Advertising Age,* September 4, 1978, pp. 32–33; and January 5, 1981, p. 56. Reprinted with permission from *Advertising Age.* Copyright 1978 and 1981 by Crain Communications Inc.

422 / Chapter 19

another advantage to advertisers — the use of preprinted inserts. Sears, A&P, and a variety of other chain retailers supply these in quantity to local newspapers and pay for them to be inserted in and circulated with regular editions of the newspapers. These inserts have also been used to distribute coupons for a variety of consumer products.

One disadvantage of advertising in newspapers is that there is little buyer selectivity. Newspapers are read by rich and poor, young and old, male and female, and persons of all social classes and vocations.

Magazines are another media choice, and they offer better production (paper, printing, color) than do newspapers. Magazines have a longer physical life; readers return to and reexamine them over a number of days or even weeks. Commitments for magazine ads must be made further in advance than is true for newspaper ads. For certain magazines, advertisers may have to buy the entire national circulation. Other magazines, like newspapers, offer advertisers regional flexibility. *Playboy*'s southeastern edition, for example, covers the states of North Carolina, South Carolina, Georgia, Florida, Tennessee, Alabama and Mississippi. Special interest magazines offer much selectivity.

Television is the number one advertising medium for national advertisers. TV is truly a mass medium, reaching more than 95 percent of American households. Combining sound, motion, and color, TV can dramatically demonstrate product features and evoke favorable product images. Advertisers can contract with individual television stations rather than with a network and thus be able to choose which stations will carry their advertisements.

Despite the strength of its impact, TV is not without its drawbacks. Commercial clutter — too many ads grouped together — can diminish the effect of a particular ad.

Radio as an advertising medium has certain advantages. It is relatively inexpensive and well within the budgets of small advertisers. Its low cost permits high levels of repetition, which can reinforce ads in other media. It offers good geographical selectivity — it can be used to reach a single city or part of a city. Finally, because ads take little time to prepare and can be placed on short notice, radio advertising is attractive to those whose advertising requirements and messages change frequently and abruptly.

Radio advertising also has some disadvantages. A radio ad is short-lived. Consumers cannot "reread" the ad as they can those in newspapers or magazines. Radio ads may not have as much impact as ads in other media because people do other things while listening to the radio.

Outdoor advertising includes billboards, painted signs on walls, and illuminated signs. Outdoor advertising can be very effective, because commuters may perceive an ad repeatedly, which will reduce the chance of forgetting the message. Copy must be short, however, because viewing is measured in seconds. In recent years, outdoor advertising has experienced a resurgence because of relatively low costs per exposure.

Advertising / 423

Scheduling. Media strategy decisions involve choosing media vehicles that will reach the target audience most effectively, and also timing decisions — when and for how long to run ads in the advertising campaign. Such decisions require marketing management to make judgments about reach, frequency, impact, and continuity.

Reach is the total number of members of the target audience to whom the campaign delivers a message at least once. The reach of a complicated media schedule is difficult if not impossible to determine. For example, Ivory soap is advertised on many programs and in many publications. Ivory brand management may know the size of the audience for each one, but adding them all together inflates the reach of Ivory's media schedule. Why? Duplication is high: many consumers will undoubtedly see the ads several times. This complicates brand managers' assessment of various media schedules.

Frequency refers to the number of times that the average member of the target audience is exposed to the campaign's message. Duplication of the type just described reduces reach but increases frequency.

Impact is the value of exposure to an ad in a particular media vehicle. This depends on the "quality" of the vehicle's audience and the appropriateness of the vehicle for the particular ad being used. An ad for racquetball equipment, for example, would have a different impact — even if audience size were held constant — in editions of *Sports Illustrated, Business Week,* the *New Yorker,* and *Southern Living.* Why? Because readers of one magazine might be heavier users of racquetball equipment than readers of another and because ads for such equipment might seem "out of place" in some of these magazines.

Continuity is a term with two different meanings. In some circumstances it refers to the length of time a campaign runs. In other circumstances it refers to the pattern of the timing of advertising within a campaign. A month-long campaign by a retailer could include one radio spot every business day or five radio spots every Monday or ten radio spots on the first and fifteenth of each month. Scheduling ads unevenly is often called flighting or pulsing.

Because it is impossible to maximize reach, frequency, impact, and continuity simultaneously when there are budget constraints, the media planner must make trade-offs. One very important trade-off is between reach and frequency. The media planner faces, at the extremes, a choice between a schedule that exposes some members of the audience very often, but others in the audience not at all (high frequency, low reach), and a schedule to which most of the audience is exposed, but not very often (high reach, low frequency).

The choice depends on the goals of the advertising campaign and the perceived value of many exposures. Advertising designed to persuade may require a greater frequency than advertising designed to build or maintain awareness. The number of exposures that is "just right" will probably always be a subject of much debate: too few exposures have no impact; too many may be wasteful, even harmful.

424 / Chapter 19

Consideration of all these issues and issues of timing has been aided substantially by the development of a variety of computer models for media selection and scheduling. All of these are to some extent artificial, and all of them depend very much on information from marketing and media researchers and judgments by media planners. But they do offer the hope of developing and testing media plans in a logical, rational way. They cannot, however, substitute for the imagination and intuition of a product manager or an advertising manager.

Budgeting

Budgeting is a planning tool that spells out the advertising program in terms of money. It cannot be separated from the ad schedule. The budget is also a control tool, because if actions go as planned, ad expenditures should not be greater than the appropriations in the budget. The two big issues in ad budgeting are how much money to spend and what to buy with it — and when. The marginal analysis we learned in Chapter 11 tells us that the size of the budget should be increased so long as each additional dollar spent increases total profit. That is the budgeting goal; but achieving it, like maximizing profits, is filled with practical problems. For example, budgeting must start with a sales forecast, even though the size of the budget obviously influences the sales volume that will be achieved. In practice, five approaches are generally used in solving the budgeting problem.

Some managers take the *affordable approach,* that is, they establish sales forecasts, estimate expenses, then determine what is available to be allocated to the ad budget. New companies and companies in trouble may be forced to budget in this way. Other firms use the approach to set an upper limit on ad spending. But the affordable approach has a major weakness that is psychological: the approach suggests that advertising is a luxury, or a way to use "surplus" money, rather than a necessary part of the marketing mix.

With the *percentage-of-sales approach* managers use a fixed percentage of last year's sales or anticipated sales to determine the overall budget or the budget for each product or brand. Such an approach ties advertising expenditures to sales, but in a convoluted way; it allows sales to cause advertising rather than vice versa. It may also lead managers into the trap of thinking that all products and all territories should have the same percentage of sales devoted to advertising. However, because it is simple to use and makes comparisons with competitors easy, this approach is probably the most popular and widely used.

Some advertisers know how much their competitors are spending on advertising, either through their own market intelligence or through organizations such as the Publishers Information Bureau, the Radio Advertising Bureau, or Leading National Advertisers. The *competitive parity approach* suggests that they match or exceed those levels. But care must be exercised with this strategy because there may be no reason to believe that competitors know any more about the optimal ad budget than we do, and our firm's goals, problems, and opportunities may be different from the competition's.

With the *task or objective approach* managers ask three questions: What are the firm's sales objectives or forecasts? What advertising is thought to be needed to make its maximum contribution to achieving that forecast? How much will that advertising cost? Clearly this approach is both logical and respectable, but it is also difficult because it depends so much on judgment. There is no known way to prejudge the effectiveness of advertising and no certain way of measuring its effects after it has been used. In theory, though, this is the best approach, particularly if the objectives are derived from a return-on-investment goal.

The *statistical approach* uses statistical methods to study historical data and identify patterns of relationships between advertising and sales. Attempts are made to determine a response curve like the one in Figure 19-2 that can help determine whether past budgets have been too high or too low. When Anheuser-Busch did such a study they discovered that they had been overspending on advertising, so they cut their ad budget until competitive threats from Miller forced them to raise the budget again.

Figure 19-2 A sales-response-to-advertising curve. This curve suggests that some sales will occur even though there is no advertising. Up to $X in spending, advertising appears to have little impact, probably because there is not yet enough to cross a threshold and enter consumers' awareness. Beyond $Y there is little or no increase in sales (perhaps even a decline), because the market is saturated or because some consumers are irritated by increased exposure.

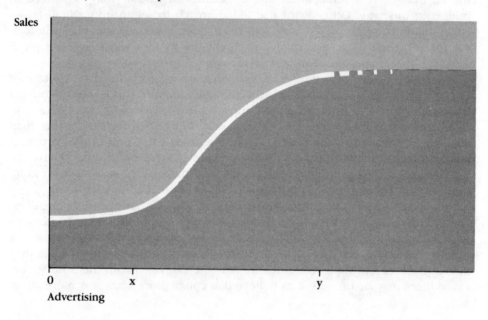

Sales

0   x   y

Advertising

No matter which approach is taken, the total advertising budget must be allocated to ads with different functions, such as ads promoting products or ads promoting the corporation; to each sales territory or market; to each media type and media vehicle; to each brand, and to each time period. These allocation decisions can be very difficult. For practical purposes allocations are often made on the basis of past sales performance or on the basis of subjective estimates of the need for advertising. If one of a firm's products produces twice the sales of another product, it may receive twice the advertising budget. Is that strategy logical? It may be, but chances are no one can say. It is simple and consistent, however, and that may be the best one can ask for in the absence of good information on the effectiveness of ads, which is our next topic.

Evaluating Advertising Effectiveness

If a firm's advertising goals are to be achieved and ad effectiveness increased, the manager must attempt evaluation. To do so requires better methods of learning how advertising affects buyers' behavior. But this is a very difficult undertaking because measurements are imperfect and imprecise. Exhibit 19-1 describes one approach to this investigation.

The advertiser can try to evaluate advertising as a sales producing force — that is, how much did advertising contribute to the attainment of sales goals? With this approach the manufacturer would try to learn how successfully its consumer ads "pulled" its brand down the distribution channel through wholesalers and retailers and into consumers' hands. How much did advertising strengthen the selling power of its sales force and its sales promotion activities? But it is difficult to isolate advertising as a cause of sales because so many other actions and events can also be influential.

The other approach is to view advertising as communication and to try to evaluate it as such. Here advertisers would ask how completely did advertising communicate to the buyers they wanted to reach. What did the message do to the attitudes and values of those buyers? Of course when ads are evaluated for their communication effectiveness it is assumed that communications success implies sales success. It is not necessarily a valid assumption.

Although measurement is difficult, the advertising manager must depend on it and apply the available techniques creatively. That means perhaps pretesting with a panel or jury of typical prospects to evaluate the ads before they are run. While the ad effort is in progress, the manager can use concurrent testing, where telephone calls are made while a show is being broadcast to check on size of audience. Or Nielsen's audimeter monitors the use of television sets in a sample of cooperating homes. This gives a measure of how large an audience the ad is reaching, but not of the ad's effectiveness.

Posttesting has difficulties, as we have already suggested. For newspaper and magazine ads, research can try to determine how many buyers recognized an ad, how many read it, and how many can recall it. The assumption, again a large one, is that the greater these three are the greater the desired response.

But often the big question remains: What did advertising do to the attitudes and buying behavior of prospects? The answer to that question determines how successful a company's advertising strategy has been. And because it cannot be answered in any definite or systematic way, at least not yet, advertising management remains a field in which experienced judgment is often the most valuable asset.

Exhibit 19-1
Television Versus Print Study: Readers More "Adtentive"

A pilot study sponsored by *Newsweek* has found that readers of the three major newsweeklies looked at 85 percent of the newsweeklies' ad pages while 70 percent of a television show's average quarter-hour audience stayed in the room during commercial breaks. Moreover, less than 30 percent of the television viewers remained mentally tuned to the broadcast ads.

The study, done by Audits & Surveys in the Philadelphia area, cost about $70,000 and evolved after advertisers and agencies asked *Newsweek*'s media researchers to help determine the actual message delivery of a television commercial or a page of advertising.

The study also found that newsweekly ad page audiences are more likely to be male and younger than television commercial break audiences. It also suggests that lower-income viewers are more likely to keep their eyes glued to the set during breaks than viewers in households with college-educated household heads.

But Frank Gromer, Jr., senior vice-president/director of marketing of Foote, Cone & Belding, said there probably will not be a great shift in budgeting because of the study. "The study is important because it adds to our limited storehouse of research in this area, but I don't think a lot of budgeting will be shifted to magazines," he noted.

And one researcher put a more practical perspective on the study: "Forty years ago someone said half the money spent in advertising is wasted. We didn't know then and we still don't know which half."

SOURCE: Bernice Kanner, "TV vs. Print Study Finds Readers More 'adtentive,' " *Advertising Age*, August 7, 1978, p. 2.

Advertisers and Advertising Agencies

Having considered some of the strategic aspects of advertising, we now step back for a moment to look at the wide variety of firms that advertise and at some of the differences in their advertising needs. Then we examine the workings of the advertising agency, an institution used almost universally by large advertisers today and by many small ones as well.

428 / Chapter 19

Advertisers

There is no "typical" advertiser. Manufacturers, retailers, schools, political parties, governments, churches, labor unions, or individuals — all these often advertise. Whether they sell consumer or industrial products, ideas or services, any one of them can engage in the different types of advertising we have mentioned: consumer versus business, brand versus corporate, national versus local.

Advertisers differ greatly in the amounts and types of advertising they do. Table 19-2 lists the largest national advertisers in the United States. The names at the top of the list are familiar to anyone who watches television or reads magazines. They are very large companies that produce or sell consumer products, especially food products, cars, toiletries and cosmetics, tobacco products, and

Table 19-2 The fifty leading national advertisers

	Advertiser	Ad dollars (millions)		Advertiser	Ad dollars (millions)
1	Procter & Gamble Co.	$614.9	26	Heublein Inc.	$155.0
2	General Foods Corp.	393.0	27	Beatrice Foods Co.	150.0
3	Sears, Roebuck & Co.	379.3	28	CBS Inc.	146.1
4	General Motors Corp.	323.4	29	U.S. Government	146.1
5	Philip Morris Inc.	291.2	30	Loews Corp.	144.5
6	K mart Corp.	287.1	31	General Electric Co.	139.4
7	R. J. Reynolds Industries	258.1	32	International Telephone & Telegraph Corp.	132.4
8	Warner-Lambert Co.	220.2	33	Pillsbury Co.	131.5
9	American Telephone & Telegraph Co.	219.8	34	American Cyanamid Co.	127.0
10	Ford Motor Co.	215.0	35	Gillette Co.	126.9
11	PepsiCo Inc.	212.0	36	Richardson-Merrell	123.8
12	Bristol-Myers Co.	210.6	37	Colgate-Palmolive Co.	122.5
13	American Home Products	206.0	38	J. C. Penney Co.	122.0
14	McDonald's Corp.	202.8	39	Kraft Inc.	119.7
15	Gulf + Western Industries	191.5	40	Chrysler Corp.	118.0
16	General Mills	190.7	41	B.A.T. Industries Ltd.	116.4
17	Esmark Inc.	170.5	42	Ralston Purina Co.	108.0
18	Coca-Cola Co.	169.3	43	SmithKline Corp.	107.7
19	Seagram Co.	168.0	44	Chesebrough-Pond's	107.3
20	Mobil Corp.	165.8	45	Consolidated Foods Corp.	105.0
21	Norton Simon Inc.	163.2	46	Time Inc.	102.4
22	Anheuser-Busch	160.5	47	Revlon Inc.	101.0
23	Unilever U.S. Inc.	160.0	48	Transamerica Corp.	95.0
24	RCA Corp.	158.6	49	Sterling Drug Co.	92.0
25	Johnson & Johnson	157.7	50	Kellogg Co.	91.6

SOURCE: *Advertising Age,* February 16, 1981, p. S–2. Reprinted with permission from *Advertising Age.* Copyright 1981 by Crain Communications Inc.

pharmaceuticals. Also prominent are large retailers such as Sears, K mart, and J. C. Penney. The United States government is consistently one of the biggest advertisers; it spent over $146 million in 1979.

Table 19-3 shows how advertising expenditures, as a percent of sales and profit margin, vary across industrial classifications. Industries like coal mining and iron and steel foundries advertise little or not at all. Why should they? Their products are all about the same; whatever selling is necessary is best carried out by salespeople because orders are typically huge. Other industries, especially the consumer-products businesses we are all familiar with — soaps and detergents, appliances, motion pictures — may devote 5 percent of sales or more to advertising. They are selling millions of low-priced units to consumers nationwide, so advertising is their most efficient selling tool.

Within these industries individual companies vary widely in the percentage of sales they spend on advertising. In the drug industry as a whole, for example, 5.7 percent of sales goes for advertising. But within the industry, Pfizer, which sells many nonconsumer drugs, spends only 3.7 percent on advertising, while Miles Laboratories, which makes Alka Seltzer among many other consumer products, devotes 13.1 percent of its sales revenue to advertising.[2]

Organizing for Advertising: The Advertising Department

Retailers and manufacturers tend to organize differently to accomplish their advertising objectives. Retailers, especially local retailers, perform relatively few advertising functions although those few are highly important. They generally run advertising regularly in the local media, especially newspapers, and the ads tend to be similar in style; only the content changes. Small retailers do not have ad departments; they handle the advertising personally, and often rely on the *cooperative advertising* offered by manufacturers. Under this arrangement the manufacturer pays part of the advertising cost and may offer suggestions and even advertising materials. In huge retail organizations the ad department is largely self-sufficient, functioning almost as an internal ad agency with only one client and using no outside specialists.

Manufacturers, by contrast, must perform many advertising functions, especially if they make several products, as most of them do. Each product may require a different advertising strategy — some relying on prime-time television, others using specialized magazines — and the strategy may require national advertising. It is not surprising, then, that manufacturers' ad departments are organized differently. The traditional organization is headed by an advertising manager, who may report to the chief executive officer of the company or to a marketing or sales executive.

[2] *Advertising Age,* September 11, 1980, p. 8.

430 / Chapter 19

Table 19-3 Estimates of advertising expenditure ratios for selected industries

Industry	Standard industrial classification (SIC) code	Advertising as % of net sales	Advertising as % of gross profit margin (net sales less cost of goods sold)
Agricultural production — livestock	200	.6	1.6
Canned/preserved fruits and vegetables	2030	2.0	8.5
Alcoholic beverages & soft drinks	2080	5.4	15.8
Cigarettes	2110	6.6	15.7
Household furniture	2510	1.6	8.7
Office furniture	2520	.9	3.2
Industrial inorganic chemicals	2810	2.2	5.4
Drugs	2830	5.6	11.7
Soap & detergent & cosmetics	2840	10.2	18.5
Iron & steel foundries	3320	N/A	N/A
Engines & turbines	3510	.9	2.9
Office computing & accounting machines	3570	1.2	2.6
Household appliances	3630	5.5	17.7
Wholesale — sporting & recreational goods	5040	2.3	10.7
Wholesale — hardware, plumbing & heating equipment	5070	1.2	13.7
Wholesale — drugs & proprietary	5120	1.4	3.1
Wholesale — groceries & related products	5140	.6	2.4
Retail — department stores	5310	3.0	9.8
Retail — grocery stores	5410	1.1	5.2
Retail — furniture stores	5710	5.8	15.8
Retail — mail order houses	5960	10.7	24.0

NOTE: All figures are averages. Specific companies may vary considerably.
SOURCE: Schonfeld & Associates, Inc., Chicago, Illinois. Reprinted by permission.

Because the firm's advertising tasks are so many and varied, it almost always uses an ad agency (sometimes an in-house agency). The ad manager plays a prominent role in selecting the agency, works closely with the account representative assigned by the agency to handle the account, and, when necessary, fires the agency.

A newer form of organization is exemplified by companies like Procter & Gamble, which pioneered the product manager system discussed in Chapter 10. Here the advertising manager is no longer the focal point of all advertising decisions: instead, responsibility is typically divided between product managers and

Advertising / 431

a department of marketing services. This department has a number of technical specialists who stand ready to provide information and advice to aid product managers in their advertising decisions. Working with these experts and their counterparts in ad agencies, the product manager makes advertising decisions with an eye to the firm's sales and profit goals.

Advertising Agencies

An *advertising agency* is a company that helps advertisers create advertising and place it with the appropriate media. An agency is purely a service business, manufacturing nothing. Its "products" are ideas for what will make good advertising; its assets are creativity and expertise. Aside from its office furniture an ad agency owns practically nothing tangible. As Fairfax Cone, one of the founders of the large Chicago agency Foote, Cone & Belding, once said: "In this business, your inventory goes down the elevator at 5 o'clock." For marketing managers advertising agencies are an important, sometimes indispensable aid in devising and implementing the advertising strategy.

How do advertising agencies work? An ad agency is staffed by people who are knowledgeable about media, copy, and art. Agencies study the products, markets, competitors, and promotional problems of their clients, whom they usually call their accounts. They draft and recommend ads and ad campaigns, evaluate and select appropriate media, and contract and pay for space and time in their own names, which is important to remember when you see how they are paid. Above all, through advertising, they attempt to build attractive, favorable images for their accounts' brands. The agency's account executive or account representative is the liaison person who manages an account.

Advertising agencies are compensated for their services by commissions from the advertising media or fees paid by clients. Because agencies bring regular business to the media, the media "recognize" agencies by giving them a commission or discount (usually 15 percent) off their list price rates for national advertising. This is their most important source of revenues. Fees are growing in popularity for noncommissionable jobs such as in-store displays for manufacturers or a thorough market survey for specific products. The agency may charge the client cost plus a fee, sometimes 25 percent. But big advertisers are not as likely to be charged for such work because the agency already receives sizable commissions on the advertising space or time they buy for the client.

Advertising agencies vary considerably in size; the largest are shown in Table 19-4. The very largest place more than a billion dollars worth of ads each year for a wide variety of accounts. By contrast, the small, local agency may place just a few hundred thousand dollars worth of advertising for only a few accounts. Most agency clients are manufacturers of consumer products or services and sell nationally, or at least regionally. The larger clients often use several different ad agencies, each responsible for a particular product or line of products. The ten manufacturers who spend the most money on advertising work with an average of eleven agencies each.

432 / Chapter 19

Table 19-4 The United States' largest advertising agencies

U.S. income rank	Agency	U.S. gross income, 1980	U.S. billing, 1980	Total U.S. employees, 1980
1	Young & Rubicam	$200.0	$1,333.7	3,804
2	J. Walter Thompson Co.	137.8	918.9	2,474
3	Ogilvy & Mather	125.5	837.1	2,160
4	Foote, Cone & Belding	109.1	749.3	2,330
5	Leo Burnett Co.	108.2	734.6	1,481
6	Ted Bates & Co.	108.0	720.3	1,884
7	BBDO International	105.8	806.4	2,049
8	Doyle Dane Bernbach	98.1	671.0	1,800
9	Grey Advertising	78.7	524.9	1,522
10	Benton & Bowles	$ 73.8	$ 492.0	1,447

NOTE: Billings and gross income are in millions; these figures do not include foreign billings.

SOURCE: *Advertising Age,* March 18, 1981, p. 8.

The Creative Side of Advertising

When advertising people refer to the "creative" side of advertising, they mean the activities involved in the actual preparation of advertisements: deciding how to appeal to the buyer, what specific headlines and illustrations to use, and what written copy will accomplish best the objectives. Seemingly small differences in an advertisement can have a dramatic impact on its effectiveness. As just one example, it has been shown that some ads are 150 percent more effective when placed on the back page of a newspaper than when placed on an inside page. Thus, choosing these elements and determining how they should be pulled together is a critical marketing activity.

The most important ingredient in an ad is the promise it makes. Why? Because the buyer responds favorably or not to what the advertiser claims its product or service will deliver. Remember, buyers do not buy products or services as such; instead, they exchange their money for what a product or service will do to or for them, for satisfaction of some sort. If consumers want a kitchen cleanser that will be gentle to their hands, that is what the product should offer and what the ad should promise.

Visualization and Layout

Once an ad's objective has been determined and its promise selected, the actual building of the ad can start. This calls for visualization and layout. Determining what elements or units an ad shall contain is called visualization. The common elements are headline, subheads, illustrations, and copy. Laying out the ad is a matter of position and relationships. Visualization decides *what* the ad will

Advertising / 433

contain, layout decides *where* each of those elements will be placed. Should a retailer's name be at the top of a newspaper ad but a manufacturer's name at the bottom of a magazine ad? If several illustrations are to be included, where should each be placed? Well laid-out ads are sound and simple; their attractiveness invites reading. The expert selection and placement of illustrations can increase advertising effectiveness and the response the advertiser wants.

Copy

The most important element in an ad's copy message, the promise, is often expressed in the headline. The major jobs of headlines are to make contact with and attract the attention of the seller's prospects — also a responsibility of the ad's illustration — and to induce prospects to read the ad.

Most strong headlines have either news content or buyer-benefit — self-interest — content "The K Cars are here," for example, a newsy headline from Chrysler, or "A better mileage rating than Audi 5000 for $1,699 less!" for the Pontiac Bonneville, stressing benefit to the buyer. Many headlines are a question — "What's Continental Telephone doing way out here?" — or a command: "Let Kelly work for you." Headlines may try to help prospects identify themselves as prospects by including such words as "motorists," or "students." Other words believed to be powerful in headlines include "free," "how to," "you," and "which."

Body copy is much like a salesperson's presentation in that it should expand on and explain the promise on which the ad is built. It should be built on a strong, persuasive sales idea. Product facts, product satisfaction, and product price are main ingredients. Body copy must be clear and believable, sincere yet interesting.

Ads should try to "close" just as salespeople do, and an ad's close is second only to its headline in importance. The close should urge some sort of immediate favorable action: "Fill out the coupon and mail it today"; "Visit your nearest dealer and ask for a demonstration"; or simply, "Try it, you'll be glad you did." Words such as "go," "try," and "ask" are often found in closes. The advertiser's name and address or the brand name are often prominent in closes.

Illustrations

Illustrations — drawings, photos, or cartoons — share with headlines the assignment of attracting the attention of prospects. They can tell a story, make a point quickly and clearly, or prove a claim; "before-and-after" photographs are an example. Art directors are always debating illustration strategies. Should the ad contain a single, dominant illustration or several small illustrations? When should the product be shown, and when should some feature or part of the product be shown? Should people be included, perhaps using the product? Proven answers are rare for these questions; as in so much of advertising, experience is often the best guide.

The Advertising Campaign Approach

Much of manufacturers' advertising and some of retailers' advertising is planned and scheduled in the form of *advertising campaigns*. What is an ad campaign? It starts with planning aimed at avoiding hasty or ill-considered decisions. Erratic advertising, approved on a day-to-day basis, is far less productive than researched, coordinated advertising.

Each campaign consists of a group of related, organized, and rather similar ads, with a single sales goal or objective. It has a specific starting date, a schedule, and an ending date. For each campaign there is a single theme or keynote idea that runs through the entire campaign, that unifies and gives focus to it. The theme summarizes the substance of the campaign message or promise. Coca-Cola has used the theme "Coke adds life." Schlitz has said, "When you're out of Schlitz, you're out of beer." For decades Morton Salt promised, "When it rains it pours." The similarity between a keynote idea and a slogan is obvious, as is the similarity between a keynote idea and a buyer benefit. Campaigns vary in length. Each can promote the image of the brand, the Chevy Citation, say, or the entire advertising firm, such as General Motors. Exhibit 19-2 discusses guidelines for successful advertising campaigns.

Exhibit 19-2
Keys to Advertising Success

Many times the business of advertising is so complex that students and advertisers alike wring their hands and cry, "Just give me a few simple rules for an effective ad campaign."

In 1972 in an advertisement (appropriately enough) in the *Wall Street Journal,* David Ogilvy of Ogilvy & Mather, one of the nation's top ad firms, listed thirty-eight pointers to the way of success in creating a good advertising campaign.

Here are a few that are common to all ads, regardless of the medium:

- The most important decision you will have to make is how to position your product. Make that decision before you begin your campaign.
- Make your promises unique and competitive. Dr. Johnson once said, "Promise, large promise, is the soul of an advertisement."
- Don't be a bore. Nobody was ever bored into buying a product yet most advertising is impersonal, detached, and cold — and boring.
- Innovate. Start trends instead of following them.
- It pays to segment your market psychologically.
- Don't bury news.
- Boil down your strategy to one simple promise and go the whole hog in delivering that promise.

Advertising / 435

> - It pays to give most products an image of quality, a first-class ticket. If your ads are ugly consumers will conclude that your product is shoddy, and they will be less likely to buy.
> - Every advertisement should contribute to the complex symbol that is the brand image. The manufacturer that dedicates its advertising to building the most sharply defined personality for its brand gets the largest share of the market.
>
> These are some of the rules Ogilvy uses in creating advertising for his clients. As his company has created more than $1.4 billion of advertising (that was before 1972), it seems safe to conclude that his formulas are successful.
>
> SOURCE: From an ad in the *Wall Street Journal,* June 14, 1972, p. 17. Reprinted by permission.

Advertising is not only the most familiar form of promotion; for many companies it is also the most important. Its best strategic use seems to be in selling many low-priced goods over a large area, which explains why most consumer-product companies depend on it so heavily. In this sense advertising seems to be almost the opposite of personal selling, which is best applied to the sale of expensive or complex goods to specifically identified customers. There are cases, however, in which neither personal selling nor advertising is precisely the promotional tool a marketer requires. In the next chapter we will turn to the tools that can be used for these other cases.

Colony's approach to its wine advertising problem described at the beginning of the chapter included many of the points we've discussed. The company worked with its advertising agency, the San Francisco branch of McCann-Erickson. Together they decided that the ads should present the results of a taste test conducted among 245 consumers and that the ads should name the competitor in the tests: Almaden Wines. The promise would be simply that Colony tastes better. Colony and its agency decided to use the ads in a campaign lasting three months, and they decided to spend $6 million on it. The media used would be mainly a combination of television and magazines. Of course Colony hoped and expected that its campaign would be effective, but the advertising of consumer products is a battle that never ends. Not long after Colony announced its plans, it became known that Almaden was planning a new campaign of its own. Its budget was to be $10 million.

436 / Chapter 19

Summary

Advertising is any paid form of nonpersonal, promotional presentation of ideas or products by a sponsor whose identity is known. The management of advertising is based on its objectives, which vary among companies but generally include selling something — a product, a service, a company, an idea — by changing buyers' attitudes and behavior. The ultimate goal, of course, is making greater profits. Advertising managers must develop a media strategy that specifies the reach, frequency, impact, and continuity of their firms' advertising. They must establish an advertising budget, and they must evaluate their advertising strategy continually.

Most retailers create their own advertising. Most manufacturers, by contrast, employ an advertising agency. A manufacturer may have a traditional organization with a single ad manager, or it may have a decentralized organization, with responsibility divided among many product managers.

Advertising consumes different percentages of sales dollars in different industries, with consumer-products companies generally spending the higher percentages.

Ad agencies are experts in the creating and placing of ads, and nearly all large manufacturers, as well as many small ones, use them. Agencies get paid either by a commission, usually 15 percent, granted by media on the amount of time or space they buy for their clients or by service charges and fees for other duties they perform.

The most important element in an ad is the promise it makes to the buyer. Of course the copy in the ad, the statement and explanation of the promise, is also extremely important. And it has been shown that such things as layout and illustrations have an important effect on an ad's success. A group of ads that are similar in approach in style and are run over a period of time constitute an advertising campaign.

Key Terms

advertising	percentage-of-sales approach
reach	competitive parity approach
frequency	task or objective approach
impact	cooperative advertising
continuity	advertising agency
affordable approach	advertising campaigns

Review Questions

1. List five possible advertising objectives.
2. Describe the factors influencing choice of advertising media.
3. What factors are involved in making media scheduling decisions?

Advertising / 437

4. How might an advertising manager evaluate the effectiveness of a firm's advertising?
5. What are some ways of determining the size of the advertising budget? Which way is most commonly used?
6. How are retail advertising departments usually organized?
7. How are manufacturers' advertising departments organized?
8. What are some typical services that ad agencies provide for their clients?
9. Explain the ways advertising agencies are compensated for their services.
10. Outline the issues involved in creating an ad or a set of ads.

Discussion Questions

1. Why do firms in some industries spend more on advertising than firms in other industries?
2. Why do some firms in an industry spend more on advertising than other firms in the same industry?
3. In the United States certain products cannot be advertised on television. In other countries no television advertising is allowed at all. In what ways do these restrictions harm or help the manufacturer of these products?
4. Suppose you want to introduce a new study aid that will help college students prepare for exams. Develop an advertising plan aimed at students in your school.
5. Look in a favorite magazine or newspaper for two ads that you feel are good ones and two that you feel are not so good. Explain why. Be sure you identify what you mean by a "good" ad.

438 / Chapter 19

Answer Key

Note: Answers are not included in this key for those exercises which require lengthy or subjective response or the underlining or marking of passages.

PART ONE

Chapter 1
How to Succeed

EXERCISE 1
1. c
2. c
3. c
4. d
5. c

Chapter 3
Organizing Your Time

EXERCISE 1
1. His choices include:
   a. reduce work hours; seek financial aid if needed
   b. settle for less than a B average in some courses
   c. ask family member to accept additional household responsibilities
   d. drop one or more courses
2. Her approach is ineffective because she plans to study the same subject continuously without taking any breaks. Susan should schedule several shorter blocks of study time instead of a single all-day session. She should also consider studying 2 or 3 hours a day for 3 days rather than spending a full day studying.
3. Mark's plan has two faults. First, he should not leave the most difficult assignment and that which requires the greatest amount of concentration until last. Second, Mark should not schedule his study of subjects according to likes or dislikes. Instead, he should select them according to the difficulty and type of assignment given.
4. You could reserve a two-hour block of time on a weekend which you could use to catch up on any assignment that you missed during the week while completing your music assignment.
5. If you follow her suggestion, you will probably not get very much accomplished. You will be studying in unfamiliar surroundings and will be easily distracted. If you plan on doing the assignment when you get back, you run the risk of being too tired to work on it. Choice d. is best because you accomplish your goal and your sister will know that you are willing to take her at another time.
6. Any honest responses are correct.
7. Problems you may have noticed with the sample schedule include:
   a. scheduling one subject per evening instead of spacing it out over several evenings
   b. scheduling fairly mechanical tasks such as typing before tasks which require intense concentration such as reading a chapter on data processing
   c. not scheduling any time for review and perhaps not enough time for initial reading and study
   d. not using some of the empty times between classes for reading or study
8. Evaluate his study plan according to the suggestions given in the section with the heading "Building a Time Schedule." He should rearrange his schedule so as to follow the scheduling suggestions presented on pages 24–25.

Chapter 4
Becoming a More Successful Learner: Principles of Learning

EXERCISE 1
1. approximately 23 percent
2. approximately 20 percent
3. Although taking the notes would serve as a form of rehearsal, without further review you should expect your recall to be fairly poor.
4. Without notes to refer to, you would not be able to recall many of the specific facts and ideas that you should comment on in your reaction paper.

EXERCISE 2
1. You could make up a word or sentence to help you remember them: GLACE or *Good Little Animals Collect Eggs*
2. You could categorize the items into groups as follows:

Clean-up	Tools	Course materials
grease remover	tire gauge	car repair manual
soap	jumper cables	car service record
hand towel	flashlight	course
paper towels	wrench	textbook
	screwdriver	notebook

3. a. Twenty pages is probably too much to review in one sitting. However, it is *not* a good idea to split up your review by working on math problems in between.
4. You could categorize the requirements using *calories* and *fluids* as headings. You would be able to remember them by thinking that protein, fat, and carbohydrates all contain calories and that mineral iron, fluoride, and vitamins can be contained in fluids. Or you could make up a mnemonic device using the first letter of each word.

Chapter 5
Improving Your Ability to Concentrate

EXERCISE 1
1. You already have associations built up for sleep and relaxation which will make studying more difficult.
2. You may be too tired to concentrate effectively.
3. You will have difficulty keeping your mind on what you are studying.
4. Your attention will be divided; at least part of the time you will be listening to and thinking about the album.
5. You already have associations built up for relaxation and/or entertainment which will conflict with your intent to study.
6. The snack bar is probably very busy during lunch hours and will be too distracting.
7. The circulation desk is one of the busiest areas in a library, and all the activities that occur there will probably be distracting.
8. You are in an unfamiliar environment, and getting down to studying will be more difficult than in your own environment.

PART TWO
Chapter 7
Prereading

EXERCISE 1
1. T   6. F
2. T   7. T
3. F   8. F
4. T   9. T
5. T   10. T

EXERCISE 2
1. The text contains a collection of articles written by different authors as well as reports of studies done on individuals.
2. a. no
   b. no
   c. yes
   d. yes
   e. no
3. The section is organized chronologically, or in order of occurrence in time.
4. The copyright date, 1951, tells you that the information may be outdated and does not include any developments or changes in business management made in the past 30 years.
5. The chapter discusses two types of learning — verbal learning and manual skill learning. The topic of forgetting is also discussed. Finally, methods and principles of study are presented.
6. a. learning occurs through three basic processes — classical conditioning, instrumental learning, and perceptual learning
   b. a description of each process with a summary of research done with animals
   c. the relationship of each of the three processes to human learning
7. The graph suggests that the production of various types of goods as it determines price is an important topic in the chapter. The cartoon indicates that a key concept in economic systems is cost as it is influenced by consumer choice. The picture tells you that currency as a means of exchange of goods is considered in the chapter.
8. The chapter is organized chronologically; it moves from the historical events to the present to projections for the future. The chapter discusses the Orient, its history, its current economy, and the directions and problems of the future.

Chapter 8
Establishing a Purpose for Reading

EXERCISE 1
1. What are the basic types of logic?
2. What is test anxiety? What are the characteristics of test anxiety?
3. What is nondirective anxiety?
4. What physical changes occur during adolescence?
5. What sociological factors are related to delinquency? Why are these factors related to delinquency?
6. Why do adolescents have a need for dependence?
7. What has been the influence of "experts" on child rearing practices?
8. How are language and memory related?
9. How are physical characteristics inherited?
10. What is the language of disadvantaged children? What affects their language? How is it different from the language of other children?

EXERCISE 2

1. What are the three branches of philosophic analysis?
2. Why do pressure and stress cause earthquakes?
3. How is information processed physically? How is it processed chemically?
4. Why has democracy not been fully realized in the United States?
5. What do astronomers learn about the stars by studying light?
6. What are the different types of drill presses? What is the function of each?
7. Why is latent heat important?
8. What rules do societies have about behavior? How are people rewarded or punished?
9. Why must the electrical terminals be insulated from the housing?
10. What insights do studies of work offer into the basic processes underlying behavior?

PART THREE

Chapter 9
Understanding Sentences

EXERCISE 1

1. S		6. N
2. N		7. S
3. N		8. N
4. S		9. S
5. N		10. S

EXERCISE 2

Subject	Verb (including Object)
1. sister	took her car
2. library	was closed
3. textbook	contains exercises
4. divorce	is
5. force	is required to change the momentum
6. relationship	was discovered
7. streets, schools, and food	are political decisions
8. reaction, compound	occurs, is formed
9. women	request abortions
10. we	saw how the colonists drew

EXERCISE 3

1. C
2. R the individual . . . effective
3. C
4. C
5. C
6. R humankind has . . . years.
7. R the Cuban economy . . . sugar

8. R the personal manager is well known . . . candidates
9. R they fall . . . air
10. R the anthropological linguist . . . form,

EXERCISE 5

1. Core parts: family — supplies affection and love
   Possible new sentences:
   a. The family teaches rules of behavior.
   b. The rules that families teach are those which are acceptable in our society.
   c. The family supplies children with love.
   d. The family supplies children with affection.
   e. Children need love to feel happy.
   f. Children need love to feel they are complete.
   g. Children need affection to feel they are complete.
   h. Children need affection to feel happy.
2. Core parts: segregation — occurs within the school
   Possible new sentences:
   a. Segregation occurs within schools.
   b. In schools students are assigned to tracks or programs.
   c. Students are assigned to different tracks according to ability.
   d. Students are assigned to different tracks according to achievement.
   e. Segregation occurs somewhere else than in schools.
   f. Segregation occurs because students are assigned to tracks.
3. Core parts: Gulf Stream — has influenced life
   Possible new sentences:
   a. The Gulf Stream is warm water.
   b. The warm water flows northward.
   c. The Gulf Stream is an ocean current.
   d. The Gulf Stream influences life on the Gulf shore.
   e. The Gulf Stream influences life on the Atlantic shore.
   f. The Gulf Stream influences life on the Atlantic shore as far north as Newfoundland.
4. Core parts: stream — is of immense size
   Possible new sentences:
   a. The Gulf Stream is of immense size.
   b. The width of the Gulf Stream is nearly a hundred miles.
   c. The Gulf Stream's depth is one mile.
   d. The Gulf Stream's volume is equal to several hundred Mississippi Rivers.
   e. The Gulf Stream passes between Cuba and Florida.
   f. The Gulf Stream goes back to the Atlantic.
5. Core parts: the rising and falling (of the barometer) — is an expression
   Possible new sentences:
   a. High pressure equals fine weather.
   b. Low pressure means rain.

c. In-between pressure means variable weather.
d. There is a relationship between pressure and weather.
e. The relationship between pressure and weather is not so simple as some barometers imply.
f. The rising and falling of the barometer is an expression of atmospheric processes.
g. Atmospheric processes determine future weather.

EXERCISE 9

Core parts	*Crossed out*
1. industrialization — made its impact	in the nineteenth century
2. member — could serve more than three years	that is
3. we — can draw conclusions	if we put together everything we have discussed about the incidence and distribution of mental retardation,
4. societies — held together	which are defined as rules . . . as well as by laws
5. man — has been labeled	(Nothing can be crossed out because the items separated by the commas are really part of the predicate of the sentence.)
6. we — perceive depth	then
7. they (humans) — know; they are thinking	perhaps even more important
8. language — can be recorded, can provide a bond	either on paper or in the folktales that survive by constant retelling
9. graphite — is made of carbon layers	on the other hand; like sheets of paper
10. it (gas) — condenses at its condensation point	when a gas is cooled; which is the same temperature as the boiling point

EXERCISE 10

Core parts	*Crossed out*
1. steel — is iron	for instance, with various other metals added, such as . . .
2. there — are three of significance	among the physical traits that, added together, separate humans from all other animals

3. cause — cannot be established
4. changes — have accelerated
5. common theme — is; behavior — is learned; they (theories) place emphasis

unfortunately, though, for all the biomedical advances
for a hundred years, wrought by humans burning fossil fuels, clearing large forests and cultivating and excavating land
accordingly,

EXERCISE 11
1. periodic table — is; we'll — be using
2. brain — sits; most — lies
3. man — has been puzzled and exasperated; teaching — has been
4. physicists — have determined
5. poverty and retardation — go; majority — are not

Chapter 10
Understanding Paragraphs

EXERCISE 1
1.	b	6.	b
2.	d	7.	d
3.	a	8.	b
4.	b	9.	b
5.	b	10.	d

EXERCISE 2
1. radiant energy
2. plant physiology
3. galvanic skin response
4. conformity or pressure to conform
5. the cell
6. reading
7. the grammar of language
8. Chinese writing system
9. the process of paper making
10. authenticity of photographs

EXERCISE 3
1. First sentence: In arithmetic. . . .
2. First sentence: To be able. . . .
3. First sentence: Sedimentary rocks are. . . .
4. First sentence: The skin itself. . . .
5. Second sentence: The key word outline. . . .
6. Second sentence: These tiny astronomical. . . .
7. First sentence: There are basically. . . .
8. First sentence: Nothing is quite. . . .
9. First sentence: In their classification. . . .
10. Second sentence: In fact, mathematics. . . .

EXERCISE 4
1. b, c, d, e
2. a, b, c, e

3. a, b, c, d
4. a, c, d, e
5. a, b, c, d, e
6. a, b, c, d, e
7. a, c, d, e
8. a, b, c, d·
9. a, b, e
10. a, b, d, e

EXERCISE 5

1. Topic: alcoholism
   Main idea: first sentence
   Key details: first step . . . stop patient's drinking/
   personality must be rebuilt/exclude . . .
   drinking/include . . . problem-solving/AA . . .
   help with the first and second/therapists . . .
   third step
2. Topic: Spanish-speaking communities
   Main idea: first sentence
   Key details: preservation . . . language and
   culture/seeks to obtain what is good . . .
   without losing ethnic identity/preserve their
   contacts . . . Old Mexico . . . pride . . . history
   and culture/recent years . . . great deal of
   interest in promoting this sense of identity and
   pride
3. Topic: objective study of dreams
   Main idea: first sentence
   Key details: experiments . . . recorded brain
   waves, body movements and eye movements
   during sleep/eye movements during sleep are
   connected with periods of dreaming
4. Topic: timing in promotional activities
   Main idea: third sentence
   Key details: special packaging may be called for/
   special seasonal pricing may be wise/demand
   occurs only for a short time . . . creating the
   need for agents
5. Topic: areas subject to earthquakes (seismic
   belts)
   Main idea: second sentence
   Key details: Circum-Pacific belt . . . Western
   highlands of South coast . . . and North
   America . . . crosses to Asia . . . extends
   southward along the eastern coast . . . loops far
   to the Southeast . . . beyond New Zealand/
   broad east-west zone . . . southern Asia and
   Mediterranean . . . to Gibraltar/Mid-Atlantic
   ridge from Arctic to Antarctic/Mid-Indian Ridge
   to unite with a belt in eastern Africa
6. Topic: light in upper atmosphere
   Main idea: second sentence
   Key details: gases in atmosphere are dense
   enough to scatter sunlight to altitudes of 200
   mi./sun must be at least 18° below the horizon
   for all traces of light to be absent/near equator
   twilight lasts only little over 1 hour . . . in far
   northern or southern latitudes . . . twilight may
   last for 2 hours/North Pole there are 6 weeks of
   twilight

7. Topic: newspapers
   Main idea: first sentence
   Key details: advantages over television/
   newspapers not performing their true function/
   television has important role/television's news
   . . . far from satisfactory
8. Topic: the media's degree of responsibility
   Main idea: first sentence
   Key details: less bias in presentation of news, less
   venality, broader coverage of national and world
   affairs, more . . . presentation of complex
   events in a perspective/even television . . .
   showing signs of recognizing its obligations/30
   percent of television and 20 percent of radio . . .
   show responsibility and quality in news
   services
9. Topic: employment letters
   Main idea: first sentence
   Key details: must pass scrutiny as a letter/the
   employer is interested in the person who wrote
   the application letter/reads character in the
   letter/correctness and neat appearance tell him
   about the writer
10. Topic: new products
    Main idea: first sentence
    Key details: many companies doing the majority
    of their business in products that were
    unknown 20 years ago/Before World War II an
    appliance . . . had only . . . few products . . . for
    distribution/Today . . . many other products are
    standard items

EXERCISE 6

1. Topic: food supplement sales
   Main idea: Food supplements are sold to people
   who are convinced that important nutrients
   have been removed from food while, in reality,
   most nutrients are preserved.
2. Topic: overweight people
   Main idea: Overweight people, regardless of age,
   suffer rejection by their peers.
3. Topic: color
   Main idea: Color has many uses and serves
   important functions in a variety of situations.
4. Topic: a speaker's purpose
   Main idea: A speaker's purpose can vary widely
   depending on the audience and situation.
5. Topic: the birth of a volcano
   Main idea: This paragraph describes the birth of a
   volcano in 1943 in Mexico.
6. Topic: the development of infant speech
   Main idea: Infant speech follows a consistent,
   regular pattern of development.
7. Topic: computers
   Main idea: computers can reduce both the time
   and cost involved in solving complex problems.
8. Topic: sources of lists of names
   Main idea: There are a variety of sources a
   business can use to obtain names.

9. Topic: the role of television
   Main idea: Television serves many different functions, depending upon the needs and interests of those involved.
10. Topic: glaciers
   Main idea: The movement and dimensions of glaciers provide historically important information.

Chapter 11
Understanding Passages

EXERCISE 1
1. a
2. c
3. b
4. b
5. d

EXERCISE 2
1. "Contests" and "matches" refer to individuals while "games" refers to individuals representing groups in various sporting events.
2. Size constancy depends on a variety of factors including learning and memory, surroundings, and brightness and color.
3. By organizing facts into theories, it is possible to process larger amounts of information and to test and make predictions.
4. Classification is a way of organizing single facts into a meaningful system.
5. Repression, a means of defending one's self against anxiety, involves forgetting certain thoughts or activities which produce anxiety.

EXERCISE 3
1. General subject: writing
   Central thought: The process of writing involves the expression of opinion and helps the writer to shape and strengthen his opinions.
   Supporting ideas:
   first paragraph — second sentence, sixth sentence
   second paragraph — first sentence, last sentence
2. General subject: department store branches
   Central thought: Branches of department stores are no longer extensions of the parent store; they are becoming specialized to service their own clientele.
   Supporting ideas:
   first paragraph — first sentence
   second paragraph — first sentence, last sentence
3. General subject: the electronic computer
   Central thought: Electronic computers process data completely within the machine at an extremely rapid rate.

Supporting ideas:
   first paragraph — first sentence, last sentence
   second paragraph — second sentence
4. General subject: parental neglect of children
   Central thought: Parents are neglecting children in terms of both physical care and personal attention.
   Supporting ideas:
   first paragraph — second sentence, third sentence
   second paragraph — second sentence, third sentence
5. General subject: corporations
   Central thought: Businesses organized as corporations have both advantages and disadvantages.
   Supporting ideas:
   first paragraph — first sentence, fourth sentence, fifth sentence
   second paragraph — first sentence
   third paragraph — second sentence, third sentence

EXERCISE 4

Directional words	Type
1. on the other hand	contrast
2. as a result	cause-effect
3. in conclusion	summary
4. for example	example
5. in other words	continuation
6. both	comparison
7. first	time sequence
8. unlike	contrast
9. then	time sequence
10. another	continuation

EXERCISE 5

Directional words	Type
1. however	contrast
2. therefore	summary
3. on the contrary	contrast
4. for this reason, however	cause-effect, contrast
5. for example	example

PART FOUR

Chapter 12
Textbook Aids to Learning

EXERCISE 1
1. Organization: the text may be organized according to types of practical situations
   Purpose: to discuss how psychology can be used or applied to real or everyday situations
   Subject: psychology

2. Organization: the text may be organized by basic principles and concepts
   Purpose: to present the basic principles and theories of American politics
   Subject: basic principles important to American politics
3. Organization: the text is organized as a series of experiments
   Purpose: to present laboratory experiments or studies important to general biology
   Subject: general biology
4. Organization: the text may be organized by author
   Purpose: to present literature by black Americans which provides insights into living as a black American
   Subject: black American literature
5. Organization: the text will be organized according to basic principles
   Purpose: to present basic principles and information about health education
   Subject: health education

EXERCISE 3
1. c
2. a
3. b
4. b
5. b

EXERCISE 4
The following texts may be outdated: 3, 5, 8, 10.

EXERCISE 5
1. Practically oriented. The text treats marketing as an "applied science."
2. The text begins with an overview of marketing, then discusses specific aspects of marketing, then reconsiders marketing as part of a larger context.
3. Yes. It contains a valuable review of text material, including important vocabulary, review questions, and case studies.
4. Each chapter contains learning objectives, summaries, key terms, review questions, and discussion questions.
5. The case studies about Levi Strauss provide practical examples of the basic marketing concepts taught.

EXERCISE 7
1. case studies
2. Chapter 5
3. proximate sociocultural, economic, and public policy
4. geographic distribution, demographic characteristics, and income characteristics

EXERCISE 8
1. b
2. a

3. a
4. a
5. c

EXERCISE 9
1. *Figure 12-2:*
   a. to show the change in percentage of blue- and white-collar workers from 1950 to 1974
   b. percentage of white-collar and blue-collar workers over time
   c. percentage of white-collar workers steadily increasing
   d. 1950
   e. 1974
2. *Figure 12-3:*
   a. unemployment rates among teen-agers, minorities, and total population
   b. unemployment
   c. unemployment consistently higher for teen-agers and minorities
   d. teen-agers
   e. 1969
3. *Figure 12-4:*
   a. The yearly income and expenditures of the federal government and whether they produced a surplus or deficit
   b. chronologically
   c. There has been a steady increase in federal spending.
   d. yes
   e. 45,095 deficit

Chapter 14
Textbook Marking

EXERCISE 1
1. most effective
2. too little underlining
3. too much underlining

PART FIVE

Chapter 15
Notetaking Techniques

EXERCISE 3
Recall Clues: Freud's psychoanalytic theory, association, repression, suppression, trauma, interpretation of dreams, three parts of personality

Questions: What is free association? What is repression? What is suppression? What is trauma? How can dreams be interpreted? What are the three parts of the personality? What does each do?

Chapter 17
Studying for and Taking Exams

EXERCISE 1
1. 1, 15, 5, 50, 4

2. 1, 7, 10, 20, 2
3. 1, 13, 1
(Other similar time plans may be correct.)

EXERCISE 2

1. no	T
2. most important	T
3. only slightly	F
4. always	F
5. sometimes	T
6. little	T
7. all	T
8. often	F
9. usually	F
10. most	T

EXERCISE 3

	Topic	Limiting word(s)	Key word
1.	trend	long-term effects	discuss
2.	monopolies	development	trace
3.	Industrial Revolution	one effect	explain
4.	cactus	reasons	discuss
5.	War of 1812	events	describe
6.	textbook marking/ lecture notetaking	purposes/ procedures	compare/ contrast
7.	textbook chapter	approach	describe
8.	memory	four factors	list/explain
9.	lecturer	techniques	summarize
10.	prereading	value/purpose/ steps	explain/list

PART SIX

Chapter 19
Effective Use of Context

EXERCISE 1
The underlined parts should be:
1. a form of government in which the people effectively participate
2. the amount of heat required to melt one gram of any substance at its melting point
3. an essentially fatty acid necessary for growth and skin integrity in infants
4. changes to a liquid
5. able to reach comfortably to the tips of all the other fingers

EXERCISE 2
1. close, dependent
2. gruesome, unwholesome

3. negative emotional experience
4. support
5. fears
6. like, or similar

EXERCISE 3
1. strong, forceful
2. authoritative, assertive
3. delay, put off
4. stubborn, persistent
5. banished, excluded from a group

EXERCISE 4
1. activities by groups that influence (pressure) legislators
2. do not go together, inconsistent
3. curses, expressions of abhorrence
4. freed from blame
5. struck out, removed

EXERCISE 5
The underlined parts should be as follows (context clues are given in parentheses):
1. the principle that the powers of government should be separated and put in the care of different parts of government (definition)
2. means of using uranium to analyze the age of rock (logic)
3. amble, stride, jog, and sprint (example-illustration)
4. large differences in the populations of Congressional districts (definition)
5. ranging from treatment as innocents to being tolerated as fools to persecution as witches (example-illustration)
6. you may notice an odor, but in a very short time, your awareness disappears (example-illustration)

Chapter 20
Learning New Terminology

EXERCISE 1
New terms: advertising, reach, frequency, impact, continuity, affordable approach, percentage of sales approach, competitive party approach, cooperative advertising, advertising agency, visualization, layout, copy, advertising campaign

Chapter 21
Organizational Approaches to Developing General Vocabulary

EXERCISE 4
1. distressed, despondent, disheartened, sorrowful, grief-stricken
2. difficult, complicated, complex, challenging
3. explaining, discussing, describing, arguing, debating, illustrating
4. lean, skinny, slender, gaunt, gawky
5. excellent, praiseworthy, pleasing, superior, laudable

PART SEVEN

Chapter 24
When Not to Read Everything

EXERCISE 1
1. a
2. c
3. b
4. a
5. b
6. b

EXERCISE 2
1. Doctors have a responsibility to be open and honest with their patients.

2. The article describes the psychological and biological aspects of aging, discusses attitudes toward death, and lists the stages of dying.
3. The article describes the change in attitude toward the use of profanity and discusses the uses of profanity.

EXERCISE 3
1. .09 cubic feet
2. anemometer
3. solar cell is 20 times as efficient as the phototube
4. shape and capacity of the brain case and proportions of the face
5. power to restrict output and hold up price
6. La Scala Opera House
7. ability of a lens to collect and transmit light rays
8. brightness of stars

References

Many of the excerpts used in this text were drawn from from the sources listed under Acknowledgments on page iv. The author also wishes to acknowledge the following sources of study material in this text.

Joseph B. Aceves and H. Gill King. *Introduction to Anthropology*. Glenview, Ill.: Scott, Foresman, 1979.

Wroe Alderson and Michael H. Halbert. *Men, Motives, and Markets*. Englewood Cliffs, N.J.: Prentice-Hall, 1968.

Hugh D. Barlow. *Introduction to Criminology*. Boston: Little, Brown and Company, 1978.

J. Darrell Barnard et al. *Science for Tomorrow's World*, Book Four. New York: Macmillan, 1966.

Erwin A. Bauer. *Outdoor Photography*. New York: Outdoor Life, 1965.

Ralph L. Beals and Harry Hoijer. *An Introduction to Anthropology*, 2nd ed. New York: Macmillan, 1963.

Louis Berman and J. C. Evans. *Exploring the Cosmos*, 2nd ed. Boston: Little, Brown and Company, 1977.

Newton H. Black and Elbert P. Little. *Introductory Course in College Physics*, 4th ed. New York: Macmillan, 1956.

Chesley Bonestell and Willy Ley. *Beyond the Solar System*. New York: Viking Press, 1964.

Elbert V. Bowden. *Economics: The Science of Common Sense*. Cincinnati: South Western Publishing, 1974.

Edgar S. Brightman. *An Introduction to Philosophy*, 3rd ed. New York: Holt, Rinehart and Winston, 1964.

Leonard Broom and Philip Selznick. *Sociology*, 2nd ed. New York: Harper & Row, 1963.

Bernard G. Campbell. *Humankind Emerging*. Boston: Little, Brown and Company, 1976.

Ruth S. Cavan. *The American Family*, 3rd ed. New York: Thomas Y. Crowell, 1966.

William R. Clark. *Explorers of the World*. Garden City, N.Y.: Natural History Press, 1964.

Luella Cole and Irma Nelson Hall. *Psychology of Adolescence*, 7th ed. New York: Holt, Rinehart and Winston, 1970.

Nelson M. Cooke. *Basic Mathematics for Electronics*, 2nd ed. New York: McGraw-Hill, 1960.

James E. Crouch and Robert McClintic. *Human Anatomy and Physiology*, 2nd ed. New York: John Wiley & Sons, 1976.

Randall C. Decker. *Patterns of Exposition 6*. Boston: Little, Brown and Company, 1978.

William H. Desmonde. *Computers and Their Uses*. Englewood Cliffs, N.J.: Prentice-Hall, 1964.

Harry Edwards. *Sociology of Sport*. Homewood Ill.: Dorsey Press, 1973.

Peter K. Eisinger et al. *American Politics*. Boston: Little, Brown and Company, 1978.

Peter Farb. *North America*. New York: Time, Inc., 1964.

John H. Ferguson and Dean E. McHenry. *The American System of Government*, 12th ed. New York: McGraw-Hill, 1973.

Gordon J. Fielding. *Geography as a Social Science*. New York: Harper & Row, 1974.

Henrietta Fleck. *Introduction to Nutrition*, 2nd ed. New York: Macmillan, 1971.

Victoria Fromkin and Robert Rodman. *An Introduction to Language*. New York: Holt, Rinehart and Winston, 1974.

Martin J. Gannon. *Management: An Organizational Perspective*. Boston: Little, Brown and Company, 1977.

Karl C. Garrison. *Psychology of Adolescence*, 6th ed. Englewood Cliffs, N.J.: Prentice-Hall, 1965.

Frans Gerritsen. *Theory and Practice of Color*. New York: Van Nostrans, 1975.

Kalman Goldberg. *Our Changing Economy*. Boston: Little, Brown, 1977.

Kennard E. Goodman. *Today's Business Law*. New York: Pitman Publishing Co., 1966.

Victor A. Greulach and J. Edison Adams. *Plants: An Introduction to Modern Botany*. New York: John Wiley & Sons, 1967.

S. I. Hayakawa. *Language in Thought and Action*, 2nd ed. New York: Harcourt Brace & World, 1964.

Gerald L. Hershey and James O. Lugo. *Living Psychology: An Experimental Approach*. New York: Macmillan, 1970.

Robert L. Hilliard. *Understanding Television*. New York: Hasting House, 1964.

Carl A. Keyser. *Materials Science in Engineering*. Columbus, Ohio: Merrill, 1968.

John Lewis. *Anthropology Made Simple*. Garden City, N.Y.: Doubleday, 1961.

William P. Lineberry, ed. *Mass Communications,* Vol. 41, No. 3. New York: Wilson, 1969.

James O. Lugo and Gerald L. Hershey. *Human Development.* New York: Macmillan, 1974.

Donald L. Macmillan. *Mental Retardation in the School and Society.* Boston: Little, Brown and Company, 1977.

John Magee and David L. Bickelhaupt. *General Insurance,* 7th ed. Homewood, Ill.: Irwin, 1964.

Abraham Marcus. *Basic Electricity,* 2nd ed. Englewood Cliffs, N.J.: Prentice-Hall, 1964.

M. Esther McClain and Shirley H. Gragg. *Scientific Principles in Nursing,* 5th ed. St. Louis: C. V. Mosby & Co., 1962.

Gene R. Medinnus and Ronald C. Johnson. *Child and Adolescent Behavior.* New York: John Wiley & Sons, 1969.

James R. Meehan, William R. Pasewark, and Mary Ellen Oliverio. *Clerical Office Procedures,* 5th ed. Cincinnati: South Western Publishing, 1973.

Alan H. Monroe and Douglas Ehninger. *Principles and Types of Speech,* 6th ed. Glenview, Ill.: Scott, Foresman, 1967.

Clifford T. Morgan. *Introduction to Psychology.* New York: McGraw-Hill, 1966.

Joseph Morgan. *Introduction to University Physics,* Vol. I. Boston: Allyn & Bacon, 1963.

Paul H. Mussen. *The Psychology and Development of the Child.* Englewood Cliffs, N.J.: Prentice-Hall, 1963.

Sydney B. Newell. *Chemistry.* Boston: Little, Brown and Company, 1977.

William F. Ogburn and Meyer F. Nimkoff. *Sociology,* 4th ed. Boston: Houghton Mifflin, 1964.

Adele Pillitteri. *Nursing Care of the Growing Family.* Boston: Little, Brown and Company, 1976.

Wilfred Robbins, T. Elliott Weier, and C. Ralph Stocking. *Botany: An Introduction to Plant Science,* 3rd ed. New York: John Wiley & Sons, 1965.

David A. Schulz. *The Changing Family,* 2nd ed. Englewood Cliffs, N.J.: Prentice-Hall, 1976.

Ernest L. Schusky and T. Patrick Culbert. *Introducing Culture,* 2nd ed. Englewood Cliffs, N.J.: Prentice-Hall, 1973.

Beverly Seidel and Matthew Resick. *Physical Education: An Overview.* Reading, Mass.: Addison-Wesley, 1972.

Robert E. Silverman. *Psychology.* New York: Appleton-Century-Crofts, 1971.

Abraham P. Sperling. *Psychology Made Simple.* Garden City, N.Y.: Doubleday, 1957.

Earl P. Strong. *The Management of Business.* New York: Harper & Row, 1965.

William Toboldt. *Diesel.* South Holland, Ill.: Goodheart-Willcox Co., 1973.

Claude A. Villee, Warren F. Walker, and Robert D. Barnes. *General Zoology,* 4th ed. Philadelphia: W. B. Saunders, 1973.

Heinz Wachter. *Meteorology.* New York: Franklin Watts, 1973.

Gary Wasserman. *The Basics of American Politics.* Boston: Little, Brown, 1976.

James P. Weinland. *How to Think Straight.* Totowa, N.J.: Littlefield, Adams, 1963.

Michael Wertheimer et al. *Psychology: A Brief Introduction.* Glenview, Ill.: Scott, Foresman, 1968.

Peter K. Weyl, *Oceanography.* New York: John Wiley & Sons, 1970.

Jesse H. Wheeler, Jr., J. Trenton Kostbade, and Richard S. Thoman. *Regional Geography of the World,* 3rd ed. New York: Holt, Rinehart and Winston, 1964.

O. G. Wilson and Roy C. McLaren. *Police Administration,* 3rd ed. New York: McGraw-Hill, 1972.

Percy M. Young. *A Concise History of Music.* New York: David White Co., 1974.

CHAPTER 8
1. Eisinger, p. 5.
2. Berman and Evans, p. 42.
3. Althouse et al., p. 25.
4. Broom and Selznick, p. 68.
5. Althouse et al., p. 221.
6. Broom and Selznick, p. 665.

CHAPTER 9
1. Goldberg, p. 15.
2. Hewitt, p. 62.
3. Perry and Perry, p. 63.
4. Hewitt, p. 204.
5. Holland, p. 23.
6. Holland, p. 9.
7. Perry and Perry, p. 20.
8. Hewitt, p. 87.
9. Hewitt, p. 188.
10. Wasserman, p. 13.
11. Newell, p. 17.
12. Pillitteri, p. 311.
13. Wasserman, p. 44.
14. Aceves and King, p. 9.
15. Aceves and King, p. 11.
16. Perry and Perry, p. 23.
17. Perry and Perry, p. 95.
18. Farb, p. 30.
19. Wachter, pp. 15–16.
20. Gardner, p. 57.
21. Wasserman, p. 23.
22. MacMillan, p. 36.
23. MacMillan, p. 13.
24. Wasserman, p. 23.
25. MacMillan, p. 73.
26. MacMillan, p. 3.
27. Campbell, pp. 8–9.
28. Geiwitz, p. 91.
29. Campbell, p. 22.
30. Geiwitz, p. 207.
31. Newell, p. 25.

32. Newell, p. 45.
33. Berman and Evans, p. 14.
34. Gardner, p. 161.
35. Newell, p. 23.
36. Campbell, p. 15.
37. MacMillan, p. 27.
38. Berman and Evans, p. 106.
39. Barlow, p. 41.
40. Newell, p. 21.
41. Geiwitz, p. 35.
42. Campbell, p. 1.
43. Campbell, p. 12.
44. MacMillan, p. 27.

CHAPTER 11
1. Holland, pp. 124, 134.
2. Holland, pp. 27, 32.
3. Holland, pp. 9–10.
4. Lewis, p. 105.
5. Guth, p. 177.
6. Arnold et al., p. 1.
7. Strong, p. 54.
8. Strong, p. 63.

CHAPTER 12
1. Russ and Kirkpatrick, pp. vii–ix.
2. Goldberg, p. 191.
3. Goldberg, p. 184.
4. Goldberg, p. 187.
5. McCarty, p. 126.
6. Geiwitz, p. 525.

7. *Webster's New World Dictionary,* College Edition. New York: World Publishing, 1966, p. 401.
8. Geiwitz, p. 578.

CHAPTER 14
1. Buskirk, p. 231.
2. Buskirk, p. 126.
3. Kohn and Drummond, p. 59.
4. Rausch, p. 246.

CHAPTER 19
1. Newell, p. 17.
2. Newell, p. 41.
3. Campbell, p. 3.
4. Campbell, p. 107.
5. Wasserman, p. 25.
6. Wasserman, p. 8.
7. Newell, p. 43.
8. Pillitteri, p. 280.
9. Newell, p. 45.
10. Campbell, p. 21.
11. Gannon, p. 20.
12. Decker, p. 9.
13. Macmillan, p. 5.
14. Campbell, p. 189.
15. Wasserman, p. 33.
16. Wasserman, p. 33.
17. Newell, p. 388.
18. Campbell, p. 16.
19. Wasserman, p. 87.
20. MacMillan, p. 11.
21. Geiwitz, p. 85.

Index

Index

TO THE STUDENT

As educational publishers, it is our job to improve our texts continually and make them more useful to instructors and students. One way to improve a book is to revise it, taking into account the experience of people who have used it. We need to know what you learned and what you found confusing, as well as what you enjoyed and what you disliked. Your instructor may be asked to comment on the second edition of *College Reading and Study Skills*. Right now we want to hear from you, the person who paid for this book and read it. Please help us by completing the questionnaire and returning it to College English Developmental Group, Little, Brown and Company, 34 Beacon Street, Boston, MA 02106.

School: _____

Instructor's Name: _____

Title of Course: _____

1. Which of Parts One to Seven did you read for class? _____

   _____

   Which part did you find the most interesting? _____

   Why? _____

   Which part did you find the least interesting? _____

   Why? _____

   Which part helped you the most in your work for other courses?

   _____

2. What useful *skills* have you learned from this text? _____

   _____

   _____

3. Did you work with the sample textbook chapter included in the appendix? ☐ Yes ☐ No
   Did you find the sample chapter a helpful way of learning to apply your skills to other classes? ☐ Yes ☐ No

4. Did you find any of the exercises in the book particularly instructive? ☐ Yes ☐ No

   Which ones? _____

   _____

Which exercises did you like the least? _____

_____

Why? _____

5. Do you like the design and cover of this text?   ☐ Yes   ☐ No

    What do you think of the size and workbook format? _____

    _____

6. Do you intend to keep this book for your personal library?
    ☐ Yes   ☐ No

7. If you have any additional comments, questions, or concerns about
    College Reading and Study Skills, Second Edition, please use the
    space below to tell us about them.

Date: _____

Signature (optional): _____

Address (optional): _____

    _____